D1535080

THE RIGHT TO MANAGE

THE
RIGHT
TO
MANAGE

Industrial Relations Policies
of American Business
in the 1940s

Howell John Harris

THE UNIVERSITY OF WISCONSIN PRESS

Published 1982

The University of Wisconsin Press
114 North Murray Street
Madison, Wisconsin 53715

The University of Wisconsin Press, Ltd.
1 Gower Street
London WC1E 6HA, England

First printing

Printed in the United States of America

For LC CIP information see the colophon

ISBN 0-299-08640-2

Contents

v

Acknowledgments

This book has been eight years in the making, seeing the light first as a thesis, then being revised for a wider audience than my supervisor and examiners, and finally experiencing numerous editorial corrections and improvements. Inevitably, in such a time I have acquired many debts of gratitude I should like to repay. I make the customary disclaimer that all remaining faults in the book are my own affair, but I cannot honestly say that its merits also are all to my own credit. Without the aid and encouragement I received, the work would never have been completed at all, and might not even have been begun; without the advice and assistance I have been offered from friends and colleagues, it would be a distinctly inferior finished product.

My thanks must go first to Toni Lacey, John Walsh, and my fellow students at Nuffield College, Oxford, for giving me good reasons not to abandon graduate work at a time when it gave precious few rewards or satisfactions; and to Philip Williams, Maldwyn Jones, and William Leuchtenburg, for guiding my path into greener pastures. Rod Martin, my supervisor, provided consistently sound advice over six years, and if it had not been for knowing that there was someone to give what I wrote an immediate, interested, careful, and critical reading, I don't think I would have bothered to write it. The U.S. — U.K. Educational Commission, my college, and Rona and Kay Rouse enabled me to go to the United States to continue my research, and the labor historians of the New York State School of Industrial and Labor Relations at Cornell University were good enough to let me base my work there. The ILR provided affordable fees, good company, an excellent library, and, in Rich Strassberg, an enthusiastic and helpful archivist who really delights in having researchers use the immense resources he and his predecessors and staff have so painstakingly collected. My advisor there, Morris Neufeld, with justice gave the term paper which grew into this book the lowest grade that I have ever received; and he went on to give yet more concrete assistance and sound advice.

Friends at Wayne State University made working in Detroit a memorable and enjoyable experience, and the resources and archivists of the Walter P. Reuther Memorial Library and the Detroit Public Library made it worthwhile. I give my special thanks to General Motors' Labor Relations section, and particularly to Ralph Deedes and Andy Court, for being most helpful and forthright.

Librarians and archivists are the historian's best friends, and I should also like to thank those of the Department of Labor, the Princeton University Industrial Relations Section, the Eleutherian Mills-Hagley Foundation, the American Management Association, and the Universities of Rochester and Syracuse, for their aid. For a British scholar attempting to work on American resources at long distance there are special problems, but successive Inter-Library Loan persons at St. Davids College, Lampeter made sure I got everything I wanted. Working in relative isolation from other people interested in, and knowledgeable about, American business and labor was sometimes difficult, but numerous correspondents provided encouragement, salutary criticism, and help in tracking down fugitive references. Bob Zieger, Kim McQuaid, Nelson Lichtenstein, and Richard Tedlow deserve special mention.

My examiners, Patrick Renshaw and David Goldey, did me the good service of accepting my thesis, while criticizing it usefully, and the anonymous readers of the University of Wisconsin Press did the same. Friends and colleagues at Durham and Newcastle Universities — Don Ratcliffe, Reg Ward, Greg Bamber, Huw Beynon, and Tony Badger — read parts or all of the manuscript and tried to help me make it more readable and orderly. And Brian Keeling, my editor, did all that could be desired.

Finally, Jenny Aworth, as friend and wife, took an interest in the project and put up with me for most of the years during which I was trying to make sense of my research and write it up. So the book's dedicated to her, for all of her practical help and for keeping me going through the sticky patches.

Abbreviations

ACWP	Automotive Council for War Production
AFL	American Federation of Labor
ALL	American Liberty League
AMA	American Management Association
BAC	Business Advisory Council
CAI	Congress of American Industry
CCUS	Chamber of Commerce of the United States
CED	Committee for Economic Development
CIO	Committee for Industrial Organization
	Congress of Industrial Organizations
FAA	Foremen's Association of America
FEE	Foundation for Economic Education
GE	General Electric Company
GM	General Motors Corporation
NAM	National Association of Manufacturers
NCF	National Civic Federation
NDMB	National Defense Mediation Board
NICB	National Industrial Conference Board
NIRA	National Industrial Recovery Act
NLRB	National Labor Relations Board
NPA	National Planning Association
NWLB	National War Labor Board
ORC	Opinion Research Corporation
SBIC	Silver Bay Industrial Conference
SCC	Special Conference Committee
UAW	United Automobile Workers
UE	United Electrical Workers
URW	United Rubber Workers

THE RIGHT TO MANAGE

Introduction

This book sets out to fill a void in the history of American business and the American labor movement in the 1930s and 1940s — or rather, two voids: business historians are interested, by tradition, in innovation in market strategy and organizational structure, and in technology, often to the neglect of the relations of managers and workers within the firm and the larger political relations of business with other social groups and the state. Labor historians have not been so free to concentrate on the institutional development of the movement to the exclusion of consideration of "outside" influences — but still, accounts of the "rise of labor" in the 1930s and after seem to have given more weight to the role of state power and exceptional instances of worker militancy than to the everyday interplay of managers and workers, corporations and unions, business and labor. Their relationships of challenge and response, conflict and accommodation, have shaped the distinctive modern American industrial relations system. This is a study of the working out of those relationships, paying special attention to one of the parties — the business community. It examines the reactions of American businessmen to the challenges to their power and authority associated with the growth of strong industrial unions in the later 1930s and 1940s. Business policy in industrial relations deserves more attention from historians who wish to understand and explain the creation of the modern American industrial relations system after the "turbulent years" of the 1930s.

In the beginning, I thought the interesting question would be how the new unionism of the 1930s had been tamed and incorporated as a junior partner within a modern, liberal capitalist political economy. The relatively unexplored territory of the war mobilization emergency and of peacetime prosperity in the first Truman administration seemed to be the critical period in which to search for answers, because many of the distinguishing features of the contemporary American labor movement clearly emerged in those years. After the dramas of the New Deal period, unions continued to grow in numbers and strength. They became firmly entrenched in the nation's basic manufacturing industries. Industrial conflict reached a high point in 1945–46, but was generally quite orderly. The institutions of collective bargaining developed rapidly toward an early maturity. The political alliance between most unions and the liberal wing of the northern, urban Democratic party became close and organized. Within the newer unions of the Congress of Industrial Organizations (CIO), power became more centralized, established leaders more secure, and the tolerance they extended to rank-and-file militancy or political radicalism declined.

My researches began with an investigation of the internal political life of the unions, and their administrative development. But this approach came to seem increasingly short-sighted and unsatisfactory. It appeared that the roots of the modern American industrial relations system were more likely to be found outside the labor movement than within it. Labor looked more like a reactive than an initiating force in the process of social change; a weak institution in a powerfully organized, pervasively capitalist society. So my attention shifted away from the unions themselves, to focus on the environment within which they had to work. I became convinced that the business community was the dynamic force in the shaping of that environment. What had begun as institutional labor history turned by degrees into business history, with special attention to business thought and practice in the areas of labor and public relations and political action designed to change public policy toward the "labor problem."

I have tried to identify the problems American management thought it faced; to examine its perception of those problems; and, in the light of management's thinking and perceptions, to evaluate its behavior. Managers' handling of their difficulties was, in the main, a success. But the favorable results they could see by the end of the 1940s often resulted from something more than the business community's exploitation of its power and opportunities. However convinced one may be by notions of business "hegemony," however impressed by the general astuteness of the managerial elite, one has to acknowledge that the situation was not in fact under the control of all-wise businessmen. They were not responsible for the climate of international relations in the war and early Cold War years, which had such immense effects upon domestic politics and, even more directly, upon the economy. And what the business community did to deal with its problems may not have been well considered in every case. Business actions certainly affected public policy and the climate of public opinoin; but one is speaking of influence, not control, and of only one influence among many. In short, many of the most important circumstances with which particular corporations and the whole business community had to reckon were outside their power to affect, or even their capacity to understand.

But even after one has deflated the significance of the business community's efforts to get the better of the labor movement in the 1940s, there is still a lot of substantial achievement left to describe, analyze, and appreciate. Business did not create its opportunities, but in the postwar collective bargaining rounds in the basic industries, the drive for the Taft-Hartley Act, and the propaganda offensive against the labor movement and its liberal allies which this work recounts, it certainly seized them — with lasting consequences.

One does not have to share the beliefs, or agree with the purposes, of those businessmen who did so much to shape the postwar industrial relations system, in order to admire their competence. They had a good understanding of their long-term objectives, and a reasonable ability to match means to ends, and to carry policy through into practical execution. It is probably easier for a British observer, who does not have to live with a system he does not altogether approve of, to respect the men who helped make it without regretting that they did their job so well.

It is impossible to explain satisfactorily the development of the ideas and practices which have made the modern American industrial relations system what it is if the focus is fixed too narrowly on one decade. Most of this study is concerned with the 1940s, but not all. Previous decades had originated many of the problems with which businessmen had to grapple, and had contributed many of the tools and weapons they would use in their complex struggle for power and influence. And the experience of past generations of businessmen was an important inheritance for the conservative, but resourceful, policymakers on whom this study concentrates. Sometimes it was burdensome, unhelpful, misleading. More often it was a source of confidence and strength.

Businessmen had a large hand in the creation of a unique industrial relations system between the rise of the large corporation and the new factory system in the late nineteenth century and the glorious heyday of the 1920s. The policies they adopted before the watershed of the Great Depression — before the rise of big labor and big government set serious restrictions on their freedom of action — are of essential interest, because many businessmen of the 1930s and 1940s continued to believe that the social order of the 1920s had been natural and right, not just desirable from their own point of view. They tried to preserve or restore as much of it as possible after the shocks of the New Deal, using and adapting the techniques and philosophies which had seemed to work so well in the lost Golden Age of Coolidge prosperity and Hoover's new era.

A situation in which business power and prestige were unquestioned was their persistent ideal. But in the disturbed conditions of the 1930s, unpleasant reality was altogether different: chronic economic failure and a steep decline in business influence; a more powerful and interventionist federal government, prepared to listen to other voices than those of businessmen and to serve other interests; and a newly powerful labor movement, which showed that forecasts of its impending demise, current in the late 1920s, were wide of the mark. Worker dissatisfaction, sometimes turning into radicalism and militancy, was channeled into the new unions of the CIO and the renascent American Federation of Labor (AFL). Aided by the federal government, encouraged by a public disillusioned with business supremacy and its consequences, it turned into a new social force with which businessmen had to reckon. Their authority was challenged, their power over their own employees and factories was threatened. The scale and severity of the new problems of labor relations may have been exaggerated — this was no revolutionary situation — but businessmen undeniably had reason to be worried, and to *act* to oppose and contain a dangerous and undesirable movement of concerted protest.

Preparing for, and fighting, the Second World War put an end to economic stagnation, mass unemployment, and the political vulnerability of businessmen and the business system. But it was not an unmixed blessing. The same conditions which allowed businessmen to make good profits, to build up reserves, to invest in new and expanded capacity, and to demand political favors from the federal government, conferred some benefits on workers and the labor movement. In an overheated economy, increased real incomes were only one index of labor's power. In the turbulent conditions of many wartime factories, workers' influence over how and how much they would produce grew; management-imposed standards of discipline and productivity suffered. Unions completed the task of organizing blue-collar workers in mass-production industries, improved their members' contractual terms of employment, and showed that the rise of labor in the 1930s was no mere flash in the pan. During the war, the CIO in particular acquired staying power. And the federal government still encouraged it: the growth of collective bargaining, as advocated by the Wagner Act, was fixed national policy. The state helped the new unions plant deep roots within the basic manufacturing industries. The aid was not given without strings, but it helped ensure that at the end of the Second World War there could be no repeat performance of the smashing of unionism which had happened in the period 1919–22. So businessmen had to learn to live with an expanded labor movement, still in many respects aggressive and undisciplined, whose members and contracts affected or even determined corporate productivity and personnel policies.

Among the new labor relations problems the war mobilization emergency loaded upon the American business community, some were purely temporary, but many were of more lasting significance. As the war drew to a close in 1944–45, businessmen could look back on a disturbed decade, and look forward to uncertain postwar prospects.

A fundamental task is, of course, to determine what was "actually" happening in wartime labor relations, to examine emerging trends, and to describe the kind of labor relations system that seemed to be developing from the rapid, complex, and confused events of 1941–45. But this study is more (or less) than an attempt to gather, relate, and interpret past "facts." It is also an investigation into past states of mind — into the way in which the businessmen who are the chief actors in this drama perceived their own times. What they did makes the fullest sense only in the context of an appreciation of why they did it, and such an appreciation requires us to try to get inside their skulls and see their own world as they did.

That is what I set out to do, first of all by examining why it was that businessmen defined certain features of the wartime labor relations scene as particularly objectionable, particularly dangerous. The study does this by trying to recreate, and analyze, the set of expectations businessmen had about the way the American economy would behave after the war, and their understanding of its effects upon their own firms and upon the political fortunes of the business community. These were key elements in businessmen's calculations of the significance of their labor relations problems, and of the need to take immediate remedial action. The stakes seemed to be very high: control over the workplace, influence in the wider political community, and perhaps the very survival of the free enterprise system itself.

Businessmen's assessments of the scale and seriousness of their problems were misjudged in some particulars, and exaggerated in general. This was partly because they did not have the time or the means to acquire full, balanced, and dispassionate information on which more accurate judgements might have been based. They were harried men, beset by many other problems than those of labor relations alone. But it was also because they were not detached observers. Rather, they were players in a power game, with a lot to lose. They were worried, sometimes even frightened. They were also affronted by what they saw. These reactions become understandable only after we have understood businessmen's ideology, values, attitudes, beliefs, and prejudices — the distorting lenses through which they looked at their world. Labor relations problems were peculiarly able to probe sensitive spots in the businessman's psyche, because they challenged his justifications of his own authority, privileges, and power. They represented a real threat to his interests too, of course. But his reactions were not purely cool and rational.

However, businessmen are practical men. They have to live in the world and work upon it. The ultimate justification of their power is not the ideology they use to rationalize it, but their continuing ability to wield it. Businessmen in the 1940s might not score very high as prophets or thinkers, but they knew how to look after themselves in a fight. In the critical years at the end of the war, they began to apply themselves seriously to the task of containing and rolling back the industrial power and political influence of the labor movement. Their objective was realistic, not utopian — and, to that extent, was somewhat at odds with their own values. They wanted to make the labor movement tolerable and manageable, and then to live with it, not to destroy it. They set about solving their problems in a number of connected ways.

One way was through political action and propaganda to change the climate of public opinion and federal policy toward organized labor. Management's success in its onslaught on the Wagner Act depended most crucially on rising public anxieties about labor power and industrial conflict. The great reconversion strike wave of 1945–46, and business propaganda, focused public and Congressional attention on the need to change the law. Republican victories in the 1946 elections provided the opportunity. Discussions within the business community had already succeeded in hammering out a working agreement on the kinds of legislative changes which were possible and desirable. The federal government was not going to be taken out of the labor relations business; instead, it could be used to help management reduce labor power, restrict union influence, and create a stable framework of law within which businessmen were happy to live and operate. This was the Taft-Hartley Act: Congressional conservatives, Republican and Democratic, were its natural parents, but the business community had played the important role of midwife in bringing it to birth.

Taft-Hartley was only part of the answer: unions also had to be confronted in day-to-day labor relations and in collective bargaining. There, too, a new and toughly realistic management approach was applied, and paid off, in the postwar years. General Motors, Ford, and other large corporations are the heroes of this story: they worked hard to limit and even reduce the degree of control workers could exert over their own conditions of employment via collective agreement or concerted pressure. Management was willing to pour resources into this task, to risk and take strikes. In return, it regained control over the workplace, and slowed, then halted, the advance of collective bargaining. What had seemed to be a rapid, remorseless movement from 1935–45, occasionally checked, as in 1937–40, only to surge forward again as in 1940–41, was stopped in its tracks by 1950. By then, the formative period of the "new" American labor movement of the 1930s was closed: the modern industrial relations system, which management had done so much to make, and which still exists in most essentials today, had been created. 1950 is not merely a convenient end point for this history: it marks the clear beginning of a present which is still inhabited by management and labor in what are now the old basic and heavy industries.

But, even at the highest point of organized labor's relative strength immediately after the war, management had many groups of employees whom unionization had scarcely touched — white-collar and supervisory workers in particular. Even in the case of blue-collar workers, most of whom were unionized, dealing with employees and dealing with the union were not the same thing. In the generally union-free atmosphere of the pre-New Deal years, American management had discovered and developed a whole variety of ways of influencing and controlling large numbers of employees. It had found out how to get them to work efficiently, and how to keep them reasonably satisfied with their station in life. These were the techniques of personnel administration and of welfare capitalism. They were not strong enough to stop the rise of labor in the 1930s. In the 1940s, however, they fitted in well with the strategies described in chapters 4 and 5. Together, they helped in the reassertion of managerial authority in the workplace, and influence in society, which this book studies. Chapter 6 examines the transformation and application of these old approaches to the problem of satisfying workers' expectations, and keeping their grievances under control.

Workers are not just employees, subordinates: they are also formally equal citizens in a political democracy where their views are presumed to count. So it was important for American management that its employees and the general public should have the "right attitude" toward managerial authority and the business system. This was the case whether the issues in question had to do with the immediate employment relationship, public policy, or large but vague concepts of liberty and free enterprise. As far as the articulate, thoughtful executives who controlled America's large corporations were concerned, there could be no rigid line between attempting to influence workers as employees and shaping their attitudes as citizens. They were engaged in a complex struggle for moral authority, not just a contest for power. The outcomes of the two battles were in any case interdependent. So, for the chief protagonists in this account, the work of labor, personnel, or industrial relations did not stop at the factory fence; it did not confine itself to the ways in which workers and their unions were actually treated. It also involved direct action, by public relations and propaganda exercises, to make sure that employees and the general public came around to the same view of the American social order as was held by business executives themselves. Therefore, one of my aims has been to illuminate the different ways in which businessmen of different political persuasions interpreted the challenges to their power in the 1940s from workers, the public, and the state. Businessmen saw things differently, and acted accordingly. What they did may not always have been particularly effective, but examining why they did it certainly helps us understand them better.

Businessmen are the subjects of this study. Their statements and their actions make up most of its sources. Their view of the full range of activities and problems to be set down under the heading "industrial relations" is the one which has determined the work's approach. But there is one important working definition employed throughout with which some of them might not have agreed, and to which certain readers will undoubtedly take exception. So it had better be explained and justified before going any further.

This essential assumption is that there *was* such a thing as an American "business community"; that there was sufficient common ground of interest and outlook among businessmen that one can make meaningful generalizations about them, can take the remarks or actions of some members of it as, in a sense, representative of all.

The business community's component parts were large corporations, the organizations they controlled, and the agencies (the trade press, consultancy firms) which existed for their service. Its viewpoint was articulated, strategic decisions taken, and interests advanced by senior executives in large firms and peak associations like the NAM (National Association of Manufacturers) and the U.S. Chamber of Commerce.

There are at least two major problems with this organizing concept of a "business community." First, and less seriously, to what extent were senior executives the authoritative representatives of the organizations for which they claimed to speak and act? Did they represent anybody, apart from themselves? Second, and much more important, what is one to do with the common objection that American businessmen and the institutions they control are in fact so heterogeneous, so lacking in unity, that one should not speak of a single business community at all?[1]

Fortunately, firm evidence on the structure of power within large business firms and peak associations exists.[2] It is usually safe to assume that senior executives really did speak and act for their corporations — either because they had determined what official policy was, and could naturally be expected to support it, or because their place in the managerial hierarchy did not encourage or allow them to step out of line. In addition, one can cross-check executive statements against corporate policy and practice. The fit is generally very close. Representatives actually are representative; spokesmen actually are speaking for the organizations with which they are identified.

There is also plentiful support for the view that senior executives constituted a distinct social type. In geographical and ethnic origins, in their parents' class and occupational backgrounds, in education, career experience, and age, in life style and even in personality and values, the American business elite displayed a remarkable degree of homogeneity.[3]

Possession of many common interests and occupation of a similar role and milieu naturally led to measurably high group consciousness. One may think of the members of the business elite in more human terms — as like-minded middle-aged men, sharing many of the same clubs and the same gossip, associating with one another in work and leisure, circulating between one another's companies and sitting on one another's boards.[4]

So much for the business community's individual members. But there is corporate membership in this community, too. And historians and political scientists have devoted considerable effort to demonstrating that there is no common ground between different corporations and their managements on a whole host of issues. Each corporation, it is said, is unique in its market situation, and hence in the interests its managers seek to protect and advance. There are big and little businesses, manufacturers of consumers' goods and of producers' goods, transport users and transport suppliers, all with their own particular problems. That must be accepted; but so must V. O. Key's assertion that "it cannot be denied that on some types of questions considerable cohesiveness prevails." A way to forestall pluralistic objections is, first, to define the centripetal issues on which to concentrate, and which highlight the measure of agreement within the business community, and second, to narrow down the operative definition of the business community so as to minimize, if possible, the degree of heterogeneity likely to be present. Once a set of shared problems is identified, problems commonly perceived by men responsible for the affairs of corporations with a large measure of similarity, then it is fair to speak of the existence of a community of interest and opinion within a significant segment of the whole entrepreneurial and managerial class.[5]

I have sought to do this by dealing with subjects on which a large measure of business class unity prevailed, not with issues that divided corporation from corporation. The relative strengths of labor and management, the status and power of businessmen as a distinct group, the legitimacy of their authority—these were the preoccupations which generated the words and actions used as evidence of the business community's state of mind. And these concerns cut right across corporate boundaries, though they were naturally more salient for some firms than for others.[6]

More significantly, this study concentrates on firms with many common characteristics, and upon their senior executives—in general, representatives of what Averitt calls the "center firms" of the American economy, the bases of its productive strength. "The center firm is large in economic size as measured by number of employees, total assets, and yearly sales. . . . Center firms excel in managerial and technical talent; their financial resources are abundant. . . . Center managements combine a long-run with a short-run perspective. . . . Their markets are commonly concentrated."[7]

Such firms included U.S. Steel and Bethlehem Steel, General Motors and Ford, Standard Oil of New Jersey, General Electric, General Foods, and their less eminent brethren in *Fortune*'s two hundred top industrial companies. Many of these, while not dominating whole sectors of the economy, were important in their own field—Allis-Chalmers in heavy electrical and mechanical equipment, Thompson Products in automotive parts.

In industrial relations matters, companies like these shared certain common problems that had to do with controlling large numbers of workers. They were necessarily bureaucratized, and they had the resources to devote to fringe activities in the areas of personnel administration and public relations. They were inevitably powerful in their home communities and in national affairs: because of their size and visibility, their managements had to adopt a definite political strategy to advance their interests and reputations, and to protect themselves against unwanted governmental interference. They provided the bulk of funds and leadership for important interfirm and interindustry national business associations.[8]

Large manufacturing firms shared other important characteristics to interest the student of labor relations. Market leaders in the steel, automotive, electrical equipment, rubber, agricultural machinery, petro-chemical, machine tool, shipbuilding, nonferrous metal, and flat glass industries established patterns of industrial relations practice which lesser firms in the same industries tended to follow. Policies on union recognition, wages, hours, working conditions and nonwage benefits tended to be established in center firms first. Moreover, the relationship between different industries became increasingly formalized over time. By the late 1940s, the "pattern" established in key bargains between the Steel or Auto Workers and U.S. Steel, Bethlehem Steel, General Motors, or Ford was followed more or less quickly and closely by center and peripheral firms in all of the above industries.[9] In addition, of course, they had all shared in the great labor relations upheaval of the 1930s and 1940s. Some had managed to keep their blue-collar workers nonunion: most could look back from the late 1940s on a dozen years of "toil and trouble."

So when the phrase "business community" is used in this study, it is not meant to embrace everything from the mom-and-pop grocery store upwards. It does not even imply that there was a perfect homogeneity of interests and perceptions amongst all corporate policymakers. Instead, it takes in the large and medium-sized manufacturing firms for whose senior managements problems of industrial relations were most similar and salient. Key policymakers and staff advisors from such firms and, to a lesser extent, organizations like the NAM which they dominated, are the human members of this community, and the players in the story which will unfold.

1

The Problem of Industrial Relations

It is probably safe to say . . . that no business generation in the history of the United States has had to cope with so many crises . . . as the generation that first sat down to its office desks as young men in the days of Woodrow Wilson. No generation has had trouble thrust upon it so fast or in so many different forms. And no generation with so much trouble safely behind it has had so much obviously ahead. The men who were twenty-three in 1912 are now approaching their fiftieth year. They are not old. On the contrary they are just in the process of inheriting the ultimate responsibilities and rewards. Yet the nature of their inheritance is not what the orators of the early twentieth century had led them to expect. They do not inherit an American dream. They inherit scarcity.[1]

Before the Deluge

Between the depression of the 1890s and the prosperity of the 1920s, American businessmen made massive strides in improving the technical processes of production and distribution. The degree of control over the economy possessed by a relatively few large corporations increased. And the influence of business men, attitudes, and institutions was pervasive. In the 1920s, it seemed that there was no serious threat to the power or status of business. Both political parties were led by conservative men, thoroughly imbued with an ideology broadly shared by the great middle class and little different from that of the business community. It was not just that government could be trusted not to interfere in business matters in any deliberately harmful way: a positive and effective collaboration had been developing since before the First World War, a more or less equal partnership between the power of the business community and of the state.[2]

In addition, most of the other groups which had seemed to threaten business power and autonomy during the "Age of Reform" — even as recently as 1919–22 — no longer offered a serious challenge. Liberal reformism was weak, leaderless, and lacking in purpose; not by any means extinct, but certainly in decline and able to win only minor victories. Internal divisions and brutal suppression in and after World War I had smashed the Socialists; there was no important radical party to take their place. And the labor movement, principally represented by the AFL, had lapsed into impotence and insignificance. Between 1917 and 1919 in particular, favorable federal legislation, high levels of economic activity, and worker militancy had increased its membership and bargaining power and helped it to penetrate the crucial mass-production industries. But the short, sharp depression of 1921–22, and the employers' American Plan antiunion offensive of the same years, had stripped it of most of its important gains. Thereafter, it aimed to regain a reputation for respectability and a safe conservatism. It hoped to win a secure place, however small, in a corporate-controlled economy, by showing how helpful it might be in fighting radicals and cooperating with managements in the solution of production and personnel problems. In fact, it demonstrated that it could safely be ignored.[3]

In the absence of effective opposition, business was free to build and dominate an industrial relations system in which independent unions and the free collective action of employees had no place. Unions were confined to the railroad operating crafts; to sick industries, such as coal mining, the garment trade, and northern textiles; and to local market industries, principally construction and some service trades. In the steel, automobile, rubber, electrical equipment, public utility, oil, chemical, and food-processing industries, the labor movement had either failed to make headway altogether, or had been pushed out in the postwar return to normalcy.

Most of the business community was therefore free to pursue whatever industrial relations policy it preferred. And in this situation, belligerency remained the typical employer's reaction to an organizing drive or a strike. To the managers of a mass of small to medium-sized manufacturing and processing firms and for some of the very largest concerns, particularly those in the steel and automotive industries, well-organized and vigorous use of the traditional weapons of industrial warfare seemed to be a sufficient response to the "labor problem."

Their antiunion efforts were as successful in the 1920s as they had been a generation earlier. So their judgment of the rightness of their course was not disturbed by doubts concerning its wisdom or practicality. Unionism they considered to be ideologically unacceptable and practically dangerous. It introduced another center of power and loyalty into the very heart of the business firm, a potential for challenge and disruption and restrictions on the pursuit of efficiency. Owners and managers fought to preserve the absolute authority they thought to be rightfully theirs, and essential for the profitable conduct of affairs.[4]

But belligerency was not the only response. In the light of future events, it was not even the most significant. An alternative strategy was supported by a strategic minority of businesses. Most of them were center firms, but some of the pioneers were small and owner-managed. The oil refining, electrical manufacturing, public utility, meat-packing, and farm equipment industries figured largely, as did some branches of the metal trades. They had been experimenting with new approaches to the problem of controlling industrial labor since the 1890s. By the 1920s they had developed a unifying rationale and a battery of techniques which promised a comprehensive solution to American management's industrial relations problems. This progressive minority constituted a self-conscious movement, with its own recognized leaders, organizations — notably the Special Conference Committee (SCC), formed of representatives from very large firms — and networks for the exchange of information, especially the American Management Association (AMA).[5]

The key elements in the progressives' program were scientific personnel administration, welfare capitalism, and employee representation through company unions. Originally, each had developed independently. The labor shortages and worker militancy of the World War I period had speeded their welding together into a common approach, and had encouraged a considerable section of the business community to support it.

Scientific personnel adminstration was part of a long-term trend toward systematization in the use of resources within the "new factory system." The objectives of this search for order were higher productivity, lower costs, and reduced levels of conflict. Its promise was that the outcome would satisfy workers as well as managers. Employees would become more efficient, more tractable, and more contented. They would neither need nor seek unionization to better their lot, because they would get all they could reasonably want at the hands of an enlightened management.[6]

Welfare capitalism depended on unilateral management action too. Its intention was to improve working conditions and the lives of employees outside working hours, beyond the factory wall. It began with the simple humanitarianism and straightforward paternalism common in late nineteenth-century family capitalism, and it offered a way of mitigating the hardness and insecurity of life in American society. Beyond this, it acquired a definite political purpose. The criticism of reformers, and the threat of positive state intervention, spurred businessmen to take the initiative to meet some of the evident social problems of the Progressive Era. The idea that businessmen had a responsibility to act positively to curb unrest, and to guide social change, was urged strongly by the National Civic Federation (NCF). But welfare capitalism also had less grand objectives. A contented workforce was reckoned to be an asset worth the expense of welfare efforts, whether or not workers or reformers were putting pressure upon management. Contented employees would be more efficient, more stable, and less receptive to "outside agitation." By the 1920s, welfarism had become an integral part of comprehensive industrial relations programs designed primarily to attach workers to their company.[7]

The first two elements in the progressive program aimed to make workers feel that unionism was unnecessary. But the company union was offered to workers as a substitute for independent, "outside" organization. It would provide machinery for consultation and communication between management and men, meeting some of the wishes of the latter while leaving the control of the former not only unimpaired, but actually enhanced. At the outset, the employee representation movement was largely an expedient reaction to outside pressures and threats. But as it developed and became consolidated in the 1920s, it represented something much more important: some managers' faith that an acceptable form of employee representation could make substantial contributions to worker satisfaction and organizational efficiency. Channels of communication in large, hierarchical corporations needed to be unblocked: in so doing, managements might acquire a new source of information and a new means to influence their subordinates. Most companies in the employee representation movement established a justifiable reputation for offering their workers good conditions, especially in terms of fringe (nonwage) benefits and the physical work environment. This was partly a result of the development of corporate personnel and welfare policies in response to workers' expressed desires.[8]

Together with the unsophisticated, but successful, antiunion efforts of the belligerents, the progressive approach seemed to be creating an unassailable, corporate-controlled industrial relations system. The AFL was unable, and seemed disinclined, to compete for the allegiance of the mass of blue-collar workers in mass-production industry. In this situation, workers had no apparent choice but grateful acceptance of whatever crumbs fell from the rich man's table. From 1922 to 1929, when moderate unemployment persisted alongside relatively high living standards for those at work, the level of workers' protests remained tolerably low. As long as business' political supremacy lasted, so also would the legal and other barriers to effective self-organization and collective action on the part of American workers.[9]

Faith in the technical competence and market power of organized business, in its ability to solve any economic or social problem, was part of the ideology of management in the New Era. That faith was accompanied by confidence in the far-sighted, socially responsible purposes to which business would give its powerful support. The air was full of self-satisfied talk about improved business ethics and the professionalization of management, of business as service and management as trustees. As long as prosperity lasted, nothing could prick this bubble of words. Businessmen were not forced to examine the flaws in the system they had created — the gaps between promise and performance, rhetoric and reality.[10]

But when prosperity disappeared, there was no delaying the day of reckoning. As businessmen had claimed credit for the good times, they had to accept blame for the bad. The inability of the managements of even the largest corporations to isolate themselves from the effects of general economic collapse was demonstrated. And the business community acting in concert, with Hoover as conductor, was powerless to counteract the decline in production, employment, and payrolls. The "new business statesmanship" was put to a severe test, and found wanting. Large corporations put out unprecedented efforts to maintain workers' incomes and to cushion them against the effects of the Depression, but even the boldest experiments failed. As the Depression persisted and deepened, corporations were forced to curtail activities and cut costs to the bone. In the process, welfare capitalism's hopes died, and personnel departments were axed altogether, or continued in shrunken form. Businessmen lost faith in Hoover, and confidence in themselves. They had been as oversold as the great American public on their own ability to keep the American economy running at a high and rising level, and were as lacking in suggestions for remedial action as were the majority of politicians.[11]

The American voting public turned against the Republican party, which had administered prosperity and disaster, and against business also. The former lost power in Congress in 1930; the latter lost prestige and its position of unquestioned authority on all matters, the economic in particular. As a result of the crisis, a revolution in public opinion and public policy was under way. Despite brutally high levels of unemployment and vicious repression, radicalism and worker militancy began to revive. The stage was set for a decade of unexpected and disquieting social change.

THE NEW DEAL

Severe though the shocks of 1929–32 were for the business community, it had begun to recover even before Roosevelt entered office at the very pit of the Depression in March 1933. Businessmen were ready to suggest measures to solve the problems of the economy and to reverse the decline in the business community's power and standing. Leaders of progressive management came forward with their idea of a corporate state as an aid to economic recovery and stability. Meanwhile, the NAM, traditional coordinator of belligerent antiunionism and conservative political action and propaganda, was also being revived. The "Brass Hats," a small group of senior executives largely recruited from middle-sized steel companies, anticipated hard struggles to come, and resurrected the NAM to lead the fight.[12]

The Roosevelt administration based its economic strategy on the progressive "industrial statesmen's" suggestions. The first New Deal had little confidence in the labor movement as an agency for social reform or economic recovery. But in the drafting of the National Industrial Recovery Act (NIRA) of 1933 there was an opportunity for the AFL and its friends in Congress to win some federal recognition of labor's right to organize and bargain collectively. They had already succeeded in lowering the legal obstacles to union growth with the Norris-La Guardia Act of 1932. Now they acted again, laying the basis for the New Deal's revolution in public policy towards the organization of labor in NIRA Section 7(a). This passed without the support of the administration, which remained cool toward labor and hesitant in taking its part in ensuing industrial conflicts. Section 7(a) condemned, in general terms, the antiunion strategies of belligerent and progressive firms. But an increase in the labor movement's numbers and strength was by no means guaranteed. The outcome would depend on the relative strength, tactical skill, and determination of particular contestants. And in 1933–35, it seemed that the business community was getting the better of the fight.[13]

Industry did not welcome 7(a). The NAM and others had lobbied hard for the protection of the open shop and the company union. Even so, they could live with their failure. The company union had not been absolutely outlawed, and the nonstatutory boards which were eventually set up to administer NIRA's labor provisions could not oppose even the cruder antiunion tactics effectively. Management succeeded in exploiting its own strength and the ambiguities in 7(a) and in the administration's attitude toward its implementation. In consequence, the upsurge of unrest in the basic industries which were to form the centers of CIO strength was headed off. Unions made few substantial gains in members, bargaining power, or contractual relations. Open shops, individual bargaining (i.e. no bargaining at all), and company unions survived and prospered. Where independent unions did win a foothold, it was only grudgingly and temporarily conceded.[14]

Businessmen certainly had to pay more attention to their industrial relations problems, and they could not always steer clear of trouble. But it still seemed that there was a realistic and acceptable alternative to union recognition and collective bargaining. As well as devoting increased recources to traditional union-busting activities, more firms began to follow the best practice of progressive companies. In particular, company unionism spread rapidly: it was a way of seeming to comply with the letter of the law, while stemming workers' own organizational efforts. No fundamental departure from opposition to independent unionism was necessary.[15]

The progressives and their agencies provided leadership in this extensive renovation. They offered a useful cadre of specialists, a battery of techniques and procedures, and a pattern of managerial organization for the systematic handling of industrial relations problems. The extension of progressive methods was encouraged by the NAM, which organized a scheme to provide its members with help in setting up company unions under the auspices of the National Industrial Conference Board (NICB) and the AMA. "The activities of the American Management Association were apparently so satisfactory that it came to be recognized by the early part of 1936 as 'the organization best qualified to give Nation-wide impetus to sound industrial relations policies.'"[16]

The SCC also used the AMA as its agent for the same purpose—less surprising, given the previous overlap in membership and approach. With such important backing, AMA conferences became much better supported and more broadly representative. The message of progressives and belligerents, and of their respective organizations, became very similar: "Put your house in order." Progressives thought they had the answers to the business community's industrial relations problems. Until 1935, it was perfectly reasonable to believe that they were right.[17]

The events of 1935–37 demonstrated that this was not so. Changes in public opinion and public policy and in the relative strength of business and organized labor invalidated many of the techniques of belligerents and progressives alike. Their common objective of freedom from outside unions became generally unattainable.

In May 1935, the NIRA, already eviscerated by lower court decisions and business resistance, was declared unconstitutional by the Supreme Court. But almost immediately Section 7(a) and the first, weak National Labor Relations Board (NLRB) were replaced by the much stronger, more comprehensive, and more definite Wagner Act. By September, a new and vigorous NLRB was in operation. Labor's allies in Congress and the administration had learnt their lessons from the experience of 1933–35. The principle of sole bargaining rights for representatives of a majority of workers in appropriate bargaining units was unequivocally endorsed, and the NLRB was given power to interpret the Wagner Act and enforce its decisions. A list of unfair labor practices, derived from experience of employer behavior, formed Section 8 of the Act. The NLRB applied these in such a way as to develop a code of positively acceptable practice. Interference of any sort with workers' exercise of their rights was forbidden, thus outlawing the old-style company union as well as more directly coercive tactics.

Until 1937, when the Supreme Court found for the constitutionality of the Wagner Act, the NLRB had to tread softly. Thereafter, until 1939–40, it was in its most active and interventionist phase. Its powers were to investigate and publicize, decide cases of representation, and to order managements to cease and desist from unfair labor practices. It could also order the reinstatement, with back pay, of workers found to have been unfairly dismissed for union activity. In addition, the NLRB brought managements and unions together in conference, and induced managerial compliance with its code of conduct in countless informal cases. The mere presence of a statute was enough to bring many companies to conform, however reluctantly. For recalcitrants, there was exposure, sometimes procedural harassment, and the difficulty and expense of protracted hearings. Gradually, the extent of blatant antiunionism subsided, as managements either complied with the developing code of practice or became much more subtle in their violations.[18]

But the federal government should not be given all of the credit for the changing character of labor relations in the late 1930s. The effective struggle of organized workers was still needed to overcome stiff employer resistance. NLRB procedures were too slow, its remedies inadequate, and judicial review made the enforcement of its orders belated and uncertain in many of the worst cases of stubborn and repeated violation. The organization strike, or the real threat of it, remained the most persuasive weapon in labor's armory. And the labor movement became more able, and willing, to use it.[19]

In and after October 1935, when the Committee for Industrial Organization (CIO) was formed, defects in the organization and leadership of the American labor movement were corrected. The established unions of the CIO — the Mine Workers, Amalgamated Clothing Workers, and Ladies' Garment Workers — provided invaluable assistance to its organizing committees in steel, textiles and meat-packing, and to the rank-and-file unions in the automobile, rubber, and electrical equipment industries. AFL unions, such as the Machinists and the Teamsters, entered fully into the competition for members and bargaining rights. They used both traditional and novel means — in particular, recourse to NLRB procedures and the sit-down strike — to bring about a great increase in labor power in the basic and strategic industries between 1935 and 1937. Corporations found themselves up against strong unions that were supported by public policy and very frequently by public opinion. Wherever the union was able to be an effective disruptive force, its pressures for recognition and contract negotiation could not long be safely ignored. The new and reinvigorated unions were formidable opponents for industrialists unprepared to deal with them.[20]

THE SPECTRUM OF BUSINESS RESPONSE

Corporations followed a variety of strategies in dealing with the labor relations problems of the later 1930s. Some of them were hangovers from the pre-Wagner Act period, but it was also in the later 1930s that the policies American business implemented much more generally in the postwar era began to take shape. Immediate business responses to the rise of labor can be fitted into three broad categories: persistent antiunionism; realistic accommodation and adaptation; and the progressive approach. Most large manufacturing firms find a place in such a classification system, but not necessarily the one one might expect on the basis of their performance in the 1920s or the later 1940s. The problems to be dealt with changed over time, and so did the character and outlook of some senior executive groups — sometimes with quite dramatic effect, as at Ford and General Electric.

Persistent Antiunionism: The Belligerents

A large and significant minority of industrialists continued to meet the challenge of labor with belligerent tactics and a reactionary political strategy. They were able, at considerable cost, to fight a determined rearguard action from 1937 until America's entry into the Second World War. Articulate opposition to the New Deal and the organization of labor was led by the NAM and the American Liberty League (ALL). Funding and direction of the two organizations came from many of the same sources. The NAM, along with other employers' organizations, had testified against the Wagner Bill in 1934–35. After it was passed, the NAM Law Department and the ALL National Lawyers' Committee reached the same conclusion — that the Act was unconstitutional. Their advice to business was to resist, to appeal to the courts for injunctive and other relief, and to await the certain overthrow of the Roosevelt administration by the electorate, or the Wagner Act by the Supreme Court.[21]

But the hoped-for deliverance was not forthcoming. Litigation to test the NLRB's interpretations of the Wagner Act continued, but usually failed; the higher federal courts, in particular, usually upheld the Board's decisions. The NAM, along with industry associations and the conservative press, made outspoken attacks on the Board, its members, and its decisions, and lobbied hard for repeal or restrictive amendment of the Act from 1937 until 1941. All this effort had some effect: the NLRB was forced onto the defensive and into moderation. But the strategy of reaction was largely a failure.

Political reaction accompanied a wave of employer antiunion belligerency. All the old weapons of coercion were deployed, and some reached new peaks of refinement. Some industrial conflicts in the late 1930s continued to be bloody affairs. Some industrialists, like Ernest Weir of National Steel and Tom Girdler of Republic Steel (both "Brass Hats"), seemed to relish the fight. But others, like the Fisher brothers of GM, were unwilling to accept the destruction of life and property, and the poisoning of community feeling, that belligerent antiunionism entailed.[22]

There were other reasons for avoiding belligerency. It was expensive, and the results were uncertain. And the costs went beyond the balance sheet: at a time when business was attempting to improve its public reputation, belligerent antiunionism won business few friends. The mass media seized on industrial violence and disseminated news and pictures of it which often, as in the case of the Battle of the Overpass at Ford's massive River Rouge complex, or the Memorial Day massacre, made it obvious that company thugs or the forces of "law and order" in antiunion communities were the instigators. In addition, crude belligerency was certain to result in complaint to the NLRB and thorough investigation — or, still worse, in exposure by the La Follette Committee of the Senate. The Committee's prolabor crusaders produced a partisan, but thorough, account of patterns of behavior which were increasingly unacceptable to the general public and to large sections of the business community itself. Sometimes the Committee's very presence was enough to limit antiunion violence. And the labor movement was given important public relations assistance when the Committee revealed corporate violations of federal law to set against business publicity protesting violations of property rights and public order by strikers in general and sitdown strikers in particular.[23]

Belligerency might well be emotionally satisfying, but it was a costly, dangerous, and crude weapon for business to deploy in the labor and public relations struggles of the later 1930s. As a result, most antiunion firms relied on less bloody, coercive, and counterproductive tactics.

Persistent Antiunionism: The Sophisticates

The objective of companies like Goodyear Tire and Rubber and International Harvester—both Special Conference firms—was, as with the belligerents, to resist outside unionism. The strategy of reaction was endorsed, and violence was used, in the proper circumstances, but the less objectionable and detectable unfair labor practices were preferred. Discriminatory hiring, firing, layoff, and recall of union members and activists, surveillance of union activity, man-to-man pressurizing by foremen, and antiunion propaganda were effective obstacles to union organization and collective action. In addition, there were yet more subtle evasions of the NLRB's code, principally assistance to company unions to become nominally independent of employer, AFL, and CIO alike, and refusal to bargain with a duly selected outside union in the hope that a demoralized membership would fall away once the futility of their action was demonstrated. Finally, individual and collective grievances were sometimes conceded, to show how unnecessary the union was.[24]

Companies were able at least to delay union penetration and the inauguration of collective bargaining. Some, like the subsidiary companies in the American Telephone and Telegraph, Standard Oil, and Du Pont empires—all of whose parent firms were SCC members—were able to steer their long-established employee representation plans toward lasting independence. The NLRB was able to investigate and disestablish "independent" unions which were nothing more than old company unions under another name, but some survived—as at American Rolling Mill Co., Armstrong Cork, and Weirton Steel, all of whose chief executives were NAM activists. In the case of corporate prevarication and refusal to bargain, the NLRB worked out a number of procedural tests of satisfactory performance—most important, the readiness to enter into a written contract—but this took until early 1941.

Accordingly, breaches and evasions of the NLRB's code remained possible and popular for many large employers. Sophisticated and belligerent antiunionism together kept substantial minorities of all of the basic and strategic industries from having to recognize unions and enter into collective bargaining with them until the war. The existence of such important union-free holdout firms as Ford Motor, the "Little Steel" companies, all but Armour and Co. of the big meat-packers, Goodyear Tire and Rubber and (in a different sense) Firestone Tire and Rubber, made organized labor insecure even where it had managed to establish workable relationships.[25]

The Realists

We signed up for two reasons. First, we believe the union has come to stay in our industry; and second, we knew we were the next citadel for assault by the CIO, and, in point of fact, we *had* to sign. Financially, we were in no position to stand a two or three months' shutdown of production or to carry the ball for the rest of the industry.[26]

A majority of American center firms were compelled to accept unionism as a fact, often after strong opposition. There was no welcome for unions: they were accepted reluctantly, under pressure, and with ill grace. Contractual improvements and increased security for the union as an organization were both strongly resisted, in the hope that, some day, the union might wither away. Managements were acutely conscious of the union as an infringement upon their power, and supported political action to amend public policy, and propaganda to reorient public opinion. General Motors is probably the best example of a large firm compelled to recognize and deal with a militant industrial union, despite its management's wishes.[27]

Managements had little choice but to be "realistic" in their dealings with labor, once their opposition had been overcome. Management's decision on when to abandon a posture of out-and-out antiunionism was determined by the intersection of two complex and variable forces: the union's bargaining power, and the management's determination to resist. The union's strength was affected by the economic condition of the firm or industry with which it had to deal, and by the state of opinion of the workers and of the communities where they lived. The size and militancy of a union's membership were partly determined by the success of industry's opposition, and in turn affected management's calculation of the costs and benefits of particular courses of action. Continued resistance might very well mean a strike, or serious, repeated interruption of production by workers on the job. Signing a contract promised some stability and continuity. Dealing with a union, either for its members only, or on behalf of all workers in the bargaining unit, signing a contract, and adjusting grievances by formal negotiation, were objectionable practices. But the law seemed to require them, and the costs of managerial obduracy, in terms of loss of control over the workforce, could be very high.

But two firms could very easily be faced with apparently similar circumstances — workers with power and unity, collective consciousness and purpose; the threat or actuality of a costly strike; local media, public opinion, and law enforcement agencies either prolabor or neutral — and *still* reach different conclusions about the proper, "realistic" course of action management should follow. This is because of the other determinant of the course of action any particular firm pursued in response to the challenge of labor: the basic outlook on industrial relations matters of its management. "In no area . . . is the character and personality of the controlling executive or group more clearly reflected than in policies dealing with labor relations."[28]

Managers are people, not calculating machines. They are influenced by more than cost factors in making industrial relations policy. Unionization and conflicts for control were very sensitive issues. Reactions to them were not necessarily "rational." To many businessmen, antiunionism was a matter of principle. Realism, practicality, problem-solving activism, and a readiness to try new approaches are important elements in the self-image of American management, and affect its behavior. But so does a deeply rooted, consistently conservative system of beliefs. The labor problems of the 1930s produced conflicting reactions from business, but certainly indicated that managers were far from being a "purely neutral technocracy." On the contrary, they had a large stake in a system of power and status which was under serious threat and which they had been brought up to consider natural and almost God-ordained. They found themselves living in "a nightmare world where the laws of capitalism, if they operated at all, worked the way the laws of gravity do in a dream." Some saw in industrial conflict and legislated social change the portents of a revolutionary conspiracy against American freedoms. Cool counsel to "get wise" and face realities could hardly prevail where issues were emotion-charged and value-laden.[29]

Or at least, it could hardly prevail generally and immediately. The outraged paternalism of the Kohlers, discovering the "disloyalty" of their prounion workers; the stubborn, entrepreneurial individualism of Ernest Weir, determined to keep strict control over the organization he had built; the reactionary, republican, High Federalist attitudes of the Du Ponts and their political allies — all of these elements of character and ideology helped condition managerial decision-making in matters of union recognition, contract negotiation, and everyday industrial conflict. Antiunion employers were willing to go to extraordinary lengths, and to incur substantial costs, in their fight against labor.

But no major American firm was willing to continue the fight into the last ditch, though some threatened to.[30] The most antiunion employers, resisting weak unions, could evade the NLRB and the labor movement for years, but for even the stubbornest corporations in the steel, automotive, electrical equipment, rubber, farm equipment, and meat-packing industries, "realism" became a distasteful, if (it was hoped) temporary necessity, in the late 1930s or the war years. The traditional armament of belligerency had been effectively depleted by law and public opinion, and countered by the organization of strong, relatively militant unions. Unions were present as a disruptive force, and were not going to go away soon. It was no use waiting for Congress to make a new law, or for a strong conservative shift in public opinion. Business was very actively in pursuit of both these objectives, but recognized that they were unlikely to bring immediate relief, whereas the labor problem had to be dealt with in the here-and-now, within the plant. Even if the power of labor should be reduced at a later date, there would still be important new operating problems in labor relations. What could be done about them? Once a corporation had rejected, or been forced to abandon, belligerency or stubborn evasion of the Wagner Act, what course was open to it?

"Swords may be beaten into plowshares, but even a plowshare can be used to clobber an opponent into insensibility."[31] The answer was to use corporate resources and available expertise to get the better of the union in orderly, institutionalized confrontations. General Motors and Allis-Chalmers typified this approach, developing a combative, hard-nosed, but fundamentally legal labor relations strategy. They put great efforts into managerial organization for contract negotiation and administration, with the aim of confining the union's intrusions into management's domain. "Management prerogatives" — the traditional authority of the employer to determine the conditions of work unilaterally — were defended, in principle and in daily practice, even at the cost of "taking a strike." The union was denied prestige, security, and legitimacy. Such a course was open and natural to a company faced with a militant union and having large reserves of strength and determination to carry on the fight against it, even after the question of recognition and collective bargaining was settled.[32]

In GM's case, the company was brought to its position of narrow and legalistic acceptance of the union by bitter experience. The great sit-down strike of 1937, which forced the corporation to recognize the UAW, was followed by a turmoil of wildcat strikes over unresolved grievances from 1937 until 1939, as the corporation refused to recognize the necessity of day-to-day negotiations over grievances, or to accept the UAW's shop steward system. Finally, in the "Strategy Strike" of 1939, a weak and divided union compelled the corporation to continue dealing with it. At last, GM management understood that it was going to be troubled by the UAW for a long time, and decided to follow a "tough but fair" labor policy of not interfering with (or supporting in any way) the UAW's drive for members. GM insisted upon the protection of management's right to manage and put pressure upon the union leadership to discipline its own members or not interfere with managerial discipline of them. GM "put its house in order": industrial relations became a top management function; contracts were negotiated, and their local administration was controlled, by a strong central staff; the wage structure was rationalized. As a result of these policies, GM, alone of all major automobile manufacturers, managed to stabilize its labor relations on more or less acceptable terms before the outbreak of the war. GM's strategy of "realism" was what came to be known, after the war, as the establishment of an "armed truce" relationship with the union. But few companies matched the speed and thoroughness of GM's adoption of this course: General Motors was a corporation with immense resources, a tradition of technical progressivism and managerial excellence, and an ingrained habit of "management by policy" — the development of a program of considered action — to handle all important problems.[33]

In contrast, the Chrysler Corporation's management, which was ideologically antiunion and politically reactionary, as were most top GM men, never translated its attitudes into organization, policies, and procedures calculated to secure the common objective of uninterrupted production and unimpaired control. Chrysler handed its labor relations problems over to the corporate attorney in New York. At the plant level, there was lasting chaos. Chrysler continued to be afflicted, into the 1950s, by unofficial workers' actions which were often successful in securing informal adjustments by production supervisors and plant management over such critical issues as discipline and workloads. The "policy," if it can be called that, which Chrysler represented was one of half-hearted defensiveness against the union, in which the avoidance of labor trouble by making expedient concessions got the better of the aim of defending managerial authority. GM adopted some of the techniques of progressive personnel administration at the same time as it developed its basic labor relations policy, trying to reduce the sources of employee dissatisfaction by unilateral management action. Chrysler did little or nothing until "labor problems" became acute, with an organizing drive or a strike. In consequence, in the 1940s, Chrysler was particularly troubled when the frontier of organization advanced from the rank-and-file into the automobile industry's white-collar and supervisory forces. As a result of its considered preemptive action, GM was relatively untouched by this new problem.[34]

Most managements which were compelled to follow the path of realism and deal with unions were evidently not as thoughtful or articulate about it as GM, and did not put as much corporate energy into the fight. Many simply tried to change as little as possible in the aftermath of unionization; to carry on as before, confining union penetration to the very minimum and granting as little recognition as possible. In the late 1930s, such a course was relatively easy to follow. It would become much more difficult once the economy got moving again. But few corporations had the foresight, time, and resources to follow GM's example and put their labor relations on a "sound business footing" before the war broke out.

This was because unions were still in the process of completing the organization of all the important units of mass-production industry when the defense period began in 1940, and their successful extension of organization into many smaller companies and smaller cities had to await favorable wartime conditions.[35] For many corporations, then, the time of decision on strategy and tactics for living with rather than holding off a union was delayed until the peculiar strains of wartime made it impossible for management to choose freely or act to secure its desired objectives. Even for corporations unionized in 1935–37, the time of decision was often deferred until too late.

It is easy to appreciate why this was so. The constitutionality of the Wagner Act was still undecided until 1937 was half over. The short, sharp recession of 1937–38 faced companies with more immediate and severe problems even than the labor movement. And, as unemployment ravaged the new unions and industrial conflict declined, the challenge with which business had to deal appeared less serious. The formation of a conservative coalition in Congress, and its strengthening in the 1938 elections, offered new hope of a legislative solution to the labor problem. The NLRB's interpretation of the Wagner Act developed quickly in 1937–39, but judicial confirmation of such crucial issues as the necessity of reaching written agreement had to wait until the defense period. The code of practice of which an employer had to be aware, even if he was intent on breaking it, was only in the process of being formed. Contracts and the machinery of collective bargaining were similarly in flux. Faced as corporations were with the speed and complexity of change, and the temptation to wait for Congress to turn up with a panacea, it is understandable that GM's self-critical, self-reliant approach to its industrial relations problems was untypical.

In addition, the resources out of which a tough, successful approach to labor relations problems might have been fashioned were scarce. Only a minority of firms had been organized to deal systematically with personnel problems in the 1920s, and many personnel departments had been scrapped in the cost-cutting disorganization of the Depression. Those which survived had neither relevant experience, the correct outlook, nor adequate staff to handle the problems posed by the organization of labor and the burden of new legislative requirements; and then the shock of transition to the new age of strong unions was great, even for such an unusually well-constructed personnel department as International Harvester's.[36] There was a shortage of knowledge and expertise to apply to new labor relations problems, and in any case managements had other, often more important preoccupations as they searched for strategies for corporate survival. Companies were going through the throes of expansion and contraction of personnel and operations, centralization and decentralization of management structures, and the problems of managerial succession (of which Ford provides the best example). In these circumstances, adoption of new policies and structures for the handling of industrial relations problems was inevitably difficult, even where it did command a high priority.[37]

Where progress was made, it was generally taking place in an atmosphere of crisis, as managements reacted to immediate pressures. There was little time for strategic thinking. Rather, companies were adopting what came to be called a "fire-fighting" approach, looking for ways to comply with increased governmental regulation and new personnel record-keeping requirements, and having to recruit or train staff, and then organize them into departments, to handle these tasks and cope with contract negotiation and administration in recently unionized plants.[38]

So it is not surprising that General Motors provided a rare example of a corporation that was able to get over the turmoil of 1935–37 before the war. GM was giving a lead many other corporations would follow in time. But most large and medium-sized firms had reached some of the same "realistic" conclusions: that unions were going to be around for the foreseeable future, and that they must be dealt with, within the law, in such a way as to preserve as much order, efficiency, and control as possible. Unfortunately, developing policy and procedures to make "living with the union" tolerable was a difficult matter which many firms were only beginning in the years 1937–40.[39]

The policy of "armed truce," though the most important, was not the only strategy for living with unionism that existed in the late 1930s. For the most liberal and constructive response to the problems of unionization, we must look to some of the heirs of 1920s-style managerial progressivism. Not all progressive firms by any means accepted change gracefully. Many, like Special Conference firms Bethlehem Steel, Standard Oil of New Jersey, Du Pont, Goodyear Tire and Rubber, and International Harvester, practiced a sophisticated antiunionism, in the later 1930s as throughout the 1920s; some, notably Westinghouse Electric, General Motors, and U.S. Steel, followed the course of realism. But a few, notably U.S. Rubber and General Electric, accepted the labor movement with little hesitation or apparent regret.

The Progressives: Divergent Responses to the Challenge of Unionism

Managerial progressivism in the 1920s had not entailed any readiness to recognize independent, outside unions as legitimate representatives of employee interests and attitudes. It had involved a certain readiness to alter industrial relations policies as a result of consultation with workers' representatives in company unions, or of some consideration of employee sentiments. But managerial authority and discretion had been unimpaired. The new facts of the 1930s produced markedly different responses from progressive firms. The essentially authoritarian objectives of progressive management, rather than its realism and tactical resourcefulness, inclined most SCC firms to resist truly independent unionism. But the deficiencies of the old solutions, and the challenge of a new situation, prompted some companies to change their tune.

They insisted that the company union remained good in principle: its dedication to harmony between management and workers in each individual plant and firm must be recreated, if possible, in the relations between companies and outside unions. But if workers wanted to organize their own unions, and the law supported them, then the company union must be abandoned. Management's task was one of constructive accommodation to the new circumstances, not outright resistance. Cyrus Ching, U.S. Rubber's Director of Industrial and Public Relations since 1919, developed a convincing rationale for a new progressive program for building an acceptable, cooperative union relationship.

In our company—I am going to try to impress this on industrialists here—we are going to get about the type of labor leadership that we develop by our own actions. If, in dealing, with labor organizations, we are ethical, are entitled to the confidence of people, use fair tactics and use friendly attitudes, we will get that in return; if we are going to be militant, use underhanded tactics and fight all the time, that is the type of organized labor leader we will get. So I think we all must realize that, where we are dealing with organized labor, we are going to get about the type of leadership that we are ourselves.[40]

Ching did not promise overnight or automatic success. But his aim was to win fellow industrialists away from belligerence, and to stir others out of inaction and fatalism in the face of the challenge of labor. He spoke from the tradition of welfarism and corporate liberalism, advising against overreliance on political action as a solution, and in favor of rapprochement at all levels between responsible leaders of business and organized labor. His aim was to build a workable union-management relationship plant by plant, company by company, and perhaps to create a new federal policy based in top level consensus. Commitment to the politics of consensus and the avoidance of conflict was Ching's hallmark. Ching asked his fellow businessmen to strip the subject of union recognition and bargaining of its overburden of emotional and ideological clutter. They should treat the labor leader or negotiator as just another trading partner or sales prospect, "realizing that the fellow on the other side of the table has his troubles and trials and tribulations also, and that you are going to try and work this thing out as well as you can."[41]

At U.S. Rubber, this is exactly what Ching did, putting no obstacles in the way of union penetration of the company's plants and representation plans. Ching and United Rubber Workers (URW) president Sherman Dalrymple met on neutral ground, secretly, each with a second, and worked out an agreement: Ching would prevent plant managers from resisting the union; Dalrymple would do all in his power to make sure that elected local union leadership was responsible, avoiding wildcat strikes and harassment of the management. The agreement worked: U.S. Rubber proceeded slowly towards recognition of the URW, plant by plant, avoiding unfair labor practices and staying clear of the NLRB, even in cases of representation, where possible. In return for its policy of enlightened voluntarism, the company was spared the sitdowns, mass pickets, wildcat strikes, slowdowns, and industrial violence that troubled the other three large rubber companies for years, and Goodyear worst of all.[42]

Ching did not see independent unionism as dangerous and ideologically unacceptable. If it had the responsible leadership management could try to produce, it promised to replace the company union as a communications device and as a means for the peaceful settlement of grievances. And the achievement of constructive and harmonious labor relations could assist in "reselling" the American public on the power and social responsibility of big business.

> Be realistic about it. If you have a union organization in your plant, there is no use ignoring it and failing to see it. You have it there with you. Why not utilize the union organization as it comes in to build confidence on the part of that organization, on the part of your employees, and on the part of the nation generally? Use it as one other avenue to demonstrate that industry has character, has intelligence, has integrity, and is entitled to the confidence not only of its own employees but of organized labor and the public generally.[43]

U.S. Rubber was the second largest firm in the rubber industry, part-owned by the Du Ponts and closely associated with GM as a primary supplier of tires as original equipment. In consequence, its management had to proceed carefully towards recognition of the URW so as not to antagonize its powerful, fundamentally antiunion associates. The other notable "corporate liberal" firm, General Electric (GE), was under no such constraints. It dominated its industry. In addition, its bargaining power against its union was greater than that of U.S. Rubber. All the latter's main tire operations were concentrated in Detroit, whereas GE's plants were already quite decentralized and it had diversified into a number of different product lines.

GE's decision to recognize the United Electrical Workers (UE) was partly triggered by UE's success in taking over company unions from the inside, as in the case of the Steel Workers Organizing Committee and U.S. Steel. But, more than that, it reflected GE management's confidence in its own power and the weakness of the UE. GE believed that it could co-opt UE leadership from the very outset, and obtain a legal substitute for the company union which fitted in well with GE's liberal and progressive public image. The substance of GE's employment relations policies at plant level hardly had to change at all: UE had insufficient membership to have won NLRB elections, and attained recognition that way, had not GE graciously conceded; and, in the stagnant economy of the late 1930s, the UE/GE master contract was little more than a formalization of the liberal personnel policies GE had long instituted. At small cost to itself, GE's constructive response to the problems of labor organizing appeared to have entirely succeeded by the end of the 1930s. It had avoided belligerency and militancy alike.[44]

The examples of U.S. Rubber and GE were well known: both firms were active in the progressive management movement, in the Business Advisory Council of the Department of Commerce, and in preaching their message to less enlightened business audiences. They were not afraid of organized labor, and they were confident that management had the power, the intelligence, and the techniques to get itself just about the kind of labor relations it wanted. Sources outside the business community reinforced this progressive message, turning it into the common currency of "enlightened" labor leaders and academic industrial relations specialists.

The contribution these men made was more than just commentary. They played an active part in teaching management that it must get down to the serious business of building a workable industrial relations system in which responsible unions played a key part. Industrial relations specialists from universities came to fill the difficult positions of final arbitrator or impartial umpire in the grievance procedures of mass-production industry. This was much more a development of the 1940s, but GM blazed the trail in 1940, agreeing to an umpire system in an endeavor to introduce order into its labor relations. Its first umpires, Harry Millis and George Taylor of the Universities of Chicago and Pennsylvania, were men with long experience in the labor relations of the garment, hosiery, and anthracite industries. They believed that collective bargaining through responsible unions could contribute to industrial efficiency and social stability. They and their like, increasing in numbers and influence in the 1940s, played their part in prodding managements to develop proper organization, policies, and procedures for getting their contractual labor relations onto a sound footing.[45]

Men with firsthand experience of the labor movement and federal policy assisted management in other respects: Radio Corporation of America, having decided to recognize the UE after years of bitter struggle, handed over its industrial relations problems to Edward F. McGrady, Assistant Secretary of Labor, experienced mediator and former AFL legislative representative. Ralph Lind, director of the NLRB in Cleveland, and one of McGrady's assistants in the adjustment of labor disputes in the crucial industrial Midwest, left the federal service to join an established firm of management consultants as their labor relations specialist. Both these men made their move in mid-1937, when an increasing number of firms responded to the Wagner Act's validation by accepting public policy and the labor movement as facts with which they had to live.[46]

Active members of the new unions' bureaucracies chipped in with their suggestions. Sidney Hillman, Amalgamated Clothing Workers president, helped persuade GM president "Engine Charlie" Wilson to institute an umpire system, citing the clothing industry's experience of its usefulness as a stabilizing factor in institutionalized conflict. The Steel Workers, centralized, bureaucratized, and responsible from the outset, campaigned to convince managements to accept unions and grant them security. In return the international union's officials could assist in taming radical local leadership, moderating contract demands, and even helping marginally competitive employers to improve productivity. Organized labor's social democratic leaders and intellectuals — Hillman, Walter Reuther, and Phillip Murray, Clinton Golden, Harold Ruttenberg, and Joseph Scanlon of the Steelworkers — were able to reach a large measure of agreement with managerial progressives on the desirability of building an efficient, orderly industrial relations system founded on collective bargaining through responsible unions.[47]

The labor relations strategy of U.S. Rubber, General Electric, and some other firms was the work of a small but prestigious minority of American business. It gained more supporters in the 1940s, and won great attention in the early 1950s. But it was never the modal strategy of American industry. Nor was it even the most significant response to the rise of labor from the ranks of managerial progressives.

Thomas Spates, who became director of General Foods' first corporation-wide industrial relations program in December 1935 after a background with the progressive Industrial Relations Counselors Inc., taught his fellow managers the same lessons of optimism and activism as Ching. But his aim was to stop or even reverse the rise of organized labor. General Foods' top management was extremely active in the NAM and in the organization of nationwide, anti-New Deal and anti-labor propaganda. In his long service with it, Spates developed an integrated personnel and labor relations program which helped keep the company weakly unionized. Spates represented the predominant authoritarian brand of managerial progressivism, committed to the rational development of an orderly industrial relations system responsive to worker's pressures but remaining under executive control. He explained worker's discontent and union consciousness as the results of management's poor industrial relations policy and practice: "If there is any single cause for 'labor trouble,' it is to be found in the inferiority of our administrative intelligence."[48]

As that was Spates' analysis of the causes of the problem, his prescription for managerial counteraction followed naturally. He looked at the figures for union membership, and concluded that "the normal thing for the American workman to do is not to join a trade union" and that "we have not missed the last boat. We still have a chance to do a good personnel job and thereby preserve our fundamental American institutions." He was "convinced that if a greater percentage of employers in this country will do an honest-to-goodness industrial relations job things do not have to go the way they have been tending during the last three years."[49]

Spates' line of argument pointed toward the further application and perfection of scientific personnel administration, not toward the encouragement or willing acceptance of union recognition and bargaining. Unionization was neither inevitable nor in some ways desirable, but an indication of managerial failure. It was unnatural, illegitimate, un-American, and to be resisted, within the law, by the more intensive practice of the sophisticated antiunionism of the 1920s progressives. Spates' prescription was important: it offered an antiunion course the NLRB could not touch, and one which was increasingly adopted in the 1940s, by firms like Fred Crawford's Thompson Products, and General Electric after the departure of its progressive top management.[50] Spates' and Ching's analyses and prescriptions were equally "progressive": their differences simply indicate the divisive nature of the new and intrusive challenges of unionism and the Wagner Act.[51]

NEW TACTICS FOR LABOR PEACE, 1939–40

In the aftermath of the Supreme Court fight and union organizing drives of 1937, the recession of 1937–38, and the evident exhaustion of the New Deal, the pendulum of public opinion swung back. A conservative coalition formed in Congress, and was strengthened in the 1938 elections. Resolutely antilabor Republicans and southern Democrats prevented further legislation for social change and began to pick off the New Deal's exposed positions. The La Follette Committee expired, and its place as a source of meaty investigative reporting was taken by the Dies (House Un-American Activities) Committee, which swiftly showed the antilabor animus and redbaiting tactics of the reinvigorated conservatives.

In industrial states like Pennsylvania, Michigan, and Wisconsin, prolabor administrations were ejected and antilabor statutes enacted reflecting successful business agitation at the grass roots and in state capitols. Law enforcement agencies moved more vigorously against strikers, and the Supreme Court, in the *Fansteel* case, effected one of its very rare reversals of the NLRB. It condemned the sit-down strike as an illegal tactic, and excluded sit-down strikers from the Wagner Act's protection. In Congress, the Smith Committee of the House, set up to investigate the NLRB and its administration of the Wagner Act, partly as a result of AFL complaints against Board policies allegedly favoring the CIO, became a platform from which conservative legislators launched their onslaught on the Board *and* the Act. Taft-Hartley was already conceived, and beginning its slow gestation which the war prolonged.[52]

Clearly, labor's moment was passing, the window of opportunity which had swung open in 1935–37 was slowly being shut. This was the background against which Harold Browne, chief of the Management Research Division of the NICB, delivered a cool evaluation of the contemporary background to industrial relations strategy. Browne observed that "time and the sobering effects of business depression have been working in the direction of greater discipline of union members and the acquisition by their officials of better control over them."[53]

The UAW, ravaged by unemployment, torn asunder by factional fights, almost displaced from General Motors in 1939, still excluded from Ford, moved against wildcat strikes by its members. Wildcats made it difficult for the union to acquire a necessary and desired public image of "responsibility." Its bargaining partners, especially GM, were putting pressure on it to stabilize labor relations and deliver continuous production in return for recognition. The Rubber Workers had many of the same problems, and its officials offered the same answers. As for the Steelworkers, the failure of the Little Steel strikes and the recession had so weakened the union that the only way it could hope to increase its membership was by the dual strategy of utilizing federal machinery, particularly that of the NLRB, and appealing to employers to recognize it as a "responsible union."[54]

Whatever the appearance and the potential of the rise of labor in 1933–37, it was clear that by 1939 not even the new unions of the CIO constituted any sort of revolutionary vanguard. In response to internal forces — the "iron law of oligarchy" — and external pressures — the necessity of dealing with federal agencies, large corporations, the mass media — even those industrial unions which had started life as rank-and-file organizations, rooted in activist militancy, were becoming bureaucratized and "responsible." It was the only way they could survive in an essentially hostile environment and meet the demands of the mass of their members for services, improved contracts, and protection against managerial arbitrariness.[55]

This was a kind of labor movement the business community could live with. Business was also learning to live with the Wagner Act, though not to love it. As Browne wrote, "More and more managements are adopting a broader philosophy of industrial relations, one in which there is no place for even indirect interference with employees' freedom of decision, and one in which belligerency is not the instinctive reaction toward anything having to do with a union. Managements are becoming accustomed to a situation that at first seemed intolerable, and are now taking in stride the various problems that arise in negotiating with established unions or in dealing with situations connected with organizing activity in the plant."[56]

This was good policy for employee and public relations alike. Overt coercion, violence, and lawbreaking hurt both.

"By ruling out fruitless opposition to a condition that, however unwelcome, exists, it clears the way for the application of management's energy and ability to working out a sane and mutually profitable *modus operandi* in labor relations."[57]

Outmoded policies had led to industrial conflict, loss of public confidence in business, and legislative interference and restriction. Now Browne was optimistic that managerial activism could deal with the problems left by the events of the 1930s, and prevent any recurrence of what another, hotter-headed observer called "the so-called social revolution, now burning out."[58]

Management's new tactics for labor peace included the progressive proposal that business should strive to achieve working harmony with organized labor, but, more important, many firms were formulating industrial relations policies leading towards "armed truce" of the kind that prevailed in the postwar years. Belligerency was on the wane: it would not disappear completely, but it became rare in large, city-based firms in the basic industries. More sophisticated antiunionism remained an option some firms were able and willing to take, coming to rely increasingly on the intensive practice of "scientific" personnel administration and "human relations" rather than on the nonviolent unfair labor practices which prevailed in the later 1930s.

All of the important strands in the postwar industrial relations policies of American business were visible by 1939. In the area of political action, the growing sophistication of the business community was also clear. Business organizations like the NAM and numerous employers' associations were belatedly recognizing that reaction and belligerency were no longer a sufficient response to challenges to business hegemony. In the late 1930s the NAM moved towards assisting its members with the difficult task of living with the new circumstances, while attempting to change them. The *Labor Relations* (once *Open Shop*) *Bulletin* provided members with important information on changes in government attitudes, policies, and administrative decisions, and on developments in collective bargaining. Biannual Industrial Relations Institutes were organized nationally, and many local "clinics" were held. The NAM made itself more useful to a growing membership, and the character of the guidance it provided became much less distinctive. It came to incorporate firms and points of view which had been "progressive" in the 1920s, but would only go as far as a provisional acceptance of the new public policy and the labor movement, and then only under duress.[59]

So business attitudes toward the NLRB and the Wagner Act remained hostile. In 1939, *Fortune's* poll of executive opinion revealed only 3.7 percent willing to keep the NLRA as it was, with 41.9 percent in favor of its modification, and 40.9 percent for repeal. The NAM reflected this overwhelmingly disapproving consensus in the substance of its legislative proposals announced in December 1939, but also showed its new-found realism. At that date, the NAM's "acceptance" of collective bargaining "in principle" had little depth or sincerity, and its attack on the Board and the Act was so severe in intent as to defeat their basic objectives. Still, the NAM had made some progress. Under the presidency of Charles Hook of American Rolling Mill Co. (ARMCO) — a long-established, but dynamic, antiunion steel firm which had succeeded in preserving its company union *and* steering clear of the NLRB's sanctions — it no longer asked for outright repeal of the Wagner Act. What it wanted instead was such thoroughgoing amendment as to make the law acceptable and useful to a business community becoming more interested in building stability in labor relations than in continued crude union-busting.[60]

In 1939 the economy was still stagnant, barely recovered from the recession. The labor movement was divided, hesitant, defensive, and as stagnant as the economy. The CIO had lost its élan. Mopping up the large unorganized sectors of industry, and improving contract terms, the working of grievance machinery, and the quality of union recognition and security were daunting problems to which no immediate solutions were available. Business and labor were settled down to a long slog, with business probably more optimistic about its prospects of winning political support.

This was the situation when war orders — particularly from Britain and France — began to revive the heavy and agricultural industries. There were powerful continuities between the industrial relations policies American business was developing in the later 1930s and those it pursued in the 1940s and after. But in the period between, the scale and character of industry's labor relations problems were transformed as a direct consequence of total mobilization of the economy for war. The pressure of events, the rapid succession of crises needing immediate attention, made it even more difficult for managements to think strategically about labor relations policy, or to act with any long-term ends in view. And by the time the war ended, and businessmen were once again comparatively free to set about actively shaping the evolving American labor relations system, they had a rather more formidable adversary to contend with than they confronted in 1937–39. But by that time they, too, were able to negotiate from a position of much greater strength.

2

Labor Relations in the 1940s

THE POLITICAL ECONOMY OF WAR

The coming of war drastically altered the context in which workers and managers, business and labor, competed with one another. Total mobilization left lasting imprints on the American industrial relations system, as well as creating serious short-term problems with which business, labor, and government had to grapple.

After the summer of 1940 the pace of mobilization, and of consequent re-employment, quickened. Unemployment fell from 7.7 to under 4 million in 1941, and factory workers began working large amounts of overtime. By the fall of 1941 existing economic capacity was fully utilized, so there were only two ways to increase production for war: increasing investment, or restricting civilian demand.[1] In practice, both courses were followed. America acquired a planned economy. To make that economy work, the cooperation of both sides of industry was required. But that of the business community was more important, and it was able to exact a high price.

Building America's war economy was a difficult task for the Roosevelt administration. It needed to win the controllers of the key institutions of the American production system over to its side: no modern war could be fought without their services and expertise, and they could not be compelled to cooperate. They had to be coaxed. They were the federal government's bitterest political opponents, and they were afraid that the war emergency would give the New Dealers an opportunity to extend and consolidate central economic control. Roosevelt reassured them. He abandoned domestic reform for the duration, and left an increasingly conservative Congress free to make much of economic and

41

social policy. It used that freedom to begin to dismantle the New Deal. Businessmen's anxieties were further allayed by giving them the largest voice in making and administering policy within America's economic mobilization agencies. America acquired a planned war economy in which business power was safe, and in which the largest corporations' interests and opinions counted most.[2]

Political concessions, by themselves, were not enough. Both in tooling up for war and in reconverting to peacetime production, businessmen were able to demand that the federal government should foot a large part of the bill, and cushion them from risk. In the months before Pearl Harbor they were reluctant to expand capacity, or to convert their plant from civilian to military production. They expected a short war, and anticipated serious postwar problems if they deserted their peacetime markets or imposed additional burdens of excess capacity upon themselves. They were also loath to lose the best, most profitable, least disruptive civilian market they had seen since before the Crash. The federal government had to woo them away from this business-as-usual mentality by providing an extremely favorable operating environment. Liberal investment grants, a cessation of antitrust prosecutions, and generous treatment of profits, expenses, and investment under the tax laws smoothed their path into war. Compensation for contract termination, the refunding of excess profits taxes, and the opportunity to acquire brand-new production facilities, created at the federal government's expense, for next to nothing or much less than their true value, made the return to "normalcy" in 1944–47 much easier than it had been after the First World War.[3]

So businessmen did very well out of the war. For the unions and their members the picture was not quite so rosy. Organized labor's participation in planning the war economy was limited: it never had more than advisory status, and its influence declined steadily from 1941 on. The labor movement was politically vulnerable: conservative legislators inflicted direct wounds, and the mass media slammed it as unpatriotic, an obstacle to all-out defense production. And the Roosevelt administration did little to protect it against these chill winds of conservative hostility. All labor could do was try hard to fight back, by strengthening its ties with the liberal wing of the northern, urban Democratic party. In 1944 the CIO, in particular, helped the Democrats get out the vote in many industrial districts, and made a strong case for a resumption and extension of the New Deal to solve the expected social and economic problems of the coming peace. Its efforts to counter the conservative drift in public opinion were certainly strenuous, but not particularly effective.[4]

The war certainly gave businessmen and conservatism a powerful boost in their climb back to political influence from the depths of 1934–37. But it also helped the labor movement to extend and consolidate its own power, as well as conferring important material benefits on the working class after more than a decade of depression. An honest balance sheet of the effects of war upon the labor movement must show many entries on the credit side.

Businessmen could exact the greatest political concessions, but labor's cooperation in the war effort was also required, and that too had its price. Labor could not and would not have refused to cooperate, in any event. But the government was able to win its consent quite cheaply. For the duration of the war a sort of synthetic social harmony prevailed, which meant that the conservatives' program of attacking the central pillars of the New Deal could not be achieved. In particular, serious and permanent attacks on the Wagner and Fair Labor Standards Acts were ruled out. Given that protection and the advantages an overheated economy gives to organized labor, the movement emerged from the war stronger than it had entered it.[5]

In the first place, organized labor's numbers rose from less than nine to almost fifteen million. More important, it had the strength arising from the near-completion of the task of organizing blue-collar workers throughout the basic and mass-production industries. In 1939–40 unions had still been struggling to win members, bargaining rights, and some basic guarantee of their future security. By 1945–46 almost 70 percent of workers in manufacturing industry were covered by union agreements. In the transportation and mining sectors, and in the agricultural equipment, aircraft, aluminum, automotive, electrical machinery, meat-packing, nonferrous metals, rubber, shipbuilding, and basic steel industries, between 80 and 100 percent of wage earners worked in unionized plants. The machinery, petroleum, and steel products industries were between 60 and 80 percent organized. Furthermore, as a result of negotiated agreements in 1940–41 and of wartime developments, unions in these industries were now much more firmly entrenched, with contractual guarantees of a secure income and membership, and a greater influence in the plant.[6]

The different political fortunes of business and labor determined their fates in the controlled wartime marketplace. Federal economic management relied on restraining wage and salary increases far more than on controlling prices and profits. The very different treatment Congress meted out to labor's program for domestic reconversion and postwar economic security, compared with the generous attention it gave to the claims of organized business and agriculture, is another instructive measure of labor's relatively small political clout and its consequences.

Nevertheless, in straight cash terms, workers did quite well out of the war. Real disposable incomes increased rapidly, particularly in the defense period, 1940–41. By 1943 a vastly expanded active labor force was more than fully employed. Opportunities were created for those at the margins of the interwar labor market: women, blacks, and other minority groups, country and small town dwellers, the young, the old, the handicapped. Money wages rose, despite federal controls over direct wage increases, high personal income taxes,and restrictions on the free mobility of labor and the use of collective power. Earnings rose more, because of overtime working, the upgrading of workers into more skilled occupations, the expansion of the well-paid durable goods industries, and extensive wage drift. The failures of price control meant that real wage increases were substantially lower. Even so, workers emerged from the war with immediate experience of full employment and relatively high standards of living which their unions aimed to protect, through collective bargaining and political action, in the postwar years.[7]

The big picture of the political economy of war shows that both business and labor garnered many advantages from those years. Business did distinctly better than labor on all counts, save one of the most important: it had to accept the growth of workers' power in its very own mines, mills, and factories. Government policy, full employment, and the threat or reality of industrial conflict all pushed in that direction. The war, which was so kind to American business in most other respects, exacerbated the labor relations problems with which management had been trying to come to grips in the later 1930s, and added many new ones to them.

WARTIME INDUSTRIAL CONFLICT AND FEDERAL POLICY

No modern state can ignore conflicts between the two sides of industry which seem to threaten the social order. State intervention in labor relations and labor disputes in America is almost as old as industrialism itself. In the 1930s the federal government had taken a decisive step toward continuous and active intervention in the labor relations system, deliberately encouraging the growth of unions and collective bargaining as agents of social reform, economic policy, and social control. In the 1940s it went further down that path.

Federal labor relations policy in wartime was largely, but not exclusively, designed to repress strikes. There were a number of reasons for this. As the final consumer, the government was obviously concerned about the quantity and cost of output from the nation's war industries, which strikes and other workers' actions could affect. More important, it wanted to be sure of uninterrupted production, and to guarantee that unrestricted wage bargaining did not cripple the wartime economy, in which inflationary pressures were in any case strong. In addition, it feared the effects social unrest and industrial conflict were supposed to have on the morale of the civilian population, the armed forces, America's allies, and her enemies. Finally, the administration had a party-political interest in the matter. Bipartisanship did not extend onto the home front. Strikes by the President's labor "clients" made good Republican propaganda, and banner headlines in the conservative press.

The state had plenty of tricks up its sleeve to keep labor in check. Even before America entered the war, the government used its coercive authority in labor disputes, smashing the one center of antiwar Trotskyist power (in the Minneapolis Teamsters union) by selective prosecution of militants, and using troops against Communist-led strikes at Allis-Chalmers and North American Aviation. As the war dragged on, and the crisis atmosphere of national unity following Pearl Harbor became less real and compelling, the state had to show its iron hand more frequently. Roosevelt and his advisors seriously considered compulsory national service laws applied to civilian work. But the means actually employed were more subtle — the War Manpower Commission and the Selective Service System hovered threateningly over the heads of strikers, and public opinion was sometimes deliberately whipped up into an antiunion rage.

And the government's intervention in wartime labor relations generally showed its preference for persuading, co-opting, and cajoling. Cooperation was what was wanted from workers and unions, and a judicious mixture of argument, favors, and veiled threats was enough to secure it. America was, after all, not simply a democratic, but a Democratic state at war. The manipulative approach the government preferred turned out to be effective in keeping industrial conflict under control, and did not alienate many of the administration's friends.

Still, the picture was not one of total success. In total war, nothing less than total industrial peace is theoretically acceptable, and that was unattainable. Wartime strikes were generally viewed as unpatriotic and inexcusable, but the strike weapon was not taken from labor's hands. It was a powerful weapon: as the Mine Workers proved in 1941 and 1943–44, only the use or the real threat of it could force major concessions from employers or the federal government. But it was also dangerous, arousing the righteous indignation of the general public and making it more likely that the state might turn toward coercion.

1940 was a relatively strike-free year. Unions made substantial organizational and economic gains, and the federal government relied on the cooperation of both sides of industry to keep disputes from interfering with defense production. But in winter 1940–spring 1941, there was a serious upsurge of strike activity over wages-and-hours issues and the completion of union organization in the heavy industries. In consequence, the government established a tripartite administrative tribunal, the National Defense Mediation Board (NDMB), to settle all serious disputes affecting the defense program. It succeeded until the fall of 1941. It had things to give the labor movement, and it had the voluntary pledge of unions not to strike once disputes had been certified to the Board. In addition, labor had an equal share with business representatives (co-opted by the administration, not nominated by the NAM or the Chamber of Commerce) and public members in determining Board policy. The patriotism of union leaders and their members, their growing commitment to the defense effort, and the threat of severe legislation to limit labor power from an outraged Congress unless they went along with government policy, further encouraged labor acceptance of NDMB rulings in which it had played a part.

But in the fall of 1941 the NDMB fell apart. Before a declaration of war, the President's emergency powers were somewhat vague, so the NDMB had to be founded on consensus, however forced. But there was one crucial issue of power and principle between business and labor on which neither side was prepared to compromise, and which was therefore not susceptible to mediation. That was the Mine Workers' demand for the union shop in the coal mines wholly owned by the steel companies — the so-called "captive mines."

All concerned recognized that the "captive mines" issue was a test case. Business representatives on the NDMB and the business community's peak associations demanded that union strength and security should be fixed for the duration of World War II, in the same way as had happened in the First World War. No union should be free to exploit a period of national emergency to further its own selfish interests, whether it did so by strike action or by twisting the arm of some government agency. Union leaders saw things very differently. They were cooperating fully in the defense program, helping the federal government keep their members on the job and limiting their use of their very real bargaining power. In return they believed they deserved some formal security of membership and income. What was more, they needed it to maintain their organizations and exert some control over the rank-and-file.[8]

Business and public members refused to grant the Mine Workers their "due." CIO representatives withdrew. But Pearl Harbor occurred before the administration could solve the immediate problem by giving in, or Congress could pass harsh antistrike measures into law. Roosevelt quickly called a conference of AFL, CIO, and business representatives to thrash out issues in dispute and give him a lasting replacement of the NDMB. They remained irreconcilable. But an interfering Congress was pushed to one side. Both sides of industry gave Roosevelt a formal pledge that there would be neither strikes nor lockouts. All matters of wartime labor relations and, initially, wage control policy were passed on to a new agency, the National War Labor Board (NWLB), to be settled case by case by representatives of business, labor, and the public.[9]

THE NATIONAL WAR LABOR BOARD, 1942–45

The NWLB came into operation on 12 January 1942. Until V-J Day it remained the most important influence on the pace and, to some extent, direction in which the American labor relations system developed. Its powers were based in the "consent" of the partisan representatives at the Labor-Management Conference of December 1941, but that was not a strong enough foundation. The Constitution does not recognize corporatist deals; in any case, the representativeness of the "representatives," and their practical ability to deliver their "constituents'" acceptance of Board rulings, were both questionable. So the war powers of the President, and statute law after the passage of the 1943 Smith-Connally (War Labor Disputes) Act, gave it a more secure basis.[10]

The NWLB inherited the NDMB's structure, approach, and problems. But it was stronger. Unions were bound by the no-strike pledge, which was in theory voluntary. In practice, it was considered to be irrevocable, and binding on unions whether or not they had been represented, however indirectly, at the 1941 conference. Where consent failed, penalties, threats, and force backed it up. Unions were compelled to take all unsettled disputes over contract negotiation and administration through the machinery of private arbitration and state and federal mediation and conciliation, leaving the NWLB to rule on any that remained unresolved.

With the passage of time, the voluntary participation of union officials and their members in the time-consuming and unsatisfactory procedures of the NWLB became increasingly qualified and reluctant. Some whole unions—the Mine Workers in particular—abrogated their no-strike pledge, and called or even engaged in official strikes. More general was an upsurge of rank-and-file unrest, directed against their employers and managers, against their "responsible" union leaders, and against the NWLB itself.[11] The NWLB also had increasing difficulty getting the business community to comply with its orders. In addition, the NWLB itself changed. As wage control became a more important priority, and stricter, it had to rule on a massively increased caseload. And it found its freedom to set wage policy restricted by presidential orders and the superimposed Office of Economic Stabilization.

So the NWLB's life was far from smooth. The first large hurdle it had to clear was the problem of union security, which had proved too much for the NDMB. During the first half of 1942 it felt its way toward a workable settlement which was also an acceptable compromise. After some hesitancy and experimentation, lasting policy was laid down in the "Little Steel" case on 15 July.

After four years of NLRB pressure, litigation, piecemeal organization by the Steelworkers, and some strikes, the four "Little Steel" companies had been forced to recognize the union in spring 1941. Negotiations for their first contract stalled, and the entire dispute was handed over to the NDMB for settlement. The combined "Little Steel" cases were by far the most important that the NWLB inherited. National counterinflation policy required that the workers should be denied any substantial wage increase. But they were already disappointed at the slow, small gains from unionization. So the union had serious problems in controlling its dwindling and disaffected membership. The NWLB took these political factors into account. It gave the union a "maintenance of membership" clause in the contract it wrote, as compensation for a poor wage award and as a reward for the union's responsibility in not pressing its members' demands more vigorously. The clause required workers who already were or subsequently became union members to remain so for the duration of the contract. A "checkoff" provision further authorized employers to deduct union dues, fines, etc. from the pay packet before handing it over to the worker, and then pass the funds on to the union direct. In return for its full-hearted cooperation in the war effort, the union was granted organizational security and a larger measure of disciplinary power over its own members — at least for the contract term.[12]

The "Little Steel" principles — strict control over direct wage increases and material aid for responsible unions — were the twin pillars of the NWLB's subsequent policies. Maintenance of membership was less than the labor movement had wanted. But it was still offensive to the libertarian principles of industrialists who had been brought up to believe in the "open shop." It went against the grain to have to recognize the institutional existence and legitimate rights of organizations widely considered un-American, antimanagement, Communistic, and not truly representative of the good body of loyal employees. Before the war no large corporation except Ford (in mid-1941) had gone very far beyond recognizing unions *either* as representatives of their members only, *or* of all workers in the bargaining unit, but for bargaining purposes only. Formal union security was rare. But now managements were compelled to accept that union membership might be a condition of their workers' continued employment. They had to assist union administration and discipline by "checking off" dues, fines, and assessments, and sacking workers ejected from their union, often for internal political opposition. The rights to hire, fire, and work were well and truly violated. This was objectionable, but in addition the more formally secure the union, the less likely it was that a company would be able to get rid of it after the war. A conservative Congress might drastically amend the Wagner Act, and the return of unemployment would surely lower workers' willingness or ability to strike effectively in defense of their union's rights. But by then it might be too late, and in the meanwhile business was being forced to live with an undesirable situation.[13]

Understandably, the NWLB ran into a lot of flak from business, the press, and conservative politicians for its decision in favor of strengthening responsible unionism as an aid to the defense effort. This bedrock principle of Board policies was the work of its four public members and their alternates. These men had a continuous, expert presence on the Board. Theirs was the deciding vote in the frequent cases, generally the most important, where the partisan representatives were at odds. As the Board's work expanded, and its staff multiplied, more and more men were called to serve as public members or staff assistants. Labor lawyers and economists, sometimes fresh from college, supplied the demand for specialist manpower. One reason that the NWLB left lasting imprints on the American labor relations system was that so many of the practicing and academic labor relations experts of the postwar years gained their most important experience in its service, and absorbed its ethos. The NWLB left an ideological as well as an institutional legacy. Both are worth exploring.

The first public members were men skilled in mediation and arbitration. They were liberal pluralists, committed to the development of a labor relations system in which the triple objectives of efficiency, order, and representative democracy could be reconciled. They believed in the Wagner Act's legislative philosophy, and in strong, responsible unions as agents for its implementation. They preferred to see industrial disputes settled in decentralized, voluntarist negotiations between the parties rather than on terms imposed by the state from the center, or unilaterally determined by employers.

They worked for the creation of a "common law" of industrial rela-

tions, formalized in written contracts, interpreted and enforced by negotiation between the parties and by the forceful intervention of expert
outsiders. The men who were cast in the latter role followed NWLB
public members' lead and were often, in any case, public members or
NWLB staffers themselves. These Impartial Umpires and Arbitrators
became common, enduring features of the American labor relations
scene during the war, and the NWLB did much to make them so.

Public members were not outright partisans of organized labor although they were sometimes accused of being so. They paid full recognition to the rights of owners and managers to direct their enterprises,
but qualified the arbitrary exercise of that power by insisting on the
rights of responsible unions to a voice in the determination of the conditions of employment of their members. Such determination was to be as
orderly and nondisruptive as possible: written contracts were to run for
fixed periods; disputes arising during their life, over their meaning or
application, were to be settled by negotiation and arbitration. The
NWLB wrote into law the contract-policing role of unions in collective
bargaining: management acts and the union grieves. To management is
left the right of initiative and a broad discretion. The union can seek redress, but not at the cost of damaging or unpredictable industrial conflict. Well-disciplined and lawful strikes, or the real threat of them, had
a part to play in making both parties take bargaining seriously. The
strike was the necessary final sanction in a voluntarist labor relations
system. But it should be used sparingly, and only after contract negotiations had reached an impasse.[14]

These principles, and their collective wisdom, informed the solutions
public members helped devise to the labor relations problems which
pressed upon them. But they also had to try to make sure that those solutions were acceptable to the contending parties and were workable. The
policies the Board developed to strengthen the machinery of collective
bargaining reflect these varying, sometimes conflicting, imperatives.

NWLB public members recognized that union officials had an important contribution to make to putting day-to-day labor relations on a
sound footing. If responsible unions were to play their part in orderly
contract administration, it followed that employers ought to grant
them, by contract, the status and facilities to do the job properly. The
NWLB used this line of argument to justify granting a variety of union
demands. Clauses allowing "outside" union officials access to their
members, on company property and during working time, and giving
local officers payment for time spent in grievance handling, or automatic top seniority rating, were inserted in contracts, often against
management protests.[15]

Public members accepted that local union stewards and grievance committeemen were often the people who defused industrial conflict. Regional and national officers acted as "fire fighters," processing diffi- cult grievances and holding the lid on local unions' discontent. What we now know of wartime labor relations suggests that these contemporary observations were generally accurate. But that was not the way man- agement saw things.

Management traditionally thought, or at any rate spoke, of its *own* men as essentially sound, though ill-informed and easily misled. Indus- trial conflict was not thought of as something occurring because of the necessary tensions and contradictions of the employment relationship. Instead, it was seen as unnatural, imported from outside the plant by labor agitators and union officials. Companies could be forced to deal with "outside" unions in the 1930s and 1940s, but that did not mean that they abandoned their basic convictions. Managerial ideology continued to be reflected in corporate labor relations policy — in particular, in re- sistance to the efforts of national unions to gain control of collective bargaining. Management preferred to negotiate directly with its em- ployees and their immediate representatives within the individual plant or firm.[16]

Management found it hard to accept that shop stewards, grievance committeemen, and — worst of all — union officials could be mediators and moderators of discontent. In the 1940s, they had some reasons for their suspicion. Some union officers were still "agitators," particularly in those CIO unions which had scarcely emerged from the insecurities of the organizing stage of their development. But, as applied to a re- sponsible union, one cooperating in the war effort and assisting man- agement with its personnel problems, any such characterization was manifestly unfair. Businessmen's principles (or prejudices) and the real- ities of wartime industrial relations as they experienced them were often at variance, on this and other similar matters.

For example, many industrialists, in practice, went along with NWLB public members, union officials, and progressive management spokes- men like NWLB industry members Ching and Roger Lapham, who un- derstood that only a strong, secure union could afford to be cooperative and thus contribute to the development of sound labor relations. But the libertarian-individualistic principles remained: management must adhere to its conscientious opposition to union security, "except that nothing is more hopeless than to have to deal with a weak union, irre- sponsible because of its weakness." Similarly, efforts of the union hier- archy to entrench itself must be fought, but "the international and local officials are often less radical in their demands than the rank and file who roll the snowballs for them to throw."[17]

As a result, the NWLB had to fight against a stubborn rearguard action by managements far from reconciled to having to deal with a union, and attempting to maintain a "hands off" or "arms' length" policy, confining recognition of the union's institutional existence and legitimacy to an absolute minimum. The NWLB had to give such firms an education in the practical and procedural necessities of labor relations, just as it had "instructed" them in the need to accept maintenance of membership.

Enhancing the status of union officials was only one part of the NWLB's program for making everyday labor relations work better. The NWLB paid particular attention to the development of improved grievance procedures in mass-production industry. Before the war, when unions had only just been organized and were still fighting for full recognition, typical grievance procedures had been either informal or extremely complex, with a series of conferences to settle disputes between different levels of the union and management hierarchy, right up to the top. In either case there was no way of settling a difference quickly, or after the breakdown of the last stage of negotiations, except a strike. Managements had little experience in contract administration, and were reluctant to extend the scope of collective bargaining to include day-to-day grievance settlement. Some unions were less interested in building grievance machinery to bring about orderly settlements than in using every dispute as an opportunity to put pressure on management. Direct action, including "quickie" strikes and the harassment of foremen, or the real threat of it, was used to bring about the speedy enforcement of workers' demands. This kind of behavior could be more effective than relying on a formal grievance system.[18]

This problem of inadequate habits and systems of grievance adjustment was carried over into wartime, when workers' intrinsic bargaining power was extremely high. In addition, responsible unions were at a disadvantage if they had to depend on formal grievance machinery, as management could always say no without even the pretense of negotiating. After all, it knew that the union was pledged not to strike. Chrysler and Ford were particularly bad offenders, stalling or refusing to negotiate altogether on grievances over matters of discipline, discharge, production standards, rates of pay, etc. They were confident that their workers would not generally strike, even under provocation. Even if they ended up with a wildcat on their hands, the union not the company suffered public condemnation, and had to try hard to get the men back to work.[19]

The NWLB had to come to grips with this problem. It had to deal with management stubbornness and union irresponsibility, as well as with parties who were simply inexperienced in collective bargaining, negotiating their first proper contract, or tempted to leave all hot and difficult issues to the Board for settlement. The result was that the Board was soon snowed under with work. Its weakened ability to respond quickly became an additional cause of unauthorized strikes by workers who supposed that only thus could they attract its attention to festering, unresolved grievances. The Board looked for answers. One was to decentralize, and set up a dozen regional boards and a number of commissions for specific industries. The more fundamental solution was to try to improve collective bargaining machinery and behavior. The Board put pressure on parties coming before it to exhaust the possibilities of negotiation and voluntary mediation before bringing their disputes to it.[20]

As far as the negotiation of new annual contracts was concerned, this approach was only partly successful. Because the Board did have powers to make and enforce policy, and its policies were uncertain and changing throughout the war, in many cases parties had no choice but to resort to it. This may well have delayed the acquisition of experience in settling "disputes of interest" through collective bargaining by both sides of industry, who were in any case often novices.[21]

But on the administration of contracts, NWLB orders had a distinct and beneficial lasting effect. Giving the Board's ruling on the 1943 Chrysler case, vice-chairman George W. Taylor, GM's second Impartial Umpire, said:

Collective bargaining is not confined to the making of an agreement once a year. It is also a day-to-day process and, on this score, the grievance procedure plays a highly important role. The grievance procedure should be set up so as to make unnecessary unresolved disputes over the application of the agreement.[22]

Efficiency and order were the Board's watchwords in establishing and improving grievance systems. It set no fixed pattern, but followed certain ground rules. There should be a limited number of stages in the procedure, with reasonable time limits, to speed settlements. Different levels of the union and management hierarchy should handle grievances at each stage, with direct, top-level contacts over those that could not be resolved lower down. Beyond that final stage of negotiation came arbitration, and the Board moved from ordering the parties to include a "mutually satisfactory" form to requiring a clear definition of the arbitrator's role and powers. It preferred to see the appointment of a permanent arbitrator, and would nominate one or designate an independent appointing agency — usually the American Arbitration Association — if the parties could not agree. From 1 July 1943, it became firm NWLB policy to order final and binding arbitration when cases came before it.[23]

Arbitration had existed before the war, notably in the garment trades and anthracite industry. But the 1940 GM-UAW contract pioneered its introduction into mass-production industry.[24] Arbitration violated management's unitary conception of the enterprise — as, indeed, did the contractual determination of conditions of employment through bargaining with an "outside" union representing employees of more than one company. But arbitration was particularly objectionable, as its results were binding on the parties, whereas in a bargaining power play management could always say no. As GM's Steve Du Brul had put it in 1934,

in any case in which any compromise would mean serious injury to the true long-term interests of the institution and the interests for which it was created, no Management can be excused if it voluntarily submits the issues to any form of arbitration which involves an irrevocable agreement to abide by the decisions of another party or agency.[25]

In accordance with this principle, GM's basic labor relations policy statement of 1934 ruled that "no case is to be submitted to the determination of any outside agency without the specific authorization of the Executive Committee." In practice, it was compelled to a limited departure from this position. But the authority of the Impartial Umpire was restricted to ruling on disputes over the application and interpretation of the contract — "disputes of right." He had no power in the most sensitive areas — production standards and wage rate grievances — where the end point of the grievance procedure was still the strike, once negotiations failed. Such strikes were not viewed as breaches of the no-strike clause, but the UAW's GM department was in practice loath to authorize them. As a result, GM management retained a large and unimpaired discretion in the areas of job control most important to it.[26]

NWLB industry and public members sometimes had to play the part GM management had been able and clear-sighted enough to in its own case. Some managements were apparently unaware of the implications of the contracts they signed: if the subject matter of arbitrable grievances was left undefined, and the arbitrator given full authority to adjudicate *any* difference arising under the contract, then the scope of his rulings would be much increased, and the temptation on the union to use the grievance procedure for continuous bargaining to extend the terms of the contract quite dangerous.[27]

NWLB public members had no sympathy for downright business opposition to arbitration. If allowed to have its way, it would perpetuate that "uncontrolled right of unilateral employer action" which was contrary to the Wagner Act and the NLRB's definition of collective bargaining. That right had only a limited place in the labor relations system public members were helping to build. But they were quite willing to support industry members in the latter's efforts to produce arbitration systems conducive to the preservation of order and managerial discretion.[28]

There were a number of ways of doing this. One was to limit the scope of authorized grievances in order to protect a broad range of managerial prerogatives from union attempts to extend the scope of joint determination between annual bargaining rounds. "Changes in business practice, the opening or closing of new units, the choice of personnel . . . or other business questions of a like nature not having to do directly and primarily with the day-to-day life of the employees and their relations with their supervisors" could be defined as subjects where management decisions simply could not be protested or affected via the grievance system.[29]

Such important issues of corporate strategy were not, however, the subjects about which unions and management struggled most frequently and bitterly. Job control was the main preoccupation of both sides in arguments over, for example, "the transfer and promotion of employees; the day-to-day adjustment of piece rates; the question whether additional employees should be hired for certain operations; the retention or discharge of probationary employees; determination of the work schedule," etc. NWLB policy was either to exempt such matters from arbitration (and the no-strike pledge effectively blocked the only other lawful way unions could hope for redress if negotiations deadlocked), or to underline that

the hallmark of a management function is the right to initiate business decisions. Thereby the interest in continuity of production is recognized, the many disputes which are bound to arise over employment problems do not interfere with the running of the business. More, the notion of business problems and conditions is advanced as an overriding set of factors which determine employment.[30]

NWLB policy on the grievance procedure and arbitration eventually proved to be acceptable even to authoritarian employers, who learned how useful it could be in helping them with the difficult business of living with a union.[31] NWLB guidance and support was valuable particularly where it helped managements with that thorniest of wartime problems, the maintenance of discipline over the workforce. The Board endorsed management's right to promulgate and change workshop rules (governing every aspect of employee behavior) without the union's prior consent. And it laid down the basic principle that "[m]anagement retains the right to discipline employees for cause and as necessary for the efficient conduct of its operation." All that the union could lawfully do was to protest any such action, after the event, through the formal grievance system. Direct action tactics to bring about immediate redress, such as walkouts, slowdowns, or physical violence against company property and management personnel, were ruled out. The NWLB threatened and penalized unions whose members used them, and sometimes punished the militants themselves.[32]

In sum, the NWLB played an important part in defending management's free exercise of a broad discretion, limiting workers' right to challenge. It built on the code of practice public members had observed and developed in the prewar garment and hosiery trades, with their long histories of relatively stable labor relations. It passed on a much larger body of principles and interpretation which the arbitral profession, staffed with its alumni and vastly expanded because of its policies, went on to apply.[33]

As NWLB vice- (later full) chairman Taylor said, "It is a tough job to develop a new institution in modern society."[34] The Board's performance was impressive, encouraging the growth of bureaucratized, centralized, responsible unions, and the improvement of the machinery of orderly, law-bound industrial conflict. The NWLB's work was creative, but it was also quite conservative. Nevertheless, it ran into stiff business opposition. On the face of it, this might be thought paradoxical: were not businessmen sufficiently far-sighted to appreciate the ultimate value of what the Board was doing for them?

The question suggests its own answer. NWLB orders on union security, union officials' status, and grievance adjustment were immediately objectionable to businessmen whose traditional convictions about labor relations were ignored or overruled. Board policies made businessmen increasingly and understandably anxious about the strengthening of labor power and the entrenchment of labor unions. Public members were convinced that a responsible labor movement was a bastion of democracy, etcetera. Businessmen were not so sure, and were certainly not convinced by the unions' claim to *be* "responsible." From where businessmen stood, unions still looked potentially dangerous, and occasionally militant. In addition, the Board gave some assistance to union pressures for an extension of the scope and area of collective bargaining. And it adopted a number of practices which raised labor costs and made them resistant to the downward adjustments management thought it had to make after the war. So, from the businessman's point of view, the Board was a very mixed blessing, and many of its policies seemed practically damaging and ideologically unacceptable.

For example, the NWLB supported union demands for "automatic wage progression," whereby workers acquired the right to expect to move steadily from a low initial rate of pay to the regular rate within a fixed period, providing they performed adequately. This deprived management of one of its customary ways of controlling labor costs and rewarding the more "meritorious" employee. Less offensive, but still inflationary, NWLB policies included the standardization of relatively liberal fringe benefits, such as shift differentials, sick leave, paid holidays, and longer paid vacations. NWLB rulings here merely formalized and attempted to control the workings of a tight labor market, and tried to keep rising worker and union opposition to the rigid "Little Steel" prohibition of direct wage increases in hand by permitting a certain amount of wage drift. But they resulted in increasingly sticky labor costs, which would be a problem in the event of a recession. Incentive pay and job reclassification schemes could also be used as collusive devices by companies and unions wishing to get around pay control. The NWLB positively encouraged the latter practice, in particular, as it wished to reduce the chaos produced by industry's irrational wage structures. But NWLB policy on job reclassification displeased management hard-liners because it gave unions the right to be consulted in drawing schemes up, and to participate directly in their administration, rather than simply allowing particular grievances after management had put a general policy into effect.[35]

As well as expanding the scope of collective bargaining in some directions, the Board also gave some tentative encouragement to union pressures for a widening of the geographical coverage of agreements. This was much more serious. Majority opinion among managers favored atomizing labor relations, confining representation and negotiations to units composed of the employees of a single firm, or even single plant, and their direct representatives. But the industrial or multi-industrial nature of unions, the multiplant structure of many large corporations, and established relationships between the wage schedules and economic fortunes of many basic industries, combined to make this policy somewhat utopian. Industrial unions recognized economic realities, and aimed for industry-wide negotiation of basic terms of employment. The NLRB gave qualified support to the establishment of multiplant or multifirm bargaining units. And the NWLB added its influence to those already making for the centralization of negotiations.[36]

For the most part, it simply wanted to reduce the number of cases coming before it by consolidating those concerning a particular, recognizable industry; and its respect for community wage structures and interregional, inter- or intraindustry wage differentials, militated against union desires for common basic wage rates. But in the basic steel and Akron rubber cases, the NWLB did seem to be encouraging true industry-wide collective bargaining. Industry was doubtful about the supposed benefits of any such system: it might lead to greater efficiency and order, as its supporters claimed; or it might lead to enhanced union power, a larger scale of industrial conflict, and, inevitably, more federal intervention.[37]

Businessmen were more suspicious of the dangers of formalized industry-wide bargaining than they were hopeful of its benefits. Insofar as the legacy of the NWLB and of the postwar fact-finding boards and wage rounds which replaced it included an encouragement of formal industry-wide negotiations, rather than simply pattern-following, it was the subject of considerable, but not unequivocal, business opposition.[38]

The NWLB was fatally weakened by the end of the war and of the no-strike pledge. It continued to make rulings and recommendations for some months after V-J Day, but they lacked binding authority. In the confused process of building a wage-price policy for the transition from war to peace, its place was taken by ad hoc fact-finding boards, and by industrial conflict of unprecedented scale.

It did not simply disappear into the dust bin of history: its rulings had exerted a profound influence on the character of the American industrial relations system and on the content of many labor contracts. It had contributed to the education of American management in labor relations matters, and had helped construct bargaining institutions which were to prove useful and lasting in the postwar years. But, in the short run, its contributions to the increase in organized labor's power and security seemed more important.

THE CHALLENGE TO MANAGEMENT CONTROL[39]

The NWLB was only a temporary feature of the American labor relations scene. Managements could hope to get rid of any unacceptable or unworkable clauses it had inserted into their union contracts after the war ended. But they were then going to be faced with labor opponents stronger in many respects than they had been in 1940–41. The power of the labor movement, which businessmen overestimated, and the character of its ambitions to limit their authority, which they exaggerated, began to look like much more serious problems.

Business magazines and conference proceedings displayed relatively little concern about the growth of unions and workers' power, and the consequences that might have for management, until 1944. There were a number of reasons for this. For one, there were simply too many immediate problems to be solved in meeting production targets in the frantic years 1942–43.⁴⁰ But by mid-1944 the war seemed to be nearly won, the first big cutbacks in defense orders hit industry, and the relaxation of day-to-day production pressures gave businessmen time to think strategically about labor relations and other problems of the impending peace. In addition, some of the most worrying features of wartime labor relations, which were sure to have some lasting effects, became sharply prominent by 1944 — wildcat strikes and other proofs of the breakdown of industrial discipline, including stirrings of militancy and union-consciousness among foremen and supervisors. Finally, 1944 was the year when the labor movement, on its side, began to think seriously about how to preserve the gains it had won during the war years, and how to build on them in the coming peace.

This was the context in which Thomas Roy Jones, president of American Type Founders, NWLB industry member, and a man long active in forming industrial relations policy for the NAM, issued a call to arms to fellow managers. He presented them with an apocalyptic vision of the likely consequences if the growth of labor power and aggressiveness, within the plant and in the world of politics, were allowed to remain unchecked.

> In the labor leader's way of thinking, there is no conceivable concession which the employer should not make, no obligation which he should not assume. Annual wages, private social security systems, early retirement, twenty-five hour weeks — all are completely within the range of economic possibility. Of course, control of management is possible, too; and so is the distribution of profits; and advertising policy; and marketing and production methods. . . . If you ask for a lot, you can always get some; and if you keep asking long enough, you get the whole thing.
>
> But there is a limit to everything. The limit here might be the relinquishment of the stockholders' last right — the ownership of the corporate stock. The one-way operation would then have achieved its ultimate goal. If this is not to be countenanced, then some limit has to be set before that end is reached. What is that limit, and who will set it?⁴¹

Jones was no rabble-rouser, but on this occasion his rhetoric was extreme. He had had a good opportunity to see what was happening in wartime labor relations, and he was frankly worried. And he was not alone. In the next three years, many other businessmen joined their voices to his, expressing concern about what seemed to be a real and threatening "union challenge to management control." They described and analyzed it, and suggested remedies. Scholars conducted enquiries into what was actually going on, and what businessmen thought about it. The results are revealing.⁴²

From 1944 to 1947, formal confrontations between organized labor and the business community became increasingly frequent and serious. There were conflicts over the negotiation and day-to-day administration of labor contracts, which spilled over into bitter propaganda battles and hard-fought political struggles. And to many contemporary businessmen, especially those in control of large firms, the stakes seemed to be dangerously high. Businessmen interviewed in the fall of 1945 were angered by the tendency of unions to incorporate extraneous considerations of "aggregate purchasing power, full employment, human rights, the American standard of living" into the arguments they used to justify wage claims to members and the public. They were irritated by the specific restrictions unions imposed on management's control of the workforce in the workplace. And they were possessed of a general uneasiness — "anxiety . . . about the future; uncertainty as to where this process will end." Another investigator reported that big business executives thought that the issue of preserving managerial prerogatives in labor relations had "significant characteristics of a power struggle." They were not just trying to reverse trends which had led to a "lessening of efficient production," but also fighting the good fight on behalf of the "general concept of authority" — against wildcat strikes and other direct challenges to managerial control, and against an "unwanted economic order."[43]

Leafing through the yellowing pages of thirty-year-old business speeches and periodicals, full of this kind of anxious analysis, and knowing that little of what was forecast has come to pass, it is difficult at first to appreciate how solid a basis there was for businessmen's fears in the 1940s. Businessmen did not always read their own times accurately, and they were, perhaps, too easily scared. But there really were many things happening in wartime labor relations which were immediately troublesome, and might, in the long term, have become very dangerous — *if* the trends businessmen observed in 1944–46 had been allowed to continue. The NWLB was responsible for some of them, as noted above. But workers and the American labor movement were the cause of many more.

The Wartime Labor Relations Problems of American Business, I: The Crisis of Discipline and Productivity

In recent years the wildcat strike wave of 1942–45 has received considerable attention from labor historians. Their analyses of the causes of these strikes have generally revived the conclusions of contemporary critics of the no-strike pledge within the unions themselves: wildcat strikes and informal pressures for job controls were a natural and right-

ful response to managerial provocation, to NWLB delays and unsatisfactory orders, and to the desertion of their members' interests by top
union leaders.[44]

Wildcat strikes were a serious problem in the automotive, steel, rubber, farm equipment, and electrical manufacturing industries in particular. They reflected union leaders' loss of influence with their membership, caused by a too faithful adherence to the no-strike pledge and the
orderly procedures of collective bargaining and the NWLB. And they
were costly: in order to escape either the loss of "union security" contractual provisions, or some more serious NWLB-imposed penalty,
unions had to intervene strongly to further repress dissident sections of
their membership. Union leaders faced an uncomfortable choice: in order to avoid inciting public opinion and the Congress to take harsh antistrike positions, and to maintain the collaboration in the war effort to
which they were committed, they sometimes had to take measures they
knew to be alienating members' loyalties and not serving their immediate interests. The NWLB's requirement that unions should not support
or condone strike action even against managerial provocation was especially galling.

The size of the wartime wildcat strike movement should not be exaggerated. Wildcat strikes were concentrated quite disproportionately
in the greater Detroit automotive industry and in the Akron rubber
plants. The peculiar organizational histories and internal character of
the unions involved, and the explosive community settings of Detroit
and Akron, help account for this. Most wildcat strikes were affairs of
the moment. Their support, even within plants badly affected, was
often small and qualified. In the long term they were not particularly
significant. But as far as harassed wartime managers were concerned,
they created practical difficulties of workplace discipline and productivity, and seemed to be one part of a disquieting struggle for power and
authority in labor relations. Management's expressed anxieties reached
a crescendo — as did wildcat strikes — in 1944–45, and helped stimulate
a determined effort to recover control over the workforce in the workplace during the reconversion years.

From a managerial perspective, the causes of wildcat strikes were
straightforward: laxity, not provocation, on the part of management,
particularly those of its representatives in daily and intimate contact
with workers; and unethical pressures from workers, individually or in
groups, led or supported by their unions' local officers. This latter viewpoint was most clearly expressed in the testimony of automotive company representatives before the Senate War Investigating (Mead) Committee in Detroit in March 1945.[45]

General Motors' position was especially noteworthy. GM had begun to apply strict penalties to ringleaders and participants in wildcat strikes before the war, and its approach toward the use of its contractual rights was intelligently unprovocative, in line with its policy of "tough but fair." GM was therefore able to help Walter Reuther impose and maintain discipline within the UAW's GM department. In consequence, GM's problem of wildcat strikes was only one-fourteenth as serious, in terms of man-days lost, as the industry average. But GM was not satisfied with a less than perfect outcome, and its wildcat problem increased throughout the war. Its explanation of the causes of the strikes and of other less open challenges to managerial control, given to the Committee by its vice-president Harry Anderson, tallies with that of more seriously affected companies.

> This barrier which disturbs me so much is represented by the apparent reluctance of too many of our production employees to work as hard as they could without undue strain on them physically. Too many employees are loafing and wasting their time despite the fact that they are getting high pay for their efforts. . . .
> [M]ost of the serious strikes which have occurred in General Motors' plants during the war were caused by the refusal of small groups of our workers to meet production standards which we know to be very reasonable.[46]

If management was silent about its role in the provocation of wildcat strikes, it was at least openly self-critical about the extent to which companies had conceded to individual and collective pressures. The problem of managerial relaxation of its controls over the workplace was much more general than the wildcat strike. It affected, in particular, the durable goods and heavy metalworking industries, only recently unionized and especially strained by wartime expansion and conversion to all-out war production. This problem was the most serious of the hidden costs of the so-called "miracle of production" which caused Westinghouse Electric's vice-president Newbury to speak of such industries as "war casualt[ies]."[47]

What determined management's actual behavior in much of workplace industrial relations in wartime was the fact that the peculiar circumstances of the war economy weakened its inclination to resist union or worker demands which increased costs, lowered labor productivity, and eroded managerial authority and control. Cost constraints were relaxed, and continuous production was the primary objective.

> Production costs are relatively unimportant during a war. Quantity and quality are uppermost in everyone's mind. Military products wholly new to industry are placed in production with little or no idea of what they should cost, and the customer cares little about their actual cost so long as the goods are delivered.

Yardsticks for cost measurement do not exist in most cases. Cost controls are relaxed or even abandoned. The manufacturer is usually assured the return of his full cost, regardless of inefficiency, with a fixed profit to boot. Renegotiation confiscates a major share, if not all, of the reward for reduced costs. These conditions soon destroy the cost-consciousness of any organization.[48]

In support of this analysis, Packard's former local union president asserted that the company had hoarded labor and tolerated loafing from 1941 until late in 1944, and NWLB chairman George Taylor believed that the major breaches in the counterinflation policy had been made by management. It had pursued labor peace and adequate manpower by the maladministration of wage systems as a way of getting around strict NWLB prohibitions against direct wage increases. Widespread practices included the "demoralization" of incentive schemes and production standards, misclassification of jobs, rapid upgrading of workers to supposedly more skilled positions, and allowing excessive overtime. Such practices might result from workers' pressures, but they were also the natural response of management to conditions of manpower shortage in a controlled, but overheated, economy.[49]

More serious than wage drift, by itself, was the underlying fact of managerial adjustment to a situation in which "labor was scarce, independent, articulate, impatient of delay or restraint." Business had to cope with "green help," not conditioned to accept industrial discipline, and with general changes in workers' attitudes and behavior once freed from the fear of unemployment. There was "a rather general lowering of employee morale . . . reflected in absenteeism, tardiness, early wash-up, disinterest in application to the job, lessened pride of workmanship, insubordination, and just plain soldiering." The old disciplinary sanctions — temporary unpaid suspension, or layoff — lost their effectiveness. The first might provide a welcome break from continuous overtime, or the opportunity to "moonlight"; the second, a chance to change jobs, free from War Manpower Commission controls.[50]

In many cases, what management saw as indiscipline — what one might term a unilateral renegotiation of the effort bargain, a disinclination to work "whistle to whistle excluding rest periods"[51] — was allowed to increase by foremen and supervisors as they learned the difficulty or futility of taking remedial action. Faced with demands by higher management for continuous production and labor peace, and with the likelihood of opposition by workers and their union stewards, members of management actually in contact with workers gave up the struggle to maintain strict control. As a result, the enforcement of shop rules prescribing management's ideas of "reasonable and orderly" behavior, the setting and enforcing of production standards, and the exercise of traditional controls over the disposition of the labor force all suffered. Forty-three percent of a sample of manufacturing firms questioned in 1943 agreed that implementation of discipline had been relaxed, though most added that the slackening was only slight.[52]

The effect of such pressures was to encourage the development of unofficial job controls which went far beyond the areas sanctioned by the language of contract, and also of some formal agreements enshrining these controls in companies which had neither the bargaining power nor the determination to resist. One major problem for management — and for federal agencies interested in maximum output — was the setting and enforcement of production quotas by groups of workers. Numerous instances of this practice were disclosed or alleged in the Detroit hearings and elsewhere.[53]

Production control and attendant matters were the thorniest problem, but there was a similar pattern of extracontractual job controls in less sensitive areas, such as the making of promotions to better paying jobs within the ranks of production workers on the basis of seniority. Management made little resistance to the rule of seniority in cases of layoff and rehire, but the de facto extension of the seniority system to cover matters of manpower utilization and placement within the plant was viewed more seriously. The contract might state that only where "merit or ability" were equal would seniority rule, but faced with the likelihood of a shop steward's protest, and the difficulty of proving one worker superior to another, foremen often conceded the right of the more senior worker.[54]

The extent to which this process of extracontractual compromise between steward and supervisor might develop is suggested by the testimony of Packard foreman Richard Bone, who was instructed by his superiors to cooperate with the union in the interest of maximum production, but given no firm guidance: "There is never a move I make in the department that he [the steward] doesn't know it. We talk things over, seniority, raises, movement of men. If the night shift is short a man, he even allows me to put an extra man in there, running, say, three men on two machines."[55]

Similar arrangements between local unions and plant managements had the same effect, increasing the degree of actual job control exercised by workers and their locals. Sometimes such arrangements were formalized; at other times they remained as "understandings." They reflected managerial adjustment to the unpleasant reality of having to take the fact or probability of union resistance into account before formulating a policy or attempting to implement it. "[T]here has been a tremendous change in labor relations. You don't run your factory if it is unionized; you merely cooperate with the union and try to get it to do the things you would like to have done."[56]

Probably the most celebrated example of the limiting of a management's formal, as well as actual, authority by local union bargaining power was given by the Brewster Aeronautical Corp.'s Long Island City plant. It was featured in journalistic exposés and a congressional investigation. Brewster exhibited common problems in an acute form: it was a "war baby," a firm with a weak management, cost-plus contracts, and a strong, militant UAW local to contend with. The union acquired a formal veto over all of the important decisions management might want and need to make affecting manpower utilization. For example, the contract stated that the union had to be notified, *and give its consent*, before the imposition of any disciplinary penalty or the transfer of any worker within the plant. Brewster also experienced chronic semi-official stoppages and a general unproductive disorder which finally led to the plant's closure even before the end of the war. It served, finally, as a sobering example for American management of where growing union power could lead, a stimulus to inspire them to attend to their own, less serious, problems.[57]

For Brewster's problems were exceptional but not unique. In the automotive industry, for example, marginal companies like Packard and Studebaker, or small parts suppliers forced to meet their powerful customers' demands for firm delivery dates, caved in before union demands for a voice in the determination of production quotas and the administration of personnel procedures. Murray Body agreed to union participation in work-measurement; Packard discontinued time studies altogether in its Naval Engine Department in response to union pressures. Studebaker shop stewards enjoyed a veto on questions of work standards and line speed. Bundy Tubing Co., forced to discontinue piecework by the UAW before the war, had turned to a form of measured daywork, abandoning that in turn in May 1944, as 65 percent of grievances involved time studies and standards. Instead, it asked simply for a "fair day's work . . . I can't honestly say that the results were better, but they were no worse, and we eliminated one type of grievance." Between 1937, when the union entered, and 1945, when joint action was taken to save the company from closure, productivity declined by an estimated 55 percent.[58]

These examples are all chosen from companies on the margins of the automotive and airplane industries, but they are not unrepresentative. They simply provided an exaggerated version of a commonly experienced crisis of productivity and authority in the durable goods industries in the war years. The compromises many managements had to make with their employees and local unions left them troubling problems of lowered labor productivity and demoralized workplace discipline which they would have to confront in the postwar years.[59]

The opportunity for tightening up on discipline and abandoning the policy of making concessions to guarantee uninterrupted production came in 1944, as war production passed its peak. With the termination of defense contracts and the first large reconversion layoffs, management was again in a favorable position both to provoke and to take strikes as the cost of reimposing control, and to launder its workforce of inefficient or disruptive workers and their leaders. For example, the Williamson Heater Company of Cincinnati chose that time to institute a model program of retrenchment. It understood well the direct connection between the manpower shortage and war economy, on the one hand, and the slippage in its productivity and workforce discipline. Actual labor costs were 65 percent over computed standards. Partial reconversion to civilian production began, and a new works manager was installed to supervise the implementation of a new hard line. Rules and regulations were reduced to writing, for uniform enforcement and compliance. Explicit penalties were prescribed, including "separation" after two fair, written warnings. The results were valuable: "Enforcing a rule which puts a man at his post of duty at the starting time, holds him there throughout the day, and prohibits leaving his post to wash up before quitting time, contributed importantly to a full day's work for a good day's pay."[60]

Reconversion and the anticipated return of unemployment were expected to help management solve many of its wartime problems. Workers would feel less secure in violating managerial directives, or in resisting its attempts to tighten up. At Packard, union officers believed their management toughened in late 1944. The company stalled on grievances, after years of cooperation with the union. It engaged in a large-scale job reclassification program, to lower overall wage costs on civilian production. It made discriminatory recommendations to local Selective Service boards, to have difficult shop stewards, who had been classified as essential war workers, reclassified as 1-A. Its objective? "[D]isintegration of the union." The reason? "I think they would [go bankrupt] if they followed the same line of thought they followed on the cost-plus contracts they are now operating."[61]

Other reports of automotive industry intentions bear out such UAW allegations. A number of companies had decided to make an issue of productivity and disciplinary matters before the war's end. Unrest was expected to ensue over layoffs, the reduction of overtime working, transfers and downgradings of workers, retiming and reclassification of jobs. These and other steps were designed to raise the amount of output per unit of labor cost, and to recover control after years of disorder. It would be no easy task. As one industrial relations director put it, in the words of the 1918 hit song, "How ya goin' to keep 'em down on the farm, after they've seen Paree?"[62]

Management considered unofficial union pressures and the actions of informal work-groups as only a part — and not the most serious — of a general "union challenge to management control." The strains of war had exacerbated problems inherited from the organizing phase of industrial union activity in the late 1930s, and had postponed managerial action for their solution. But management was confident that it had the resources to stabilize the situation on acceptable terms, given the return of normal circumstances — a euphemism for unemployment. A happy outcome was not likely to be entirely automatic, but there was a large element of simple "What goes up, must come down" reasoning in management's predictions for the future of workplace labor relations.[63]

Radical labor historians of recent years have concentrated their attention on wildcat strikes and other efforts at job control. At the time, however, observers among management were much more impressed by the serious and lasting limitations on their freedom of action resulting from the orderly collective bargaining achievements of bureaucratic unionism, assisted by the orders of arbitrators and the NWLB. The crisis of authority which worried them most was not the temporary, reversible loss of control and productivity at the workplace, but the almost political, highly formalized challenge offered by industrial unions, no matter how "responsible." They realistically expected to have to continue to deal with a historically strong labor movement. They attached great importance to the formal industrial conflict in which they were active participants, and which was much more visible to them than the pattern of day-to-day accommodation at the workplace.

II: "Dynamic Job-Consciousness":[64]
The Extension of Official Union Power and Influence in the 1940s

Lee H. Hill, industrial relations director of the Allis-Chalmers Manufacturing Co., was one of the most outspoken and perceptive business commentators on the union challenge to management control in the 1940s. He was one of the first to awaken his fellow managers to the problem, to identify and anatomize it, and to suggest solutions. He also played an important part in the managerial counteroffensive which he had helped to promote, as an active member of the AMA, an industry representative on the NWLB, a delegate at the President's Labor-Management Conference of November 1945, and a member of the NAM committee whose proposals of 1946 helped shape the Taft-Hartley Act. Hill was versatile as well as ubiquitous — besides being responsible for handling the labor relations problems of an important, troubled firm, he was a lecturer, writer, management theorist, and political activist. If we examine his experiences in dealing with the notoriously "red" Local 248 of the UAW at the West Allis main plant, we can understand some of the urgency of his message to other businessmen whose problems were less immediately serious.[65]

Allis-Chalmers' management was powerful, authoritarian, and determined. But it was up against an exceptionally aggressive opponent in Local 248. According to A-C, Local 248's tactics consisted of a "campaign of lying propaganda" designed to lower the company's standing in the eyes of employees and the community, and the use of the grievance procedure as a means for agitation and the harassment of production supervisors.[66] A-C's problems and complaints on this score were different in degree, but not in kind, from those of other firms dealing with new, raw industrial unions.

Local 248 requested that shop rules governing seniority, transfers, promotions and demotions, apprenticeship, leaves of absence, and vacations be jointly determined and applied only when union and management were in agreement upon particular cases. The union aimed at eliminating shop rules governing falsification of time and work records, insubordination and "soldiering," repeated negligence, deliberate damage to equipment or materials, and wandering around the plant. These were the rules whose enforcement was crucial to the maintenance of managerial control over the workforce and its productivity. The union also aimed to undermine managerial control by eliminating the contract provisions excluding certain categories of "confidential" nonsupervisory employees from union membership. Inspectors, timekeepers, and plant protection men were vital adjuncts to the supervisory force, and their being subject to a measure of union control would surely dilute their effectiveness.[67]

Local 248 applied pressure to make seniority determining in questions of shift preference, promotion, and transfers within the nonsupervisory group. It attacked management's right to designate 5 percent of the workforce "whose work in the judgement of the Company is of exceptional value and whose length of service is three years or more" as being secure in their job tenure against being "bumped" out by less desirable employees of greater seniority. And it wanted to eliminate the super-seniority of foremen and supervisors, i.e. their right to retain and accumulate seniority after promotion, and thus "bump" production workers out of a job in the event of their subsequent demotion because of a reduction in the labor force. Such demands were quite normal, but affronted management's determination to retain control over the makeup and utilization of the workforce, to be able to reward the "loyal employee," and to keep minor supervisory positions attractive. The seniority clause — long, complicated, and difficult to administer — was one of the important battlefronts along the frontier of control. Unions aimed to give their members protection against managerial arbitrariness and some definite sequence of limited promotion opportunities. From management's viewpoint, its rights and necessary discretion were needlessly impaired. "We do a better job alone than when you interfere with us. You are trying to tie management up in knots."[68]

As for the grievance and arbitration procedures, their intended purpose was to contribute to stable and orderly industrial relations. But they could be used as a means to hinder, harass, and weaken management. Local 248 wanted to see a grievance defined as "any controversy . . . which is raised by the Union, under the agreement," which would "make bargaining a twelve-months-in-the-year proposition" and leave all undecided matters to the arbitrator's discretion. The union wanted, in particular, to make issues concerning promotion and wage rates (piece rates or time standards) arbitrable. It wanted to free itself of grievances brought against it by the management. At the same time, it wished to subject the actions of management representatives to which it disapproved to union grievances, on which the arbitrator would be final judge. Finally, Local 248 wanted to turn the grievance procedure into a device for increasing the union's status and power. Allis-Chalmers pursued a "hands off" policy on union membership, neither granting union security nor recognizing the union's legitimate institutional existence. Employees were supposed to present their grievances to their foremen first, in order to bolster up his authority and weaken that of the union steward. One of Local 248's more important objectives was to gain sole control over access to the grievance procedure for its own officers, thereby raising their status and increasing their ability to press nonmembers to join the union as the only guarantee of equitable treatment. The union also wanted to increase the burden of grievance handling on management, by insisting that all union-management conferences be held in working time, and that time limits in the first steps of the procedure be very short. This suggestion threatened real problems for production management, especially in the context of 248's tactic of "swamping" the grievance procedure, particularly before annual contract negotiations.[69]

Local 248's proposals for new contract clauses were similar to the more radical demands which were being made by many other union bargainers (particularly within the UAW) during and after the war.[70] Local 248's strategy was more in line with that of the rest of the labor movement than its extremist tactics and rhetoric would suggest. Had its demands for formal, contractual job controls been won, management's authority over the workforce would have been seriously impaired. Informal or local agreements in weak firms like Brewster Aeronautical and Packard, although disturbing auguries, were at least confined. If major unions had been able to extend their gains into strong companies like Allis-Chalmers and General Motors, and to fix them in legally recognized written agreements, the challenge to management control would have been much more serious.

Fortunately for Allis-Chalmers, such union demands were so controversial and potentially damaging that the NWLB would not order them, and it is unlikely in any case that Local 248 could have won them in a free trial of strength against A-C's determined management. Until 1945, Local 248's hands were tied by the national UAW's no-strike pledge, and all it could do was skirmish with A-C management. After 1945, both parties were free to resolve their differences. In the succeeding years many other firms, determined to hang onto their power or to grab back what bits the labor unions had torn from them, met unions wanting to extend and consolidate their gains while the going was good. They clashed head-on, and management usually emerged the victor. One reason for this was that most unions actually had quite unambitious bargaining objectives, and even those whose members wanted more turned out to be willing to settle for less.

Most unions, in practice, only wanted to acquire influence over important aspects of corporate personnel policy directly affecting their members' interests. Most of their bargaining objectives related to the immediate "job territory." As well as negotiating on wages and hours, they sought to create rights to predictable conditions of employment for their members. They wanted workers to have job tenure, i.e. freedom from the threat of arbitrary dismissal. Management had to show a reasonable cause for its actions in the exercise of discipline, as well as in the layoff and rehiring of workers and the making of promotions. Unions were usually content to negotiate with management to establish the rules determining what was fair treatment of workers, leaving management to enforce them on its own initiative, with the union's role confined to policing management actions through the grievance procedure. The same principle was followed in determining what output was expected of a worker, and how much he should be paid for it. Unions were interested in the joint development of rules, systems, and standards governing personnel policy, but not in sharing directly in its administration.[71] As a senior Steelworkers official said to calm business fears of union aggression, "We have no desire to control industry. All we desire is to bargain collectively for wages, hours, and working conditions. The responsibility for controlling industry as such rests with industry."[72]

This was the frequently reiterated position of "responsible" labor leaders. It was a model of union behavior with which NWLB public members were in full agreement, and which they tried to encourage. In time, as unions followed this line more closely in practice, they even became acceptable to many businessmen as useful institutions for regulating aspects of workplace industrial relations.

But, in the 1940s, and in the mass-production industries, *all* aspects of corporate personnel policy had been very largely under unilateral management control until very recently. The modest gains of responsible unions had been made very rapidly and, however much they denied the accusations of limitless appetite for power leveled at them, they could not stop many businessmen from believing the worst about their actual intentions.

This was partly because, as the realities of workplace industrial relations in wartime showed, many union members and local activists were neither so responsible nor so unaggressive as their national officers. In addition, contract clauses that were won at firms like Brewster Aeronautical, and demanded at Allis-Chalmers, Ford, General Motors, et al., indicated that some unions clearly were not satisfied with the gains they had made. They wanted to continue to expand the amount of the "job territory" subject to joint regulation, and to advance into the joint administration of policy instead of having a limited, reactive role. Thus Lee H. Hill warned his fellow managers of the dangerous potential of union demands to establish joint committees with a more than consultative or advisory status, and to restrict management's right to initiate and implement change by insisting on the "mutual consent" of company and union beforehand. Such demands for a direct union stake in management were more threatening in principle even than unrestricted arbitration and the extension of the seniority system.[73]

All of the discussion so far has centered on union bargaining objectives in workplace labor relations. More worrying still were evidences — only straws in the wind in the 1940s — which seemed to demonstrate that *some* union leaders were ready to claim a voice in the management process far beyond the limited field of personnel policy, and to challenge business in political action. Phillip Murray of the Steelworkers, Walter Reuther of the UAW, and Sidney Hillman of the Amalgamated

Clothing Workers were the real villains of the piece. These respectable, responsible men, not a host of miscellaneous rank-and-file militants and political activists, produced the most extreme reactions from American businessmen. Fear and loathing of their supposed intentions inspired George Romney, spokesman for the automotive industry, to describe the CIO program as "a selfish drive . . . for more, more, and more power — political, social, and economic power" aiming ultimately at the creation of a "CIO superstate" and "cartelization of American industry."[74]

There *was* a measure of truth in businessmen's analyses of the collectivist, corporatist proposals made, but not strenuously pursued, by middle-of-the-road Democrats like Murray, and ex-social democrats like Reuther and Hillman. In the defense period, Murray and Reuther suggested the establishment of a hierarchy of joint labor-management councils, stretching from the workplace right up to Washington, to coordinate the defense production effort. They wanted to protect their members' interests, and to give their organizations some more effective representation in the mobilization program than purely advisory participation in federal agencies afforded.[75]

Nothing came of these proposals, except perhaps in the very dilute form of plant-level War Production Drive committees set up at the suggestion of the War Production Board. These committees were dedicated to promoting union-management cooperation to maximize output, boost morale, and solve some practical problems of wartime living. Even such innocuous bodies aroused the suspicion of authority-conscious managements, like that of General Motors, which did not accept them during the war, or terminated them once it was over.[76]

Far more serious a danger than the interest of some unions in plant-level cooperation was the apparent threat to the autonomy of individual managements represented by the industrial unions' drive for industry-wide determination of, first of all, basic labor conditions, and beyond that, such important matters as corporate pricing policy. Organized labor's "industrial statesmen," Reuther above all, appreciated that corporate decisions on pricing, investment, and plant location could undermine the union's strength, its members' employment opportunities, and the value of negotiated economic gains. In the transition from war to peace, they were extremely concerned about the prospects of postwar recession, unemployment, and/or inflation. It was natural for union leaders to make what use they could of collective bargaining to forestall these anticipated problems, particularly after their preferred approach, political action, failed.[77]

The CIO Political Action Committee (PAC) was set up in 1944 to strengthen the forces of political liberalism, in the country and in Congress. It was largely a defensive move: working-class nonvoting in the 1942 elections, the increased strength of the Republican-conservative Democrat coalition, the power of business in the war agencies and in Congress, and the threat of postwar antilabor legislation foreshadowed by the 1943 Smith-Connally Act, stirred the CIO into action. It realized that it could not rely on Roosevelt forever, and must try to protect itself and advance its members' interests. As far as the CIO was concerned, these had to do with what it called the "human side of reconversion." After the war, the CIO wanted to see an Americanized version of the Beveridge Plan implemented. It wanted to see federal price controls extended into peacetime, to counter the immediate danger of inflation, together with improved social security policies and a federal commitment to support continued high-level economic activity, to fend off the universally forecast impending recession.[78]

The CIO-PAC did much good work, stemmed defections of workers from the Democratic fold, and earned an entirely unjustified reputation for fearsome political power and effectiveness. In fact, attempts at a New Deal revival in Congress in 1944–45 failed miserably, and the assaults of business on price control in the early reconversion period, 1945–46, were wholly successful. The Employment Act of 1946, as finally enacted, did not guarantee liberal Keynesian intervention by the federal government to support capital formation and effective demand at or near full employment levels. And the PAC's very limited successes in returning liberals to Congress and booting out reactionaries in 1944 were not repeated in 1946, when the staunchly reactionary 80th Congress was elected.[79]

The industrial unions' second strategy was to attempt to gain some of their political objectives, admittedly for members only, through collective bargaining. They aimed to establish liberal welfare funds, employer-financed, to safeguard workers' purchasing power against inflation and the reduction of overtime, and to influence corporate management's exercise of its market power over prices. The postwar bargaining rounds were therefore, and inevitably, highly politicized, the "First Round" of fall 1945–spring 1946 most of all. And, of all the First Round strikes, the massive dispute between Walter Reuther's section of the UAW and General Motors summed up the manifold struggles between business and labor best.

The postwar bargaining rounds had several peculiar features which help to explain their overtly political nature. Federal economic controls were still in existence, though under attack. There was, in fact, an unprecedented degree of federal interference in the peacetime settlement of basic wage disputes in the pattern-setting heavy industries, through the use of "fact-finding boards." So unions (and managements) had to "play to the gallery," couching their bargaining demands in terms of the "public interest," and using propaganda to try to line up public support for them. This was important, as the federal government was sure to be the final arbiter.[80]

But even when this is accepted, there was something new, and perhaps dangerous, in unions' overtly linking their bargaining objectives to the large matters of public policy. In the language of the UAW-GM department's economic brief in the 1945–46 strike, the union aimed to secure "Purchasing Power for Prosperity" and "Higher Wages Without Price Increases." Reuther promised the American public that his members' take-home pay could be protected, in real terms, against postwar readjustments without causing inflation. But this argument depended on making large assumptions about the level at which the corporation, and the economy, would be operating, about the level of its investment, and about the level of profit the corporation could make, consistent with the public interest. In doing so, the union was intruding on the holy-of-holies of managerial power, and offering a real threat to its traditional freedom to make the key decisions affecting the future of the firm.[81]

Thirty-five years' hindsight allows us to conclude that both the collective-bargaining and the political-action routes to the transformation of American society have turned out to be dead-end streets. Even at the time, thoughtful independent observers doubted the depth and sincerity of the CIO's commitment to radical reform.[82] But businessmen did not know the future, and did not feel like taking chances. What so disturbed them was not so much what had already happened as what seemed to be in prospect. Elements in some unions' tactics and strategy which really did constitute a serious challenge to managerial power and authority colored business reactions to the whole labor movement. The modest achievements and ambitions of responsible unions were not a source of reassurance. Maybe they were just a Trojan Horse, or, to change the metaphor, an insidious entering wedge. If business allowed the slightest union challenge to management control to succeed, it would be started irreversibly down the slippery slope to perdition . . .[83]

III: The Issue of Supervisory Unionism

Blue-collar production workers and their unions were the source of most of management's actual labor relations problems of the war years, and of most of its anxieties about the future. But, whether it is measured by the volume or intensity of business comment about it, or the amount of energy employers dedicated to countering it, no *single* part of the rank-and-file challenge to management control was as important as a threat from an unexpected quarter which exercised businessmen in the 1940s. All of a sudden, tens of thousands of foremen and lower-level production supervisors in the automotive, airplane manufacturing, rubber, steel, shipbuilding, coal, and other heavy industries showed themselves ready to form and join unions, and to strike. They behaved just like the blue-collar workers they were supposed to help management control.

Supervisory unionism was just the tip of an iceberg of discontentment in the lower levels of the management hierarchy in the 1940s. The two most important independent foremen's unions had a combined membership of 90–100,000 by 1945–46, and several thousand more foremen were recruited by blue-collar unions. But in December of 1945 a sample survey indicated that while only 7 percent of foremen actually were union members, 11 percent wanted to be, 33 percent thought foremen needed to get organized, and 38 percent thought it was "all right" for them to join unions. As far as senior managers in the affected industries were concerned, their lowly subordinates' behavior, intentions, and even prounion attitudes were problems to be dealt with aggressively and decisively. This was not a situation management could come to tolerate: it was "a threat to the very structure of management itself," and "the most serious problem facing industry today."[84]

Like most of the labor relations problems of the 1940s, supervisory unionism was not altogether new, but the conditions of war brought it to a head. The roots of foremen's discontentment stretched back well beyond the 1930s, right into the formative period of large-scale, bureaucratized capitalism around the turn of the century. The foreman in mass-production industry was a creature of the "new factory system" which reached its maturity in the 1920s. He no longer possessed the power or the status of his nineteenth-century forebears, or of his contemporaries in small-scale, technically unprogressive industries. The mass-production foreman did not rule over a little "empire," an autonomous shop or department, and he did not have a direct line to higher management. Production processes had become complex and minutely subdivided. Staff specialists had taken over most actual management functions in the areas of design, organization of production, and budgetary control. As foremen lost independence and responsibility, they also suffered a decline in status. Foremen continued to be recruited very largely from the ranks of blue-collar workers, but now their positions were about the best to which a man without a college education of some sort could aspire. For all the talk of the foreman as a vital part of management, he could see that the door of the executive suite did not swing beckoningly open before him.

Production supervisors in large firms were the lowest-ranking members in the distended hierarchy of line management, with several levels of superiors above them to insulate them from the policymaking heights. They were responsible for executing policies decided elsewhere, according to procedures they had little part in determining. They had to keep records and make reports to prove how closely and successfully they had followed orders. They were kept under quite tight supervision themselves, and subject to the kind of arbitrary exercise of authority and favoritism that they themselves showed toward their subordinates. These features of the foreman's life persisted through the late 1930s and 1940s. But at least, until the mid-1930s, foremen enjoyed a few substantial advantages to compensate them for the difficulties and hardships of their work — a few status symbols, greater job security, better fringe benefits, and, usually, more pay had given them the edge over their blue-collar brethren. However, in the late 1930s and through the 1940s foremen's jobs became relatively less attractive and absolutely more difficult as a direct consequence of the rise of mass-production industrial unionism.

The essential core of the foreman's job was day-to-day man-management at the point of production. He had to get out production and meet the standards of cost, speed, and quality which the company set him. To do this, he was left with extensive powers over the rank-and-file: he could hire workers, place them at work, assign them to jobs or shifts, train them, drive them, reward, promote, discipline, and fire them. Even in the minority of companies which had a personnel staff in the 1920s, his powers were only restricted, not destroyed. The foreman could use his powers for the company's purposes or for his own — finding jobs for family and friends, demanding bribes and sexual or other favors, lining his own pocket — secure in the knowledge that unorganized workers could not protest his actions effectively, and that higher management would not intervene.[85]

Union organization in the later 1930s made the jobs of production foremen much more difficult and less attractive, and undermined the vestigial independence and remaining powers of these petty barons in America's industrial feudalism. Abuses of power by supervisors supplied many of the grievances which caused industrial workers to form and join the new unions. Workers wanted protection against foremen's "discretion." In a time of mass unemployment it was particularly objectionable to have to pay, in money or kind, to get or keep a job, or for minor promotions, and to be threatened with the sack for small breaches of discipline or just getting on the wrong side of the foreman. Foremen were also the traditional factory regime's trusty agents in maintaining output standards and enforcing the "speedup," and in opposing independent unionization.[86]

For all of these reasons the industrial unions concentrated heavily on reducing the foreman's power in order to strengthen their own organizations and win their members a measure of job security and job control. This was the effect of the development of contractual clauses covering employment decisions the foreman had once been able to make on his own. It was also the result of the elaboration of grievance procedures, and of the ability of workers and unions to complain to the NLRB, to take direct action against any particular supervisory decision, or to threaten convincingly that they would follow one course or the other. So the autonomy once enjoyed by the shop foreman in his relations with his subordinates was decisively ended as union organization spread in the later 1930s. Indeed, a powerful "outsider" intruded: the union steward or grievance committeeman was a formal competitor in the workplace, with the right to challenge the foreman's decisions. Stewards and committeemen could often depend on the support of the rank-and-file in cases of conflict. They also had the backing of the official union bureaucracy if they prosecuted a formal grievance, and enjoyed a direct line to higher management when the time came to settle a grievance or negotiate the contract.[87]

The foreman's discretion in man-management was steadily ground down between an upper millstone of union challenge and a nether of managerial response. Some managements tried to give the foreman an important part in implementing labor relations policy, and to improve his status vis-à-vis his subordinates and their union. They required workers to present grievances to the foreman first, in person, rather than to go to a union officer who might bypass the foreman altogether and take the case directly to higher management. And they resisted union demands for the shop steward system, holding out instead for the appointment of grievance committeemen — much less numerous, but full-time, officials, who would not compete with every foreman in every department. Other firms recognized that unionization had created new and difficult problems for their foremen, which they were neither trained nor competent to handle. They could not be trusted with the responsibility for making important decisions which might prove costly or set dangerous precedents. Such firms centralized grievance-handling and much more of man-management in a personnel staff. But whatever course a company took, its foremen found their authority over the rank-and-file restricted. In the one case, a labor relations department would provide them with firm guidelines, and take over any tricky cases very quickly. In the other, they were simply displaced from the very start of the grievance adjustment process. Such an outcome was the inevitable result of the imposition of a "reign of rules" in the workplace.[88]

Unionization of rank-and-file workers led to a sudden and drastic increase in the difficulties of the foreman's job of maintaining discipline and meeting management's production targets. He was no longer so free to punish and reward. It also led to a decline in his status and working conditions relative to his subordinates and their union officers. Foremen were often the last to hear of the terms of contracts or grievance settlements which affected them, or of changes in company policy. Management's internal communications system was revealed in all of its inadequacy. Foremen lacked formal job security, grievance procedures, and fair or rational payment systems. They were still just as exposed to their superiors' arbitrary control as they had been before the New Deal, while their subordinates had largely escaped the old degrading conditions. Management's desire for labor peace, and the strength of organized workers, brought real improvements in direct pay and fringe benefits for blue-collar employees. The Social Security and Wage and Hour Acts had similar effects. Foremen missed out on these advantages, and found their extra margin of reward over the rank-and-file distressingly compressed.[89]

This was the situation in which the first, abortive union of supervisors in mass-production industry was organized — the United Foremen and Supervisors–CIO, established in Greater Detroit in 1938–39. Deserted by the UAW, attacked by automotive managements (Chrysler's in particular), it came to nothing. At the same time, some management observers began to express their anxieties about the morale of the non-commissioned officers in the production army, and a very few far-sighted companies began to take corrective action.[90] But before either the awareness or the remedial action could become more general, the war came to make the immediate problems much worse, and prevent considered action even to deal with symptoms of poor morale, let alone the underlying causes.

Mobilization of the economy for war accelerated, then substantially completed, the unionization of blue-collar workers in mass-production and basic industries. Workers' wartime restiveness, strong bargaining power, and direct actions created important additional problems for foremen. Furthermore, the ranks of supervision were greatly diluted by the rapid upgrading of production workers, given crash courses in basic foremanship by individual companies and the federal Training Within

Industry organization. Wartime foremen were thus likely to have had direct personal experience of the benefits of unionization. Even the old-timers could not help but observe what the rank-and-file had won. Many wartime foremen, in addition, could expect to return to the ranks once war ended, the veterans returned, and industry's manpower needs shrank. As a result, they were preoccupied with the protection of their job security, and naturally turned to contractual seniority as the way to get it. Furthermore, they were concerned to maximize the direct economic rewards of their, perhaps temporary, jobs.

But without collective power they missed out on many of the benefits conceded by management or the NWLB, or exacted by groups of workers. Traditional differentials of 25–60 percent on basic pay were further compressed, and in some cases differentials on earnings were even reversed. Salaried foremen had less opportunity than hourly paid or piecework employees to inflate their earnings by overtime and increased production, or to create wage drift by "demoralizing" time-keeping and production standards. Blue collar workers' fringe benefits — shift premiums, sick pay, holiday and vacation pay — similarly became as good as, or rather better than, their immediate superiors'.

In the early years of the war, these supervisory grievances tended to be ignored by management as they were not protested effectively — here as elsewhere, management greased the wheel that squeaked the loudest. By the time it realized something was seriously amiss, federal salary stabilization (a fancy term for wage control) policy made adjustments much more difficult to implement.[91]

These were the immediate grievances, acutely felt, which accounted for the organization and growth of the Foremen's Association of America (FAA). Fundamental alterations in the foreman's status brought about by the bureaucratization of management and the growth of blue-collar unions also played a part. The FAA was born in 1941 at the Ford River Rouge plant, where foremen suffered from all of their fellows' general problems, but in an extreme form.[92]

In June of that year, Ford's management made its surprising decision not only to recognize the UAW, but to grant it a better contract than it had yet obtained from any other major automobile company. Ford foremen were suddenly exposed to a militant workforce that was able powerfully to resist their authority, which had traditionally been very extensive. Meanwhile, higher management's importunate demands for increased — and uninterrupted — production continued. Ford foremen did not receive the pay increases, the security against dismissal or arbitrary treatment, or the relaxation of the work pace their subordinates were able to win, and remained at the mercy of their own superiors.

They were neither consulted nor officially informed about the change in Ford's labor relations policy, nor were they given any assistance in adjusting to the new factory regime. As a last straw, the UAW contract provided — as was not unusual — that any worker promoted out of the ranks of the bargaining unit thereby stopped accumulating seniority. In the summer of 1941, the mobilization emergency was not expected to last very long; reconversion would inevitably come, and then foremen, generally long-serving, reliable workers, would find themselves demoted, competing on unfavorable terms for preferable jobs, shifts, or even the right to work in any production or maintenance occupation.[93]

Against the background of these specific grievances and anxieties, a group of foremen from the aircraft engine plant within the massive River Rouge complex began to meet in late August. This band of associates met to bowl and drink after hours, but from the very outset they were more than just a social club. They were planning to form a union patterned after the UAW and seeking similar objectives for its members. The UAW was obliged by contract not to organize supervisors or accept them into membership. The UAW held to this principle, so the overtures the FAA's founders made to Ford Local 600 were rejected. Accordingly, they acted independently, signing up members clandestinely and then holding their first public meeting on 2 November 1941. Twelve hundred Ford foremen attended. Officers were elected, a constitution adopted, and an organizing campaign inaugurated, directed in the first instance only at Ford plants in Greater Detroit.

Expansion was rapid, but progress toward recognition and meaningful bargaining slight. The FAA found itself besieged by representatives of other companies' aggrieved foremen, often undertaking their own spontaneous organizational efforts and seeking its advice and assistance. By newspaper advertising, a radio campaign in metropolitan Detroit, and the appointment of a membership director and staff, it began to actively seek members at large in 1943. It emphasized that the foreman was the "forgotten man" of mass production industry and likely to "become a victim" in the "ceaseless struggle between ownership and wage labor."[94]

The FAA gained members in the Midwestern automotive, steel, rubber, and metalworking industries, and by the end of the war had made significant inroads in the aircraft industries of the Pacific coast and Middle Atlantic states, as well as in miscellaneous and scattered manufacturing enterprises and in some nonmanufacturing sectors. However, the Detroit automotive industry remained its base, and the Ford Motor Company the only major manufacturer with whom, after years of negotiation and a number of strikes, it negotiated a written agreement.[95]

At the same time, other unions were actively recruiting supervisors in newly organized mass-production industries. Independent, autonomous supervisors' unions sprang up, particularly in aircraft plants, and some of them subsequently became affiliated with the FAA; the Mechanics' Educational Society of America competed with the FAA in its Midwestern heartland; the CIO Longshore, Packinghouse, Steel, and Shipbuilding Workers' unions acted independently, within their own sectors, to recruit and act for the lowest level of supervision. Somewhat analogously, the UAW recruited the vastly expanded security forces of war plants, and routine white-collar workers, whose grievances over pay and conditions were similar to those of foremen. Finally, the Mine Workers took over the newly formed, militant Mine Officials' Union of America and transformed it into the United Clerical, Technical and Supervisory Employees (UCTSE), which threatened to go on the offensive in recruiting outside its own industry.[96]

Even in the favorable conditions of wartime, the gains which foremen's unions actually registered, in membership and bargaining rights, were quite small. FAA membership fluctuated between thirty and forty thousand in 1945–46, while UCTSE acquired sixty thousand at the same time, but did not spread beyond the mining industry. But union-consciousness was more common than union membership, and if it turned into actual membership then foremen's unions would become a formidable new problem. The Detroit foremen's strikes of 1943–44 showed how much disruption such a strategic minority of workers could cause. If every firm had been as badly hit as Ford, American industry would have found it hard to deny the FAA or other foremen's unions the status they were seeking.

Luckily, Ford's problems were exceptional. Most of industrial management was determined to deny recognition to foremen's unions, to stop the rot of labor organization from spreading beyond the blue-collar working class. They used all of the traditional stratagems of nonviolent antiunionism to win this objective. So the FAA's life was more troubled than that of most other unions. It encountered espionage, discriminatory discharges, threats and blandishments from superiors, attempts to buy off its officers, hostile propaganda, promotion of what were, in effect, company unions for foremen, refusal to recognize or bargain, and protracted litigation. Right through the war, the FAA's usual experience at the hands of management remained strongly reminiscent of the relations between business and the new unions of the 1930s. But the FAA did not have the power, or the outside assistance, to enable it to make the kind of progress toward forced managerial "acceptance" of its existence and rights that the CIO had been able to win after 1937. Most firms fought its attempts to use the Wagner Act and NLRB procedures to strengthen its hand. Even when the union won cases, late in the war and immediately after, those decisions were contested by management, never enforced, and consequently of no practical value.

The FAA's peculiar vulnerability resulted from its questionable legal status under the Wagner Act: were supervisors "employees" within the meaning of the Act at all? The union said yes; management, forcefully, no; and the NLRB wavered, answering, at various times from 1942 to 1946, yes, no, maybe, yes again, first with reservations, later without. It could always find plenty of plausible arguments for its changes of opinion, but the essential reason was that, on this of all sensitive issues, it was subject to powerful, conflicting pressures. In 1943, when it delivered the crucial *Maryland Drydock* decision, denying foremen protection of the right to unionize, the important, and conservative, House Military Affairs Committee was holding hearings on restrictive legislation sponsored by a consortium of large, heavy-industrial firms led by GM. The Board brought out its opinion, industrialists turned off the heat, and the hearings ended with no action.

Managements exploited the free hand the Board had given them by firing FAA members and activists. The FAA replied by forging an understanding with UAW and Steel Workers/CIO presidents Thomas and Murray which increased the effectiveness of any strike action it might take. And in 1943–44 it organized massively disruptive recognition strikes in key defense industries. The FAA and UCTSE might not have much political clout, but they had plenty of industrial muscle. The FAA's main objective remained the winning of full recognition, by peaceful means if possible—either by negotiation, or through NLRB and NWLB orders. But when this avenue was blocked, it turned to the strike weapon. It used strikes (or the threat of them) to win recognition, to speed negotiations to a successful conclusion, or to bring pressure on the NLRB and NWLB to alter their policies in favor of supervisory unionism. Strikes were dangerous: they exposed members to possible job loss, as the NLRB's leaky umbrella did not shelter them at all; and members and their unions felt the full weight of a hostile press and the very real pressures managements, the NWLB, and the armed services brought to bear. So the FAA did not call or authorize strikes often or hastily, but it recognized that in the last resort it had no other way to protect its members' interests or advance them.

And, in the short term, the strategy worked. In the 1944 *Republic Steel* and *Soss Manufacturing* cases the NLRB partially reversed itself, giving individual foremen protection against job loss for union membership or activity. And the NWLB set up a prestigious investigative panel composed of three public members led by Sumner Slichter, to look into foremen's grievances. The NLRB was now under pressure from two fronts: from the NWLB, interested in uninterrupted war production; and from the FAA itself, which had proved its strength and its determination to use it. In January 1945 the NWLB recommended that grievance procedures for foremen should be established. And the NLRB set up the *Packard* case as the occasion for it to alter its past policies. The FAA was exceptionally strong at Packard. In due time, the NLRB came out in favor of granting a foremen's union independent of the rank-and-file free and equal access to its procedures and the full protection of the Wagner Act. In 1946, in the *Jones & Loughlin Steel Co.* case, it removed the stipulation that foremen should be organized into a fully autonomous union. The last legal barriers to the growth of supervisory unionism and its collaboration with, if not incorporation into, the rest of the labor movement seemed on the way to being removed, especially once the Supreme Court endorsed the *Packard* decision in 1947.

But by that time the ball was in the other court. In early 1945 General Motors once again began to muster business opposition to supervisory unionism. GM was not seriously affected by the problem itself; Chrysler, its sidekick, was. They and others lobbied against the FAA before the NWLB, weighed in with amicus curiae briefs in the *Packard* case, and helped fight it all the way to the Supreme Court. They did not rely on their forensic campaign alone. They also took the issue back to Congress, asking for a return to the *Maryland Drydock* doctrine to be written unequivocally into federal law for all time. This demand became one of the main specific objectives in the business community's struggle to amend the Wagner Act after the war.[97]

Supervisory unionism was never a particularly large movement. Admittedly, it made an important localized impact within the Midwestern automotive industry and its corporate cousins — airplane and steel companies in particular. But even there it was quite a temporary phenomenon. The FAA had begun to lose members even before the Taft-Hartley Act deprived it and them of legal protection in their fight for organizational survival against business hostility. Reconversion brought the demotion or layoff of many wartime foremen; some plants where the FAA had been particularly strong, notably the Ford bomber plant at Willow Run, closed down or shed most of their workforce. And, in the difficult economic circumstances of the postwar years, foremen's unions simply had less appeal and less strength. Reconversion brought wage cuts and unemployment for blue-collar workers, and restored some of the relative attractiveness of foremen's jobs. Foremen were certainly more apprehensive about losing them. And they had less bargaining power than they had possessed in the war. Some unions, the UAW for one, were less willing to give striking foremen their passive support. Foremen's strikes affected their own members, many of whom were heartily sick of the effects of strikes — their own and other people's — and shortages of parts and raw materials upon earnings and employment. In addition, companies found it easier to take foremen's strikes than they had during the war. Continuous production was no longer an overriding imperative, and managers were free to provoke or ride out foremen's strikes without pressure from the military or the NWLB to reach a truce. They also had a much better opportunity — which many firms took — to do something to remove the root causes of many of the most acute grievances foremen had felt over pay and conditions.

When we look at the brief, unsuccessful history of the FAA — aptly termed a "meteor on the industrial relations horizon" — and the ease with which management was able to squash it and other foremen's unions, we may be forgiven for wondering what all the fuss was about at the time. Why were businessmen so worried by this new development which did not, in any case, affect most of them directly?

The answer to this particular question throws light on the general response of the business community to other elements in the "union challenge to management control" in the 1940s. Businessmen did not react simply to what had *already* happened to their *own* companies. They read or heard about the experience and troubles of firms in a much worse fix. What had happened to Ford or Packard today might happen to them tomorrow. Supervisory unionism was a new phenomenon. Until 1945, it appeared to be a growing one. Businessmen projected apparent trends into the future, and constructed worst-case scenarios that frightened themselves and their fellows into taking corrective action.

In addition, the growth of union-consciousness among foremen seemed to indicate that it would be impossible to limit labor organization to the ranks of the blue-collar working class. By the mid-1940s industrial management had, by and large, come to terms with the fact that most production and maintenance workers had been enrolled into unions and were going to stay there. Such unions caused management many day-to-day headaches, as well as more important problems of control. But management was confident that the situation, once stabilized, could be lived with.

"Stabilization" meant, first of all, making sure that the growth in union membership slowed down, or even went into reverse. This required keeping some blue-collar workers nonunion, and then preventing union fever from spreading into the ranks of routine white-collar workers, foremen and supervisors, and even middle management. All such groups showed stirrings of discontent and union-consciousness in the late 1930s and '40s. They were all potentially organizable, but it was even more important for management to retain their loyalty and obedience, to keep its firm control over them, than it was to win back unilateral control over blue-collar workers. After all, they were its essential agents in any program to regain influence over the attitudes and behavior of workers. Top policymakers could only chart a course for the organization. To do so, they depended largely on the technical expertise, advice, and information their subordinates supplied. To see it followed through, they were even more dependent on their subordinates, especially those in line management, as executors. If top management wanted some way of communicating with the rank-and-file other than through union leadership and machinery, it had to turn to line managers and supervisors. If it wanted to compete with union committeemen and shop stewards for influence over the workforce in the workplace, it only had one numerous group of subordinates—its foremen—in intimate, day-to-day contact with workers *and yet* directly subject to its own authority. In the struggle to regain control over production and discipline, foremen would surely play a key role.

Thus, the fight to prevent the unionization of foremen and supervisors was, as far as management saw it, a vital engagement in its battle to keep and recover control. It would be an important victory in its own right, and a precondition of later success in the broad-front assault against the power of industrial unionism which management planned and commenced in 1944–46.

And the price of failure would be high.

Take away from us our foremen and we are lost; because they are the people . . . that have got to be held responsible for production, for cost, for accident prevention, and for all the various phases of the business. They are the representatives of management out there on the firing line.[98]

[W]e must rely upon the foremen to try and keep down those emotional surges [i.e. wildcat strikes], to keep the men in the plants, and to urge them to rely upon the grievance procedure. If we do not have the foremen to do that, who is going to do it?[99]

Managers did not believe that unionized foremen would or could be satisfactory agents. This was partly a matter of "common sense": freed from the strict control of their superiors as a result of unionization, foremen would serve their own interests first. It was only human nature. Businessmen's prejudices on this score were backed up by good authorities: the Bible (Matt. 6:24) said, and common law confirmed, that no man could serve two masters (company and union); nor could any agent be allowed to have interests independent of or opposed to those of his principal.

What little experience businessmen had of the actual consequences of supervisory unionism confirmed them in their fearful suspicions of it. Foremen joined unions, in part at least, to win some limitation of higher management's hitherto unquestioned power over them. But "if management is not able to control those within its own group, then it loses effective control of the business and the result is chaotic and injurious to the successful operation of the business."[100]

It was not just that unionization weakened management's control over foremen. It also gave the union of blue-collar workers a dangerous degree of influence. That was because, as the FAA-UAW understanding of 1943–46 showed, foremen's strikes could only really cripple production if they enjoyed some support from the rank-and-file. If unionized skilled workers, maintenance men, set-up men, gang bosses, etc. refused to substitute for striking foremen (which they were quite capable of doing, as a stopgap measure), productivity and discipline collapsed. If they and semiskilled or unskilled workers observed foremen's picket lines, the effects were even more immediate and extreme. In return, foremen might agree not to cross workers' picket lines nor to try to keep production going with skeleton crews of managerial and white-collar staff, or scab labor. Such well-developed cooperation and solidarity was rare, but not unknown: occurrences at Ford, the Murray Corporation of America, B. F. Goodrich, and Westinghouse Electric lent credibility to predictions of the awful consequences of allowing foremen to form and join unions. Businessmen believed, or asserted, that there was no chance of any foremen's union, however formally independent, being able to stay free from the influence of the unions representing their blue-collar subordinates and fellow workers. Either the blue-collar union would take over the supervisors' union, or their alliance would grow. "'Solidarity of labor' is not an empty phrase, but a strong and active force."[101]

If the foremen are unionized, if they are just as quick to strike as the rank-and-file, if they are dependent, wholly dependent, upon the rank-and-file union for their very existence, for their effectiveness, why, of course, they are going to be beholden to the rank-and-file union, and they are not going to try and dissuade the rank-and-file from going out and kicking the grievance procedure over and saying, "Let us strike."[102]

Foremen would be even more likely to "[grant] the rank-and-file favors at our expense" than they were already inclined to do in response to informal, everyday pressure in the workplace. If worst came to worst, and blue-collar unions gained control over unions representing foremen, supervisors, company policemen, and other middle-management elements of top management's control system, the consequences would be disastrous: "the workmen will take the plants over."[103]

In practice, union fever was largely confined to the lowest level of supervisors who were little more than production workers elevated to higher office (perhaps temporarily) and given a white coat. But the FAA, for example, opened its doors to all middle-management personnel who did not have an actual voice in policymaking. And the NLRB, in a case involving chain-store managers, seemed to agree that all but the highest circles of management could be considered as "employees" within the meaning of the Wagner Act—that is, they were eligible for union membership. So top management men could see an awful possibility of being effectively isolated at the pinnacles of their organizations, without any remaining subordinates over whom they had unchallenged unilateral authority. They were not worried about being lonely, but about being made powerless.[104]

[I]f you destroy this leadership of ours and take our management away from us, then you have taken over our company and our organization. . . . [O]ur management will be gone, and . . . we will have nobody to represent us and represent our stockholders and the owners of the business. . . . [I]t might even go from mass production into just sheer mob production, with no boss and no leadership there to run it. . . .
It is a movement that will lead—well, where will it stop?[105]

The same question could be asked about any element in the union challenge to management control, and no definite answer could be given. There was no answer, apart from the one that would result from the determined application of the business community's power and influence in the immediate postwar years.

In assessing the nature and importance of the different strands in the business community's labor relations problems, it is hard to avoid the conclusion that businessmen misjudged the seriousness of many of the separate issues. And they were certainly too worried by the nightmare they conjured up of a sustained, concerted attack on their authority. There was no such attack. There were many localized, particular, often temporary problems; threats which gained significance as they seemed to fit into a pattern. And there was the large difficulty that American business was having to adjust its manner of handling labor relations, and even its ways of thinking about them, in a time of rapid and unpredictable social change.

In the late 1930s businessmen had begun to show that they were capable of living with the new world of post-CIO, post-Wagner Act labor relations. They began to learn new tactics, adopt new strategies, and come to terms with their new adversaries. The rise of labor slowed down; it looked as if it would soon be contained.

Wondering what would have happened if the war had not is an academic exercise in the pejorative sense — futile. The war's impact on American society was large enough to destroy the possibility of projecting apparent trends of 1937–39 into the future. Businessmen needed stability to complete the process of accommodating themselves to the new unions. They did not get it. Working out a new balance of power in industry and society, consigning labor to its place somewhere below the salt at the great American banquet, would in any case have been a difficult task. The war made it much more so.

During the war businessmen had to deal with the impact of full employment, worker militancy, and federal intervention on a labor relations system still troubled and unsettled after the transformations of the 1930s. The war did not simply prolong the period of turbulence — it also extended it to new areas of the country, new industries, new sections of the workforce. The emerging American labor movement, stronger in many respects than it had been in 1939, talked in terms of a role for itself in politics, economic management, and workplace industrial relations which was larger than most businessmen were willing to allow. There was more talk than action, more ambition than achievement, but there was enough real growth in labor power to make even responsible unionism seem quite formidable.

What businessmen could see around them was bad enough; what they feared might be in prospect, if current trends were allowed to develop unchecked, might become intolerable. This explains the saliency of the "management prerogatives" issue in 1944–47 — the anxious, detailed discussion of how those prerogatives had been eroded, and how they could be defended and recovered.

But that is not the whole story. It has been impossible to write this chapter without a liberal use of the words "seem," "appear," etc. I have attempted both to explain what was actually happening in the period of war and reconversion, and to give the "view from the top" — to show what businessmen thought was happening. Policy decisions are made by men enmeshed in present problems and concerns, acting with partial or inadequate information about the way things actually are, and with only their best guesses about the future to guide their choices between options. To explain the matrix in which labor relations policy was formed in 1944–47, we need to understand both what businessmen thought had been happening during the war, and what they thought might happen after it. This chapter has only served the first purpose.

Furthermore, it is too easy in writing business history to treat businessmen as purely rational calculators, to take their frame of reference as the historian's own, rather than to question its premises. The union challenge to management control in the 1940s undoubtedly produced serious operating difficulties, but the management response was not just automatic, that is, an attempt to deal with "real" situations which any "reasonable man" in an executive position would think of as unacceptable. Businessmen were flesh-and-blood characters, often, to judge by their words and actions, passionate in their approach to labor relations problems. The extravagant rhetoric and large, costly effort with which management defended its power and autonomy were out of proportion to the modest threats labor actually posed. Possibly this strikes a British observer more forcibly than an American, because he has seen managers in his own country and Europe accept limitations on their power by workers, unions, and the state with a lot less fuss and resistance.

What is the peculiar element in the makeup of the American businessman? Why, in the 1940s, did he define certain situations as problematic, certain goals as desirable? To answer this question, we need to know something about the way businessmen looked at, and thought about, the structure and purposes of the enterprise, and their place in it; the rights of managers, the responsibilities of workers — in short, their ideology, the way businessmen attempted to justify their own power and status to themselves and others. Their perception of the seriousness of union challenges to the business community's power and authority was heavily influenced by immediate considerations — notably the forecasts of economic and political trends with which they worked. But the ideological framework in terms of which businessmen interpreted those challenges was relatively timeless.

3

The "View from the Top"[1]

ECONOMIC FORECASTS AND LABOR RELATIONS POLICY

The economic outlook was uncertain and disturbing in 1944–47, at the very time when businessmen were formulating and trying to implement their labor relations strategies for the reconversion period. The wartime "miracle of production" had left firms with a very mixed legacy of gains and losses. Management had learned, or more generally applied, more efficient methods of production. After a series of fat years, industry also had plenty of investment reserves for re-equipment with the most up-to-date machinery. Set against those advantages were the harmful consequences of the wartime sellers' market. The absence of cost contraints had led to an increase in industry's fixed costs and "break-even points." If companies were to continue to be profitable in peacetime, they would need to be able to make and sell a greater proportion of their maximum theoretical output than they had been able to survive on in the 1930s. And they must be able to sell it at a price which gave them a margin over their higher costs. If the economy failed to operate at a much higher level than it had achieved in the 1930s, they would be in difficulties. And in the short term, as long as federal price controls lasted, they might be trapped in a profitless squeeze.[2]

Management's awareness that it was facing a potential crisis resulted in widespread action, both to provide the business community with a more favorable operating environment of federal tax and price control policies, and to improve the productivity and cost-control of individual firms. Manpower management obviously had a large contribution to make toward achieving the latter objective.[3]

This was particularly true in those durable goods industries which

91

had converted totally to war production. They had been most seriously affected by the loss of labor discipline which had resulted from overfull employment and management's relaxation of its usual intense concern for labor productivity, unit cost, and orderly behavior. Businessmen were not sure how serious the problem was, but they tried very hard to find out. Impressionistic evidence and their own gut feelings told them that since 1940 there had been a decline in management's ability to control the workforce and get the most out of it. In 1944–47 they attempted to give the consequences of this decline some numerical value. They succeeded, after a fashion. One industrial relations consultant was willing to "hazard a guess that in the typical war plant labor cost (sic) are roughly 25 to 60 percent higher than they should be on comparable civilian work." His broad estimate was quite representative of the range of employer opinion, most of it gloomy.[4] "It is a matter of record that the real productive efficiency of most workers is now substantially lower than it was before the war, even though production in terms of tons or dollars per man-year may have increased."[5]

Any improvements in productivity levels were to be attributed to managerial actions — technical breakthroughs, capital investment, improved organization, etc. — and were not as high as they could and should have been, because of worker resistance or lack of cooperation. Every decline was largely the worker's fault.[6]

Businessmen were far more definite about the extent of the problem, and the reasons for it, than the information at their disposal warranted. The best productivity figures they could offer in public debate, for example, had to be obtained by comparing the amount and cost of labor required for a particular product or process before and after the war. Like was compared with unlike, and all sorts of complicating and distorting factors left out of the picture. Usually the evidence they used to support their arguments was even scantier and more questionable, nothing more than the estimates of worried and prejudiced men.[7]

A part of the reason for this was that there were no accepted, reliable, comprehensive, or meaningful productivity statistics to which they could turn for support. The war had disrupted the U.S. Bureau of Labor Statistics' series by transforming many of the industries to which they referred, making comparison between prewar and wartime figures impossible and extrapolation of wartime "trends" into the postwar period unrealistic. The economy had to reconvert to civilian production and settle down into peacetime "normality" before BLS statistics became useful once again. There was, for example, a three-and-a-half-year hiatus in passenger car production, while the making of airplanes and cargo ships had been revolutionized, and some whole new industries — e.g. synthetic rubber — invented.

The war had battered and twisted the data base for productivity measurement in less obvious ways, too. In the converted durable goods industries, proportionately less semiskilled machine tenders and assembly-line workers were required, and the demand for skilled labor had to be met by rapid training and upgrading of the less skilled. Companies had been unable to retool in many cases, and had not been able to achieve the full economies of continuous production because of shortages of manpower and materials and rapidly changing requirements from military procurement agencies. The immediate postwar period was also exceptional, with serious strikes, continuing shortages, and the difficulties of reconverting plant and workforce to meet the unfamiliar demands of the civilian market.[8]

All of these factors made the measurement of productivity movements difficult, and explanation hazardous. Workforce behavior was obviously not the only reason for whatever temporary and transitional difficulties management had. But it was one factor which was, at least in theory, under management's control, which businessmen could see and understand, and which was objectionable to them on moral and ideological grounds, as well as being potentially a threat.

Poor labor productivity might not be an immediate danger to the profitability of a firm in the consumer boom which was expected to occur during the early reconversion period. But the middle-term outlook was distinctly less reassuring. In two, or three, or four years' time, a recession or depression might come, and then success in the restoration of productivity and cost-control might make the difference between survival and bankruptcy. Even if things did not turn out so badly, the successful management could hope to see higher profit as a reward for its efforts.[9]

So the economic outlook provided plenty of good reasons to persuade firms to pay attention to manpower management as well as to other ways of boosting productivity and reducing costs in the immediate postwar period. But arguments related to the viability and profitability of particular companies were not the only ones employed at the time. Businessmen were also aware that the success or failure of their efforts to improve their own firms' chances of survival and growth had a much broader significance. The postwar recession, "corrective dip," or full-blown depression which was almost universally forecast seemed likely to be more than a crisis in the life of individual firms which had not yet managed to recover from the effects of war. It would also be a challenge to the "American individual enterprise system" which they were so determined to preserve.[10]

Businessmen were not the only group in American society to suffer from the "depression psychosis," and to worry about the impact of the return of mass unemployment on the political climate. Such fears also conditioned the thinking and planning of the CIO and liberal Democrats for the postwar era. And there were good reasons for their concern. After all, America had only returned to full employment and economic growth on a tide of federal dollars. By the end of the 1930s it had seemed as if the American economy was irredeemably stagnant, that the wellsprings of economic growth had dried up. A successful experiment in military Keynesianism in 1939–45 had temporarily solved the chronic problems of overcapacity (or insufficient purchasing power) which had plagued the 1930s. But, to most observers, the long-run prospects for the American economy in times when there was no such artificial stimulus still did not look bright.[11]

Businessmen had clear memories of the serious political and ideological challenges which mass unemployment and chronic economic failure had created for them in the 1930s. They congratulated themselves on the wartime "miracle of production" and were understandably pleased by the recovery in business prestige that it had caused. But they were uneasily aware that their wartime achievements only testified to the massive technical resourcefulness of the American economy. There had been no shortage of effective demand, no problems of marketing, and central controls had managed many of the tasks of coordination which a decentralized system of decision-making had earlier proven unable to handle. They were not altogether sure that they could guarantee lasting peacetime prosperity. And they knew that the lessons which liberals read from the experience of wartime economic controls and federal support of the level of effective demand were unacceptable to them. Liberals assumed that the war had proved that Keynesianism worked, and offered the only sure path away from stagnation. Demand management, microeconomic control, and the expansion of the welfare state were the ingredients in their recipe for prosperity.[12]

Businessmen wanted prosperity too, but most of them were not prepared to swallow any such liberal Keynesian nostrums. They wanted to travel a different road to postwar economic salvation, one which did not involve what they saw as a further weakening of the capitalist system. Instead, that system was to be strengthened by decontrolling the economy, lowering taxes, and letting the "spirit of enterprise" have its head. Businessmen's postwar political program would build on the good work of conservative Congressmen during the war and continue their onslaught on liberal reform's beleaguered garrisons. Republican successes in the 1946 elections seemed to promise that this dismantling of the New Deal would proceed apace.[13]

But this political strategy depended on continued prosperity for its hopes of success. Popular support of the existing economic system and of conservative economic and social policies depended on works, not faith. The only guarantee of a conservative or moderate public opinion, and hence of a political climate favorable to business, was the system's performance in meeting demands made of it. Among these, full employment ranked first. Economic collapse would surely be followed by a permanent New Deal—or worse![14] To be really frightened about the political consequences of economic failure and social upheaval, businessmen had only to look abroad. They could look around them at a world full of the debris of war, and appreciate, with Henry Ford II, that "it is not merely *things* which have been destroyed. The landscape is littered with wrecked ideas and faiths. Political and economic systems have been torn up and lie twisted and broken like a great railroad yard after a bombing raid."[15]

America seemed to be the last outpost of western liberalism and more-or-less intact capitalism. Communism was advancing across central and eastern Europe, democratic socialism was scoring victories in western European countries more important to the United States. And the example of Britain under the 1945 Labour government was particularly worrying—the Labour program reflected what American businessmen thought they could expect from a revitalized liberal coalition at home, and they did not like what they saw. As far as businessmen were concerned, America was the last bastion of the freedoms they held most dear, and it seemed to be disturbingly fragile.[16]

At the level of the firm, it looked as if management might have only a very few years in which to win back territory it had lost to workers and their unions during the war. Moving from the grass roots to the national level, and from labor relations into more conventional interest-group politics, it seemed that there was a similar urgency for the business community to "seize the time," to get labor relations law reforms on the statute book and to get Congress to implement its conservative economic strategy. The immediate reconversion years, 1945–47, were busy ones for labor-management conflict at all levels, partly because the business community (represented by the NAM in particular) and many large firms turned on the heat, feeling that they had to act decisively while the time was right.

MANAGEMENT'S UNITARY IDEOLOGY

Workers and their unions challenged American businessmen's power and authority in the 1940s—not for the first time, but in an unprecedentedly organized way, and right across the spectrum of mass-production and basic industries. In the "good old days" before the New Deal, businessmen had been able to deal with less serious challenges relying on their own resources, with occasional — but important — assistance from the state. But in the 1940s businessmen could no longer depend altogether on the old unilateral strategies. They could not set the limits to their own power on their own say-so. Workers and unions had actually infringed on business sovereignty, with the backing of public opinion and public policy. If businessmen wanted to win back some lost territory, and make a new definition of the legitimate spheres of influence of labor and management stick, they had to have some assistance from groups outside their own ranks — their bargaining partners (or adversaries) in union leadership, arbitrators, Congress, the courts, and administrative agencies. Businessmen found that they had to make a case for the restoration and preservation of their own authority which would have at least some appeal among these other groups, the media, and the general public. The result of this situation — new in degree, not kind — was that businessmen bombarded these various "publics" with justifications of their own claims to sovereign power within industry. Much of this barrage was crude propaganda, and will be dealt with later. But some of it was much more sophisticated, consisting of quite elaborate, connected, and reasoned arguments, addressed to potential sympathizers for the most part.

These ideological constructions were also an important constituent of the "stream of information" within the business community itself. Ideology is a two-edged sword, justifying power to those who hold it, who need and want some legitimate basis for authority, as well as to those over whom it is exercised or whose compliance is required. The political thought of businessmen in the 1940s served a number of different purposes, but one of them, undoubtedly, was reassurance — confirming a threatened elite in the belief that it was right and good, as well as privileged and strong. It often seems that businessmen were the most important, as well as the most receptive, audience for their own propaganda and rationales. Often what they said and thought was more a thin tissue of shared assumptions than a case likely to convince anyone outside of their own ranks who was not already disposed to accept it. But the intellectual poverty of business theorizing should not lead us to ignore it. It offers us a way to see the world as businessmen wanted themselves and others to see it — a way to understand their own view of their role, their power and its justification, the rights they had over others, and the attitude and behavior subordinates should adopt towards them.

Businessmen were not given to much disagreement about the justification for *their* control over *their* enterprises. On this matter more than most, they spoke with one firm voice. It expressed their timeless faith that their power was founded essentially on property right, and that their chief responsibility was to maximize profitable production in the interests of shareholders before anybody else. These propositions were central to so-called "managerial" as well as older "entrepreneurial" ideologies. But in the former they were supported and overlain by other arguments from the structure of large business enterprises, the function of modern management, and its supposed broad social accountability.[17]

The main function of managerial ideology was (and is) to justify the continued possession of power and autonomy by the business elite in a pluralistic and democratic society. In twentieth-century America other claims on corporate resources than that of profit-maximizing, and other stakes in the enterprise than that of ownership, have come to be recognized as legitimate. In response, businessmen have tried to bolster their own authority and interests with more sophisticated arguments than sufficed in earlier, simpler times. In managerial ideology, businessmen are held to be accountable to a variety of pressures and "constituencies" — the state, the public interest, the consumer, the local community, the business community, employees, et al., variously ranked. But it is up to the management of any particular firm to decide what its obligations are, how to meet them, and when they have been met. Management is the "trustee" or "steward" of the various groups with an interest in the firm; it devotes itself to "service" to them, and gains legitimacy thereby. Management claims that it is in the best position to reconcile and satisfy the numerous and conflicting demands made of it, and that its performance in doing so is adequate. There is no need for unions, the state, or others to impose specific, enforceable obligations upon it.[18]

Ideology, by itself, is not a strong enough shield for business interests. Business claims have to be supported by business power, and in the 1930s there was not enough of that precious commodity to prevent unions and the state from restricting management's right to take unilateral action. Businessmen could no longer enforce their own definition of the proper scope of their rights and responsibilities. Employees, in particular, showed by their actions that they were not content with the way management had looked after them, and the Wagner Act supported their efforts to build collective power to look after themselves. These developments threatened managerial control at its point of greatest practical and theoretical sensitivity — *within* the firm.

Businessmen soon came around to a practical acceptance of the new public policy and of the facts of union presence and pressure. But that is not to say that they accepted the pluralistic ideology of labor relations which the NLRB embraced. Some did, but most did not, or had very

substantial reservations. So there was an enduring contradiction between the "real world," in which businessmen had to operate, and the
ideal world of labor relations which their ideology described. Changes
in business ideology were slow and slight. Instead, business bent its
strength to try to make the real world look more like its ideal world once
again. In that counterattack against the strength of organized labor in
the mid- to late 1940s, management ideology provided inspiration,
guidance, and rationale.

Lee Hill of Allis-Chalmers was the management ideologue who did
more to determine the tone of the debate about prerogatives than any
other single spokesman. At a conference of the AMA's Personnel Division in 1944 an unidentified speaker — almost certainly Hill — provided
the keynote for all later discussion. The consensus of conference participants was that the danger of union erosion of managerial prerogatives
had become real and pressing, particularly since the start of the war.
The speaker turned the discussion away from details and toward basic
theory. Prerogatives, he said,

are not conferred by the Ten Commandments, the Magna Carta, or the Constitution. These prerogatives are merely the powers necessary to run the plant efficiently, and they are management prerogatives rather than union prerogatives
simply because management is solely responsible for the operation of the plant
and for perpetuation of it.[19]

But Hill did not rely entirely on structural-functional arguments in
justifying management's authority. Underlying such modern and sophisticated reasoning was the classical bedrock of property right, the
common law, and the formal authority of owners and masters, dele-
gated to their supposedly chosen management. The collective bargaining agreement and statute law imposed some specific restrictions. Where
they were silent, Hill advised managers to assume that all of the right,
and all of the power, were reserved to them.[20]

Such a traditional and absolutist argument might be agreeable to
businessmen, but it was not much use in giving answers to hard questions about where and how to draw the line when unions had acquired
a real, lawful, and growing status in the enterprise. For this purpose,
Hill and others fell back on their more subtle analysis, to fill in the details of management's case and to strengthen it against challenge.

What were the functions and responsibilities of management? First
of all, management occupied the central, coordinating position in the
firm.

Management is obviously not the sole component of a successful enterprise. A
manufacturing plant requires (i) men, (ii) materials, (iii) machines, (iv) money,

as well as managements to allocate, direct, schedule and otherwise manipulate these four components to produce useful goods at a competitive cost, in order that they may be sold at a hoped-for profit for those who furnish the money to pay for the machines, materials, salaries and wages. Management is selected by the owners of the enterprise and is held responsible for its successful operation. To assert that management has the sole responsibility for the success of an enterprise is not a reflection on the importance of the other essential components. It is simply a statement of fact, for that is management's reason for existence.[21]

Large, modern business organizations were complex. In order to be efficient, they had to be well managed. And the only way to manage them effectively was to follow the same principles of administration as had been proved to work in other similar situations — the armed forces, or governmental bureaucracies. Technical necessity denied the possibility of any nonhierarchical power structure in industry. There had to be a single source of authority, a single line of command, with no confusion. "Industry could not, any more than an army could, take orders from every private in the rear ranks and operate successfully."[22] "In industry as in government or anywhere else, there are two classes of people; there are those who decide and those who carry out. You cannot organize human society on any other basis than that. . . . In private enterprise management is the decider."[23]

Businessmen made it perfectly clear that there was no room for democracy in industry, but couched their claim to power in flat, neutral, technical language. And they buttressed it by arguing that the equation of hierarchy and efficiency in complex organizations was universally valid. To prove this they pointed to the experience of France under the Popular Front, and of the Soviet Union before it began to grant large powers to responsible, qualified executives. There was no middle way between managed mass production and "just sheer mob production." And in the 1940s no one questioned the importance of production — it was the only way to meet the needs of America's war machine before 1945, and to satisfy the overwhelming demand from domestic consumers and the shattered economies of the rest of the Free World after the war. So the argument that managers must be free to exercise a broadly unobstructed discretion to initiate change and respond rapidly to events struck them as reasonable and unobjectionable.[24]

Management, secondly, was responsible for deciding on the allocation of corporate net income among the various claimants upon it. Management therefore had a broad social accountability, and did not represent any single, narrow interest group. This gave it the most legitimate claim to the power to make important decisions affecting the future of the enterprise and the interests of all parties involved in it. By virtue of its strategic location, it also had a monopoly of the information, expertise, and present power needed to make and carry out the best decisions, for all concerned.[25]

Moving from generalities to particulars, what were the powers businessmen thought they needed to possess in order to perform their manifold functions and discharge their responsibilities? There were, first, those rights whose exercise was "seldom questioned because they usually do not directly affect the employees" — control of financial, investment, marketing, and sales policy; selection of material, processes, and products to be manufactured; location and structure of plants; selection and location of machine tools; determination of production schedules. The list was meant to be illustrative, rather than exhaustive.[26]

One thing the list illustrates, of course, is the limited ambitions of most unions. But managers were not even really willing to allow labor's modest bargaining objectives, which usually did not touch the above important issues. Businessmen wanted the narrowest possible definition of "wages, hours, and working conditions" so as to keep for themselves the greatest possible latitude in determining how workers behaved on the job. Hill recognized that such matters "do immediately affect employees" but that the rights to

hire, discharge, promote, discipline, train, secure deferments, grant leaves of absence, and determine employee classifications and merit wage increases are rights which management must retain, because the right to make decisions on these matters is essential if management is to discharge its responsibility creditably for the successful operation of and perpetuation of the enterprise.[27]

What Hill was doing, of course, was to use rather shallow reasoning to oppose exactly the kinds of bargaining demands job-conscious unions legitimately made, in order to justify leaving management with most of the powers it had had before unionization. So the prerogative argument amounted to nothing less than an attempt by management to reassert the scope of its own authority unilaterally. Things had always been thus, and the habits of a long period of conveniently unopposed control died hard. And American business, long a respected ruling elite, thought it perfectly right that it should still be the judge in cases where its rights were disputed. In all such cases, managers were ready to pass a vote of confidence in themselves, because "management is usually best qualified by specific training and ability to exercize such rights" and "[t]he employer must decide what is necessary for him to retain the flexibility of working forces essential for efficient production."[28]

Hill and his fellows made perfectly clear the essential ideological bases of industrial management's opposition even to narrowly job-conscious, responsible unionism. They showed how few and how slight were the concessions they would willingly make to the collective-bargaining model of "industrial democracy" which had been written into law. A limited form of pluralism was the aim of unions, the goal of arbitrators and other labor relations experts, and the policy of the NLRB and NWLB. Businessmen had to live with that pluralism in practice, and had formally accepted it. But their idea of the limits of collective bargaining was still very restrictive, and most of them had hardly advanced beyond regarding unions as an unavoidable problem — an evil, more or less, and not really a necessary one.

Businessmen were usually unwilling to allow unions any more than a minimal stake in the making and administering of policy because, at the most basic level, "a union is somebody opposed to management."[29] There was no room in the unitary ideology of the greatest part of the business community for any *theoretical* acceptance of the view that unions could play a useful role in helping management solve many of its personnel problems. The practice might be different, but in principle most businessmen continued to see unions and collective bargaining as a problem, not a resource.

The unitary ideology provided a model of the ideal distribution of power within the enterprise. It also included a very unflattering picture, a product of the experience and folklore of management, of the workers and their unions. A union was an organization of outsiders, intruding with disruptive consequences into the naturally close, smooth, and friendly relations between master and man. By its very nature, a union was in the agitation business, concerned with the promotion of bad feeling and the stirring up of unreal grievances, or grievances which nobody worried about until the union came on the scene to foment discontent. The union could only be a source of confusion, divided loyalties, friction, and restriction on management, which after all best knew and served the real interests of its employees.[30]

Unions were thoroughly bad, and workers were not much better. Managers described workers as fundamentally loyal, honest, hard-working, and thoroughly American (i.e. bourgeois in their values), but easily misled by union agitators, radicals, and others into thinking and acting in ways contrary to those management required. At its most charitable, then, management described workers as just too stupid and too ignorant to know their own best interests and pursue them without firm guidance from their employers and superiors. But there was yet a darker side to this managerial view of the American worker.[31]

Business rhetoric usually described the workplace as naturally free from tension. Ideally, it was a place of harmonious relations between master and man, employer and employee, superior and subordinate, with both sides accepting their roles and working smoothly together to further the common interests of the enterprise. The firm could be spoken of as a "family" or a "team" — not, it must be said, a body of equals, but a collection of people with common views and purposes, abiding by agreed rules, content with their place, however lowly, in the great scheme of things. But there was another, tougher metaphor in common use: the firm was an army. Managers were the top brass, foremen and supervisors the noncommissioned officers, and the rank-and-file were, well, they were the rank-and-file.[32]

But who was the enemy? There wasn't one, outside of the organization. Management faced the great problems of any conscript army, especially one without a real enemy to fight. It had to maintain morale — that is to say, it had to preserve the efficiency of the organization against the inherent laziness and selfishness of the rank-and-file, who were inclined to "soldier" (shirk their duties); it had to keep discipline; it might even have to stave off mutiny. The workplace was the "firing line," and workers were the cause of most everyday problems.

Workers, then, were seen as unsatisfactory, unreliable, and refractory agents for the achievement of management's purposes. They had to be driven. Their behavior had to be governed by strict rules, minutely enforced. They had to be controlled by loyal, obedient foremen and supervisors. Their autonomy had to be limited by the design of production processes. They were what an elitist from a less mealy-mouthed age would have called a "swinish multitude," needing to be kept in the proper, inferior place. The working man "is not interested in the whole picture. . . . He has no responsibility and does not want it."[33]

This harsh view of American workers was only an undertone in the 1940s. It had been much stronger in the 1920s, when the manager's feeling of moral and intellectual superiority was bolstered by ideas of social Darwinism, eugenics, and Anglo-Saxon superiority still common among the old-stock, middle-aged men who made up much of the business elite. But managers in the 1940s still felt themselves to be the other side of a wide cultural divide from their workers. "The man in the shop may be a foreigner with only a fourth-grade education," while the manager was likely to be a college-educated WASP. He thought of himself as a rational, public-spirited man, brimming over with integrity and a Calvinistic will to work. Workers were not such admirable characters.[34]

The industrialist . . . is in a state of confusion and resentment, but (sic) of fear not for himself but for a society which is rejecting the principles which to him are not only good economics but good morals. He fears the increasing dependency, increasing leisure, increasing lack of personal responsibility, leveling down of workers by equal pay for equal work, decreasing pride in good workmanship . . .[35]

Workers' morale had been undermined by subversive ideologies, the welfare state, and the temptations of an overheated economy. They could not be trusted to act in an orderly manner, or to work efficiently, unless they were disciplined. Managers in the 1940s, with rare exceptions, believed firmly in what Douglas McGregor would later call "Theory X" — a connected set of assumptions, underwritten by experience, about the character and motivations of their subordinates. Their unavoidable conclusion was that there was no alternative to the present, hierarchical and authoritarian, adminstrative and political structure of the business firm.[36]

"Theory X" thinking reinforced the conclusions managers derived from their formal theory of the structure of the firm. Workers who behaved in the manner to be expected of alienated labor in the everyday business of production had to be confined to their duty to obey work rules and their superiors' commands. To secure that compliance, management had to keep hold of the maximum possible latitude to direct, reward, and punish its subordinates. The presence of a union was an admitted but regrettable infringement on this freedom: for that reason it had to be resisted and ultimately weakened, if not eliminated.

The "historic compromise" most industrialists were willing to make with the unions of their employees in the 1940s accordingly only went so far. The law — even after Taft-Hartley — and the actual presence, strength, and sometimes militancy of their bargaining partners compelled them to grant recognition, to negotiate, to achieve collective agreements covering a range of employment-related matters. They could come to accept unions and collective bargaining as in some respects a managerial convenience, in that their presence encouraged management to handle its industrial relations generally in a more orderly and systematic fashion, and defused many individual grievances. But that was the limit of the cool "welcome" most managers extended; it was only a limited, provisional tolerance. Few accepted industrial pluralism wholeheartedly; fewer still were prepared to depart from managerial styles and structures which rested on the implicit assumption of conflict between superior and subordinate, to experiment with consultative and participative approaches later summed up by McGregor as the products of his alternative "Theory Y." For most, unions were still, at least potentially, a disloyal and disruptive opposition; blue-collar workers and their organizations should be decision-takers and executors, not accepted as active partners in any firm's decision-making process, at any level.

American management's economic outlook, political forecasts, and ideological convictions all helped shape the objectives of the labor and industrial relations policies pursued in and after the war. But economic outlooks change, political forecasts prove to be incorrect, and practical men are often willing to change plans, and modify their assumptions, in the light of experience. This chapter has given an indication of what businessmen would try to do in the industrial relations field, and why; but the actual implementation of their plans was affected by circumstances beyond their control. So the kind of labor relations system that resulted from, amongst other things, businessmen's postwar policies and actions, was not one which perfectly reflected their ideal of unilateral control. But it was pretty close, and they were quite happy to live with and profit by it.

4

Recovery of the Initiative, I

In the last year of the war, and the reconversion period which followed, managements of large manufacturing firms took action in day-to-day workplace labor relations and at annual bargaining sessions to roll back and then stabilize the power of work-groups and official unions. They followed the course of realism: however objectionable unionism might be in principle, the aim of corporate labor relations policy had become the achievement of stable and efficient union-management arrangements, not the destruction of union power. They were able to exploit favorable political and economic circumstances, and to mobilize their own immense resources, to get the better of unions and their members.

This was an important development, but it was not particularly dramatic: most union-management skirmishes along the frontier of control were quite private affairs. But there were some actions the business community took to redress the balance between itself and labor which did take place in a public arena. In 1944–46, the pressure group which best represented the practical conservatism of heavy manufacturing industry — the NAM — developed proposals to change public policy toward organized labor to aid and complement what individual corporations were doing to improve relations with their own workers and unions. The NAM, too, abandoned reaction. Instead, it produced a labor relations program supported by a broad consensus of business opinion — a comparatively moderate set of workable proposals which had an undeniable influence on the legislative process which resulted in the Taft-Hartley Act of 1947. NAM's road from reaction toward effective influence was the first part of the successful "recovery of the initiative" in labor relations by conservative managements which took place in the postwar years.

THE POLITICS OF WARTIME LABOR RELATIONS POLICY

The opposition of the business community and of its peak associations, the NAM in particular, to the Wagner Act and the NLRB from 1935 to 1941 was largely ineffective. Federal labor relations policy was unchanged in all essentials, and still developing new pro-union measures, when the war came. The immediate problems thrown up by the emergency of economic mobilization diverted the attention of the NAM and its members from long-run considerations of peacetime labor relations policy. They also made it impossible for the NAM to make any progress toward its goal from 1941 until 1945.

Initially, the NAM was just as ineffective a pressure group on the matters of wartime labor relations policy most directly affecting its members as it had been in the immediate prewar years. The NAM advanced a wartime labor relations program involving suspension of the Wage and Hour Act's overtime provisions, a binding no-strike policy, and no alteration in the status of "open" and "organized" shops for the duration. It failed in every particular, the last worst of all. On the first two matters, federal policy slowly moved some distance in the direction business wanted. But on the third, federal policy, as implemented by the NLRB, the NDMB, and the NWLB, recognized that organized labor could not be prevented from using wartime full employment and high bargaining power in order to grow. Instead, federal policy was to try to make the process of growth as orderly as possible, and to guide the development of stronger unions in the direction of "responsibility."[1]

The NAM was not even strong enough to demand that it should be consulted in working out wartime labor policies. At the President's Labor-Management Conference in December 1941 industry members were not the authorized delegates of the NAM and the U.S. Chamber of Commerce (CCUS), which claimed the right to nominate members of such bodies. Instead, members were selected by William Batt, president of S.K.F. Industries, Inc. (ball bearing manufacturers) and of both the AMA and the Department of Commerce's Business Advisory Council. Batt was also a senior member of the government's chief war production agency. His closest ties were to the business community's "corporate liberal" minority; like them, he gained in influence by his acceptability to the federal government, his understanding of its policies, and his readiness to work with it.

The men Batt chose, after informal consultations with business leaders and organizations, included Ching of U.S. Rubber, Paul Hoffman of Studebaker Motors, Roger Lapham of American-Hawaiian Steamship Co., and Charles E. Wilson of General Electric, all "corporate liberals" like himself. He also picked noted NAM activists Robert M. Gaylord of Ingersoll Milling Machine Co., Thomas R. Jones of American Type Founders, and Charles Hook of American Rolling Mill. But an anonymous critic complained to the *New York Times* that "only five" of the twelve representatives were "truly representative of industry." Even so, the delegation fought hard for the freezing of union status in organized and unorganized plants for the duration of the war. But when the conference deadlocked on this issue, Roosevelt overruled them.[2]

NWLB industry members were initially of the same, generally liberal, stamp, including Ching, Lapham, and Walter Teagle of Standard Oil of New Jersey, all carried over from the NDMB. As senior executives of New York-based companies, the "country club set," as they were called, gave little time to Board duties in Washington, and neither prepared their cases well nor fought for them very vigorously. They objected to the Little Steel policy on union security, but without success. Thereafter, they occasionally voted in favor of granting membership maintenance to "responsible" unions, but more generally pursued the moderate policy of entering *pro forma* objections and seeking to modify NWLB orders. They did not fight for the right to work (or hire). Instead, they tried to reach workable and mutually acceptable compromises which gave unions greater security of membership and income, but reserved the right of workers not to join under certain conditions. They also wanted to subject internal union affairs to a greater degree of federal supervision and control than the law then required. Their pragmatism and moderation were in marked contrast to the determined opposition of the NAM to any form of enforced union security.[3]

Industry members were free to ignore their constituents' principles, as the NAM reflected them, in 1942–43. The NAM continued to be weakened by its political distance from the federal government. And it neglected the opportunities for influencing NWLB policy presented by industry members' repeated requests for closer contacts between them. Industry members were distressed by the results of poor liaison: NWLB labor members were much better briefed by their constituents, and much more single-minded in advancing their interests, despite occasional AFL-CIO differences. Companies made relatively ineffectual cases when they came before the Board, and did not seek industry members' aid and advice. The consequence of this miserable performance was an accumulation of NWLB orders which might turn out to the disadvantage of the whole business community.[4]

But it was 1944 before the NAM and CCUS did something to meet the need for closer coordination. By that time, the problem of presenting industry's case before the NWLB had grown much greater, with the establishment of a dozen regional boards and a number of commissions for particular industries. To fill the resulting vacancies for industry members, the previous method of co-optation was supplemented by using the NAM and the CCUS as the appointing bodies they claimed to be. Industry members thereby became more formally representative, but the problem of securing effective cooperation between themselves and their constituents remained.[5]

At the same time, fierce opposition to the course of NWLB orders, particularly on union security, was rising. There were two centers of irreconcilable antiunionism: the industrial South, especially the Texan oil and chemicals industry, where federal intervention was breaking down traditional local obstacles to effective labor organization; and reactionary Midwestern industrialists. The entrepreneurial Hughes Tool Co. and the Humble Oil and Refining Co. (a subsidiary of Standard Oil of New Jersey which still held to the Rockefeller principle of company unionism) typified the first group; Sewell Avery, controller of Montgomery Ward and U.S. Gypsum, symbolized the second.[6]

Organized business, particularly the NAM, belatedly recognized the importance of effective representation before the War Labor Boards for the successful defense of business interests and principles. In February 1944 close liaison was established between industry members and a joint NAM-CCUS committee, on the initiative of 1943 NAM president Frederick Coolidge Crawford. Crawford was president of Thompson Products of Cleveland, a resourceful and resolutely antiunion medium-sized automotive manufacturer. The committee appointed William Frew Long of the Associated Industries of Cleveland, a long-established belligerent employers' association, as the executive assistant to the NWLB industry members. From then on, the organized business community was better placed to influence NWLB decisions, to make the best possible presentation of industry's case, and to "whip" industry members into line behind considered conservative positions — even if, as one industry member and NAM activist ruefully said, it was "attempting to find keys and locks to lock a stable out of which most of the horses had already been stolen."[7]

There *were* some concrete results. When the *Humble* case finally came before the NWLB in the spring of 1944, industry members made a strong, closely argued attack on the union security policy — much more than the previous *pro forma* dissent. And they went against custom in refusing to unanimously endorse the decision of the majority granting the CIO Oil Workers maintenance of membership. In the summer, the system of liaison committees was carried out from Washington into the regions, so that industry members became directly representative of state trade associations and important local industry groups. More uniformity was secured by policy conferences for board members and prehearing consultations between industry members and representatives of companies with cases before the board.[8]

The war experience gave businessmen a practical education in the importance of tackling labor relations problems collectively. By the summer of 1944, their national organizations were at last pushing a considered common policy for wartime. But the prospects for working out a single, comprehensive, realistic and attainable program for postwar labor law revision were still uncertain.

While the war lasted, reform of the Wagner Act was impossible: it would have been against the spirit of the no-strike pledge, and in any case continuing Democratic majorities in the House and Senate Labor Committees blocked it. Nor did it interest the NAM or the CCUS as much as more immediate problems. There was a surprising lack of specific business proposals on this important matter from either of the most prominent business pressure groups, and no apparent consensus to support them.

The NAM and its spokesmen maintained, as they had since 1939, that the Wagner Act should be amended to equalize the rights of employers and unions, and to protect employees against unions and "the public" against many kinds of industrial conflict and the supposedly monopolistic power of organized labor. "Equalization" involved, in particular, guaranteeing employers free speech — that is, the right to issue propaganda during union organizing drives, representation elections, strikes, or indeed on any occasion when unionism could be attacked. The Supreme Court's *Virginia Electric* (1941) and *American Tube Bending* (1942) decisions severely restricted the NLRB's powers to discourage or penalize such propaganda, but the NAM wanted something much more definite. On this and other matters, NLRB interpretations and Supreme Court rulings had begun to move in favor of business viewpoints and interests after 1941, but the NAM persisted in wanting firm statute law to rely on in its dealings with labor, not the changeable and unpredictable policies of the Roosevelt Court and administrative agencies.

Protection of employees involved restricting or prohibiting any contractual union security clause, in the name of the right to work, and extensive regulation of unions' internal affairs. Protection of the public required the prohibition — by injunction if need be — of strikes whose aims and tactics were particularly objectionable, for example sit-down strikes or boycotts. It also involved the limitation of collective bargaining units to one plant, one locality, or the employees of one employer, in such a way as to atomize the industrial unions and reduce labor's "monopoly power."[9]

These principles were not fleshed out to produce detailed legislative recommendations, at least, not by the NAM itself; no attempt was made to mobilize industry behind them; and they were not pressed upon Congress. But they demonstrated the depth of senior NAM officials' continuing antiunionism and reluctance to accept orderly collective bargaining through strong, independent unions as basic national policy, or as an objective which, properly defined, business might seek for its own interests.

The NAM began to give some thought to postwar labor relations policy in 1944–45, but it was not the only business group in the field. Indeed, until the fall of 1945 extremists on both wings of the business community made much more of the running. One group centered on the automotive industry, and was led by the Chrysler Corporation — its management still personal, entrepreneurial, and politically reactionary, its labor relations disturbed. Eric Johnston, president of a small West Coast building firm and of the U.S. Chamber of Commerce, was chief spokesman for the other — the most liberal but, as it turned out, least influential section of corporate management.[10]

In March 1945 Johnston produced a "Charter" for postwar labor-management relations, signed by himself, William Green of the AFL, and Phillip Murray of the CIO. The Charter itself was brief and platitudinous, but quite significant. It proposed a linked pair of deals: business would recognize labor's right to organize and bargain collectively, and would not press for revisions in public policy on labor relations. In return, labor would recognize management's right to manage, and continue a no-strike policy into the reconversion period. The right or power of any one of the three men to sign on behalf of his organization, to say nothing of actually delivering the membership's practical assent, was very questionable. But the Charter showed the readiness of labor officialdom and a section of the business community to continue into peacetime the wartime practice of high-level accommodation between leaders of both sides of industry. It was backed by noted corporate liberals Paul Hoffman of Studebaker, Henry Kaiser, and J. D. Zellerbach of Crown Zellerbach, as well as the chairman of the CCUS Labor Relations Committee and E. J. Thomas, president of Goodyear Tire and Rubber.[11]

But the Charter's chances of success, never very great, quickly faded as automotive industry activists led by Chrysler's chairman B. E.

Hutchinson fought it within the NAM and the CCUS. Johnston was discredited by the revelation that the Chamber had been exploring the possibility of a common program of labor law revision with the NAM at the same time as he had been negotiating with Green and Murray. The NAM gave the Charter's unobjectionable ends its rhetorical support, but insisted that the Wagner Act must be heavily amended. The NAM's empty endorsement sealed the Charter's fate.[12]

Even before they had helped torpedo the corporate liberals' attempt at interest-group diplomacy, the automotive industry's powerful reactionaries had begun their move to push business opinion and national labor policy far to the right. They began their campaign with a propaganda blast from Chrysler's labor economist, John Scoville, delivered to the Detroit Kiwanis on 8 August 1944 and given wide distribution as a pamphlet. Scoville spoke of collective bargaining as "an assault on liberty, as an evil thing which is against the public interest, as something which will increase poverty. . . . one chick in the foul brood of vultures that seek to pick the meat from the bones of honest men."[13]

Automotive industry antiunionism evidently had a strong ideological dynamic, but it was also the result of real difficulties in collective bargaining with the largest, most democratic, and probably most militant industrial union. Anxieties about postwar productivity, competitiveness, and industrial peace made it more acute. As such, the specific program the industry advanced through its trade association, the Automotive Council for War Production (ACWP), had to address itself to real problems as well as to ideologically sound, but unattainable, objectives.

The Council's general manager, George Romney, presented this program throughout 1945 and 1946, attacking the UAW as antimanagement, antiproduction, and implicitly un-American. The program aimed to weaken the UAW in particular, and industrial unionism in general, by calling for the "equalization" of legal treatment of organized labor, removing its privileged position (including immunity from lawsuits and injunctions for breach of contract); supporting the "right to work" against any union security device; and insisting on the confinement of collective bargaining to individual company or employer units. The ACWP's program was neither very well articulated nor fully comprehensive, but it represented an important contribution to the debate within the business community on needed Wagner Act amendments.[14]

RECONVERSION AND THE PRESIDENT'S LABOR-MANAGEMENT CONFERENCE

One reason for the lack of detailed preparation for the coming peace which would bring the need and possibility for Wagner Act revision was that no one expected the V-E/V-J Day interval to be so short. Quite naturally, the atomic bomb was not a factor in anybody's planning for the reconversion period. In the area of labor relations in particular, it threw everybody's calculations into confusion.

With the sudden end of the war in Asia, the no-strike pledge lost all its dwindling effectiveness, the NWLB its compulsory powers. The federal government found itself embarrassed for lack of a wage-price policy, and business and labor squared up for a mighty scrap. The issues were, on one side, the protection of workers' living standards and job security, and the defense of unions' recognition and bargaining rights; on the other, the restoration and preservation of corporate profitability, viability, and managerial prerogatives. Conflict, mediated by the federal government, settled these matters. Workers' real incomes slumped, but few union-busting efforts were undertaken or succeeded. Union power and job control did not increase, but they remained essentially intact.[15]

At the suggestion of Senator Arthur Vandenberg (Rep., Michigan), President Truman attempted to get business and labor representatives to settle their differences in conference and make the process of reconversion easier. The conference assembled in November, and *this* time the business delegation comprised the unofficial leaders of the organized business community, nominated in equal numbers by the NAM and the CCUS. They were presidents and chairmen of large corporations or senior trade association executives. American Rolling Mill, Consolidation Coal, General Motors, the Pennsylvania Railroad, Swift & Co., Monsanto Chemical Co., Radio Corporation of America, Goodyear Tire and Rubber, and Consolidated Vultee Aircraft were represented by their presidents as full delegates; so also were Armstrong Cork, Servel, Inc. (electrical appliances), and Bridgeport Brass, providing two former NAM chairmen and one CCUS president-to-be. The current NAM and CCUS chiefs, Ira Mosher and Eric Johnston, also figured prominently. Alternate delegates included representatives of Hughes Tool, Newport News Shipbuilding, the Texas Co., Aluminum Co. of America (Alcoa), U.S. Steel, Union Carbide, and a host of trade associations — the National Sand and Gravel Association, the New Jersey State Chamber of Commerce, the Automotive and Aviation Parts Manufacturers, the Wisconsin Manufacturing Association, the Toledo Chamber of Commerce, and the National Federation of American Shipping. Of the thirty-six full and alternate delegates, only one — Eric Johnston — was an indentifiable corporate liberal. Given his office, he could hardly have been left out. Six were former NWLB industry members. The delegation was dominated by representatives of medium to large-scale manufacturing firms, overwhelmingly conservative in their politics and long active in the business community's peak associations.[16]

Business delegates to the Conference did not come unprepared. They had to guide them the recommendations that came of two years' research and consultations by the respected think tank, Industrial Relations Counselors, Inc. [IRC], published in early Fall. This report had been reviewed and approved by the Committee on Labor Policy of the Business Advisory Council, and by the full Council itself, in October. The BAC itself is usually identified with the "corporate liberal" wing of the American big-business community. But its committee was stacked with NAM stalwarts: of its eight members, six were from firms which were members of the NAM's active minority, and the chairman and vice-chairman were NAM ex-presidents. Of these six, the two NAM ex-presidents, Charles Hook of ARMCO and Henning W. Prentis of Armstrong Cork, were also full management delegates at the November conference, and the firm of a third, Newport News Shipbuilding and Drydock Co., provided an alternate. The program which they brought with them was detailed and pragmatic: the fit between it and the management delegates' unanimous recommendations at the conference itself is close and suggestive, but of course it cannot be demonstrated conclusively that the IRC/BAC "wrote" those recommendations. Rather, they provided a well-argued, defensible focus around which a consensus of practical conservative industrial managements could gather. The IRC/BAC proposals gave such business politicians a sense of direction; more important, the direction in which they pointed was towards an attainable, realistic goal of labor law reform, not Wagner Act repeal. The November 1945 conference saw these proposals acquire further definition, concreteness, and the public support of the business community's chosen representatives. The December 1945 Congress of American Industry gave them the backing of the NAM itself, fast approaching the peak of its lobbying effectiveness and membership.[17]

The conference took place while unprecedented numbers of workers were on strike or locked out, between representatives of the corporations and the unions involved in some of the bitterest fights. Understandably, it was unable to deliver the recipe for industrial peace, even in the short term, for which its proponents had hoped. But its participants displayed a remarkable degree of agreement among themselves and chalked up some worthwhile achievements. Three of the conference's six working committees reported unanimously, and its proceedings showed how far American business and labor leaders had moved toward one another in the ten crowded years since unions began to invade the mass-production industries. "Only the pressing and critical needs of reconversion made these accomplishments appear insignificant."[18]

Committee V on Initial Collective Agreements and Committee VI on

Existing Collective Agreements produced unanimous reports which were essentially general guides to good labor relations procedure. Committee V recommended that employers not question their obligation to bargain in good faith with a duly chosen union—an implicit endorsement of the Wagner Act and support for the hard-pressed NLRB—while Committee VI summed up best practice in long-organized industries and NWLB policy on grievance settlement and arbitration. Grievances were accepted as natural and legitimate—a position that Harry Coen, GM's vice-president for employee relations, for one, was not ready to countenance, given the common belief that few difficulties arose within the employment relationship unless agitators were at work. Furthermore, the grievance procedure was seen as a means of orderly contract administration. Unions and managements were advised not to use it as a way of continuing industrial conflict between annual negotiations. Impartial arbitration was to be the final guarantee of order, empowered to rule on disputes of right under the contract, not to "add to, subtract from, change, or modify any provision of the agreement."[19]

Management concurrence in the reports of Committees V and VI indicated great progress toward practical acceptance of the system of collective bargaining in the mass-production industries. Committee IV, on Conciliation Services, similarly testified to the interests of both sides in institutionalizing industrial conflict. Its recommendations on the improvement of the Conciliation Service, as an alternative both to strike action and to undesired compulsory federal intervention, were largely accepted and implemented by executive action in 1946–47, and endorsed by the relevant provisions of Taft-Hartley.[20]

Harmony was not entirely absent in Committees I–III, but the disagreement between business and labor representatives was much more significant. Management spokesmen worked out a common position on those subjects where, agreement with organized labor failing, legislation was the only possible recourse. The NAM's legislative proposals of 1946–47 grew directly out of these committee deliberations.

Committee I, on Collective Bargaining, was not fundamentally divided. Its management members accepted the principle of collective bargaining and supported ways of making it work in a more orderly fashion. But their repeated emphasis that the bargaining agent should be the *free* choice of the workers reflected their dissatisfaction with NLRB procedures and union security policies; they were distinctly cool on labor's proposal—with which corporate liberal managements would have agreed—that as collective bargaining matured, the subject matter admitted for discussion should broaden; and they insisted on a definition of good-faith bargaining, allowing either party to reject the other's proposals if it thought them contrary to the interest of "the employer, employees, the union, or the public." Management fended off any presumption in favor of broadening the scope of collective bargaining agreements, and stated its objection to the NLRB's interpreting the "duty to bargain collectively" as requiring something more than discussion of issues of wages, hours, and working conditions, narrowly defined. Management members also implicitly endorsed the "public interest" rationales GM and other corporations were currently using to oppose union demands.[21]

These reservations were important enough, but there were others even more substantial. Together they underpinned many of the NAM's proposals for labor law reform in 1946–47.

Voluntary negotiations or free collective bargaining is (sic) not possible except under conditions of law and order and the absence of force. . . . The public has the right to insist that management and labor at all times practice collective bargaining with full regard for protection of individuals and property against unlawful acts. . . .

In order to provide effective measures to carry out the letter and spirit of the labor agreement, it is recommended that each agreement . . . provide for appropriate guarantees to insure complete and effective compliance with provisions . . . prohibiting strikes, lockouts, or boycotts.

For years, in the public interest, legislation and government regulation have controlled the activities and defined the responsibilities of employers. Likewise in the public interest, the activities of labor organizations should be controlled and their responsibilities appropriately defined to assure equality of status before the law.[22]

Notable in these rather unspecific propositions is the emphasis on the regulation of industrial conflict in the *public* interest, and the demand for equalization of management and labor rights and responsibilities under the Wagner Act. Business made it absolutely clear that thorough revision of federal labor policy was required, and pointed in the desired direction. It also endorsed corporate demands for "company security" against official or unofficial strikes during the term of any contract currently being pressed by Ford and other large firms. The law was to be used to foster order in industrial relations.[23]

If Committee I illustrated the limits of labor-management consensus, Committees II and III were the scenes of the greatest business hostility to labor claims, and produced the most specific legislative recommendations. Committee III, on Representation and Jurisdictional Questions, was at least agreed on some important matters. Management members accepted that the NLRB should continue in existence as an independent agency, and advised companies not to oppose voluntary or informal means of settling union representation issues, which was a far cry from widespread business behavior in the late 1930s and lingering hostility in 1945–46. But they insisted that any representation question must be protected against direct action from the side of labor until it had been settled — either by voluntary agreement, or by state or federal agencies. Once such a question had been decided, no attempt to alter it by strike or boycott should be allowed. Business was demanding that unions lose the right to short-circuit the time-consuming and often unsatisfactory procedures of the NLRB and the courts, and wanted to be protected against such powerful unions as the Teamsters which relied on direct action to win bargaining rights. Management had discovered that federal regulation of labor relations could be to its advantage, so long as the government entered on the side of "order" and against the exercise of labor power, where that was overwhelming.

The same was true in the case of jurisdictional disputes, where binding NLRB determinations were to have precedence over "voluntarist" settlements by labor unions and employers, and no settlement was to involve the employment of "unnecessary" employees, or "featherbedding." Against powerful AFL Teamsters, or strong craft unions in the Federation's Construction and Metal Trades Departments, American business was quite willing to seek federal protection.

More directly relevant to the labor relations problems of large-scale manufacturing industry were propositions A-6 and A-7. The employer was to be given the right to question the representativeness of the union bargaining for his workers at each contract-termination date — an obvious weapon for any antiunion employer to use, as Sewell Avery's Montgomery Ward and Co. had demonstrated in its long-drawn-out, successful struggle with a weak CIO union. And, most important of all, no state or federal agency should be able to order the establishment of an appropriate bargaining unit larger than a single plant or store, unless sanctioned by past practice *of the employer* or mutually agreed. Such a provision would allow any automotive employer to resist UAW demands for corporation- or industry-wide bargaining, while it would not prohibit employers in competitive, decentralized industries like trucking, building, or longshoring from getting together the better to resist union demands.[24]

Management proposals at the 1945 conference displayed a new sophistication, a readiness to use the law selectively to assist in the solution of labor relations problems, rather than to seek freedom from legislative intervention and administrative action. The latter were perfectly welcome, provided they were on the right side, helping management to deal with, and get the better of, a powerful labor movement that existed and would continue.

Despite a "conscientious effort" by labor representatives "to arrive at an understanding along the lines proposed by management," Committee II reached no shared conclusions. If the two sides of industry on Committees I and III were some distance apart, in Committee II — on Management's Right to Manage — they were a world apart. Management representatives were all heavyweights: two NAM past presidents, Charles Hook of American Rolling Mill and Henning W. Prentis, Jr., of Armstrong Cork, plus GM's "Engine Charlie" Wilson as full delegates, with representatives from Newport News Shipbuilding, the Toledo Chamber of Commerce, and the Automotive and Aviation Parts Manufacturers (another former GM man) as alternates. These men spoke for the heavy industries where anxiety about union intrusion on management's prerogatives and the issue of supervisory unionism was greatest.[25]

They asked, in plain terms, for an amendment of the Wagner Act to exclude supervisors and other managerial personnel from its protection once and for all, and for organized labor's acceptance of Lee Hill's simple division of managerial "functions and responsibilities" into two categories. The first was to be not at all subject to collective bargaining, and went well beyond the determination and implementation of central corporate strategy to include "[t]he determination of job content [and] of the size of the workforce; the allocation and assignment of work to workers; determination of policies affecting the selection of employees; establishment of quality standards and judgement of workmanship required; and the maintenance of discipline and control and use of plant property; the scheduling of operations and the number of shifts."[26]

These were clearly matters of direct, intimate, and legitimate concern to job-conscious unions under the Wagner Act. On such matters as discharges and disciplinary action, and the application of the seniority provisions, management must be free to act promptly, in the first instance, but the union was permitted to grieve. Management members of Committee II did not propose legislation to secure the protection of their prerogatives, except on the supervisor question. They asked instead for labor's acquiescence. No law could encompass all possible situations — nor, perhaps, could any administrative agency be trusted to interpret and implement any general provisions in such a sensitive area. The strong and determined management could look after its own interests better.[27]

Labor members replied, in very moderate and conciliatory terms, that it was "unwise to specify and classify," to restrict the flexibility of individual union-management adjustment, and to obstruct the evolutionary broadening of the scope of collective bargaining. But they accepted management's basic proposition that its rights needed defense against some union intrusions. "The functions and responsibilities of management must be preserved if business and industry is to be efficient, progressive, and provide more good jobs" — shades of the aborted consensus of Johnston, Green, and Murray eight months earlier.[28]

The Conference's deliberations were rather overshadowed by the mounting wave of industrial conflict beyond its doors, which occasionally seeped under or washed right over them. For example, the crisis provoked management members to propose cooling-off periods of fifty days and the appointment of independent fact-finding boards by state governors or the President, where possible strikes threatened to cause an undefined "emergency" or to endanger public health or safety. But the Conference's work should not be forgotten.[29]

On some issues, it was clear, consensus between business and labor leaders existed. Both had an interest in the orderly institutionalization of conflict. Where they differed, management was ready to act. Lee Hill summed up the conference's real achievements most thoroughly and convincingly, from a business standpoint. Its successes were "the nailing down of the union delegates' positions on fundamental issues," and

the development of a newly improved pattern of agreement among thirty-six principal and alternate delegates from management.

These men met daily for almost five weeks, and . . . they succeeded in unanimously developing a program which, if it can be made effective by appropriate legislation, will definitely minimize future labor disputes. . . .

(1) It goes far to crystallize certain management viewpoints that were previously nebulous or inadequately defined, and it has come far to provide a platform on which management, often divided within itself heretofore, can now find a much larger basis for its own unity.

(2) Thus it can serve management as a valuable supplementary guide in future negotiations or conferences with labor.

(3) It should point out clearly to members of Congress a carefully considered, logical, and practical program for minimizing labor disputes.

If properly implemented by appropriate legislation, [it] should go a long way toward solving the country's Number 1 problem.[30]

THE NAM AND THE LEGISLATIVE STRUGGLE

At the NAM's annual Congress of American Industry (CAI) in December 1945, the work of the management representatives at the conference was endorsed, and the legislative proposals in committee reports I, II, and III formed the bases of the CAI's resolutions on labor law reform. Meanwhile, the reconversion strike wave was helping to create a political climate in the country at large in which chances of severe amendment of the Wagner Act were good. NAM propaganda encouraged a receptive public to believe that industrial conflict, shortages, and inflation were the fault of organized labor and of the federal government's economic mismanagement. President Truman also played an important part in bringing labor law reform to the public's attention by introducing his own proposals for federal intervention in peacetime labor disputes to protect the "public interest." Congress exceeded his wishes, and passed the Case Bill in the summer of 1946 — a compendium of conservative attacks on the NLRB and the Wagner Act which the NAM generally supported. Truman vetoed it, but Republican prospects in the off-year elections in November were good, so the likelihood of passage of antilabor measures in 1947 was high.[31]

In these circumstances, there was an obvious need for the organized business community to be united behind a well-considered, comprehensive program, if it was to have the greatest influence on the legislative process. Accordingly, the NAM's Industrial Relations Department and Industrial Relations Program Committee worked throughout the year, with increasing urgency toward the fall. November brought the election, December the CAI. By that time, differences of opinion within the NAM had been as nearly as possible eliminated.

Under the presidency of Clarence Randall, vice-president of Inland Steel, senior executives from NAM's activist minority met in October and November, together with important trade association executives. Companies represented included Alcoa, American Cyanamid, Armour and Co., Eastman Kodak, Island Creek Coal, Pratt and Whitney, Warner and Swasey (machine tools), Worthington Pump and Machinery, and Standard Oil of New Jersey; trade association delegates came from the utility industries (Lee H. Hill), the CCUS (Homer Hartz, a Chicago machinery manufacturer), the Associated Industries of Cleveland (William Frew Long), the Automotive Manufacturers Association (George Romney), the Michigan Manufacturers Association, and the St. Paul (Minn.) Committee on Industrial Relations.[32]

After protracted discussions, the committee produced an agreed draft, which was endorsed by the NAM's Board of Directors and thereafter rubber-stamped by the CAI. Within the committee and the board, the Midwestern steel and automotive industries' last-ditch opposition to the Wagner Act *in principle* continued. But moderation prevailed: even after the Republicans' smashing electoral victory, the NAM resisted the temptation to "go for broke," that is, outright repeal of the Wagner Act. There were two basic reasons for this: first, NAM strategists understood that reactionary legislative proposals would not square with their attempt in their massive propaganda campaign to portray the NAM in particular, and business in general, as moderate, reason-able, and unselfishly pursuing the public interest. Second, and more important, they appreciated that repeal would not "provide the neces-sary answers to our labor relations problems, the core of which involves the enormous exercise of monopolistic power by unions." Only further governmental intervention, in the right spirit, could measure up to the task. In addition, at least a minority of the Program Committee be-lieved that "employers, quite aside from their legal obligation to bar-gain collectively, should work sincerely to make such bargaining effective — recognizing that sound collective bargaining is a useful tool for the maintenance of good employee relations."[33]

That phrase did not survive the last compromises within the committee — its elimination was part of the reactionaries' price for their reluctant acceptance of a strategy of amendment, not repeal. But it represented the management position at the President's Labor-Management Con-ference, and it became the accepted policy of the NAM Industrial Rela-tions Department in its advice to members. The Department came under the control of Carroll E. French, an alumnus of the progressive firm of Industrial Relations Counselors, Inc. French only accepted the position on the understanding that the NAM had finally abandoned re-action. Chrysler's Hutchinson might not be reconciled to the labor movement, but the NAM in 1946 had finally accepted the realistic, re-formist approach to labor relations problems — in its practice if not al-ways in its rhetoric.[34]

NAM's 1946 Declaration of Principles began with a brief but signifi-cant call to employers to implement personnel policies of a generally "progressive" character:

(1) High wages based on high productivity, with incentives to encourage supe-rior performance and output;
(2) Working conditions that safeguard the health, dignity and self-respect of the individual employee;
(3) Employment that is stabilized to as great a degree as possible, through intel-ligent direction of all the factors that are under management's control;
(4) A spirit of cooperation between employees and the management, through ex-planation to employees of the policies, problems and prospects of the company.[35]

The NAM encouraged member companies to turn those platitudes into practice, not as an overtly antiunion device, but because "[i]n many companies, particularly where such a spirit of cooperation has been maintained effectively, employees have felt no need to organize to secure these benefits." Reflecting the realistic conservatism of many of its member companies, the NAM accepted much of the labor relations status quo, but thought it right to resist the further expansion of union-ism by legal means. The NAM still preferred to work for an industrial relations system in which management remained free to deal directly with workers and to keep them contented with progressive personnel policies. Carroll French firmly believed in this strategy: under his con-trol the Industrial Relations Department expanded the services of ad-vice and assistance to member firms to encourage its implementation.[36]

But in the many circumstances where such an ideal, union-free state was unattainable, NAM and many of its members aimed for decentral-ized collective bargaining in which the law assisted management in keeping the upper hand. That was the object of the remainder of NAM's principles, upon which Congress was invited to act.

First, and crucially, while "the right of employees to organize in unions is, and should continue to be protected by law," the right *not* to join should be accorded equal status. The presumption in favor of in-creasing union membership which underpinned the Wagner Act and NLRB policy should be ended. Similarly, "[i]n exercising the right to or-ganize in unions or the right not to organize, employees should be pro-tected against coercion from any source." The Wagner Act had only conceived of employer restrictions on workers' free exercise of the right to organize and bargain collectively. NAM called now, as it had since 1935, for *balance*. In practice, the defense of individual rights meant le-gal restrictions on many of the customary organizing tactics of the labor movement. Taft-Hartley accepted these principles wholeheartedly.[37]

Second, both union and management should be obliged to bargain in good faith, so long as the union was the freely chosen representative of workers in the bargaining unit. Congressional acceptance of this bal-ancing principle opened the way to employer accusations of "refusal to bargain" against strong unions. It also allowed the employer to question the representativeness of his workers' union, as NAM had long re-quested, most recently at the November 1945 conference.[38]

Third, union and employer "should be obligated by law, to adhere to the terms of collective agreements." As well as contractual no-strike and company security provisions, federal intervention to guarantee orderly contractual relations was desired. In addition, agreements "should pro-vide that disputes over the meaning or interpretation of a provision should be settled by peaceful procedures" — by which was meant, pri-marily, binding arbitration.[39]

Fourth, under the guise of protecting the public against labor mo-nopoly, bargaining should be restricted to the employees of one em-ployer, their local union, and the firm employing them. After much debate, NAM had decided in favor of a strict preference for atomized bargaining, as the steel and automotive reactionaries desired, rather than have any truck with the multiemployer bargaining which was customary in many competitive and local market industries, and advantageous to the companies concerned.[40]

Fifth, the right to strike over legitimate differences — concerning wages, hours, or working conditions — was accepted, where peaceful procedures had failed to bring a settlement. But the exercise of that right was to be conditional on a majority vote, in a secret ballot by an outside agency, on the employer's last offer. In every case, NAM's presumption was in favor of industrial peace and against the representativeness of any union, however local.[41]

Sixth, a broad category of strike actions was to be excluded from legal protection. Strikers would lack status before the NLRB, and have no right to vote in representation elections or to be reinstated after the strike; and the union, or its members, might be laid open to legal proceedings. These could include judicial injunctions, so undoing much of the benefit of the Norris-La Guardia Act of 1932 (but not repealing it altogether, as the reactionary NAM minority demanded), and overruling a decade of interpretation of it by the Supreme Court. The NLRB had been moving in the direction of excluding certain categories of strikers from its protections on the grounds of unacceptable aims or methods of conflict. NAM wanted the law to be made much more sweeping and explicit: jurisdictional strikes, sympathy strikes, strikes against the government or to force employers to ignore or violate the law, strikes to force recognition of an uncertified union, or to enforce "featherbedding" or other work-restrictive demands, or secondary boycotts, were all to be made illegal. Congress accepted most of these recommendations: it shared NAM's hope that industrial conflict could be restricted to well-regulated, nonviolent disputes between particular companies and their employees.[42]

Seventh, any kind of union security provision was to be outlawed. The staff of the Industrial Relations Department, and some Program Committee members, were willing to consider the individual, revocable checkoff, or even a modified form of union security, subject to the 75 percent vote of workers in the bargaining unit in its favor. But the majority, and the Board of Directors, plumped for the "right to work," without qualification. In addition, individual employees were to be protected by law against violence or intimidation, while "the public" was to be protected against mass picketing or any other form of coercion. NAM's aim here was to defend the nonunion worker, the scab, or the struck enterprise against the effective, if objectionable, direct-action tactics of unions and their members which local law enforcement agencies and the courts could not cope with, either because of political reluctance or the slow course of the law. Here again, Congress acted, but neither as effectively as NAM had hoped, nor with quite the results it had expected.[43]

Finally, two glaring abuses of the Wagner Act, perpetrated by the NLRB and countenanced by the Supreme Court, were to be remedied. Supervisors' unions were to be excluded from the law's protection once and for all, and employers were to be allowed "free speech" — the use of all of their resources for antilabor propaganda — without any risk of unfair labor practice charges being brought against them.[44]

Once the NAM had produced its new Declaration of Principles, it rallied a united membership behind them and bent itself to try to affect the legislative process. A massive propaganda campaign, always couched in "public interest" terms, was mounted to influence the climate of opinion in the country, and thereby bring indirect pressure on the Congress. NAM officials and member firms testified before the House and Senate committees; committee members and Congressmen were deluged with mail and pamphlets supporting NAM's proposals; and Republican majorities on the House and Senate labor committees consulted corporate attorneys representing the NAM and member firms. The House majority was advised by, amongst others, General Motors, General Electric, Chrysler's economist Scoville and attorney Iserman, and by William Ingles, lobbyist for antiunion Inland Steel, Allis-Chalmers, Fruehauf Trailer, and J. I. Case (farm equipment); while the Senate majority was ably served by its counsel, Gerard Reilly, an ex-NLRB member who had won industry's affection with his ringing dissents, particularly over the issue of supervisory unionism, and had entered the service of GM and GE.[45]

But this is not to say that the NAM, or industry representatives, "wrote" the bills which led to the final Act, as organized labor and some Democratic Congressmen alleged at the time. The NAM's was only one influence among many, and only influential because the time was ripe for legislating and the Republican party was looking around for proposals to enact. The legislative process was not under NAM control.

Thus, hard-line Republicans and conservative southern Democrats on the House committee included draft proposals reflecting the views of the defeated NAM minority and its advisors, which the Program Committee and Board of Directors had rejected as unwise. Such provisions included: strict regulation of the internal affairs of unions; exclusion of confidential employees (including "labor relations, personnel, employment, police, or time-study" employees by name, and other white-collar employees implicitly) as well as supervisors from the Act's protection; the non-Communist rule, barring unions with Communist officers from access to the NLRB; and the definition of "collective bargaining" in strictly procedural terms, so as to forbid the NLRB from ordering an employer to bargain on any specific issue except "wages, hours, and working conditions," which terms were not to be interpreted loosely. Similarly, the final Act included "national emergency strike" provisions, involving cooling-off periods and federal fact-finding of a sort the NAM had considered, but had rejected at the insistence of Lee H. Hill and the public utility industries most likely to be affected.[46]

The Senate presented different, and more difficult, problems. Its composition had altered less in the 1946 elections than had that of the House, it had a closer Republican-Democrat balance, and it overrepresented rural districts rather less flagrantly. So the two-thirds majority needed to overrule the likely Truman veto could not be guaranteed — it had not, after all, been available in 1946. In this situation, the three Republican moderates on the Senate committee — Aiken of Vermont, labor relations expert Ives of New York, and ex-NWLB public member Morse of Oregon — played a crucial role in helping to produce a workable and broadly acceptable draft bill. On the sensitive issues of industry-wide bargaining and union security, it reflected the opinions of the NAM Industrial Relations Program Committee, rather than of the more conservative Board of Directors. Republican leaders Taft of Ohio and Ball of Minnesota attempted to reintroduce strict provisions covering those subjects, but the Senate did not support them. (On other issues, however, the bill was toughened on the floor of the Senate, and made even more antilabor as a result of the Senate-House conference to resolve differences between the two chambers.)[47]

The NAM certainly influenced the legislative package Republicans and southern Democrats put together, but obviously the final outcome was affected by many other considerations. One of them, clearly, was the climate of public opinion, as reflected in the biased press and as perceived by a prejudiced Congress. NAM claimed much of the credit for shaping public opinion toward labor and public policy, especially when justifying its expenditures on public relations activities and propaganda to its membership.[48] But it is more difficult to make a firm assessment of the business community's work in this respect than it is when concentrating more narrowly on lobbying activities in Congress. Admittedly, in 1946–47 public opinion did seem to shift in a direction businessmen had wanted and worked to achieve. Nevertheless, the opinion-forming process is not a simple machine, on which one or another organized interest group can pull the lever marked "propaganda" to good effect, simply as a result of devoting increased resources to the business of influencing people. The business community's propaganda may have focused and directed public opinion to some extent, but only because it was swimming with a strongly flowing tide. Nobody can doubt that public dissatisfaction about the way the Truman administration handled reconversion was much more important in causing the decisive swing away from the liberal Democrats in 1946, or that the reconversion strike wave and well-publicized abuses of power by an unprecedentedly strong labor movement made the public receptive to proposals for Wagner Act reform.

It is also difficult to trace the linkage between the climate of opinion and the legislative process with any certainty, even in a representative democracy like the United States. Businessmen assumed that public opinion counted, and believed that their propaganda activities helped to shape it. The detached observer may wonder how accurate those positions were, and may believe that old-fashioned lobbying was more significant in shaping Taft-Hartley than the mechanisms of indirect influence NAM's public relations department relied upon. At any rate, it is clear that the NAM thought itself responsible for the character and passage of Taft-Hartley, and under a continuing obligation to defend it.

It showed this in many ways. To safeguard the Act's reputation, NAM advised its members not to abuse the rights it had granted or restored to them, and encouraged them to do all in their power to tell employees and the public that Taft-Hartley was fair, was not a "slave labor law," and should be maintained. NAM had to continue its pro–Taft-Hartley lobbying and propaganda after 1947, as the Act had revitalized the political action campaigns of the CIO and AFL, and brought them into much closer alliance with Truman and the liberal Democrats. Labor hoped for repeal of Taft-Hartley after the 1948 elections, and wanted to influence its administration via the appointing power of the President, who could thereby shape NLRB policy indirectly. Taft-Hartley was not really secure until the Democrats failed in their first attempt to repeal or amend it in 1949.[49]

And NAM's big-business supporters evidently shared in its appreciation of the importance of Taft-Hartley, and of the NAM's contribution to winning and securing it. They showed this, rather ungratefully, by withdrawing from active membership after Taft-Hartley was safely in place. Once the long campaign against the Wagner Act, the NLRB, and the labor movement had been won, there was no other common political objective to keep them interested in supporting the NAM with all of the time, energy, and money it had been able to command while "the enemy" had been powerful.[50]

THE TAFT-HARTLEY LAW

Taft-Hartley was a complex and poorly drafted measure. Some of the remedies Congress provided to the problem of labor power were inadequate; some of the law's provisions even had results quite the reverse of what its supporters had intended and expected. The antiboycott and antifeatherbedding clauses proved to be particularly weak, while those designed to make it more difficult for unions to win union shops and bargaining rights on fringe benefits and health-and-welfare funds actually made it much easier, to the chagrin of business and Congressional conservatives.[51]

Many contemporary observers foresaw these and other defects in the new federal law, so it is understandable that the enthusiasm with which Taft-Hartley was greeted by the business community was neither universal, unqualified, nor immoderate. And even Taft-Hartley's greatest supporters knew that it was not the whole answer to the labor problem. Industrial relations specialists understood that it might well prove burdensome in dealing with a strong, established union with which a firm's management wanted to maintain stable relations.

NAM's general counsel Raymond Smethurst and industrial relations director Carroll French recognized that there were imperfections in the law business had helped draft: there was a feeling that the Act had "seriously encumbered the formulation of sound industrial relations' (sic) programs by so involving industrial relations in legal technicalities that . . . the administration of sound programs is now a very serious problem." As a "good many employers" who "were somewhat lukewarm" about it pointed out, "the status of their relationships with their employees did not depend upon legislation, and they were not expecting any set of laws to work new miracles in their labor relations." A survey of executives' attitudes taken immediately after passage of the Act revealed two-thirds expecting "little or no effect on their day-to-day relations," with the next most popular response "don't know." They expected the free speech provision to be useful, and anticipated a more responsible approach to collective bargaining from the union side. But they did not intend to "get technical" or take unfair advantage of the law, as they knew such a course could produce its own crop of labor relations problems. Management had many more opportunities to take unions to court under Taft-Hartley, but should not rely on the courts or the NLRB for the answers to most of its difficulties — the help they gave came slowly, and might well be illusory. The law had an important but restricted part to play — "the provision of more equitable rules of the game"; but the outcome of union-management struggles was still more likely to depend upon "economic pressures" and "informed personnel practice." This was a position the NAM officially endorsed.[52]

Business in general, then, had rather limited and realistic expectations of the contributions Taft-Hartley could make to solving the labor relations problems of middling to large-scale manufacturing industry. Those expectations have since been supported by expert assessments of its actual effects. Taft-Hartley certainly made it easier for antiunion firms to resist the expansion of union membership and bargaining rights: the provisions on supervisory and white-collar unionism, and the freedom given to states to pass "right-to-work" laws against any form of union security, have certainly made it more difficult for unionism to spread into those areas of the country and the workforce which have shown the greatest growth since the Second World War. Taft-Hartley has played its part in confining American labor to the strongholds among blue-collar workers in the traditional manufacturing industries and regions which it had gained by the end of the Second World War. Within those organized sectors, Taft-Hartley systematically increased the forces of law and orderliness in American labor relations, increasing the pressures upon unions to act "responsibly," to centralize control over bargaining and strike policy, and to develop the bureaucratic apparatus essential for institutions living within such a law-bound system.[53]

Taft-Hartley, whatever its defects, certainly brought American business tangible long-term benefits. In the short term, it proved useful for firms like General Electric and International Harvester in their fight against Communist influence in the unions they dealt with, and Ford in its attempt to persuade the UAW to accept its ideas about responsible union behavior. But of course, some years were required for the law to be tested and interpreted by the NLRB and the courts, so perhaps its most important immediate value to the business community was as a source of reassurance, a sign that the social and political "revolutions" of the New Deal years were well and truly burnt out. "Coming out of the long period of confusion under the Wagner Act is something like coming out of a tunnel wherein one has grasped toward the light. There is suddenly much more clarity, much more assurance of sound footing, much fresher air to breathe. We sense the closing of confusion."[54]

This reassurance was very welcome in the later 1940s, "a period of precarious prosperity, threatened by insecurity and torn by strife."[55] Taft-Hartley showed that, after years of uncertainty, the practical conservatism of American business was once again triumphant in national politics. It provided a legal framework for labor relations within which business would be happy to operate. But it had not provided all the answers.

5

Recovery of the Initiative, II

BIG BUSINESS AND BIG LABOR IN THE POSTWAR YEARS

Management and unions, for rather different reasons, both anticipated the tapering-off of wartime demand with considerable anxiety.
But in fact the reconversion years were a period of shortages rather than
overcapacity in American industry; of insatiable consumer demand and
massive corporate reinvestment, with no hint of a return to economic
stagnation. The Truman administration found itself faced, quite unexpectedly, with the problems of inflation, not depression. No one was entirely confident, as the postwar consumer boom rolled on, that the specter of mass unemployment would not return to haunt the great American
banquet. The question remained not whether but when the postwar
"corrective dip," recession, or depression would arrive. The bargaining
behavior and political strategies of business and labor have to be set
against this background of middle-term pessimism and uncertainty.

Unions wanted to put a floor beneath their members' living standards, to entrench their organizations, to consolidate their contractual
gains of the previous ten years, and to provide for a more secure future
by the extension of private social welfare systems via collective bargaining. They also had to try to protect members' real incomes in a time of
galloping inflation, especially after the death of the Office of Price Administration in 1946.

Companies wanted to set their houses in order before the return of a
buyer's market; they wanted to make sure they were "prepared for
rough weather." To meet the demands of the home market, to support
the continuing relatively high level of military effort, and to provide the
requirements of a shattered Western Europe, industry had to expand its

productive capacity in the short term. This it was ready and able to do. New investment brought its own productivity gains. But, if a company was to be able to exploit the seller's market most profitably as long as it lasted, and yet to remain competitive in anticipation of the coming downturn in demand, it had also to pay attention to lowering labor cost, increasing its productivity, and guaranteeing continuity of output — particularly where labor was a key factor of production.[1]

The postwar years were extremely profitable for American business: the cost of wage increases was easily passed on to final consumers, so the resistance of center firms to substantial annual money wage rises was not strong. The patterns they established in national-level bargaining were followed more or less swiftly and closely in peripheral firms and industries. But postwar wage bargaining was not a smoothly functioning process. Each wage round — 1946, 1947, and 1949 — was marked by large, though generally orderly, official strikes, and by bitter, violent propaganda wars between companies and unions. The economic conflict had its political dimension, as business fought, successfully, for the decontrol of prices in 1946, and resisted, much less successfully, federal intervention in all of the major disputes of 1945–46, and in the steel industry dispute over welfare funds in 1949. The industrial conflicts of the late 1940s were about much more than wages-and-hours issues: fundamentally, they revolved around issues of control. How strong were unions to be, and how much influence should they and their members have over working conditions via collective bargaining and direct-action tactics? These were the questions that stirred business to take aggressive action in negotiations and everyday labor relations in the postwar years.[2]

Orderly mass strikes in a buoyant economy helped protect unions' basic contractual rights and bargaining relations, and their members' living standards, against the worst effects of what appeared in 1945–46 to be a determined and concerted attack by organized business. But conflict, however immediately successful, had its political costs — notably the conservative triumphs in the 1946 elections and the Taft-Hartley Act. Accordingly, unions, particularly those of the CIO, exercised considerable self-restraint in their use of the strike weapon through 1947 and 1948. They wanted to restore their public image and not embarrass the Truman administration, their only, if imperfect, political ally. At the same time they gave the Democrats more support than ever before, hoping for the restoration of price control and belated enactment, in the form of the "Fair Deal," of labor's program of increased federal social welfare activities, as well as for the repeal of Taft-Hartley.[3]

Organized labor's alliance with the liberal wing of the Democratic party also led to a "cold war" within the CIO, because of a desire to co-operate with the anti-Communist Truman administration and to make the labor movement less politically vulnerable. Taft-Hartley's provision that no union with officers who had not taken a non-Communist oath enjoyed any rights under the Act helped right-wing social democrats like Phil Murray and Walter Reuther to purge their own organizations and CIO-affiliated unions. The CIO was not immediately strengthened by its public purging: rather, in 1948–49 it became preoccupied with its internal divisions. A labor movement which needed unified strength crippled itself. The Electrical, Farm Equipment, and Mine, Mill, and Smelter Workers left the CIO, or were forced to leave. Their bargaining rights unprotected by law, they became fair game for rival CIO and AFL unions, and labor's internecine wars created opportunities for an-tiunion corporations like Allis-Chalmers, J. I. Case, International Harvester, Servel, and General Electric to exploit.[4]

Finally, in 1948–49, the long-awaited recession came, but it was shallower and briefer than had been expected. Marshall Plan aid and other exports to Europe aided recovery; the massive expansion of the military budget resulting from the increase in international tension in 1949–50 guaranteed high-level prosperity into the next decade.[5]

Throughout the postwar years, industrial unions continued to possess a large measure of economic bargaining power. But, because of their political weakness, they were increasingly unable to mobilize it effectively. In this situation, their large bargaining partners saw an opportunity to alter the content of collective agreements, and the way they actually worked out, to their own advantage — an opportunity which they seized. However, the labor relations strategy of realistic corporate managements in the later 1940s was much more than simple opportunism. It also reflected the application of a well-articulated program of labor relations reform which had been more than a decade in the making. Once the NWLB had disappeared from the scene, business was again free to try to build an industrial relations system in which collective bargaining with responsible unions played an important, but limited, role. It could use its own resources, including valuable accumulated experience, and build on the habits and machinery of orderly labor relations the NWLB had bequeathed. This course, much more than Taft-Hartley, offered hope of long-run success.

"Realistic" Collective Bargaining

From the management side, collective bargaining cannot be conceived of as the forcing of grudging concessions by pressures of various kinds. It does not imply a

situation in which management fights a rearguard action to preserve its prerogatives; such a negative approach can hardly produce a vital mechanism. . . .

It is management's duty to make such demands on the union as are necessary
to preserve its ability to perform its functions. Collective bargaining is by no
means a one-way street.[6]

NWLB vice-chairman George W. Taylor still felt it necessary in 1944
to preach to a business audience that collective bargaining had something positive to offer. They should seize it rather than longing hopelessly
— and dangerously — for a return to the good old days before labor had
raised its ugly head. General Motors, whom Taylor had served as its second Impartial Umpire, had already learned that lesson for itself.

GM was the originator of what it liked to call the "man bites dog"
technique in labor relations — that is, a program of action aimed at limiting union influence by, amongst other things, making demands of the
union rather than being passive, defensive, or purely reactive in collective bargaining, with the union always taking the initiative. In 1942
GM began to put pressure on the UAW to behave in ways management
defined as "responsible," by accusing it of being an obstacle to all-out
production in a time of national crisis. There was a large element of
public relations in GM's bargaining posture, as it was striking back
against Walter Reuther's recent, accurate charge that the automotive
industry as a whole had obstructed the defense effort. Also, it was attempting to defend itself against the probability that the NWLB would
grant the UAW some kind of union security on the grounds that it *was*
responsible.[7]

But GM's bargaining posture was more than propaganda alone. It
went on to make specific requests for alterations in contract terms
which added up to a sustained criticism of the UAW's record, combined
with a presentation of the kind of labor relationship GM would consider
to be acceptable. General Motors demanded that the union should discontinue attacks on the company; allow the elimination of double-time
pay; allow management to establish "any shift system which it feels is
efficient"; permit the introduction of piecework systems; sanction pay
differentials, promotions, and transfers on a merit, not seniority, basis;
halve the number of union committeemen and eliminate their special
privileges (paid time off for union business and special seniority rating);
and allow a general reform of the grievance procedure in the interest of
efficiency.[8]

GM's immediate success was limited. It had asked the UAW to abandon its agitational character and to give up its claims to exercise a degree of formal job control. In response, the UAW only agreed to censor
the local union press to get rid of antimanagement diatribes, a promise

which such a decentralized and democratic union could not easily or quickly fulfill. GM's demands could not be achieved through negotiation at that time, and were of such a controversial character that the NWLB would not order them. GM's bargaining posture was perhaps more successful in showing how a large and aggressive corporation could take on a powerful and publicity-conscious union at the difficult business of making a case to win public favor. Throughout the war, GM continued with the same policy. Its demands of the union, and attacks upon it, continued in the same vein. GM made its position absolutely clear, and tried to win public support for it — a valuable asset for such a large and visible corporation, any of whose major industrial disputes was certain to involve federal intervention.[9]

In wartime just as in the years immediately before, GM's labor relations policy was unusually single-minded. Few corporations followed its lead. Most were content to pursue immediate industrial peace by making expedient concessions, leaving the resolution of tricky issues to the WLB's. In consequence, WLB industry members were excellently placed to observe the weaknesses in most of the business community's preparation for collective bargaining and labor relations. They "receive[d] a liberal education in other people's problems," and were most strongly — and disagreeably — impressed by the poor presentation of management's case. This resulted from and reflected the poor quality of the labor relations staff in many companies (or indeed their utter absence). Companies were inexperienced in having to make a case for their labor relations policy and practice before any outside body — be it union, arbitrator, or government agency. The habits of a long period of unquestioned authority died hard: getting used to having to negotiate took time, and acquiring the skill to do so in such a new and difficult area as labor relations was no small task. There was a shortage of experienced personnel, and also of agreement on the course they should follow. In this situation, WLB industry members had an important part to play in influencing the thought and practice of the whole business community. They gave concrete assistance in the writing and enforcement of better contracts. They tried to unscramble the mess made by companies which had already made unwise concessions to their unions because they failed to appreciate the consequences of their acts. And they advised companies on how to improve their own labor relations performance through the usual channels — conferences and publications of the AMA, NICB, and NAM, and other membership services of trade associations and consulting firms, as well as the business press.[10]

WLB industry members' were only some of the voices in this chorus. The common program of labor relations reform that it recommended sounded fairly simple. It began with a call for improvements in the supply, utilization, and organization of managerial expertise to handle the complexities of contract negotiation and administration. But competence and success in collective bargaining and labor relations required more than just technical preparedness. It had to be accompanied by hard thinking about what new strategy the "personnel," "labor," or "industrial relations" department was designed to carry out.

One thing was absolutely insisted upon: labor relations policy must be based in an acceptance of unions and of the essentials of public policy as lasting facts. Management must be determined to make collective bargaining work as a way of arriving at and enforcing acceptable agreements, and not try to continue antiunion struggles with a view to the eventual elimination of the "outside" organization. Whether union power resulted from direct action or federal policy, whether the management concerned liked it or not, it had to be accepted and dealt with within the law. Antiunionism might still be the "right" course, but it was not generally wise, and was liable to be costly — resulting in industrial conflict, legal proceedings, and bad publicity.[11]

Once management had accepted labor relations as a permanent problem, it must treat it just as it did problems in other areas of business administration. It must be realistic, practical, constructive, objective, astute, ethical — in short, *businesslike*. Management's task was to resolve immediate problems in line with long-run objectives, which must be generally acceptable and attainable. Indiscriminate and bloody-minded antiunionism was ruled out on both counts.

In addition, labor relations policy should be well worked out, consistently implemented, and dynamic. There must be an end to defeatism, to the tendency to sit back and wait for union demands, and then reach a compromise settlement. Collective bargaining must be recognized as a game management could play aggressively, to maximize productive efficiency and minimize union interference with management's discretionary powers essential for the success of the enterprise. In return for the contractual benefits it received, the union should be forced to deliver something — its members' acceptance of managerial authority, continuity of production, adherence to orderly procedures. Each company should work out precisely what it wanted. Management policy must be based in detailed knowledge of what was going on within the firm — not just of the formalities of contract language, but of how stewards and supervisors actually interacted on the factory floor. The management which knew what its operating problems were, had firm objectives, and had the expertise to meet with organized labor on a footing of equality or better, could go about the job of bargaining with confidence. It should attempt to influence the content of the final agreement, either by laying a preemptive offer on the table, or by making a considered counterproposal to the union's demands along the lines General Motors had sketched out.

It was not enough simply to negotiate a satisfactory agreement. It must also be consistently enforced right down the line if it was to work as intended. Here again, the well-set-up industrial relations staff had its part to play, setting up feedback and monitoring systems, making sure supervisors did not depart from formal labor relations policies, and in general policing the administration of the contract with the assistance of orderly grievance systems and arbitration.

Underlying the managerial program of labor relations reform was a recognition of the profound importance of policy and practice in this area to the success of any drive to cut costs and restore discipline and productivity in the postwar era. Management aimed for stability, predictability, and order in labor relations; for the confinement and gradual reduction of the scope of union influence through formal collective bargaining and informal pressure; and for the elimination of direct action tactics on the part of workers of any but the least disruptive sort — the official strike, called in due season at one, two, or even more years' interval, at the contract termination date.[12]

In the long run, this realistic program swept all before it, becoming the accepted best practice of American industry. It was also by far the most important tendency in the late 1940s, enjoying the support of many large firms. But it was not the only strategy advocated and adopted at the time, and it certainly was not the most prestigious.

THE PROGRESSIVE ALTERNATIVE

In the late 1930s, the realistic strategy was not the only constructive response to the problem of labor. Indeed, the policy recommendations of U.S. Rubber's Cyrus Ching, and the practice of the General Electric Corporation while it was headed by Owen D. Young and Gerard Swope, seemed to offer much more. They promised social harmony, a way to square America's commitment to use collective bargaining as the way to extend some kind of industrial democracy with the continuation of private capitalism and managerial authority.[13]

These three elder statesmen of progressive business moved on from active participation in industrial management after the war. Swope and Young retired for good in 1945; Ching became head of the newly independent and more powerful Federal Mediation and Conciliation Service established by Taft-Hartley in 1947. But the progressive strategy still had influential supporters: Paul Hoffman of Studebaker Motors, J. D. Zellerbach of Crown Zellerbach, Eric Johnston (who moved on from the presidency of the CCUS to head up the Motion Picture Association of America), Robert Wood Johnson of Johnson & Johnson (pharmaceuticals and textiles), Walter H. Wheeler of Pitney-Bowes (postage meters), and numerous executives from the garment and textile industries, together with some from smaller steel-making and -fabricating firms. Their message was endorsed from the side of organized labor, particularly by CIO Steelworkers' officials Clinton Golden, Harold Ruttenberg, and Joseph Scanlon, by Solomon Barkin of the CIO Textile Workers, and by Edward Cheyfitz of the Mine, Mill, and Smelter Workers.[14]

Business and labor advocates of the progressive approach worked together to turn their vision of union-management accommodation into reality. Edward Cheyfitz became Eric Johnston's assistant; the Steel Workers, through their famous Scanlon Plan, helped managements of small steel firms improve productivity by cooperative action; Botany Worsted Mills and the CIO Textile Workers organized joint foreman — shop steward training programs to help the lower-level members of both organizations reach common understandings and work together more smoothly.[15]

Leading business supporters of union-management rapprochement were the kind of men historians have termed "corporate liberals" — sophisticated conservatives who were not unduly perturbed by the recent increases in power of unions and the federal government. They viewed these two great institutions as forces for improved social stability and efficiency rather than as threats to the Free Enterprise System and the American Way of Life. They associated with one another in organizations they controlled — notably the Committee for Economic Development (CED) and the National Planning Association (NPA). Their ties with one another and their understanding of government and labor were further strengthened by common service under Democratic administrations, particularly after the war. Hoffman and Zellerbach, for example, together supported the Johnson-Green-Murray Charter of 1945, served on the CED's Special Policy Committee on Collective Bargaining, and held senior positions in the Economic Cooperation Administration set up to implement the Marshall Plan in Europe. Hoffman, in addition, was chosen as one of six management advisers to Ching's Conciliation Service.[16]

In their European service, such men as Hoffman, Zellerbach, and NPA trustee William K. Batt of S.K.F. worked with social democratic union leaders and staff members like Golden, Victor Reuther, and James Carey. They helped rebuild non-Communist labor movements in

Western Europe, and tried to encourage over there the kind of union-management cooperation to increase productivity that they practiced and preached in their own country. In the process, they came to see responsible labor leaders as "free men on the same team of democracy." These Cold War liberals found new arguments in the necessities of international relations to strengthen their case for the pursuit of rapprochement between all levels of labor and management. America had to present a united front to the outside world, to eliminate flaws in its democratic institutions, and to remove obstacles to the increase of production so essential to sustain a new world role.[17]

The progressives' strategy for improving in-plant labor relations was quite straightforward. It had many features in common with the realists' program, but it went much further toward willing acceptance of the new labor relations system. And it had an altogether different emphasis: there was less concern for fixing boundaries between union and management spheres of influence, and a rejection of the idea that labor relations was a zero-sum game.

The fundamental question management should ask itself was: did it accept the permanency of the union? If the answer was "yes," management policy "should be designed to make the union a reliable, helpful, and cooperative factor in the operation of the company's business."

> To this end, the policy of management would be to deal fairly at all times with the union and its officers. It would want the union to participate actively in the accomplishment of all objectives requiring the teamwork of employees.
>
> Management representatives would treat the union representatives with the same respect and good will as they would like to have from the union representatives. They would do nothing to discredit the union. They would give credit where credit was due to union representatives.[18]

The rhetoric is soft — the "Golden Rule" lurks in the shadows; but the practical program was quite well worked out. It involved: granting the union security of membership and income; allowing the scope of collective bargaining to grow, with notification, discussion, and even negotiations on issues of corporate policy well beyond wages, hours, and working conditions; making no distinction between "the union" (radical, subversive, "outside") and "our men"; using the union as a channel of communication with employees, not treating it as a barrier to be vaulted over. Management should try to build up the status of established, responsible union leaders, and even consider its shop stewards as "departmental morale executive[s]."[19]

This program represented American management's closest approach to a fully "pluralistic" ideology of labor relations, giving unions a positive welcome rather than simply granting them a limited legitimacy, and seeing real advantages in joint regulation. Still, there was to be no abdication by management: it would only share some of its power and knowledge in order to use the remainder more effectively. Management would retain the right to take the initiative, and to make the final decision, on most subjects, industrial relations among them. In most cases union participation was to be restricted to the right to be notified or consulted, or to protest management's decisions after the fact. Where labor acquired a real voice in policymaking and administration, the subjects involved were either unimportant — for example, welfare and recreation programs — or concerned ways to increase productivity in marginal companies. The price of a share in power over the heart of the enterprise in such situations was union acquiescence or assistance in implementing speedups or layoffs.[20]

Collective bargaining relationships in progressive firms attracted considerable attention at the time. Academic industrial relations experts looked into them, wrote of their virtues, and spoke of "working harmony" or "union-management cooperation" as the goals toward which labor relations generally would and *should* mature. Many of the case studies which provided the foundations on which this interpretation rested were conducted under the auspices of the NPA, with Clinton Golden as director of this project on the "Causes of Industrial Peace under Collective Bargaining."[21]

But whatever its apparent successes and its appeal to a broad range of liberal Americans, the progressive strategy simply failed to win the support of most nationally important firms. One survey found no company with more than a thousand employees enjoying an actively cooperative relationship with its union; no establishment with more than five thousand employees where union-management relations were those of working harmony. The progressive strategy flourished, if at all, in medium-sized and closely held firms, or in marginal companies operating on the periphery of America's "dual economy."[22]

It was also a fairly tender flower, needing special circumstances in which to survive and prosper even in those firms most noted for their management's commitment to political liberalism and union-management accommodation. In 1968 Herbert Northrup and Harvey Young turned a fierce critical gaze on the companies involved in the original "Causes of Industrial Peace" study. Twenty years after the first case studies had been made, they reexamined the fortunes of the companies involved in the intervening years, and questioned the reasons NPA investigators had cited to support their conclusion that union-management relations at an earlier date were good. They found that, even in the 1940s, the situation had not been as rosy as NPA investigators glowingly depicted it. Union-management accommodation had depended, sometimes, on the unresponsiveness of union leadership to membership pressures. More often, it had been bought by managerial laxity in a period of prosperity. "Progressive" and peaceful firms had paid top dollar, matching or exceeding wage rates negotiated by the large firms in their industries. Sometimes they actually *had* abdicated control over workplace labor relations and working practices, and hence over labor cost and productivity, in a way they could afford in the late 1940s, but not in the post-Korean War and Eisenhower depressions of the 1950s. Other firms in the NPA spotlight had been in industries where labor costs had been a relatively unimportant element in final costs, or which had not had to worry too much about price competition. Lessons learned in such situations were not universally applicable. Certainly they were neither useful nor attractive to large firms which did not occupy such sheltered havens, which had to negotiate the pattern-setting deals with the great industrial unions, and which were determined to regain, and keep, strict control over worker behavior and productivity.[23]

COLLECTIVE BARGAINING AFTER THE WAR

During the war, companies accumulated skill and experience in handling labor relations, and acquired a more sophisticated approach, as well as new and serious problems. When reconversion came, some of them were ready to use it for "a well planned program of recovery [of management rights] to be negotiated into their agreements as opportunity offers over a period of years," and for "straightening out the salients in the management front created by government and union offensives."[24]

In the first postwar bargaining round, General Motors occupied the center of attention as it fought off the demands of the largest and most militant industrial union, and tried to pursue its own objectives. The UAW insisted on: a 30 percent wage increase predicated on the need to protect workers' take-home pay and purchasing power in a time of reduced working hours and accelerating inflation; the payment of such an increase without any compensatory price increases, on the grounds that corporate reserves and anticipated profits were more than adequate; and an extension of union security and contractually protected job controls well beyond those which the UAW had gained before the war, or the NWLB had ordered during it. Walter Reuther, head of the UAW's GM department, chose which one of the Big Three automobile firms to strike, named the issues of the dispute, and largely determined the tone of the contest. There were really two struggles going on at the same time: an orderly mass strike, involving almost 300 thousand workers directly, and lasting for 113 days nationally and up to sixty more in many locations; and a bitter propaganda battle, carried out over the radio, in pampheteering, through paid advertisements and carefully engineered news releases, and in testimony before federal fact-finders and Congressional committees.[25]

General Motors did not choose the ground, but it won the battle. The corporation simply gave a "pattern" wage increase, following the steel and electrical industry settlements, and matching those negotiated between the UAW, Ford, and Chrysler. It won permission to raise its prices from the federal government, which more than paid for the wage hike. The long strike was not even as costly to GM as might have been expected. The federal government repaid some excess profits taxes, part of a general policy to cushion corporations during reconversion. And the corporation was able to retool and to accumulate scarce raw materials during the strike, getting itself ready to make cars and trucks for the awaiting civilian market. The UAW had hoped to force GM to a quick settlement by allowing its competitors to keep working and steal a march on it in the battle for postwar markets. In fact, shortages of power, raw materials, and bought-in parts (for example, spark plugs from one of GM's subsidiaries), which the strike wave of 1945–46 made worse, meant that they were unable to make anything of that "opportunity." GM's sense of its own market power and bargaining position was much superior to that of the UAW.[26]

Reuther lost on all of the "economic" issues of the strike. He had to move much further from his initial demand than GM did from its first wage offer, and he failed utterly in his attempt to introduce corporate pricing policy as a proper subject for bargaining or arbitration. The sovereign power of corporate management to make investment and pricing policy — "the very heart of management judgement and discretion in private industry" — was protected absolutely. GM did not even have to disclose any of the confidential information on which forecasts and decisions were based. Reuther also lost the war of words. For three months before the strike he attempted to soften up the corporation with a preliminary propaganda bombardment, composed of equal parts of liberal Keynesian economic analysis and of claims to be more "socially responsible" than the "small group of industrial and financial bureaucrats who control General Motors." His special pleading and elaborate briefs were simply not accepted — if indeed they had registered with any important section of the public. A poll in December 1945, conducted in industrial states north of the Ohio and east of the Mississippi, showed that 42 percent of the sample blamed the UAW for the strike (19 percent blamed the company, 26 percent both sides). Forty-two percent, again, thought GM had been "more reasonable" (23 percent rated the UAW higher, but 15 percent said neither had been reasonable). Fifty-five percent rejected the union's wage claim, while only 35 percent thought it fair. Public opinion shifted somewhat during the strike, but on balance GM retained the advantage.[27]

The union's only real success was in resisting GM's concerted effort to weaken its ability to influence its members' working conditions. There were no major union victories in the "noneconomic" clauses of the contract, but it was lucky to avoid utter defeat. GM locals advanced an ambitious set of demands for increased formal job control: they wanted to eliminate remaining piecework and bonus systems, and to abolish "merit spreads" (variable rates on the same production jobs, at management's discretion). They wanted a strict seniority rule on such matters as shift preference, job transfers, and promotions; an increase in the numbers, powers, and freedom of action of union committeemen; and an end to management's unilateral right, according to the existing contract, to set time and production standards (the union theoretically retained the right to strike over such issues during the life of the agreement, but only used it once, ineffectively, between 1940 and 1948).[28]

An aggressive union met a rather more single-minded management head-on in a struggle for authority in the workplace, and lost. GM did not simply resist UAW demands. It had its own proposals to make, beginning with the striking out of nineteen clauses the NWLB had inserted and which, GM made it clear, it had only accepted under duress, for the duration of the war. Beyond that, it wanted to restore the more stringent terms of the last prewar agreement, or even to go further and regain the maximum possible degree of managerial authority and discretion. It aimed to "improve" the contract in line with its basic principles and objectives, a plan the UAW and the NWLB had only delayed.

The clauses GM wanted to strike out covered: maintenance of union membership; the numbers and powers of committeemen; union officials' rights of plant entrance; the working of the grievance procedure and the powers of the Umpire; the acquisition of seniority and its application to promotions and transfers; the imposition of discipline; and numerous liberalized fringe benefits—equal pay for women on the same jobs as men, call-in pay, night shift premiums, and vacation allowances. The NWLB had even tampered with such minor regulations as those covering smoking, and GM was determined to undo *all* the damage.[29]

The principles on which GM wanted to insist stemmed from its Statement of Basic Policies first issued in 1934. It was dogged and consistent in its attempt to regain the powers it had possessed in the preunion era. GM's major demands were:

1. That wages, hours of employment and other conditions of employment are the only matters which are subject to collective bargaining.
3. That the products to be manufactured, the location of plants, the schedules of production, the methods, processes, and means of manufacturing, the right to hire, promote, transfer, discharge or discipline for cause, and to maintain discipline and efficiency of employees, are the sole responsibility of the Corporation.
7. That there be appropriate penalties, including loss of seniority, against any employe (sic) taking part in any strike or work stoppage in violation of the agreement.[30]

Other demands included, once again, an end to antimanagement diatribes in union publications; full protection of the "right to work"; prohibition of union recruitment and fund-raising on company time; restriction of the rights of committeemen and "streamlining" of the grievance procedure, to cut down on costly, frivolous, or disruptive activity; formal processing of all narrowly defined grievances, not continuous bargaining and direct action on a wide range of issues; an increase from ninety days to twelve months of the probationary period during which no seniority rights were acquired; and the withdrawal of union opposition to new and existing incentive plans. During the negotiations, GM added to this impressive list demands for a guarantee of no official union opposition to any management effort to speed up production, and for an absolute no-strike pledge for the life of the contract, with no exceptions to cover issues on which the union had no appeal to the Umpire against management's decisions.[31]

These proposals added up to GM's opinion of what was needed to make a union-management relationship truly acceptable. But the corporation had to live in the real world, and recognized that compromise would still leave it with a very good contract, one with which it could operate, and on which it could hope to make future improvements. General Motors ended up accepting most of the NWLB's innovations, except that the maintenance of membership clause was eliminated, and that 1941 contract terms on the rule of seniority in promotions and transfers only where "ability, merit, and capacity are equal" were restored. The union retained the weakest form of income security, the checkoff of dues from members' pay packets — and even here GM protected the rights of any UAW member to escape from his financial responsibilities.[32]

General Motors' success in rolling back union power was limited, but it had not been forced to give any ground. The formative period of job rights for GM workers was over. Stabilization also resulted from the extension of the time between negotiations on all issues except wages from one to two years. Decreasing the frequency of bargaining rounds and possible mass strikes remained one of GM's objectives between 1946 and 1950. The 1945–46 strike and negotiations were the first step toward making labor relations a source of stability, not unpredictability, in GM's operations.

General Motors considered its investment in the great strike well worth while. The UAW and its members had learned of the corporation's will to resist: it was to be twenty-five years before the union again attempted to use a strike against GM to set the automobile industry pattern, preferring to take on the weaker Ford and Chrysler. The corporation had made its point, on behalf of the entire business community, that basic management rights were not negotiable. The scope of collective bargaining had been narrowly confined to wages, hours, and working conditions, and even there the corporation's power to take the initiative in instituting change was adequately broad. General Motors was well placed, as most-efficient, lowest-cost producer, with guaranteed uninterrupted production, to consolidate its position of market leadership.[33]

While the GM strike dragged on, the UAW attempted to settle with Ford, Chrysler, and the "independents" — Studebaker, Packard, Hudson, Nash, Willys-Overland, and Kaiser-Frazer — in line with Walter Reuther's totally misconceived "one-at-a-time" strategy. The UAW found itself banking everything on a hopeless struggle with GM, and unable to bargain effectively with Ford or Chrysler at all. It needed a quick settlement much more than they did, and it had no realistic strike threat to bring to bear. Ford Motor Co. took advantage of this favorable situation to begin to practice an aggressive program of labor relations reform on its own account.

Ford faced extremely grave problems as it entered the postwar era under the recently installed command of Henry Ford II. The company's management "structure" was a shambles, after decades of "Old Henry's" erratic, personal, unsystematic, and production-oriented control. There was no financial control or corporate planning activity to speak of. And Ford labor relations between 1941 and 1945 had been extremely disturbed; Ford foremen were solidly unionized; labor costs and productivity were at such levels that the company was guaranteed a loss on every car it made under government-controlled prices. In the whole of Ford management, after the removal of the old thug Harry Bennett and his cronies, there was only one really bright spot: the Labor Relations

Staff, under ex-FBI man John Bugas. However, Ford also had certain compensatory advantages: massive investment reserves, and the freedom of a closely owned family business to carry losses for some years while it rebuilt its production facilities, its model range, and its management structure. Ford did not have to worry about the reactions of stockholders denied dividends, or financial backers unconvinced of corporate strategy.[34]

In the 1945–46 bargaining round, Ford knew it was as nearly free to write its own contract as it ever would be. The Labor Relations Staff — upgraded into an Industrial Relations Department on 27 September 1945, just six days after young Henry became president — proceeded to do so. Ford followed classic reformist strategy, and kicked off the negotiations with its own list of thirty-one demands for contract changes, which were given wide publicity. It insisted that there was no hint of union-busting in its intentions. It simply wanted to obtain the benefits the UAW had promised from collective bargaining, back in 1941: freedom from unauthorized strikes, and freedom to maximize production, as the company's return for paying the industry's highest wages and giving the UAW an unprecedentedly liberal contract and a large measure of security. The way to do this was to go for the same kind of contract as GM already possessed, in much the same way as GM went about its labor relations business. In labor relations, as in other aspects of Ford's managerial renaissance, it paid GM the sincerest form of flattery — hiring in GM executives, copying GM management structure and techniques, and setting the Ford "team" the simple goal of "Beat Chevrolet."[35]

But there were differences: GM's management group was toughly realistic, but politically very conservative, staunchly entrepreneurial and authoritarian, unreconciled to the principles of unionism and the "welfare state" but readily dealing with unions as a "necessary evil." Ford's style, on the other hand, was more freewheeling. Young Henry hired himself a progressive public relations consultant, and set about reestablishing the corporate reputation for liberalism so badly dented by Old Henry's penchant for antisemitism, fascism, and isolationism in the 1920s and '30s. Rebuilding the corporate image was one part of the program designed to improve Ford's market position. But in addition, Young Henry allied himself in politics, quite sincerely, with the CED and corporate liberalism. GM management members, individually and collectively, supported radical-rightist causes; Ford was much less vocally and ideologically conservative. It is interesting to compare the two former chief executives of GM and Ford who served as Secretaries of Defense to Eisenhower and Kennedy on this score — the practical conservative, production-oriented Engine Charlie Wilson, and the sophisticated whiz kid Robert McNamara, representative of a younger, more pragmatic executive style.[36]

Nevertheless, the practice of labor relations was much the same in both corporations. Ford conducted its negotiations in private, wherever possible, without ringing appeals to "the public" and self-righteous proclamations that it was fighting the good fight for managerial authority and the free-enterprise system on behalf of the entire business community. Still, it had the same basic objectives in in-plant relations: improved control, efficiency, stability, predictability, and order; and it had even worse problems than GM, having to deal with a less-disciplined, more militant body than Walter Reuther's relatively "businesslike" and "responsible" GM Department of the UAW.

Ford's thirty-one demands were all directed at its problems of job control. At the head of the list stood a requirement for clarification of the "excluded categories" of workers whom neither the UAW *nor any other* CIO union should either organize actively or even admit into membership. These included supervisors, timekeepers, pay clerks, draughtsmen, and white-collar workers generally Ford wanted to isolate the FAA from the UAW and the rest of the labor movement, and to make sure that unionization was confined to production and maintenance workers.

Second, Ford wanted the union to give it some real security against unofficial stoppages, by making the union itself financially responsible for each man-day's loss. Third, Ford wanted much more extensive and explicit protection of managerial prerogatives. Fourth, it wanted to reduce the numbers of union committeemen, to streamline the grievance procedure, and to insist on the first presentation of grievances by workers to foremen in person, without any intermediary. These were the most important provisions; others included a many-sided attack on the seniority system; unilateral management control over all bulletin boards, all union handouts, etc., posted or distributed about the plant; explicit recognition of management's right to make, change, and enforce rules unilaterally; permission for supervisors to do production work; and a narrowing of the powers of the Umpire, including prohibiting him from making any ruling restrictive of the prerogatives of management. This was a complete, General Motors-type package.[37]

What was new in 1945–46 was not just that Ford knew what it wanted, but also that the company was prepared for businesslike negotiations, and had a well-articulated philosophy to give its labor relations program conscious purpose. From 1941 to 1945, Ford had followed the inconsistent policy of trying to buy industrial peace with a liberal contract, at the same time as continuing with an antiunion, authoritarian, provocative supervisory style. Now there was to be an end to that period of drift and miscalculation.[38]

Young Henry outlined Ford's whole postwar strategy in his keynote speech to the Society of Automotive Engineers in January 1946.

[W]e of the Ford Motor Company have no desire to "break the Unions," to turn back the clock to days which sometimes look in retrospect much more attractive than they really were. . . . We do not want to destroy the Unions. We want to strengthen their leadership by urging and helping them to assume the responsibilities they must assume if the public interest is to be served. . . .

[W]e must look to an improved and increasingly responsible Union leadership for help in solving the human equation in mass production. . . .

If we are to have industrial relations programs and labor relations staffs, and spend as much money on them as we do, we should do it expertly and efficiently, bringing to the task the same technical skill and determination that the engineer brings to mechanical problems. . . .

There is no reason why a union contract could not be written and agreed upon with the same efficiency and good temper that marks the negotiation of a commercial contract between two companies.

Ford determined to take the initiative, and to rely upon its own considerable bargaining power and managerial resources to get a solution. "We cannot . . . expect legislation to solve our problems. . . . [M]anagement must take the initiative for developing the relationships between labor and management. . . . [M]anagement is in charge."[39]

UAW negotiators seemed to agree. They understood and sympathized with Ford's problems, and replied to its central suggestion that the union should be responsible for its members' unofficial actions by proposing that members alone should be. Around this desperately unpopular compromise the final contract was written, giving Ford full freedom to discipline those who led, instigated, or fomented a strike, or participated in more than one, with penalties up to immediate discharge, and to discipline mere first-time participants with lesser penalties. The Umpire's role in this procedure was very limited — he could not set aside any penalty, merely investigate the facts of guilt. Management prerogatives were extensively defined; union committeemen's numbers, and thus the effectiveness of the grievance procedure, reduced; excluded categories of white-collar and supervisory employees very clearly defined, to the company's satisfaction (though not that of the union rank-and-file); and the company was guaranteed that the only kind of strike it need fear or expect would be the orderly mass walkout.[40]

With this contract as security, Ford began its great postwar program of increasing productivity — hiring in, for example, management engineers who had straightened out GM's wage and salary structure in

1940–41 and would go on to perform the same task for Chrysler in 1956–57. Unofficial strikes evaporated, though a great pressure of resentment was in fact building up — to explode, ineffectively, in the form of the company-wide 1949 "Speedup Strike." Ford Industrial Relations Department (Labor Relations Section) had registered one GM-style postwar victory. It went on to record several more, finding collective bargaining to be a "flexible and useful instrument" which "makes it possible for us to handle many of our labor-management problems on a mature basis, and without strife."[41]

The 1945–46 negotiations set the pattern for those that followed.

> We prepared for the negotiations with great care. We spent nearly a month in the preparation of our basic data — . . . the very meat and sinew of modern collective bargaining. We could not have conducted responsible negotiations without it.
>
> The men who represented the company, moreover, were not selected merely for their skill as negotiators. They were experts in various aspects of company operations.[42]

Ford held to this strategy of detailed preparation, of "businesslike" collective bargaining, and of treating the negotiations as a "two-way street" along which company and union proceeded from different ends, seeking contractual improvements and making "fair and valid concessions" in return.[43]

In the 1947 negotiations, Ford showed how this favor-trading could work. It continued its union shop agreement for twelve months by signing the contract just before Taft-Hartley took effect, and it was ready to abandon its right under the Act to sue the union for breach of contract in the event of unofficial strikes. The second concession was conditioned on the UAW's good behavior: it operated only when the union had neither inspired nor authorized the strike, had promptly and publicly denounced it, and had done its best to prevent or end it. Ford's realistic management knew that, in return for not using one of Taft-Hartley's least worthwhile provisions, it could secure the union's cooperation or acquiescence in imposing a stricter and more effective control over dissident groups in the workforce.[44]

The UAW did not immediately agree, but Ford still waived its right to sue for one year to allow time for negotiations to secure the company's objective and give the union freedom from legal liability. During this period, the UAW lived up to the spirit of this bootlegal arrangement. Ford was able to dislodge and destroy the Foremen's Association of America chapters in its plants even before the FAA lost its legal protection under the expiring Wagner Act, in part because the UAW gave the foremen no help, and kept on working. The FAA was defenseless once denied the solidarity which had been common during the war. The FAA's destruction removed another obstacle to Ford's program for the recovery of workplace control. The company began to take action to answer foremen's long-standing complaints, even offering FAA president Carl Brown a position in the new Management Relations Section of the Industrial Relations Department. Unilateral management action would be an alternative to independent unionism for supervisors, who could be developed into loyal instruments for more effective labor control.[45]

Ford used all of GM's bargaining stratagems — massive preparation, counterproposals, appeals to union members over the heads of their officials, carefully timed press releases — and, in addition, was ready to make concessions to the UAW. It was not uncommon for firms to practically abandon their legal right to sue unions under the Taft-Hartley Act (International Harvester, for example, did so). But Ford was remarkably open in its use of this particular bargaining counter to secure greater union "responsibility." Ford workers became rebellious under this regime, and their local union leadership was a thorn in Reuther's side. They asked for the extension of formal job control at each negotiating session, but all they received were higher money wages and, in 1949, a pension plan, according to the pattern.[46]

By 1946–48, the pattern of postwar contractual relations at Ford had been set. Formal job rights were fixed by agreement at a level which represented a retreat from wartime achievements. Actual practice was even more restrictive in a situation where production pressures were no longer so acute, unemployment was creeping up, and management resistance was more determined. This picture holds true for other large industrial firms, but Ford's program for the recovery of control was notably successful. It had seen its productivity fall by over 34 percent in wartime: as a result of its postwar efforts, the figure was restored to roughly 15 percent less than GM, with Chrysler, under its unreconstructed management, as far behind again. As well as undertaking a sustained, considered counteroffensive in 1945–49, Ford became more like GM in its rhetoric and other personnel practices. Vice-president Bugas hammered away at the point that collective bargaining was not the answer to all industrial relations problems, and that the union leadership only imperfectly reflected the interests and opinions of the rank-and-file. And, with the assistance of the most liberal opinion pollster, *Fortune*'s Elmo Roper, the company began to look for employee grievances on its own initiative, with a view to remedying them.[47]

The strategy of Ford and GM became the model for other large corporations. It emphasized the need for managerial preparedness for bargaining. "It is an around-the-calendar job, just like engineering, purchasing, manufacturing, or any other phase of the automobile business." Contemporary practitioners and observers of labor relations had no doubts as to the effectiveness of their new techniques. In the war period, the lack of managerial skill and preparedness in this area had worried businessmen. The unions were the competition, and they had seemed to be ahead on points.[48] In the postwar years, Ford and GM led the way in showing how they could be beaten. In the long run, in bargaining relationships where outcomes depended on forensic skills, detailed preparatory investigation, plentiful factual evidence, and clear objectives, the scales were clearly weighted to favor business. In businesslike collective bargaining, management's superior resources of information, expertise, and economic muscle gave it a real advantage.

Ford's entire postwar program was designed to beat GM by imitating it. GM remained the prototype, and at the same time that Ford was toughening up its approach to industrial relations, GM was discarding some of its remaining antiunion inclinations, and building a remarkably efficient and civilized relationship with the UAW. The result of these two contrary movements was that, by 1950, GM's labor relations practice was still more sophisticated than Ford's, even though Ford management's rhetoric was more liberal.

After the 1945–46 debacle, GM workers were not about to be the guinea pigs in any subsequent bargaining round. As a result, GM was in the favorable position of not having to expect a strike at each contract termination; the pressure was off. GM was consequently even freer than Ford to design a contract according to its wishes. The noneconomic provisions were about right: all that was necessary was to further stabilize relations with the UAW.

GM was already extremely well prepared for the labor relations job *technically*, but the experience of the big strike persuaded the corporation to adopt a less aggressive tone and posture in its relations with unions. GM's bitter and extreme propaganda during the strike had won it few friends. The corporation, embarrassingly massive and profitable, wanted less risky public exposure in future than convulsive industrial confrontations had given it in the past decade. GM learned that, as realists advised, conservative and individualist principles were out of place at the bargaining table. The two negotiators most wedded to such principles were therefore shunted into staff positions where they did not come into direct contact with unions: Stephen Du Brul and Harry Coen, who had been openly antagonistic toward Reuther, were confined to putting together the wage packages GM would use in its bargaining coups of 1948–50, and to the vice-presidency of a new Employee Relations department which had no responsibility for collective bargaining. Future negotiations were conducted by the very capable Harry Anderson and Lou Seaton, men with a background in the law and marketing. GM's decision, consistent with the conventional wisdom of realism, assumed that such men were likely to be more flexible and smooth in negotiations than those who had clawed their way up through line management and become used to getting things done by issuing orders rather than by persuasion.[49]

GM's preparation for collective bargaining was much more thorough than even the research-conscious UAW could match. This became increasingly important as negotiations came to center on such complex issues as those involved in setting up and administering health-and-welfare funds. GM knew what it wanted, knew what had happened under the old contract and how it had worked out on the shop floor, and was easily able to shrug off repeated union demands for contract changes to extend "job rights." Such rights were now fixed; where there was slight movement, it was in GM's favor.

What GM did, in 1948 and again in 1950, was to buy out possible UAW resistance to its refusal to bargain about job rights by being relatively generous with wage increases and better fringe benefits. Since 1941, GM had been looking for a way to stabilize labor relations and labor costs for more than one year at a time, and to find a rational, factual basis for any adjustments. In the 1948 and 1950 agreements, by taking the initiative and getting the UAW to negotiate on — actually, to accept — its proposals, it secured this objective.

GM offered more than the pattern of wage and fringe-benefit settlements in other firms and industries, and added its own unique features: wages were tied to the Bureau of Labor Statistics cost of living index, and an annual "Improvement Factor" of 2 percent in 1948 (4 percent in 1950) for anticipated productivity rises was built into the contract. GM workers were put on an elevator which was much more ready to move up than down, while GM secured a measure of downward flexibility in its labor costs — useful in the 1948–49 recession. More important, it won the union's endorsement of management efforts to raise productivity; and the long-term goal of stability and predictability in labor relations was brought closer. The 1948 contract ran for two years, without a "wage reopening" clause; the 1950 contract, incorporating the most generous fringe benefits in American industry, ran for an unprecedented five-year term. GM won recognition for the sophistication of its labor relations program, as well as some condemnation from other industrialists for selling the pass on fringe benefits and inflationary wage increases — quite a change from 1945–46.[50]

GM's contractual labor relations were stabilized by the declining frequency of rebargaining, the growing inflexibility of the contract, and the increased "responsibility" of the UAW, once the Reuther caucus had defeated its Communist and rank-and-file radical opponents. GM was very satisfied with the extent of control it retained in all important areas, but, after the 1948 negotiations, determined to aim for even better labor relations in the future—to make achievement in this area dynamic, as in other fields of a technically progressive corporation's activities. GM aimed to do a good labor relations job between negotiations. In line with its basic policy of "tough but fair," it would try to settle legitimate grievances and even take the initiative to remove sources of discontent. This program, and the growing "maturity" of the UAW, meant that labor relations lost its status as a crisis area in the eyes of GM's top policymakers. Good relations became routine.

From 1948 through to the current negotiations, the union . . . did a remarkable job of administering the contract that we had. When a fire would start they would put it out, and if they thought we were wrong they would come to us and say, "We think you are a little wrong and get into it yourself," which we did on a number of occasions. The experience through the period from 1948 to 1950 was very, very good. On the basis of this performance, we were satisfied that if we could put a five-year agreement across, which was something new, something unheard of, it would be the right thing to do.[51]

The fire had gone out of GM's antiunionism. It was still unwilling to allow the area of joint regulation to expand, but reactionary inclinations no longer impeded its pursuit of a "realistic" course. GM even laid aside its traditional commitment to the "right to work," and gave some help to the Reuther administration in keeping members attached to the union now that it could no longer deliver "annual dividends" in the shape of contract improvements. In 1948, GM held the UAW to the checkoff agreement conceded in 1946, refused to allow it immunity from Taft-Hartley lawsuits, and resisted its request for NLRB union-shop elections to be held on company property—the only way, GM and the UAW calculated, that the union could win. By 1950, GM saw some merit in the union's contention that it deserved a reward for its good behavior, and the one remaining problem in the UAW-GM relationship was removed by allowing the union-shop election procedure to take its course.[52]

The 1946 UAW-Ford contract and the 1950 "Treaty of Detroit" have a significance reaching far beyond two large companies and their half million employees. Ford is remarkable for the extent of the improvement in its managerial policy and performance; GM, for the consolidation of its already strong position. But they were not alone in the kinds of policies they pursued. Negotiation of company security and management's rights clauses in the postwar bargaining rounds was common, and other elements in the GM and Ford strategies can also be seen in the performance of other large companies in similar heavy manufacturing industries. In the electrical equipment industry, for example, there were strikes at both General Electric and Westinghouse Electric in 1946, when both were imitating GM and Ford in trying to recover lost ground. Westinghouse endured a long strike, but succeeded in laying the contractual basis for tightening up a demoralized incentive system, won protected seniority rights for supervisors upgraded during the war who might have to be sent back to the ranks in future, got the union to agree to pay one-half the cost of the time stewards and committeemen spent in grievance handling, and modified the union shop agreement to allow an annual "escape period" of one week. Like GM, the company made a large investment in a costly strike, but reaped immediate benefits in increased productivity, and had "clarified" its union-management relations for the longer term.[53]

General Electric's experience was rather different. GE was anxious about its relations with a Communist-controlled union turning toward militancy after wartime collaboration, and was concerned about labor cost and productivity levels. It tried to eliminate the maintenance-of-membership clause from its contract, and to get the union to agree not to oppose any steps management might take to improve worker discipline and efficiency. In a strike of exceptional bitterness and, for 1946, violence, GE won nothing and was forced to match the wage increase negotiated between the United Electrical Workers and GM. After this shocking defeat, GE began a total rethink of its labor relations policies which, since the late 1930s, had been based upon a thorough acceptance of unionism. The union had failed to meet its side of the bargain.[54]

The same pattern of management counterattack can be observed in the farm equipment industry. All of the large firms were fundamentally antiunion, but they operated within the law to weaken union power. International Harvester, J. I. Case, and Allis-Chalmers all took long strikes. International Harvester wanted to end maintenance-of-membership, halve the payments to stewards for time consumed in grievance handling, and restrict the power of the arbitrator. At the cost of a three-month strike it won its first and third objectives. The farm equipment industry's "acceptance" of collective bargaining was minimal.[55]

Probably because of having to deal with a more compliant union, the basic steel industry was more fortunate than the automotive, electrical equipment, or farm equipment firms in winning the common objective of minimal contractual restraint on management without much of an argument. The pattern-setting Steelworkers/Carnegie-Illinois contract

of 1946 provided for union cooperation, or at least official acquiescence, in the attainment of management goals:

It is the intent of the parties to secure and sustain maximum productivity per
employee during the term of the . . . Agreement. . . . In return to the Company for the wage increase herein provided and consistent with the principle of a
fair day's work for a fair day's pay, the Union re-emphasizes its agreement with
the objective of achieving the highest level of employee performance and efficiency consistent with safety, good health, and sustained effort, and agrees that
the Union, its agents and its members will not take, authorize, or condone any
action which interferes with the attainment of such objective.

The Union agrees that during the term of the . . . Agreement . . . neither the
union nor its agents, nor its members will authorize, instigate, aid, condone, or
engage in a work stoppage or strike.[56]

The union had bound itself to an ironclad no-strike clause, and to a
rather less watertight statement of cooperative intent. The union lived
up to its promise, collaborating with management to complete the joint
study of the industry's chaotic wage structure which the NWLB had ordered and to implement its proposals for rationalization. In 1947, Big
Steel and the union made further progress toward mutual accommodation on terms perfectly acceptable to management, agreeing that the
aim of their relationship was "to promote orderly and peaceful relations
with the employees . . . and to achieve the highest level of employee
performance . . . ; Company and union encourage the highest possible
degree of friendly, cooperative relationships between their respective
representatives at all levels." The cosy arrangements between two centralized bureaucracies were cemented into place. Thereafter, contract
language was stabilized. Steel industry labor relations were not without
bitterness, but until the big strike of 1959–60 the issues of conflict at the
national level did not include workplace order and control.[57]

Postwar bargaining rounds in several key industries show certain
common features in the policies managements pursued and the results
they achieved. Formal labor relations were stabilized, partly as a consequence of management's considered counteroffensive. But there were
other factors involved. Some companies used the political bargaining
power Taft-Hartley gave them in order to persuade unions to behave
more "responsibly"; others exploited the Act in their continuing struggles against labor militancy, sometimes with official union support.
Allis-Chalmers, for example, had Walter Reuther's assistance in 1947
when it finally rid itself of the Communist leadership of UAW Local 248
at its West Allis plant. International Harvester used the "employer's free
speech" provision and the UAW's willingness to raid unprotected Farm
Equipment Workers' locals for membership, in the hope that ridding

the company of Communist labor agitators would bring industrial peace. The electrical industry used similar tactics, and the net effect on the labor movement was certainly debilitating. But it is worth noting that even such hard-nosed firms no longer aimed to break the law in the interests of unilateral management control. Instead, they used it, and were even prepared to collaborate with the "right kind" of labor leadership too.[58]

THE MODERN LABOR RELATIONS SYSTEM TAKES SHAPE

By 1950, large corporations like GM, Ford, U.S. Steel, and Westinghouse Electric had all, in their different ways, accepted the permanency of some limited role for responsible unionism within their enterprises. They were ready to use many of the same tactics to get the stable and efficient labor relations they desired. "Realism," the strategy of these center firms, was not the only strategy on offer for dealing with and incorporating labor unions within the corporate economy, but it was the most important. Antiunionism of the old sort was banished to the industrializing fringes of the South and West, though it occasionally showed up in small to middling northern firms with authoritarian managements located outside of the great industrial centers. The progressive strategy of union-management accommodation attracted more academic attention than it won managerial followers. In those firms where it was adopted, it showed less staying power and adaptability than the realistic approach. Its limited and temporary successes depended on circumstances which could not be found in large, multiplant companies, and also on the extraordinary prosperity of the long postwar boom. Brief recessions in 1948–49 and after the Korean War did not show up the weaknesses in some of the most notable progressive firms. The more serious economic slowdown of the late 1950s revealed that working harmony had often been bought at a price, in terms of management concessions, that could not be sustained. Realistic firms kept control over their workforces throughout, and did not have to go in for agonizing reappraisals like Studebaker's.[59]

The triumph of realism was not complete, even in large manufacturing firms, by the end of the 1940s. Chrysler, for example, was still willing to embark on a three-month strike in 1950 to resist the UAW's demand for a pension and welfare program without even rudimentary actuarial information. It had not balanced the costs of concession and resistance, and had clearly miscalculated its own bargaining power and the depth of the UAW's determination. Chrysler still had no in-house labor relations department. But such ineptitude was increasingly rare amongst large corporations.[60]

The period of contract development in American labor relations was largely completed by the end of the 1940s. But fixing contract language is one thing; stabilizing the pattern of informal and day-to-day relations between workers and supervisors, management and union representatives, quite another. Substantial areas of American manufacturing industry remained in which the kinds of job controls work-groups and local unions had developed in the war period continued well into the 1950s. The explanation for this is the same as that for the apparent success of some progressive experiments in formal union-management accommodation: namely, the long postwar boom. Production pressures and lax labor relations practices went along with one another. When economic stagnation and cost pressures hurt profit margins and corporate viability in the late 1950s, more firms adopted a thoroughly realistic strategy, opposing wildcat strikes effectively, defending management rights with determination, and raising discipline and output standards unilaterally. Market conditions thus affected the cosy relations between the basic steel industry and its union, as management's need to install new technologies and meet foreign competition led it to ask for an end to local unions' control over working conditions. The result was a massive strike, and political turmoil within the union.[61]

General Motors and Ford had led the way, but it took time and the pressure of the market to make the ground rules laid down in the 1940s more generally accepted and observed. By the late 1950s, it seemed to have been proved that realism alone offered a reliable and generally applicable way to maintain efficiency and order in a unionized plant. Summing up the findings of an investigation into labor relations practice in manufacturing industries, Robert Livernash identified four key elements in successful corporations' experience: first, management by policy, not purely reactive decision-making with no long-term objectives; second, "a high degree of management initiative in formulating and carrying out labor relations policies"; third, developing labor relations staffs and training managers and supervisors in day-to-day contract administration; and fourth, carrying out "a balanced policy of firmness and fairness." Other researchers reached the same conclusions, and discovered that more and more companies had learned the same lessons.[62]

An overview of important trends in postwar labor-management relations suggests that challenges to business power and managerial authority which seemed so serious and threatening in the last years of the war and the early years of reconversion have been successfully put down. Union membership has been falling, as a proportion of the labor force, for a quarter-century. Formal job controls have been stabilized and even reduced, actual job control has ebbed way even more. Collective bargaining as a means for extending workers' participation in the decisions affecting their own lives, as the American way to industrial democracy, has failed to make significant progress. So should we conclude that the policies American businessmen pursued which looked toward these ends were actually responsible for the desirable outcomes which could already be seen by the end of the 1940s? They were not a sufficient cause. Perhaps they were not even necessary factors. But they certainly made an important contribution to the way things actually panned out.

Favorable circumstances were of the greatest importance. The general conservatism of the American political climate; the anti-Communist and antiradical ethos of Cold War America; and the general success and stability of the postwar economy, which allowed business to buy the acquiescence of the organized working class in the entrenchment of managerial control with job security, real wage increases, and fringe benefits, are clearly the basic explanations. In addition, the new-style business unionism of the CIO as it became "mature" and more like the AFL, even before the merger, lessened the possibility of any effective labor counterthrust. By and large, the system appeared to deliver much of what the members wanted. Union leaders in the 1950s were not subject to very great rank-and-file pressures, so they were free to build the centralized, "apolitical" bureaucracies needed to conduct businesslike labor relations. They could discipline workers and discourage local union militancy, where outbreaks of it occurred. American business was blessed with responsible, and responsive, bargaining partners. It had helped shape the environment in which they operated, but the forces making American trade unions the distinctive institutions they are were much larger, some of them as old as American industrial society.[63]

Nevertheless, what business did to meet the challenge of labor in the postwar years certainly added up to a well-considered exploitation of favorable circumstances, some of which business had also helped to make. Competent handling of labor relations problems, combined with a thoughtful and aggressive bargaining strategy, made the best use of these opportunities. American management did not wait until it had the advantage to develop this approach. It was one large element in the immediate response business made to the rise of labor in the late 1930s. At first it had to contend with serious rivals — continuing antiunionism and "progressive" union-management accommodation. But, in time, it carried all before it, with middle-sized firms coming to follow the lead large firms had given.

Realism has been a dynamic and adaptable approach to the containment of labor power and the defense of managerial authority in principle and practice. But labor has had another avenue, political action, toward influence over working conditions. It has been useful. Objectives which collective bargaining could not secure — particularly for the unorganized majority of the working class — have been won, infringing directly on management's power and increasing costs. Pension fund reform and regulation, and health and safety controls, are notable examples. So business has had to play the same game, resisting prolabor legislation (recently through its own "political action committees") and seeking to increase state and federal controls over the unions. The 1959 Landrum-Griffin Act and the "Right to Work" movement at state level witness to its influence. Clearly, realistic collective bargaining has not been the whole answer to the labor problem for American management in the last three decades. It has used many other devices which can only be mentioned here — installing new technologies which have the added benefit of weakening or eliminating strongly unionized, strategically located work-groups; decentralizing production facilities into lower-wage, union-free sunbelt states with their right to work laws and anti-union local culture; diversifying, by investment or merger, into a range of disconnected industries whose workers have no bargaining alliances; exporting technology and establishing overseas operations and profit centers. All of these techniques have helped to reduce the vulnerability of large firms to direct union pressure which was such a feature of the 1930s and 1940s. Ford, with most of its activities concentrated in one industry, on one huge site, was only an extreme case.[64]

One company which has made skillful use of the above techniques is General Electric. After the debacle of the 1946 strike, it went to war against the Communist-controlled United Electrical Workers. Under a new vice-president, Lemuel Boulware, it embarked on a successful campaign to divide and undermine its unionized workforce. The corporation became stridently anti-Communist, and used the Taft-Hartley law, churchmen, rightist labor leaders, Cold War liberal Democrats, and McCarthy himself — the man, not just the ism — to help it smash the UE. Boulware made many practical and rhetorical attacks on the strength and the very legitimacy of unionism. GE's tone and posture harked back to an earlier and cruder age of industrial conflict, but its collective bargaining tactics were bang up-to-date. It used all of the stratagems which had served Ford and GM so well in their postwar struggles for managerial control, and gave them its own particular emphases. It showed the hardest face of managerial realism in its determination to confine unionism to the declining blue-collar labor force in traditional industrial districts, to weaken and dominate the blue-collar unions it tolerated, and to get rid of them altogether where it lawfully could.

GE also showed the technical resourcefulness of conservative management by its use of all of the tactics of personnel administration and advertising or "public relations" in order to support its new labor relations program. GE had been "progressive" in its employment of those same techniques since the 1920s. But until 1946 it used them to support a relatively liberal, "enlightened" industrial relations policy. After 1946 it developed them further, and applied them more intensively, to make important contributions to the lethal cocktail it served up to the weak and divided unions of its workers. GE was certainly the most notorious, and possibly the most thorough and single-minded, among business exponents of the manifold skills and tricks needed to keep workers contented with their lot, and out of unions.[65]

General Electric, under Lemuel Boulware, showed what could be done to support a conservative management's determination to preserve and retain the greatest possible degree of unilateral control over its employees. But the techniques of personnel administration, in particular, found a place in companies whose political outlook and labor relations strategy were much more liberal. Personnel administration was versatile. It became an important, integral part of American business' approach to industrial relations problems in the 1930s and '40s. Boulware's tactics of using the mass media and other machinery of persuasion to try to win employee and public support for management's objectives and authority were also adopted by many other large business firms at the same time.

6

Beyond Collective Bargaining

During the first third of the twentieth century, American business had developed and used a variety of sophisticated means to achieve its connected objectives — maximum influence and effective control over the workforce, in and outside of the workplace, and maximum prestige and power for business men and institutions in society at large. Progressive firms were the originators of this approach, which did not depend on the crude use of employers' economic power. It attempted to build islands of benevolent rationalization in the midst of social upheaval.[1]

Changes in public policy, and the rise of strong unions, represented an important defeat for this strategy during the 1930s. But that defeat was neither total nor permanent. Admittedly, most company unions disappeared, and it was often impossible to keep production and maintenance workers from unionization. But there were many tools left in the progressives' cupboard, and it was not difficult to adapt them to the needs of the new world of Big Labor and Big Government. The objective of progressive man-management — the building of efficient factory communities free of conflict and friction — naturally remained attractive to businessmen. And the presence of unprecedentedly strong centers of opposition to management's power and moral authority provided new incentives for the adoption of progressive techniques. They promised to control the behavior and influence the attitudes of workers, manipulating them until they conformed with management's stereotype of the ideal employee: efficient, disciplined, willing, cheerfully obedient, and loyal.

The techniques and the experience of managerial progressives were well suited to more thorough application, in modified forms, by corpo-

159

rations trying to keep all or part of their workforces nonunion by legal methods, to undermine the labor movement's following among its members, or to achieve less troublesome relations with unionized workers. Progressive man-management in the 1940s and after was not necessarily a flank attack on unionism, but very frequently it did amount to an attempt to thwart the growth of pluralistic power-relations in industry. And that attempt has often been successful, with the result that "where management acts in faithful performance of its responsibilities in handling grievances, in promoting extracurricular employee activities, and where more than a majority hold an implicit faith in the idea that their management and directors have their best interests at heart. . . . there is unity of purpose and teamwork in the attainment of progress toward the company's objectives."[2]

In much of personnel work, we can see clear traces of the implications of management's unitary ideology and theories of worker motivation for business policy and business action. By and large, businessmen were still quite free to take unilateral action in the personnel field. And they were not forced to compromise their principles in response to the pressure of awkward, resistant realities to the same extent as in the area of labor relations. This style and method of man-management is of more than intellectual interest to the business historian. To some extent, it seems to have worked — in combination with other elements in management's control system, it has made it easier to get workers to do what is required of them, to mobilize and order the human resources of the large modern corporation.

HUMAN ENGINEERING AND THE PERSONNEL SPECIALISTS

Personnel administration, as the term is commonly understood, began with World War I. It grew out of the recruiting, training, and payment of vast masses of new workers in the war-production effort. . . . [E]verything we know about Personnel Administration was known in the early twenties, everything we practise was practised then. There have been refinements, but little else.[3]

Much of the outlook, and most of the techniques, of "scientific" personnel administration developed independently of the need to combat labor unions. They were aspects of the growing rationalism of the modern industrial bureaucracy. Changes in the technology and organization of production, increases in the size of workforces, and a mechanistic attitude toward problems of social organization exemplified by the scientific management movement, combined to encourage the more systematic use of human resources within the firm. The expanding corporations of the early twentieth century tried to gain control over their complex internal operations as well as over their markets. Systematic personnel management was born in that period, and was a part of that organizing process. Its approach to the management of men was attractive partly because it fitted well into a developing philosophy of industrial administration.[4]

"[M]anagement must set up objective measures of everything that can be measured and supplement this (sic) with semi-objective ratings of those items for which there are not as yet reliable yardsticks." "[T]he proper approach . . . to the satisfactory solution of problems in industrial relations should be as scientific as the approach to problems in sales, production, corporate finance, or in the development and marketing of a new product."[5]

Personnel administration really had three parent disciplines: organizational design, employment management, and industrial psychology. Their particular contributions blended well, offering senior management an integrated way to improve their control over their subordinates' actions and to influence attitudes as well as behavior.

In the area of organizational design and development, personnel men introduced a collection of administrative procedures to improve managerial control and information systems in large and complex firms. They developed and published written personnel policies, and then established machinery for their implementation and reporting systems to check up on actual practice. Personnel staffs were involved in research inside and outside their own firms to put more useful information about best and actual practice at the disposal of top management. Their overall objective was to make the firm a perfect hierarchical system of functions and functionaries, which would minimize the common problems of overlapping areas of responsibility and imperfect compliance with orders on the part of subordinates. Personnel specialists were wedded to a military concept of business organization, in which they would occupy a valuable and valued staff role. They had a vision of the ideal corporation as a perfectly engineered social mechanism, and of themselves as its respected chief engineers. In practice, their chief activities were the diligent production of organization charts and job descriptions covering ever larger proportions of the workforce, and the setting of standard rules to govern decisions about the employment of masses of low-status blue- and white-collar employees.[6]

Employment management was the everyday work of personnel men. It was a collection of techniques tied together by the desire to systematize and centralize control over the workforce. Personnel men believed that rules of their own making should determine how workers were to be hired, placed at jobs, trained, promoted, paid, disciplined, and fired. Proper wage and salary administration should guarantee efficient and equitable payment for carefully classified jobs, and minimize sources of friction in the employment relationship. Arbitrary and uncoordinated decisions affecting these matters made by line management and supervisors could be limited by giving personnel men power over them, and by setting up reporting systems and appeals machinery to further strengthen central control and uniform compliance.[7]

Employment management shared with scientific management a rather limited, mechanistic and economistic view of worker motivation. It believed that workers wanted little more than "fair" payment and predictable treatment according to standards rationally determined and uniformly applied by management and its staff specialists. Industrial psychology offered a rather more complex and rounded explanation of human needs and aspirations, and a variety of techniques to combine with systematic employment procedures in the realization of the ideal of the efficient, conflict-free workplace full of contented employees.[8]

Industrial psychologists recognized that every person had certain specific attributes. These could best be employed by placing him in the right job, giving him appropriate training, and promoting him in line with his capability. Testing of the individual could identify and select "square pegs"; scientific job design should already have created a variety of "square holes." Different aptitudes and the hierarchy of job opportunities in industry could therefore be matched perfectly, minimizing worker dissatisfaction and maximizing efficiency — both individual and organizational. In addition, industrial psychologists insisted that all individuals needed the recognition of others and the protection of *amour propre*. They had a right to expect and receive fair, respectful treatment. People were not all equally capable or ambitious, but they all wanted to progress as far as their abilities could carry them, and they needed the sense of personal security and dignity which arbitrary treatment destroyed.[9]

Industrial psychology's view of human needs and abilities was based in primitive behavioral science, and supported by a set of normative principles. The scientific element was mostly European in origin, but the values were all-American, and in the mainstream of the American cult of democratic opportunity. Industrial psychologists believed that workers carried their expectations of equal rights and individual achievement into working life, where they had to seek most of life's necessary satisfactions. The difficulty was that American workers had to pursue happiness, their birthright, in new and unfamiliar surround-

ings. They could look forward to working lives as dependent subordinates in large, impersonal, and generally authoritarian organizations.
But progressive management could satisfy the desires of the mass of employed Americans, and turn them into efficient workers and contented
citizens, by treating them at work as industrial psychologists recommended. It could fight alienation, preserve the American Dream, and
protect middle-class values against the consequences of widespread
proletarianization.

As well as scientific placement of employees, industrial psychology's
most important practical contribution was a new style of man-
management. The worker's contacts with the organization should be
softened and humanized. Crude authoritarianism should be abandoned, and replaced by smooth manipulation and persuasion. All-
American salesmanship should be applied to industry: hiring and firing
should be courteously done; supervisors should lead their men to do
what they wanted by instruction and example, rather than rely on pe-
remptory orders, issued without ceremony or explanation, and backed
up by the real threat of harsh discipline. Discipline itself should be
treated as a branch of adult education in the reasonableness of following rules. Industrial psychology could even be taken to require the
adoption of a consultative or participative managerial style, as the most
efficient because the most in line with American mores and workers'
expectations.[10]

Personnel administration developed its techniques and its ethos in the
1920s, and these persisted throughout the period under consideration,
with remarkably little change. But personnel men found it easier to
preach and write about how useful they could be, and how important
they should be, than actually to win authority and status. They were
hard-pressed to find employment and influence outside of large and
progressive firms. They met powerful resistance from line managers
and foremen, who thought they imposed unconscionable restrictions on
supervisory control over the rank-and-file. And many top managements
were apparently convinced that personnel work was a frill, an overhead
cost producing few discernible benefits, something to be sacrificed in a
recession. So even where personnel men managed to get a foot in the
door, they often found themselves out in the cold again after a short and
unhappy trial period.[11]

However, in the 1930s and 1940s personnel men finally made an entrance into most medium- and large-scale firms, not so much because of
their own efforts and arguments as because of a change in the business
community's operating environment. Personnel men proved useful in
meeting the industrial relations problems of the time. Their established

techniques were more extensively applied — there were few important innovations.

The social legislation of 1935 and after multiplied the openings for personnel men by creating a need for more systematic employment procedures and higher standards of record-keeping in all but the smallest firms. The Social Security and Wage-and-Hour Administrations spewed forth regulations, forms, and requests for data. The NLRB imposed its own demands: to prove that union members had not been discriminated against in hiring, placement, promotion, discipline, layoff, or recall, a company had to have definite rules, uniformly implemented, with the results centrally recorded. Bargaining with a union had the same effect: seniority systems, grievance procedures, and contract negotiations required expertise in their administration, produced new demands for data and record-keeping, and strengthened the inexorable tendency toward centralization of control of the employment relationship in a particular staff department. The further elaboration of formal rules governing man-management strengthened the hand of the personnel staff as against line managers and supervisors.[12]

Personnel departments lived in an atmosphere of crisis throughout the later 1930s, searching for men and methods to handle manifold new problems and, hopefully, to forestall unionism. Coordination and consolidation of the new activities had to wait: personnel work was a matter of "fire fighting," meeting immediate problems rather than planning for the long term. Then came the war, bringing new difficulties for established personnel departments and stimulating the creation of others.

Personnel departments and other similar fringe activities met less resistance from cost-conscious policymakers when overheads were relatively unimportant, during a period when gross profits and corporation taxes were both high. And personnel men promised to help solve that pressing problem of war industry — getting and keeping workers. War agencies further increased the unavoidable administrative burdens on employers: records had to be kept for the purposes of the draft, the War Manpower Commission's labor stabilization controls, the Office of Price Administration's rationing schemes, pay-as-you-go taxation, and enforced savings programs. NWLB orders compelled companies to systematize their job classifications and wage schedules, and brought other innovations requiring the accumulation of specific data on each employee. Checkoff of union dues, maintenance of membership, and the voluntary or bargained extension of fringe benefits all increased the complexity of record-keeping and personnel administration.[13]

Outside agencies' requirements encouraged personnel departments' natural tendency to systematize and centralize control over the employment function. The need to maximize manpower utilization in a tight labor market had the same effect. New sources of labor were developed — women, minority groups, the disabled, the very old and the very young were recruited, placed at redesigned jobs where their skills could best be used, and trained. Once new or nonmarginal (adult white male) workers had been hired, they had to be kept at work. Absenteeism and turnover were the key problems, and personnel men set about tackling them. Car pools were organized to solve transport difficulties; services were provided within the plant to dissuade workers from taking time off. In-plant catering expanded enormously, as did childcare services and even assistance with shopping for women workers. Counseling also experienced an upsurge of popularity, as firms realized that their workers' morale and effectiveness were impaired by factors outside the plant as well as within it. Much of the assistance given was practical — help and advice on housing, legal, financial, and family problems in the disturbed conditions of war-boom communities with many single-parent families. The more problematic side of counseling aimed at adjusting workers to their work situation by giving them a chance to talk through their problems, and perhaps have them solved.[14]

Personnel departments were also responsible for the less direct means companies used to relieve the tensions of continuous maximum production and increase worker morale — music while you work, recreation and entertainment programs, and the in-plant broadcasting of pep talks. They also supervised War Production Drive committees and the other media — films, house magazines, posters — that firms used in an attempt to turn patriotism into productivity.[15]

New personnel departments, like many of the plants possessing them, were often "war babies"; and after the war was over some of them expired, and the others changed the emphasis of their activities. Labor-supply difficulties eased. Pressures within industry for all staff departments to make direct, measurable contributions to cost-reduction and the improvement of productivity increased. Once again, personnel departments had to prove their usefulness and justify their share of the corporate budget. Marginal, morale-boosting programs and employee services were trimmed or eliminated altogether. In the more questioning, economistic climate of management decision-making in the late 1940s, personnel specialists returned to the argument for their own value which they had long stressed, emphasizing the contributions effective handling of human resources could make to productivity and profitability.[16]

In a slacker labor market, there was more opportunity for personnel specialists to use selection and placement tests. Testing would help management build an efficient, well-adjusted workforce, weeding out less serviceable employees. This could be done by screening job-seekers before they were hired, or by examining new employees before the end of the probationary period, after which they acquired seniority rights and job tenure conditional on good behavior under standard union contract terms. Test criteria included readiness to obey orders and follow rules as well as ability to perform the job. GM's Delco-Remy division even began to experiment with straight attitude tests, aiming to build a domesticated workforce in the atmosphere of industrial and ideological conflict after the war. Basic political beliefs and social values were plumbed, alongside matters of more obvious relevance to an employer — attitudes toward the necessity and value of work; toward supervision and authority; toward the company and its property; toward quantity and quality of output; toward membership in a work-team; and toward acceptance of "necessary changes."[17]

But most personnel work was more directly concerned with keeping labor cost and productivity under systematic control. Job analysis and evaluation were increasingly used. They built sound, defensible rate structures, thwarting unions' exploitation of inequities to promote wage drift, and minimizing employee discontent over relative pay. Merit rating was similarly employed to restrict the influence of unions and workgroups over corporate manpower management, by determining whether or not employees were suited to the jobs to which their seniority otherwise entitled them. Supervisors were forced to follow standard rating procedures and were less likely to make arbitrary decisions which were vulnerable to criticism and alteration via the grievance system. And management regained some flexibility in making decisions on manpower allocation, as plausible, quasi-objective standards were used to discriminate between two or more employees of comparable seniority, selecting the one most acceptable to management for preferment.[18]

Personnel administration therefore helped limit union incursions along the frontier of everyday job control, complementing the work of labor relations staffs in bargaining, enforcing the contract, and adjusting grievances. It also offered a solution to the worrying problems of supervisory dissatisfaction and union-consciousness. Its analysis of the reasons for "low morale" among foremen agreed with the bargaining objectives of their unions and the evidence of attitude surveys: foremen were concerned about the insecurity of their employment, the decline in direct and indirect pay relative to the rank-and-file, wage inequities within the supervisory group, and the uncertain scope of their authority and responsibilities. As an alternative to collective bargaining, far-sighted managements went beyond the simple step of reestablishing, and then determinedly maintaining, supervisors' differentials over their subordinates. In addition, they gave supervisors the benefits of progressive personnel administration. Foremen were provided with formal or informal appeal procedures against arbitrary decisions (particularly discharge) made by their own bosses. Seniority was given some weight, with "ability and merit," in matters of job tenure and promotion. Supervisory jobs were analyzed, and fair or rational payment systems established. All of this was intended to enable the foreman to function more effectively, and to give him some assurance of equitable treatment and protection against his immediate superiors in line management.[19]

White-collar employees were restive in the 1930s and 1940s for reasons similar to those of mass-production supervisors. Here too, preemptive personnel work could remove grievances at source, and assist managements determined to resist the spread of unionism, if possible by legal means. For example, the autonomous Society of Designing Engineers— later incorporated into the UAW—won its first and most important beachhead at Chrysler, in December 1941, as a result of managerial ineptness, and without significant opposition. Chrysler's mistakes included "a chaotic white-collar rate structure and job classification system. Merit increases were widely misused by supervisors. Favoritism, arbitrary promotions, demotions, and discharges, and salary 'secrecy' were prominent features of the white-collar worker's life."[20]

Wartime neglect by management, at a time of rank-and-file pressures and liberal NWLB orders on fringe benefits for them, compressed or even reversed traditional differentials. But here, just as with supervisors, well-managed companies moved quickly to guarantee fair, rational, and predictable conditions of employment. General Motors, for example, introduced a modified seniority system, a regular performance-review procedure, and a union-free grievance system, with appeal to higher stages of the management. Differentials were maintained by increasing white-collar pay and fringe benefits in tune with improvements in the basic UAW contract. After the war, managerial malpractice and favorable organizing opportunities for white-collar unions continued to go hand in hand: companies like GM and Ford, which used aggressive antiunion propaganda and other illegitimate pressure tactics as well as progressive personnel administration, were able to stay union-free.[21]

Personnel specialists found the most convincing arguments for the value of their services to management in their "successes" with supervisors, white-collar workers, or companies like Thompson Products, which managed to keep their rank-and-file employees nonunion in strongly organized industries and communities.[22] But personnel work was not necessarily antiunion. Its basic purpose was to increase higher management's effective control over the activities of employees, particularly those affecting productivity, costs, and overall efficiency. It promised to create a stable, contented, orderly, and hard-working labor force — something of obvious value in a period of continuing relatively high employment and production pressures, when serious industrial conflict was a recent memory and remained a real and present danger.

"Progressive" personnel administration at Eli Lilly and Co. (pharmaceuticals) or General Electric, after 1946, certainly was an updated, sophisticated antiunion device. But at Ford and General Motors, in their dealings with blue-collar workers, it was intended to take the fire of employee discontentment out from under responsible labor leadership. And at Johnson and Johnson, or Bigelow-Sanford Carpet Co., it was just part of a liberal management's program designed to achieve the maximum possible management-worker *and* employer-union harmony. Personnel men's techniques were flexible enough to have a place in companies pursuing altogether different courses in labor relations policy.[23] In any case, the practice of personnel administration inevitably increased as the growth of firms, the imposition of administrative burdens by the state, and the problems of control created by unionized workers all encouraged the more widespread adoption of what had been distinctively "progressive" in the 1920s.

The strategy of personnel administration depended on managerial action to solve its own problems within the firm. The firm was considered to be the essential unit of society. Work and workplace relations were taken to be the "central life interest" of most employed Americans. Management was constantly being advised to take the initiative to satisfy its subordinates' needs, or face the consequences — lowered morale and productivity, workers who abandoned their proper loyalties, more conflict and problems of control.[24]

This was also the outlook of advocates of corporate welfarism in the pre-New Deal era. Welfare capitalism and personnel administration were closely related, with common purposes and a similarly "unilateralist" method of action. Welfare capitalism also had to adapt itself to a new situation and new problems in the 1940s, when the state had assumed some of the functions of "progressive" firms' welfare programs, and collective bargaining limited the freedom of action of individual managements.

WELFARE CAPITALISM IN THE 1940s

Welfare capitalism was both a collection of practices, which were subject to change, and a philosophy of action, which was much more stable. Its aim was to attach individual workers to the corporate system by ties of self-interested "loyalty" and frank dependence. Traditional welfarism, developed in the 1890s–1900s, involved active managerial concern for the housing, education, religion, recreation, health, occupational safety, economic security, and even morality and "character" of workers and their families. By the 1920s, it had developed a hard, economic core: the systematic provision of accident, sickness, and retirement or death benefits. Profit-sharing or stock ownership programs were less common; guarantees of stability of income and employment least common of all, though efforts were made by individual firms like General Electric and some industrial communities like Rochester, N.Y. to soften the impact of layoffs by severance pay and unemployment insurance plans.[25]

Such programs had many defects. They only covered a minority of large and progressive firms, and did not include all of the latter's employees, or treat them all equally. Benefit levels were inadequate, and conditions were often very restrictive; benefits were firm-specific, not transferable, and entitlement could be lost, without appeal, in the event of layoff or disciplinary discharge—a powerful sanction against, for example, union activity. Worst of all, programs were not actuarially sound: benefits were only "guaranteed" as long as companies were willing to meet the cost. In consequence, they provided fragile defenses against the social costs of the Depression. In cost-cutting exercises, most were curtailed or scrapped.[26]

In the mid-1930s, with the return of some prosperity, and the need to compete with unions for the "loyalty" of employees, welfare plans enjoyed renewed corporate support. But at the same time the federal government and the states began to provide standard benefits, tax- or contribution-funded, on a much wider basis than the efforts of large and progressive corporations had achieved. And, in the 1940s, unions began to make serious encroachments upon what had once been management's undisputed territory. They wanted to be able to negotiate with management about the terms and operation of benefit programs. They aimed to limit management's freedom to improve fringe benefits without consulting union representatives—one of the employer's tactics in the "competition for leadership in a welfare economy." Union policy also resulted from the NWLB's encouragement of bargaining on fringe benefits as an alternative to direct wage increases, and from the needs of a security-conscious membership, facing uncertain postwar economic prospects. Costs of medical services and insurance were increasing; Social Security benefits stood still in inflationary times, and their coverage was even cut by economizing Congressmen.[27]

Accordingly, in the late 1940s unions tried to win liberalized, preferably employer-financed benefit programs, and a voice in determining and administering their provisions. Curiously enough, Taft-Hartley widened the trail the Steelworkers and UAW blazed toward managerial acceptance of the expansion of the scope of collective bargaining to cover welfare issues. The law had been intended to prevent the spread of union-dominated, employer-financed benefit plans of the kind the pioneering and aggressive Mine Workers had won. In fact, it was interpreted by the NLRB and the Supreme Court, in the precedent-setting *Inland Steel* case of 1949, as legitimizing more moderate union demands to be allowed to negotiate on benefit levels and terms.[28]

Labor's bargaining strategies affected the practice of corporate welfarism, and its political action on behalf of an enlarged welfare state threatened further to reduce the direct dependence of employee on employing firm — a basic theme in corporatist, managerial views of the proper organization of society. Unions were also ready to compete in the provision of the other services welfarist companies had traditionally provided: in the postwar years, "social unionism" of the UAW/needle trades variety, in particular, expanded the range of benefits available to members in the form of organized recreation and entertainments, adult education, legal, financial, and medical advice and assistance. Unions, as well as firms, tried to strengthen the ties which bound plant communities together.[29]

In the new world of the late 1940s, the practice of welfare capitalism was obviously much modified, and the scope for unilateral action much reduced — but not eliminated. For managements in nonunion plants, or in their dealings with supervisors and white-collar workers, the freedom to implement and administer welfare benefits was as great as ever. And of course, the incentive to do so was much larger than it had been in the 1920s, as unionization remained a real possibility. In addition, even bargained fringe benefits continued to serve many of the old purposes of stabilizing the employee population of the plant and increasing its attachment, if not to the work, then at least to the job. Reducing labor turnover of prime adult males, and increasing the seriousness of the threat of disciplinary discharge (which came to mean loss of accrued seniority and welfare entitlements), increased management's control over the workforce.[30]

Welfare capitalism often continued to have an explicitly antiunion purpose. American workers were thought to be rational, security-conscious, and self-interested individuals, taking collective action only if their management defaulted on its obligation of supplying them with the material and other benefits they wanted. The management which wanted its authority unchallenged had to deserve and win the compliance of its subordinates by its performance in satisfying their needs by remedial and preventive action within the corporate system. "Our people look to us first; only when we fail them do they look elsewhere."[31] This line of thinking pointed toward an attack on the legitimacy of, or the necessity for, unionism. Unions were considered to be a very imperfect way for workers to protest managerial action and pursue their own interests. They might be justified where the management was incompetent or inconsiderate. Otherwise, they only caused needless conflict and intruded into an essentially stable and naturally harmonious relationship. The way for a management to get the union-free, or at any rate peaceful, employment relations that it wanted was to take the initiative in finding out what workers wanted and then, if possible, give it to them. Management should identify and remove sources of potential conflict, and emphasize the community of interests and personal ties between superior and subordinate within the plant.[32]

So welfare capitalism had many other devices at its disposal as well as fringe benefits, however liberal. And the others were much less affected by unions and the state. The most important of them were the attitude survey and first-line supervisors, which were used to discover workers' grievances and, it was hoped, affect their opinions. Both of them ignored or circumvented any union that might be present; both were kept under close management control, and supplied the information it needed as a basis for effective remedial action.

The attitude survey, modeled on market research and public opinion polling techniques, had obvious advantages for the management which wanted to identify the sore points in its organization. Information was obtained which was neither filtered nor distorted — by union machinery *or* supervisory hierarchy. Respondents were guaranteed anonymity, and surveys were frequently conducted by outside agencies with an air of independence. Prominent among these were industrial relations specialists from respected universities, and consulting firms which made all the expertise of applied social science (particularly psychology) available to industry. The oldest firms of consultants, including J. David Houser and Associates and the Psychological Corporation, dated back to the 1920s, but most, including the Gallup, Roper, and Robinson (Opinion Research Corporation) organizations, were more recent.

The benefits to be expected from attitude surveys were twofold. In the first place, areas of managerial deficiency could be spotted. Morale in a particular department might be unusually low; workers could be shown to be dissatisfied with, or ill informed about, some particular phase of corporate personnel policy. Personnel men were able to find evidence—often alarming, always apparently conclusive—to help them convince higher management of the need to introduce progressive techniques to solve the problems that were revealed. Repeated surveys checked up on the success or failure of personnel programs after they had been introduced. Attitude surveying offered a plausible, "scientific" or at least semiobjective method for the concerned management to produce a "fever chart" of the soundness or otherwise of organizational morale, and to run "quality controls" on its personnel policies.[33]

Best practice, according to personnel specialists, included managerial willingness to alter policies or practices in response to revealed dissatisfaction or deficiencies. There had to be a change in workers' actual on-the-job experiences if they were to be convinced of management's good intentions. But there was another dividend to be reaped from the morale survey: the very act of taking one assured workers that "their" management was concerned about what they thought and felt. The mere opportunity of expressing an opinion might be therapeutic. The cathartic effect of talking through a grievance might be valuable, even if there was no change in managerial policy on the basis of information received.[34]

Attitude surveys were generally, and deliberately, impersonal. Use of production supervisors for similar purposes had a very different character, because it was intended to recreate the warm, friendly "human relations" which had supposedly existed between master and man in the lost Golden Age before the rise of mass-production industry. This was the strategy of "man to man on the job," designed to rebuild union-free relations between superior and subordinate in large-scale industry. It had been advocated since the First World War, and was still practiced by companies including General Electric, General Motors, General Foods, Thompson Products, Armstrong Cork, and American Rolling Mill in the 1940s, with white-collar and blue-collar workers alike.

The strategy aimed to create a parallel to, or a substitute for, the union's shopfloor organization of stewards and grievance committeemen. Supervisors were trained and encouraged to take a personal interest in their men's problems, to exercise authority in a nonabrasive manner ("how to reprimand a worker and make him like it"), to remove the causes of grievances, if possible, and to try to solve those that occurred by personal negotiation with the worker or workers involved. Supervisors were further supposed to act on their men's behalf, bringing problems with which they were unauthorized and incompetent to deal to the attention of higher management. The supervisor was supposed to turn into the accepted, not just the designated, leader of his work-group, manipulative in his style of interpersonal relations, building a "democratic," "participative," or at least "consultative" organizational climate at the grass roots. Management-oriented shopfloor solidarity would remove the need for unionism and solve many everyday problems.[35]

Undeniably, personnel administration gained itself a place in the sun during the 1930s and 1940s. In part, this was simply a function of the increasing administrative burden imposed by the state, and of the growing bureaucratization of large firms in general. The war, with its rapid — and usually not temporary — increases in the size of companies' labor forces, and its "cost-plus" accounting, also encouraged firms to expand the numbers of their staff members performing functions once considered to be of doubtful value and at best marginal to the central purposes of the enterprise. Since the war, most firms have not shed labor, most have experienced an unbroken period of prosperity and growth, the state has continued to impose yet more administrative burdens, and the habit of orderly management by policy in all areas of a company's operations has become firmly established. So many of the indices of the rising status and power of personnel administrators, to which they point, over and over again, with a mixture of pride and the desire for reassurance, have continued to point upwards — not, perhaps, as sharply as in the heady days of the 1930s and 1940s, but it has still been possible for the history of personnel administration's "growth as a profession" to be written in confident, Whiggish terms. More firms have established central personnel departments and developed written policies; more chief personnel officers have been granted vice-presidential rank and a place on the board; some have even become chief executives. Courses in personnel administration at universities have proliferated, textbooks been written, quasi-learned and practitioners' journals and boosterish "professional associations" founded. Personnel work, in short, has followed the same course towards institutionalization as some of the other fringe managerial specialities — notably public relations — to which it is indirectly related.

So, to a large extent, the history of personnel administration is just one, not unimportant, chapter in the larger account of the growth of firms and the "bureaucratization of practically everything" in twentieth-century and "post-industrial" America. But in examining its development and application in the 1930s and '40s, it is hard to avoid the conclusion that, for many firms which devoted increased energies to systematizing personnel policies and procedures at this time, this was just another way of bolstering up their power and authority against the threats posed by workers, unions, and the state. Of course, a part of the promise and the appeal of personnel administration and welfare capitalism had always been that they represented an alternative, softer, more manipulative approach to problems of everyday man-management and improving the long-run security and legitimacy of corporate enterprise — a more acceptable, durable, and successful way to achieve the same ends of efficiency, order, and social stability than was offered by authoritarian and coercive control techniques alone. But in the post-New Deal era, the personnel men's rationale became more generally persuasive: it finally seemed as if they *did* possess worthwhile skills, as if they *could* help management with intractable and unavoidable industrial relations problems, and even begin to rebuild "harmony" from the shop floor upwards.

It is impossible to be certain about the importance and relative contribution of developments in the fields of personnel administration and welfare capitalism to the restoration of managerial authority in postwar America, within the employment relationship and in the larger society. Probably one must discount personnel men's larger claims, and conclude that their chief impact was on the improvement of everyday man-management: reducing supervisors' arbitrary power, introducing and applying rules of "fairness" and regularity into the making of decisions affecting employees' working life, encouraging the widening and standardization of a whole range of fringe benefits and employee services, and providing another channel of communication within the enterprise, giving higher management the possibility of responding to employee grievances before a crisis. Well-managed and successful companies which have made use of personnel administrators for these purposes — *and* have been able to provide pay and conditions equal to, or better than, those set in the unionized sector of their industries, *and* have been able to combat unionization within the generous boundaries of the law, as well as to "play dirty" when occasion requires — have been able to keep all or part of their workforces nonunion, or even to drive back the boundaries of unionization within the blue-collar group itself. This objective is ideologically attractive to management, but one may also assume that firms devote large resources to maintaining or establishing a "union-free environment" because it is their considered opinion that unilateral control still works more smoothly and efficiently, from their point of view, than the most generally available alternative: bilateral negotiation. The collective bargaining model of industrial democracy evidently has little intrinsic appeal to most employers: attempts to combat alienation, or to compete with the Japanese, have led to a recent renewed interest in experimenting with consultative and participative management, in departing from traditional hierarchies, in establishing "quality-control circles" and the like in order to improve organizational morale and tap the latent resources of the rank-and-file. These steps toward humanizing the workplace may be well and good, but they point toward a future which may be just as inhospitable for traditional, multifirm, truly independent unions dedicated to the narrow defense of their members' material interests, and resorting to industrial conflict if necessary, as has been the last generation of managerial unilateralism.

If it is difficult to be definite about the impact of the work of personnel administration within the firm, it is even more so when one turns to the subject of the next, and final, chapter in this work: the efforts of businessmen of varying political persuasions, "corporate liberal" or sophisticated conservative, and reactionary or traditional conservative, to restore the power and prestige of business men and institutions after the shocks and blows described earlier.

7

Hearts and Minds:
The Search for Public Favor

The business community's most important political objective in the 1940s was to change federal labor relations policy. In the fight for the Taft-Hartley law, the NAM in particular used all of the techniques of the traditional and the modern lobbyist to influence the legislative process. But that was only one engagement, albeit the most successful, in a complex struggle for power and influence between businessmen and their liberal Democratic and labor opponents in the 1940s. Most of the business community's political action was not centered on Congress, and did not have such explicit legislative objectives. It was closely and directly related to the contest for authority and control within industry which management fought with the weapons provided by labor relations experts and personnel specialists.

Business was involved in much more than a naked conflict for power between interest groups of unequal strength. It was also, necessarily, involved in an effort to win and keep public support — to maintain the moral legitimacy of its power, its prestige, its privileges, its objectives, and its definition of the good society, the "public interest." Businessmen saw themselves as an embattled, threatened elite, their traditional dominance challenged within their own firms and in the larger community outside the factory fence. Political scientists may talk of bourgeois hegemony and of the mobilization of bias within a rigged political system, and be impressed by how far America actually departs from the ideal of an open, responsive, democratic polity. But thoughtful, articulate businessmen who observed and reflected on their own times, and

177

tried to affect their own political fortunes, believed that they really did live in such an open society—that what the masses of workers and citizens thought about public issues mattered, because it had an important bearing on public policy.

Similarly, it was once fashionable for historians to look at the course of American history in terms of economic growth, moral consensus, social stability, political conservatism, and overall business preeminence. But businessmen active in the 1940s were not so convinced that that was the natural state of affairs, though it was certainly their dream, best realized in the Golden Age of the 1920s. And they did not have the gift of second sight, so they could not foretell that all of their fears of economic collapse and political radicalism coming after the wartime prosperity would prove to be exaggerated—but *not* unfounded, though the affluence of Cold War America and its conservative mood obliterated most of the causes for reasoned anxiety.

It is easy for a detached, present-day observer, who knows the final score, to think that the outcome of the power games of the 1940s was inevitable. But that trap of hindsight is one to be avoided, if possible. Business leaders in the 1940s had to handle seemingly intractable problems in unfamiliar and worrying times. And they could look back on career experiences which told them that neither the economic nor the political fortunes of the American business community were fixed or guaranteed. For a man whose memory reached back to the early years of the twentieth century, affluence and tranquillity were not sure things. He could recall, from personal experience or that of acquaintances, or from the images of American life presented in the mass media, a turbulent period which taught that nothing could be relied upon absolutely.

Most of all, he could remember how easily and unexpectedly the "Dollar Decade" of the 1920s was cut short by the Depression, and replaced by the nightmare of the New Deal, when businessmen suffered much more than a loss of self-confidence and prestige. There was a real reduction in their power vis-à-vis a burgeoning interventionist state, which they could no longer control, and the labor movement it fostered. Their traditional freedom to manage their own affairs was impaired, and the political environment in which they had to operate became much less certain and secure. The defense and war periods had brought temporary deliverance, but had further strengthened the power of the state and, perhaps, unbalanced the economy.

There was nothing in this recent history to persuade American business leaders that their political fortunes could safely be left to chance. The future was clouded, political and economic prospects uncertain, and businessmen had a great deal to fear from any radical disturbance of the social order. As Senator Ralph Flanders (Rep., Vermont), ex-president of Jones and Lamson Machine Co., coolly explained, "In this age of management, in which the manager enjoys power, material reward, and a feeling of satisfaction in exercising his experience and abilities, the preservation of his position must be to him and his class a matter of serious consideration."[1] It was.

No significant section of American business opinion was anything other than conservative. But the business community was not monolithic. There was room for a range of opinions, and occasional deep disagreements, about political action, just as there was about many of the subjects discussed earlier in this work. Disagreement was not about ultimate objectives: all articulate businessmen were committed to the defense of the American social order, from which they drew the greatest benefits as its most important ruling group. Argument centered on identifying threats to American stability and business power, explaining their causes, and recommending the most appropriate strategies and tactics for dealing with them.

The debate within the business community about the seriousness of the challenge New Deal liberalism posed to business power, and about the best ways for businessmen to fight liberal politicians and labor leaders for the "hearts and minds" of American working people, followed familiar lines. The disputing parties were the sophisticated conservatives or "corporate liberals," and the traditional or "practical" conservatives. Deep down, many of the practical conservative majority were certainly reactionary, but it was tactically unwise for them to admit as much in their quest of public support. Still, the extremism of their objectives belies the moderation of some of their rhetoric. They were committed to doing away with as much of the New Deal as possible — its social reforms, new fiscal policies, and labor unions in particular. What could not be destroyed was to be gradually weakened, and prevented from doing any further damage. Sophisticated conservatism was much less alarmed by the developments of the 1930s and 1940s, could see in them some advantages for itself, and was accordingly ready to live with them and even accept further moderate progress down the collectivist path.

These two competing political persuasions within the business community reflected different ideas about how best to preserve business power within the American free enterprise system. They involved different understandings of the way people made up their minds about political issues, and of how these decisions could best be affected. But they are both interesting examples of the adjustments businessmen have had to make in order to influence the political climate. In a mass society, that is no mean task. But when the state is acquiring ever-greater power to stimulate and regulate the economy, and to interfere in relations between social groups, it is one that cannot long be safely avoided.

WELFARE CAPITALISM AS A POLITICAL STRATEGY

In the work of personnel departments in the 1940s and after, welfare capitalism has been one control technique among many used by firms whose managements have different political attitudes, and a variety of motives and objectives in industrial relations policy. But, from its beginnings, welfare capitalism has also been an approach to the problem of safeguarding businessmen's power and status in society at large. As such, it aroused renewed interest and won more support in the 1930s and 1940s. And in this case it kept its distinctively liberal coloration.

The welfare capitalist model of the American political system recognized that in a representative democracy like the United States, with an egalitarian political creed, owners' and managers' power and privilege had to rest on public support to be safe. Public acquiescence in the continuation of a social system which distributed authority and other rewards very unequally could be neither guaranteed nor simply enforced. It had to be won. The power of the elite would be most secure when the consent of the governed was freely given. Business could win that consent by demonstrating its "social responsibility," justifying its claim to power by pointing to a believable record of operating the corporate sector of the economy in the general interest. The business elite had to behave "politically," accommodating itself to at least some of the demands American workers and the public made upon it, responding to or anticipating the pressures of its "constituents" in order to retain the maximum possible freedom of unilateral action. If constructive business leadership was not forthcoming, the public would turn to rival elites — union leaders, liberal or radical politicians — for answers.[2]

This political outlook had a half-century of history behind it, but it had made much more impact on businessmen's rhetoric than on their actual behavior. Before the Depression, there was much more promise than performance. Popular and working-class pressures were easily managed, more often by using business-class power to resist change and repress dissent than by making expedient concessions. Business in the 1920s *claimed* to be socially responsible, but there was small cause for that self-congratulation. The 1930s came as a rude shock, and educated businessmen in the political consequences of their actual failure to meet the basic demands the public made of the system they controlled.

The great majority of the business community, after a brief "honey-moon" in 1933–34, was soon alienated from the Roosevelt administration and almost all its works. They went over into relentless, purely negative, and largely ineffective opposition. They provided the business community with its reactionary heart, and its practical conservative head. But a small minority of progressive firms recognized that a more constructive response to the revealed weaknesses of the American business system was required. The corporate liberal senior managers of a few large companies like General Electric and Eastman Kodak, and of rather more medium-sized, family-controlled firms like Jones & Lamson (machine tools) and Leeds & Northrup (precision instruments), were more significant than their numbers would suggest, though they were not immediately influential. They recognized that the state could play a vital role in stabilizing and regenerating the economy. Some of them were even willing to grant a small place to a cooperative, responsible labor movement in the new, pluralistic system which was being built, inside and outside of the firm. They provided the few business-men who collaborated in drafting the Social Security Act, and who served faithfully on the Department of Commerce's Business Advisory Council (BAC). A handful were among the first American disciples of Keynes, seeing in his teachings the outlines of an acceptable way of restoring the American economy to life after a decade of stagnation.[3]

Corporate liberals were ready to work with the government to try to, as they saw it, moderate the New Deal's worst excesses and restore the influence of the business community in the nation's inner councils.[4] They received their great challenge and opportunity during the Second World War. The administration turned to them to staff mobilization agencies at the highest levels; it also turned to the BAC to help answer the question plaguing so many politicians, economists, union leaders, and businessmen: "After the War, WHAT?" The economy had only recovered from the depression as a result of the war boom. For the moment, it provided jobs for all. People's expectations were thereby raised: demonstrably, state expenditure, intervention, and coordination of economic activity on a scale the New Deal never dreamed of could provide prosperity. If in war, why not in peace also?

Businessmen's minds were exercised by this question. Some of them disputed its facts or its logic.[5] Others created a new organization of businessmen to give constructive, probusiness answers to the problems of reconverting the economy to a peace footing, and thereafter maintaining stable prosperity. This organization was the Committee for Economic Development (CED), officially established in September 1942. Secretary of Commerce Jesse Jones urged and helped the BAC to set it up, but there had been talk and planning about such a body earlier, particularly among top managers of General Electric and Studebaker Motors.

The CED was a new type of business organization: it had close links with the corporate liberal minority, but it also established good working relations with the more inclusive, conservative NAM and CCUS. It aimed to develop proposals for national economic policy acceptable both to businessmen and to moderate elements in the New Deal's ranks. To this end, it actively cooperated with economists of reformist, Keynesian temper, and sought to "educate" the conservative business community, "to rescue the businessman from his own intellectual neanderthalism, to wash the clichés of an outworn ideology from his mind."[6] It sponsored research into the problems of reconversion and longer-range economic policy. And it encouraged businessmen to think and plan about their companies' contributions to easing the transition to peace, and then working for full employment and economic growth.[7]

The CED's work in the economic education of businessmen was helpful and influential, but its lessons in American political realities were more interesting, and in the long run more important. CED members, overlapping with liberal elements in the NAM and the CCUS, realized that it was no longer enough to resist all proposals for legislated social change on the grounds that they were unconstitutional, immoral, subversive, contrary to human nature, against the laws of supply and demand, un-American, etc. Conservative businessmen had spoken thus for generations, but their arguments seemed to have lost whatever reason and persuasive force they had ever had. Instead, "[b]usiness can capture the leadership of public opinion only if it makes, and dramatizes, a conscientious and determined effort to solve the nation's legitimate economic problems when they exist."[8]

"This does not mean that we can or should sponsor every scheme for welfare and security that comes along. We can't. But we can effectively oppose those things which are unsound only if we have associated ourselves with social objectives that are sound.[9]

Stable prosperity and social security in a mixed economy were what the American people apparently wanted, and the CED was willing that they should have them. It made constructive proposals about these subjects, encouraged businessmen to take the initiative to supply them, as far as they were able, and accepted that the government had a useful and necessary role to play. The CED attempted to influence government policies, not fight against intervention. Accordingly, it threw its influence against NAM policy on the abolition of price controls in 1946, and helped save the Employment Bill of the same year from a conservative attack masterminded by Donaldson Brown of GM.[10]

The CED was not strong enough to save price control, and its help to the Employment Act may not have been decisive. But at least it had presented a new image of enlightened business activism to the American people after years when the business community's collective response to any novel proposal had been perfectly predictable, and "always . . . in the form of objections."[11]

The sophisticated conservative leaders of the CED were outstandingly optimistic about the chances for survival of a form of free enterprise in postwar America, and its compatibility with an enhanced interventionist role for the federal government. Control of the mixed economy would remain, for the most part, dispersed in private hands. They believed in the essential stability of the American social order, barring economic collapse. Federal economic management could help stave off that catastrophe.[12] This confidence was strengthened by the findings of their favorite opinion pollster, Elmo Roper. Contrary to the gloomy interpretations of his more conservative brethren, Gallup and Claud Robinson, Roper emphasized that the American people believed in the principles upon which the free enterprise system was based and were generally satisfied with the way it operated for them. If it provided full employment, a measure of economic security in times of ill health, temporary worklessness, and old age, the chance of advancement, and the promise of fair treatment for its employees which good personnel administration guaranteed, it was safe. The American people's hostility and suspicion toward business management, evident in the 1930s, waning in the 1940s, was not based in any deep-seated, revolutionary ideology, but in their doubts as to its ability or willingness to satisfy the reasonable and limited instrumental demands they made of it.[13]

Corporate liberal businessmen were true "conservators," who believed that "the best in the past was not static. It was moving. Our problem is to see that we keep on moving ahead in our own time, in an orderly manner, as fast as we can go, without recklessness."[14] They wanted to guide, rather than resist or reverse, social change. They were not worried men, living in a time they could not understand and a climate of opinion of which they did not approve.

CED activists like Ralph Flanders, Studebaker's Paul Hoffman, and Eastman Kodak's Marion Folsom accordingly found themselves a congenial home in the liberal consensus of Cold War America and followed active careers in government service. They and their fellows represented that important section of American business which had come to terms with the institutional legacy of the New Deal. They appreciated its contributions to the rationalizing of American capitalism, which had made the system more secure and more acceptable to the people. CED members led the rest of the business community in the "conservative acquiescence in the changed economic system" which took place in the postwar era. They understood that businessmen still had most economic power in the mixed economy, and that the balance between public and private power could be kept fairly stable. They appreciated that businessmen could colonize and direct important parts of the government apparatus, if only they were willing to work with it on its own terms and be co-opted by it. Keynesianism was no radical or revolutionary economic dogma: it was a very practical, flexible tool of macroeconomic management.[15]

In the long run, this viewpoint gained followers, and became almost orthodox in the 1950s and 1960s. But in the anxious years of the late 1940s, most of the business community was not so reconciled to the present, nor so sanguine about the future, as the corporate liberal minority. The CED and its allies have had plenty of attention from historians, but their practical conservative and reactionary colleagues were more numerous and more immediately influential within the business community itself. And their outlook was altogether different.

THE GREAT FREE ENTERPRISE CAMPAIGN

The CED did not publicize its ideas or its activities very extensively. It was an elite organization, doing most of its work by private contact, in small conferences, or through diplomatic alliances with nonbusiness elites—politicians, administrators, labor leaders, academics. It believed that experience of the benefits flowing from the policies of corporate liberalism would restore the American people's faith in material progress under business leadership. In any case, that faith had only been shaken in the 1930s, not destroyed. Sophisticated conservatives were reassured both by the picture they had of public opinion, and by their forecast of the success of America's new mixed economy. The problem of winning public support for the business system did not seem to be too serious.

For practical conservatives, the problem was different in kind and scale. They, too, believed in the importance of public opinion, but they distrusted it. They wanted to win support for their own, often reactionary, views. Unlike the corporate liberals, they were not free to curry favor by committing themselves to full employment and social security. Instead, they had to try to swim against the tide of public opinion, as they saw it, or even make it flow in the direction they wanted to go.

This is never an easy job for even the most practiced politician. The way conservative businessmen went about it made the task more difficult.

Conservative businessmen's approach to the problem of public opinion was rooted in the need they felt to fight the kind of proposals liberal Democrats, labor leaders, and even some businessmen were making for social reforms in the 1940s. Conservatives were not ready to admit that there were any serious imperfections in the internal operations of large business firms, or in the workings of the American economy, that a dose of deregulation would not cure. America was not perfect — none of man's creations was. But it was as near perfect as any society could be. America was a success. It only needed to be defended against governmental meddling and the criticisms of the ignorant or the hostile.[16]

Practical conservatism, then, was stand-pat at best, reactionary at worst. Businessmen of this temper were elitists — authoritarian believers in the justice of an unequal society. But they were also American, through and through. They had an uneasy, paradoxical democratic faith. They knew that businessmen had to be able to justify their power by claiming they had a mandate, that the majority of real Americans supported them and their objectives. America's political creed did not offer them alternative claims to legitimacy.

[M]anagement is, or at least would like to be elected representatives of the employees with whom and the communities in which we work. Is it not true that the power of industrial management is limited by the degree and kind of popular support which it can command? Maybe the obvious conclusion is that modern industrial management is, strictly speaking, in politics, and if it is to have the power commensurate with its responsibilities, it must literally seek that power in the political arena. . . .

Power is exercized through leadership, and it takes followers to make a leader. We in industrial management had better make a serious bid for leadership, not only of our own fellow employees, but the whole community. We have the opportunity and the challenge and the responsibility.[17]

Businessmen wanted moral authority as well as power, and they needed compliance. If their program for the recovery of control inside the firm, and in society at large, was to succeed, it had to have broad public support. What worried businessmen in the 1940s was that the evidence of their own eyes and of attitude surveys suggested that that objective was a long way off.

Whichever part of the postwar American scene managers examined, they found plentiful evidence of conflict — industrial, political, ideological — in which majorities or significant minorities of American workers were lined up against the values and objectives business held most dear. This threatened businessmen's power over their own firms and their influence in large areas of American life. It was dangerous, and it was also extremely offensive to their conceptions of the right ways of ordering society.

Speaking about "Current Human Problems in Quality and Productivity" in 1949, Scoville Manufacturing Co.'s vice-president Alan Curtis complained about a widespread demoralization, characteristic of industrial workers. It made them think and act in ways contrary to those management required, and knew to be in their best interests. His opinion on this score was shared by many other commentators, anxious about workers' indiscipline, poor productivity, indifference to managerial appeals, and support of undesirable union objectives. The symptoms of demoralization included "[f]ailure of the individual to realize that good work and quantity output are in his own self interest," the "too prevalent belief that reducing production will gain job security" and that "the worker gets but a small part of the company's income and that profits range between 20 and 30 percent," the "don't care attitude of individuals, developed by the belief that they will be taken care of by the government or some other agency," lack of interest in the job, and "the belief that there is no road to advancement."[18]

It is not unusual for managers to make slighting comments about the degeneracy and sheer cussedness of the rank-and-file. Whatever may be said in other contexts about the good American worker, it is clear that s/he often turns out to be disappointingly refractory material. Curtis was hardly a dispassionate observer of the contemporary scene, but his remarks cannot be explained away as the product of mere irritation. They had a real basis. They were confirmed by the evidence of contemporary attitudes revealed in opinion surveys, the objectives of labor unions and liberal Democrats enjoying workers' active support, and workers' on-the-job behavior.

In 1950, the Opinion Research Corporation (ORC) reported that 35 percent of a sample of industrial workers believed that labor-saving machinery destroyed jobs; the same percentage thought that employee and stockholder interests were in conflict. Sixty-one percent denied that the chief benefit from increased productivity went to workers; the same proportion believed that monopoly or oligopoly, not free competition, was the predominant condition in most industries. Fifty-two percent declined to believe that more of company income went on wages and salaries than on dividends and top management pay, and 51 percent that wealth was not becoming increasingly concentrated. In these and similar "fallacious" beliefs about the structure and working of the economy, businessmen thought they saw part of the explanation for employees' endorsement of programs their superiors knew to be wrong, and detrimental to their subordinates' best interests.[19]

Attitude surveys also produced disquieting information about job satisfaction. Success was a part of the promise of American life; the individual's desire for personal recognition and advancement was a motivating force upon which much of personnel administration relied. But a belief that extra effort brought no payoffs appeared to be widespread. "A danger signal for management is that workers are beginning to feel that opportunity is dead." Only 14 percent of the ORC's sample believed they had a very good chance of promotion; 46 percent thought their chances small. Most employees were reasonably confident of the security of their jobs, but expected not to rise in status. In consequence, they supported collective action to improve their conditions — including welfare programs and claims for higher wages without price increases, that is, for a larger share of corporate income. They gave a formal, verbal assent to the individual incentive principles management espoused, but in practice supported seniority rules and across-the-board wage increases.[20]

ORC's image of the American worker is of a skeptical, group-minded character, resistant to management's appeals. *Factory's* annual surveys of "what the worker really thinks" produced similar evidence. In 1945, for example, 40 percent of its sample thought that "[w]hen a man takes a job in a factory, . . . he should turn out . . . as much, say, as the average man in his group" rather than maximizing his individual output, as management said he should. If he turned out more than the norm, "Management would raise production quotas" (30 percent) or reduce piece rates (11 percent); in any case, "It would be unpopular with other workers" (23 percent). "Only" 61 percent said yes to the loaded proposition that elimination of loafing would help workers. In these and similar responses, management could see the causes of union members' support for programs and unofficial actions designed to sabotage its productionist efforts — output restriction, opposition to incentive schemes, objection to technological innovation, support of work-sharing and of reduction in the length of the working week, or working life, as devices to stave off unemployment.[21]

Workers' opinions about their jobs needed to be corrected, and so did their attitudes to managerial authority and large public issues. In 1947, 42 percent of union members in *Factory's* sample believed the "head men" of their companies had "not much" interest in what happened to them, and 60 percent considered union leaders "more interested in the personal welfare of the working man." Workers did not follow management's leadership trustingly and with gratitude. Instead, on issues such as price control, profit and salary limitation, government ownership, state provision of Social Security benefits, guarantees of full employment, and the legitimacy of strong unions, workers and management were on opposing sides of a real political divide.[22]

Opinion polls seemed to demonstrate that unions and their leaders, and the liberal politicians they backed, represented what their members and supporters thought, in a very accurate manner and on a wide range of issues. Reformist programs had a legitimate basis in a real popular mandate. America's democratic public ideology and the realities of its political system made this widespread opposition to managerial authority and management's world-view seem to be truly threatening to American business. The ideological distance between the managements of large firms and their rank-and-file workers was particularly large. This was worrying, and it could be dangerous. ORC's surveys revealed that workers making the most favorable responses to its questions about job satisfaction tended to live in small cities, to be found in nonunion or white-collar jobs, and to have a high-school education or better; those making the least lived in medium-sized and large cities, were unionized, worked at manual jobs, and had a grade-school education at best. *Factory*'s polls showed consistently more antibusiness responses from CIO members and workers in medium-sized and large plants in the industrial heartland east of the Mississippi and north of the Ohio than from any other group.[23]

This was the problem with which managers, concerned for their power and prestige, had to deal. ORC spelt it out clearly:

> The battle for men's minds and loyalties is thus one of the realities of corporate existence. Member companies [customers for the ORC's polling service] frequently ask . . . :
> Why won't our own people listen to us? Here we are, joined together in one enterprise, all of us dependent on the company's prosperity for our good fortune.
> When management decides what needs to be done, why doesn't everybody go along?[24]

The problem of alienation in industry, and of class conflict in society, loomed large. Personnel administration and welfare capitalism offered one answer. But the more traditional conservative's preferred solution involved less flexibility of outlook on his part, required minimal changes in corporate policy, and expected all of the burden of adjustment to be borne by workers and citizens. Their attitudes and perceptions were the problem — not the performance of the system, under his control.

Nevertheless, businessmen had to acknowledge that public opinion was "partially hostile and largely indifferent"[25] to their sincere claims for the superiority of the American system, under their control, over any actual or recorded competitor. This was a phenomenon that had to be explained before it could be dealt with adequately. And of course, the effectiveness of the remedies they decided to use to cure the disease would depend in large part on the accuracy of their diagnosis.

As far as practical conservative businessmen were concerned, the problem was that the American public — especially the working class — was ignorant, or misinformed, and had been misled. Management had not done enough to inform and persuade Americans of the virtues of private enterprise. Meanwhile, purveyors of false doctrine had been active and effective in filling the gap thus left. The conclusion was inescapable: the business community must make up for lost time and get fully involved in the tasks of indoctrination and propaganda. The need was for mass persuasion and the "engineering of consent." Advertising would provide the tools, and business ideology itself would be the message, in a great campaign to lead the American people back into the paths of righteousness from which some of them had temporarily strayed

Businessmen's campaigns of mass persuasion fell into two broad categories. The first complemented the work of personnel management. It was targeted at the employee public, and its primary concern was to build correct attitudes toward work and managerial authority. In the same way as much of personnel work, it could be politically neutral, and have no direct bearing on the struggle for influence between business and its antagonists in the larger society. The second was an extension of business' political action, and consisted of an attempt to use the mass media to communicate businessmen's ideas about the economy and large social issues to the general public. The first may be called the "Communications in Industry" movement, and the second the "Great Free Enterprise Campaign." Many progressive firms were deeply involved in communicating with their workers, or trying to, but practical conservatives and reactionaries were the greatest supporters of the idea of "selling" their favored version of the free enterprise system to the American people.[26]

So much for the contrasts. But there were also significant continuities. While progressive firms were more likely to be silent about the virtues of managerial capitalism in general, conservative supporters of the Great Free Enterprise Campaign were often deeply involved in attempting to indoctrinate their own employees with the right approach to work. Concern for the restoration of managerial authority and employee morale was shared by managements of differing political persuasions, but making a fighting attack on the supposed drift toward statist collectivism was naturally the more traditional conservative's preoccupation.

In addition, shared assumptions underpinned both campaigns. Supporters of both believed that there was a true unity of interest between superior and subordinate, elite and mass, in industry and society. As is normal for members of an elite group, they thought that the leader's program and world-view were in the general interest, and allowed of no legitimate opposition. If those who should have been loyal followers actually displayed contrary attitudes, by word or action, that was to be explained by their ignorance of the true facts, or by their having been deceived and misinformed. The solution to the problem therefore consisted of "information" — the transmission, with all of the skill and force of the mass media, of the superior's viewpoint to his constituent publics.

The Communications in Industry movement concentrated on the American working class because its ideas were obviously most wrongheaded and it was most exposed to labor and liberal propaganda. Of all sections of the American public, it was most at risk. But it was also reckoned to be more accessible than any other to management's attempts to convert it.

Think of it! About fifteen million American men and women spend eight or more hours a day, five or six days a week, in the mills, factories, or plants of America — figuratively at the very elbows of the managers of manufacturing industry. . . . Armed with the economic facts, these millions with their families could be a mighty force, probably a determining factor, in the growing struggle between American individualism and foreign-bred collectivism. So in our plants we're not only manufacturing goods. We're manufacturing reactions to our way of life . . .[27]

The job was the "center of the employee's universe"; his experiences at work shaped his attitude towards the whole of the free enterprise system. These experiences should include being told, and convinced, that management's view of the enterprise and of society was the correct one.[28]

Every employee who understands in reasonable degree how his company operates, and who is proud of his company and its products, who has a sense of participating in a worthwhile effort and of being treated fairly and with dignity is, perhaps without realizing it, an advocate of our competitive economy and our system of political freedom.

Every employee who has to do simply what he is told with no understanding of why, who doesn't care about his company or its product, who works reluctantly and only for his wages, who has no feeling of job pride and is dissatisfied is, again perhaps without realizing it, a real or potential enemy. . . . The front line in the battle to preserve a free America may well be at the work bench as well as at the polling booth or in the halls of Congress.[29]

Management's message had to be supported by employees' experience of the proper working of good personnel policies, but would only be properly received if it was rammed home repeatedly and forcefully, in such a way that no reasonably right-thinking American could fail to accept it.[30]

Add it up for the employee: 2 + 2 = 4; repeat 4; repeat 4.

[D]istribution of information about the economic system is not enough; companies need to draw ideological conclusions from economic information if they want to build attitudes favorable to the continuance of competitive capitalism.[31]

The distinctive message of the Communications in Industry movement had to do with the job. Working rules, which were in fact determined by management for its own purposes, were rationalized as expressing the collective will and experience of the whole plant community, and in the best interests of the group and its members. An attempt was made to restore meaning to subdivided, deskilled, and alienating labor by making employees aware of their place in the whole complex, interdependent scheme of company operations, and of the end product of their collective endeavor. And there was an unmistakable emphasis on the firm as a human community in which there is an accepted hierarchy of power, skill, responsibility, and reward, but in which common objectives and values provide organic unity. The firm is a "family" or a "team"; the bosses are real people, kind and wise. Employees were told of all the benefits they got from work, of all the opportunities they had, and of what was reasonably expected of them in return.[32]

Putting employees right about their status and duties, and management's power and responsibilities, was an objective both liberal and traditional conservative managements could endorse. But in the late 1940s the traditionalists were in the ascendancy, so increasing numbers of large firms went beyond this common ground to treat their workers to the same diet of "economic truth" as was offered to the mass public. It involved a straightforward, repetitious presentation of the central tenets of the American Business Creed. The message of this Great Free Enterprise Campaign was that government regulation of the economy was inefficient, unAmerican, dangerous to national morals and the basic liberties enshrined in the Constitution. Decentralized managerial control, on the other hand, delivered economic progress for all, threatened the liberties of no one, and produced fair shares of the fruits of profitable, dynamic business enterprise for all parties with an interest in it.[33]

Just as there was an overlap in the message of the two campaigns, they also used many common media to communicate it. In approaching their workers, firms used bulletin board notices, pamphlets, brief messages in the pay envelope, posters, direct mail to the employee's home, employee handbooks, magazines, newspapers, and films. They made somewhat less use of social gatherings, occasional lectures and addresses, and formal courses — for the orientation of new employees, or to tell workers about the structure of the business enterprise and the workings of the economic system. Some managements realized that they had to reinforce the message their in-plant media put over by trying to shape the climate of opinion of the communities where their workers lived. So they used advertisements in local newspapers, or on radio and TV stations, and organized courses with community groups, to get at their workers in their leisure hours and to reach out to their neighbors too.[34]

In the Great Free Enterprise Campaign in particular, the line between employee, community, and public relations work was very indistinct. The Campaign took up where the work of the NAM's National Industrial Information Committee of the late 1930s had left off. In the years of its activity, the Committee's expenditures had grown geometrically. During the postwar boom, industry had more money to pour into propaganda, and the useful experience of wartime "institutional advertising" to guide it.[35]

At the national level, the Campaign used paid press advertisements, "planted" editorials, syndicated news and comment, billboards, pamphlets, sponsored programs on radio and TV, widely distributed films, and every other media outlet. It even used the press agent's established technique of the "created event": the Advertising Council sent its Freedom Train, with the Liberty Bell on board, around the country to rekindle the patriotism of right-thinking Americans. Organizations active in the Campaign were, overwhelmingly, those of the business community, or those which, while claiming to act in the public interest, depended on businessmen for their funding and direction. The NAM, the CCUS, the Advertising Council, and the Association of National Advertisers–American Association of Advertising Agencies, together with trade associations, were most active at the national level; local chambers of commerce, manufacturers' associations, and individual firms participated on a smaller scale in America's industrial communities.[36]

Businessmen supporting the Campaign did not have even a minimally adequate and disinterested system of measuring the effects of what they did. But they funded it generously for years regardless of that. If the sponsors were in the dark about the real impact of their work, we are no more enlightened now. Measuring the results of propaganda is never easy, especially as it is impossible to state with confidence that observable changes in the climate of public opinion in the desired direction were consequent, not just subsequent and best explained in other ways. In any case, between the mid-1940s and the mid-1950s public opinion toward business seems to have remained stubbornly suspicious. Polls continued to detect the same patterns of belief as had spurred business-men to get into public "education" in a big way after the war. At the start of the new decade, General Motors financed a study which re-vealed that "the predominant impressions of big business management are that it is 'impersonal and distant.'" Only 14 percent of the sample saw management as "conscientious and principled." There was wide-spread acceptance of state regulation of business in the public interest, and the "great majority of persons interviewed (71 percent) regarded big business profits as excessive." Even after the installation of the first Republican administration in twenty years, workers still credited unions, not management, with raising their living standards. Workers rated their managements very poorly on the amount of concern they had for their employees. And they distrusted the business community as an advisor to government on large issues of public policy, where they persisted in seeing a necessary conflict of class interests — this at the very time that Eisenhower's cabinet consisted of "nine millionaires and a plumber."[37]

Business propaganda seemingly had little effect on the climate of public opinion, still less on workers' behavior and citizens' political ac-tion, which were supposedly determined by their attitudes and beliefs. But that is no reason for neglecting it. The message of business propa-ganda tells us what worried, conservative businessmen believed them-selves, and what they wanted and needed to have their subordinates accept. The groups management identified as the sources of the wrong ideas it fought against clearly demonstrate the extent of lasting business hostility to the New Deal. And the media the campaign employed, to-gether with its underlying premises, show how businessmen understood their own society, and hoped to act upon it.

The "competition" which practical conservative businessmen feared consisted of America's labor leaders, liberal sections of the intelligen-tsia, and the liberal wing of the northern, urban, Democratic party. Businessmen's rhetoric often equated liberal or radical ideas with "god-less Communism," which was a good, though unfair, debating ploy in the context of American-Soviet tension and growing anti-Communist hysteria, which some elements in the business community helped to create. But the real target was not the tiny American CP. Instead, it was the CP's old allies from Popular Front days, elements in the New Deal coalition which were becoming vociferously anti-Communist supporters of Cold War orthodoxy in their own right. Anti-Communism was the cover, antiliberalism the essence of the Great Free Enterprise Campaign.[38]

The New Deal-Fair Deal program was dangerous precisely because of its proven attractiveness to masses of Americans. The basic cause of industry's political problems, conservative businessmen believed, was that the public was ignorant of proper principles of economics and social organization. The false preaching of liberal propagandists had filled that void. As a result, union members and citizens supported their leaders' unreasonable pressures on the business community. Fire had to be fought with fire.

The untruths must be destroyed at their source—in the colleges, national union headquarters, political headquarters, religious headquarters, even business offices—because the thought leaders there get their stuff into our plant cities and into our employees' minds through the wire material on the front pages of the local newspapers, through union and religious and educational publications, through contact with our extremely mobile population from everywhere, through subversive agents in and out of the unions and government and business.[39]

Businessmen believed that they faced a real political challenge, and were meeting stiff competition in the marketplace of ideas. Speeches on the subject by these practical, conservative men and their public relations advisors still convey a sense of urgency—"Madame Guillotine, it almost seems, is just around the corner for every speaker." They were staple fare on the menu at business conferences in the later 1940s, and speakers insisted on the need to seek a cure before the disease of popular ignorance proved fatal.[40]

Our competitive enterprise system must have the vote of confidence of our citizens. To get this vote, we must be understood. To be understood, our actions and the reasons for our actions must be made known to, and believed by, the people of our community. That is our job. If we fail, there will be no second chance in our lifetime, or that of our grandchildren.[41]

But they were not pessimistic. The apparent support a confused public gave to the lies and distortions of the opposition simply resulted from the greater vigor and astuteness with which the false prophets had presented their case. "The bright side of the picture is this. When the citizens of Main Street are given the facts, almost invariably they come to sensible conclusions about what should be done. Public opinion in America rarely goes off on crazy, impractical tangents."[42] So there was nothing natural or inevitable in the present, gloomy state of affairs. Americans actually wanted and were waiting for the kind of leadership businessmen were uniquely qualified to give. If businessmen provided the truth, they would find a willing and receptive audience.

Conservative businessmen believed in an ideal of society as organic, holistic, homogeneous, united by a value-consensus — and at the same time hierarchical and deferential. They also thought that America was not far from being the land of their dreams, and that they could close the gap between ideal and reality. They stereotyped the "real," average American, including the workingman, as fundamentally middle-class in his values. So they had high hopes of success in their propaganda campaigns. Any ideology at odds with the Business Creed could be written off as un-American, any support it might possess belittled as unnatural and easily eroded. If businessmen and their audience had a common fund of symbols and prejudices, then businessmen could hope that the "facts" which fitted with their own ideology would go down well with the public too.[43]

The greater reason for business optimism was a confidence that, given the resolve to use its resources, it had the ability to convey its sense of the "truth" and the "facts" to the American people. "We have worked miracles in mass production and mass distribution, but now we must have mass understanding." This was imperative, and it was also expected to be quite easy. A generation of American businessmen had witnessed the effectiveness of advertising in creating public demand for new consumer products, in changing and reinforcing brand loyalties, and even — during the late war — in persuading people to change their habits on, for example, fat conservation! Many senior executives themselves had an advertising and sales background, and the metaphor of the sales campaign sprang easily to their lips when they wanted to describe the political strategy they recommended for getting the better of the "competition" in the "marketplace of ideas."[44]

Advertising was also a source of much more substantial things than metaphors. It provided a body of experience and techniques for using the mass media to greatest effect. It had a vision of the audience, the potential consumer, as essentially materialistic and self-interested, but also susceptible to emotional, nonrational appeals; and it had a conviction of the power and value of sheer volume and repetition. The skills and the folklore of advertising could be directly applied to the "selling" of the Free Enterprise System. Achievement in ideological merchandising might not be very great, but the potential seemed enormous; once the essential task of fighting misinformation with the truth, false prophecy with the American Business Creed, had been successfully undertaken, then opposition to managerial leadership within the firm and in the larger society would subside. The interests of the public and of the business community, of workers and management, were actually the same. If the followers could be brought to recognize the fact, to share their leaders' enlightened world-view, desirable consequences would ensue. The person who came to "think straight" would surely come to act and "vote straight" too.[45]

This was obviously not a very sophisticated approach to the "engineering of consent." It was roundly attacked at the time by social scientists and more liberal businessmen. But it was influential within the business community, and it was important for demonstrating how unhappy a large section of that community was with the political climate of postwar America. The businessmen who supported this approach to the merchandising of ideas were not just owner-managers and family capitalists of the kind who became associated with the organized "radical right" of the 1950s. If we examine the contributors' lists for extreme conservative pressure groups in the late 1940s, we find instead that they are liberally spattered with the names of some of America's great industrial dynasties, as well as of the blue riband corporations dominant within the NAM. The hard core of the practical conservative majority within the business community supported this reactionary program and extremist propaganda — it was not the work of a lunatic fringe.[46]

For example, the Committee for Constitutional Government was a seasoned anti-New Deal campaigner, rabidly antilabor and reactionary in its tone. Its supporters included nonunion Eli Lilly and Co., the antiunion Fruehauf family (supporters of the abortive "Society of Sentinels" in Detroit in 1946), and J. Howard Pew of Sun Oil (Pew was also high in the councils of the NAM, chairing its public relations committee in 1946). The National Economic Council, a more secretive lobbying organization, had behind it Gulf Oil (the Mellon family), the Texas Co., Armco Steel and Monsanto Chemical Co. (both extremely active in the NAM), American Cyanamid, Sears, Roebuck & Co. (mail order and associated manufacturing, controlled by extreme conservative isolationist Gen. Robert E. Wood), and J. I. Case (antiunion farm equipment makers) as only the more notable of its corporate providers.[47]

But the most generously funded and broadly based of all of the conservative business pressure groups was the Foundation for Economic Education, established in 1947. The three groups' aims and supporters interlocked. Behind them all, as large contributors and activists, were members of the Du Pont clan — Lammot, Irenée, John J. Raskob, and, from General Motors, Donaldson Brown and Alfred Sloan. These were the men who had funded and directed the American Liberty League's anti-New Deal crusade in the mid-1930s; they overlapped with the group of "Brass Hats" who had revitalized the NAM at the same time.[48]

The Foundation's donors list was large and impressive. It included sixteen of the fifty largest manufacturing corporations. Some firms whose managements were undoubtedly conservative in their political outlook — Allis-Chalmers, for example — did not contribute; and of those which did, Ford, Esso, and U.S. Steel seem to belong at the liberal end of any spectrum of big business political outlook, whether evaluated according to their labor relations policies or the tone of their official pronouncements.[49] These caveats aside, the Foundation's organizers and chief contributors illustrate the extent of support for the practical conservative political viewpoint, and its propagandist strategy, in the executive suites of many of America's center firms. All three big automobile firms supported it, and Chrysler's B. E. Hutchinson, together with GM's Donaldson Brown, were responsible for getting it off the ground. (These were also the two who had led conservative resistance to the NAM's "liberal" labor policy of December 1946, and to the Full Employment Bill.) Five of the eight major steel firms, including U.S. Steel, and both main electrical manufacturing firms, GE and Westinghouse, were large contributors, together with Du Pont, two of the big five meat-packers (Armour and Co. and Swift and Co.), one of the big four rubber companies (B. F. Goodrich), and Pittsburgh Plate Glass, one of the automotive industry's major outside suppliers. These firms, clustered around the automotive industry, were at the heart of American manufacturing and in the storm centers of CIO activity. Other Foundation backers were also large and important — Standard Oil of New Jersey, Consolidated Edison, International Nickel, the three giant mail order houses, and U.S. Gypsum, controlled by Sewell Avery of Montgomery Ward. Even the less important contributors included nationally known firms: Armstrong Cork, Caterpillar Tractor, Champion Spark Plug, Chase National Bank, Electric Auto-Lite, Humble Oil and Refining, Johns-Manville (building materials), Kohler Co., Libbey-Owens-Ford Glass, Owens-Illinois Glass, Seiberling Rubber, Timken Roller Bearing, and Union Carbide.[50]

Only one firm on this list, Libbey-Owens-Ford Glass, figured in any of the case-studies of good and peaceful labor relations conducted in the postwar years.[51] Most of the rest followed the course of realism in labor relations, often reluctantly, and worked out an "armed truce" through institutionalized conflict. Some of them — American Rolling Mill, Armstrong Cork, Du Pont, Esso, and Humble — belonged to that small group of pre-New Deal "progressive" firms which had managed to maintain the substance of "independent" (i.e. company) unionism after the passage of the Wagner Act and the rise of the CIO; while others —

Montgomery Ward, J. I. Case, and Kohler — were in that even smaller minority of large firms that were still, in the 1940s and even 1950s, able and willing to resist unionization, within the law if possible, outside of it, and violently, if necessary. The fit between labor relations strategy and tactics and managerial political outlook is not perfect, either for the 1930s or 1940s; but it is close, and suggestive.

This chapter has been more of an examination of businessmen's ideas — occasionally sophisticated, more often simplistic and even laughable when dealing with the awkward and unfamiliar tasks of public opinion-shaping and political manipulation — and of the practical consequences for business behavior of their worried, sometimes extravagantly anxious state of mind in the 1940s, than of the actual impact of the policies they adopted on the nation's political climate. As far as the businessmen funding and supporting the very different efforts of the CED and the FEE were concerned, for example, there was a real connection between those activities and what they themselves were doing, more directly, in their labor and industrial relations policies, and in their more hard-headed political action. The ultimate objectives were either the same or complementary, and the methods were rationalized by similar models of the "American character" and the state of public opinion, how it was formed, how it could be influenced, and how it could eventuate in favorable patterns of behavior and acceptable political outcomes. Whether one is dealing with labor relations policy at the level of the firm, personnel and welfare policies, public relations exercises, or direct attempts to influence national political behavior, a fairly simple and consistent twofold categorization of American managements — as "corporate liberals" or traditionalists, progressives or reactionaries, sophisticated or practical conservatives — seems to fit. These categories are not new, they have not been tightly defined, and they are not entirely satisfactory. What may be even less satisfactory to students of the political behavior of twentieth-century American business and its response to social protest and reform currents, who may have been informed and persuaded by the interesting and stimulating interpretations and investigations of William Appleman Williams, Gabriel Kolko, James Weinstein, and others of the "New Left," is that it is very difficult to conclude that most large firms and their managements were "corporate liberal," etc., and that *that* political orientation was the more important and impressive of those I have observed.

Indeed, my conclusion is quite the reverse. Practical conservatism and merely tactical flexibility won out in every aspect of labor relations policy and the reshaping of federal labor law. And when one examines the "political thought" of senior managers of practical conservative firms, it is clear that their patterns of analysis and behavior could not be more different from those of the minority of business liberals who have preoccupied most of those historians who have been interested in business political action. Corporate liberals — the kin of Roosevelt's "tame millionaires" — have been good self-publicists, and they have often risen to prominence because of filling important positions in government service. This is particularly true when one examines the interpenetration of members of the corporate elite and of the "national security establishment" — the Departments of State and Defense, their advisory committees, and the semiofficial bodies to which they turn for advice and political support. And in the 1950s and '60s it did seem as if there was an emerging liberal consensus on issues of domestic policy too, with businessmen serving and encouraging the slow growth of the welfare state, committed to Keynesian economic management, and trying to find safe solutions to the crises of American race relations and urban life.

But it would be a mistake to interpret the domestic politics of the 1930s and 1940s in terms of a model of business behavior which finds whatever value it possesses in a debatable reading of the Progressive Era, and in an understandable attempt to account for the limited achievement and disappointingly narrow horizons of postwar American liberalism by finding millionaires under the bed, or between the sheets. American businessmen in the 1930s and '40s, according to my alternative reading, were overwhelmingly conservative, even reactionary, in terms of their values and political predilections; disarmingly open in declaring their social objectives; and quite straightforward in the way they went about winning them. They were not devious or subtle; their political knowledge was neither vast nor deep; they were moved by a passionate self-interest. They were tactically innovative, even imaginative, and were prepared to compromise, to move toward their objectives by degrees. But they were not the men an investigator wishing to find "corporate liberal" wellsprings of industrial relations and domestic social policy would wish, and have, to find.

Perhaps this alternative reading will find some passing favor, and receive some credence, in this new age of reaction. The business community's united efforts to defeat the 1978 Labor Law Reform Bill, the NAM's establishment of the Council on a Union-Free Environment, the proliferation of business-sponsored political action committees (PACs) and "new right" public policy foundations and overt propaganda agencies, should remind us that the leopard hasn't changed his spots over time, but has merely chosen and been free to pose as a big pussycat.

Epilogue:
"Getting Everybody
Back on the Same Team"

In the fall of 1949 Raymond S. Livingstone, Thompson Products' vice-president in charge of personnel, gave one of his frequent inspirational addresses to fellow businessmen. Against a fairly dismal background—economic recession at home, a Democratic administration still in Washington after the surprise and disappointment of the 1948 elections, the fourth postwar bargaining round, and tense international relations—Livingstone was remarkably confident and reassuring. He directed his audience's attention to the success of management's strategy for the recovery of the initiative in industrial relations, and the restoration of its power and status in society.[1]

Why had the sense of crisis which had seemed to grip so much of the business community in the late years of the war and the early years of reconversion relaxed so much? Livingstone pointed to grounds for real optimism. First, there was the "tremendously more informed and sober thinking on the part of virtually all American workmen." They had accurate information on, and understanding of, business economics; they had pride in the American way of life and standard of living, especially in comparison with conditions they observed in Western Europe or the Eastern Bloc. In their relations with management, amicable fair-mindedness prevailed. Thompson Products was a very survey-minded company, but what Livingstone was showing here was the decline of his own anxiety, rather than a confidence born of measurement of changes in the climate of public opinion.[2]

Second, he mentioned "the general employer enlightenment and earnest desire to do better in all his relations, and particularly those with his own people." At last, the business community at large had adopted as standard practice the progressive techniques of personnel administration which had once been reserved to vanguard companies.[3]

Third, Livingstone was reassured by

the fairness and equity of the Taft-Hartley Act as compared with the almost incredible Wagner Act, and its morally dishonest administration. Witness how a power-grasping and politically motivated horde [Q: the labor movement or the Democratic 81st Congress, or both?] that intended to emasculate the Taft-Hartley Act was successfully fought off. Mark the serious concern with which Committees of Congress are now directing their attention to the subject of labor monopoly. Note the laws that are being passed in state legislatures for peaceful regulation of labor relationships within the state. Judges are applying the same principles of law to labor matters as apply to all other types of human controversies, and police bodies are beginning to require unions to respect the laws of peace and order in the same manner as do other groups of citizens.[4]

Of course, it is impossible to speak with certainty on the actual impact of Taft-Hartley. Some of its provisions backfired, others simply disappointed their proponents' hopes, and when Livingstone spoke many of the clauses of that immensely complicated law had yet to be infused with meaning by the NLRB and the courts. All the same, Livingstone was in no doubt that the supersession of the reviled Wagner Act and old NLRB had cleared the air and opened the way to behavior by agencies of the state at all levels which did not encourage the spread of the labor movement, nor the increase of its power.

Fourth — presumably as a result of the experience of the postwar strike wave, and of the beneficial effects of the Great Free Enterprise Campaign — "[t]he public is not blindly tolerant or sympathetic today to strikes, and the public now has a vastly increased understanding of some of the problems faced by industry." Even the unions had become more tolerable, as a result of the CIO's war on Communism in its ranks. They had become responsible. "In many instances, within the four walls of the company, healthy relationships exist between employee members of the local union committee and the management. It's not until the international interjects its own theories and ultimatums that difficulty occurs." Livingstone's remarks indicated the extent of the practical and ideological accommodation with unionism possible even for an authoritarian progressive, erstwhile open shop, management. "Our boys" were still all right even if they did happen to be union members, even committeemen. Labor relations strategy had altered its aims from fighting off unionism to attempting to confine the scope of bargaining, limit it to local levels, and turn the union machinery into a force for stability within the plant. The International might still be a disruptive force, bringing its claims for industry-wide increases in wages and for novel fringe benefits. But it could also be a force for stability, helping management to manage local militancy and discontent. Collective bargaining, as a way of handling much of in-plant labor relations which was *not* threatening to the fundamentals of management's power, had won a substantial measure of acceptance.[5]

And so my point is this: During the past fifteen years we have been through a veritable hurricane of social and economic revolution. Today the storm is all but blown out, and incredibly good things are rising all about the horizon.[6]

Livingstone's speech marks the effective end of an era of profound anxieties for the business community, generated by real challenges to its power and authority. Immediately after the war, it had still been possible to believe that liberal or radical reformism remained on the American political agenda. A labor movement of unprecedented size and real militancy was a force to reckon with. The threat to the viability of individual firms, and the survival of what was left of the free enterprise system after the ravages of the New Deal, might depend on the economic and political consequences of the inevitable, however long-delayed, postwar recession.

The concern American businessmen felt and expressed about the postwar political climate, especially in 1944–46, was reasonable though perhaps exaggerated. Forces over which most of the business community had no control, and little direct influence, brought it deliverance. The Marshall Plan, European recovery, and the dramatic (and permanent) increase in American military spending consequent on the Korean War brought the American economy through a rough patch in the late 1940s. Thereafter, the system did deliver the material benefits businessmen understood to be fundamental to the American people's continuing satisfaction with an economy of private capitalism. The Cold War at home aided in the ejection of Communists and other radicals from a divided labor movement, and made serious criticism of the institutions of a liberal capitalist political economy into something quite beyond the pale. This was the favorable environment in which businessmen carried on their struggle for influence, within the plant and outside it. By 1950 it was more or less over. America speeded into the age of affluence, the "era of no hard feelings" within the bounds of consensus politics. Businessmen were once again in the saddle, though not quite so firmly as they had thought they were in the 1920s. They had had to share a little of their power, but the rest of it was quite secure.

Businessmen did not make the context in which they had to operate, and in which their programs succeeded. Some of the ways in which they sought to strengthen their power and authority—notably the Great Free Enterprise Campaign—were surely misconceived. As for the others, in labor relations, personnel administration, and political action, where there was a clearer appreciation of the problem, even there it is not possible to state categorically that what businessmen did was decisive. But it would be hard to deny that they made an important contribution to the favorable results they enjoyed, exploiting immediate opportunities and reinforcing the advantages America naturally gave them. They helped reorientate the climate of public opinion and public policy towards organized labor; they stabilized workplace and contractual labor relations on terms they were willing to accept; and they confined unionism to already-organized sections of the workforce. All of these gains were valuable, and businessmen's own thinking, planning, and actions were important in winning them.

A Note on Sources

Thirty years ago, the doyen of American business historians wrote:

Business men have not left large collections of "public papers" deposited in libraries for perusal by graduate students; their debates have not been preserved in congressional records or legislative journals; their policies were not broadcast for the benefit of constituents. They went quietly, often secretly, about their tasks.[1]

Since Thomas Cochran made those assertions about nineteenth-century businessmen, the situation has improved. Some larger businesses still in operation have liberalized their policies on scholarly access to historical files. Some important businessmen have bequeathed their papers to libraries and foundations.[2] And the archives of many smaller firms, particularly those which have gone broke, been merged with others, or otherwise lost the continuity and independence of their corporate existence, have been deposited in research collections.

But there are still serious problems for the person who wants to rely on corporate archives in an attempt to reconstruct the pattern of business thought and action in a relatively recent historical period. This study would certainly have been very different, and might well have been better, if I had been able to get free and privileged access to the intimate records of a number of the large corporations and organizations in which I was interested. Business historians who have enjoyed such access have ordinarily not been especially interested in industrial relations matters. The one notable exception — Robert Ozanne's *A Century of Labor-Management Relations at McCormick and International Harvester*[3] — is a model of what one would like to have available on General Motors, or General Electric, for example. But it stands more or

205

less by itself. Problems of access, in the first instance, have inclined me to make this work rest on something other than a number of micro-studies of particular firms and business associations. Such studies do not exist in sufficient numbers and quality to make a synthesis of published work worthwhile by itself, and the lack of time, money, and success in approaches to firms or business archives dissuaded me from attempting to fill the gap.

It may be worth exploring why intimate and accessible material for recent business history should be so relatively scarce. The answer lies, I believe, in the process by which public archives are created. Business in America has generally been a secure and legitimate institution, privileged with a protective privacy. Hostility, in the shape of legal or administrative harrassment, systematic investigation, or enforced disclosure of sensitive information, can help create an accessible and rewarding archival record. So can the consequent need some underdog organizations have felt to justify their existence, objectives, and actions before the public.

But, for the most part, large corporations and business organizations have not felt compelled to open their files to public inspection. So important decisions have continued to be taken within the managerial group, behind closed doors, free from the pressures of public responsibility and accountability, and of the need to influence a wider constituency than the decision-makers alone. And large firms have endured remarkably well over time. The great businesses established in the merger movements of the early twentieth century, or created to exploit the new technologies of its first quarter, were mature by the time of which I write, and are generally vigorous today. The records of transitory or defunct organizations are still more likely to enter the public domain than those of the long-lived giants.

In the last dozen years or so, pressures for disclosure on large firms have certainly increased. But that does not help the historian interested in the previous age of privacy very much. There are additional problems if the material in which one is interested is sensitive. And, finally, even in the rare cases when business archives are freely available, the purposes for which corporations have kept and preserved their records are not those the historian might prefer. Records are kept to satisfy the law's requirements and for a corporation's own administrative reasons. They may be excellent for a study of some phases of its developing structure and procedures, but otherwise useless.

These general points can be illustrated from my experience in trying to root out materials on automobile companies' industrial relations policies. Of the Big Three carmakers, the least helpful was Chrysler, which failed to answer even preliminary requests. Ford has donated most of its records to the Ford Historical Archives, which are excellent for many periods and purposes. But material on industrial relations in the 1940s was in a reserved classification, and subsequent specific requests to the company for information on documents known to exist, or to have existed, produced denials that the material was in Ford's hands. General Motors was courteous and helpful. I was told that the materials I wanted were available, but was not allowed to see them. Instead, the company answered some requests for copies of specific documents of which I was aware from other sources, and was generous in giving me documents it had published or circulated privately in the 1940s. Much of this was in any case to be found in good research collections. The Studebaker Company, largest of the "independents" in the 1940s, went out of the automotive business in the 1960s. All of its voluminous records have been deposited at SUNY-Syracuse. But for this student of industrial relations they were disappointing. One could have reconstructed statistical series on manpower utilization from them, but not a broad understanding of managerial motivation in industrial relations policy.

This experience—of knocking one's head against a brick wall, and only occasionally being able to see something the other side through the odd crack—was not unusual. The senior archivist at the Walter P. Reuther Memorial Library in Detroit opined that no file was ever "dead" as far as managements of the Big Three firms were concerned; and a middle-ranking executive of GM's Labor Relations staff further explained that there was material in their files of which the corporation was still somewhat embarrassed. It enjoyed a good relationship with the United Automobile Workers now: it wanted nothing published to disturb the civilized state of affairs between itself and the UAW, whose top leaders had already been on the scene in the late 1940s when things had been rather different.[4]

Of course, there is no reason why firms should bother to keep archives for researchers' convenience, or allow them open access. But it can cause ill feeling, and it does arouse a certain suspicion, usually I am sure groundless, that there are skeletons rattling in the cupboard.

Attempts to get around the deficiencies of the archival record by selective interviewing were equally frustrating. Most senior executives active in the late 1940s were in their fifties or sixties, with those in heavy manufacturing—steel, automobiles and auto parts, and the metal trades —older than the average.[5] Where death had not thinned the ranks of those in whom I was interested, retirement, separation from their firms, and migration from the industrial Northeast to Florida, Arizona, or in one extraordinary case Alaska, had made them untraceable or effectively inaccessible. Some interviews with former businessmen and retired labor leaders were quite rewarding, but some of the subjects were, unfortunately, well past their prime; and in general the information they provided was only of marginal or incidental value.

Despite these difficulties, there turned out to be plenty of rewarding material to study. What I had to do was to cast my net wider, though perhaps shallower, and make a meal of the *little* fishes that came swimming along. American businessmen may not open their archives, but they do open their mouths. There is consequently a vast quantity of published and privately circulated, generally printed material in existence which reports what businessmen have said or written, usually to one another, though sometimes for other audiences. It does not usually allow one to reconstruct the making of a particular firm's policy in the way that interoffice memoranda, position papers, minutes of executive committee meetings, and confidential reports would allow. But it does allow one to make reasonable interpretations of the thinking and action of a section of the business community at large.

The primary material for this study is therefore what Arthur Cole called the "stream of information" within the business community,[6] or at least that part of it which I was able to discover and tap. Organizations which generated it include business associations, large corporations, the business press, and firms supplying specialized services to the business community.[7] Not all of the material is the output of impersonal agencies. Much of it was written by, or issued in the name of, senior executive officers. It can be identified with them as individuals expressing their own opinions and, sometimes a little less surely, with the organizations in which they functioned. In addition, many expert commentators and advisors on business affairs were associated with particular magazines, research agencies, and consultancy firms.

There are problems in relying too much on the information, analysis, and advice produced by members of the business community for one another, because what one is dealing with is not so much a record of decisions taken and their rationale, but a rather softer, less specific, more rhetorical material. Accordingly, before admitting material as "evidence" to be used at all, or deciding quite how to use it, questions must be asked — about the author, the intended audience, the forum, the desired effect. Is a man speaking authoritatively, for his firm? Is he representing facts fairly? If he is speaking for a business association, what is its constituency? How representative is it? Is the speaker engaged in "consciousness raising," or is he giving hard, practical advice?

Much of the discussion at business conferences and in the business press served the former, ideological purpose: it selected and distorted the "facts" it presented, encouraging in-group unity by exaggerating the seriousness of out-group threats, creating and exploiting a paranoid extremism of the right. It was designed to increase businessmen's sense of shared interests, shared dangers, and common obligation to support one another and to follow uniform and consistent courses of action. The associations themselves, the conferences they held, the rhetoric they employed, were deliberate attempts to increase the centripetal tendencies within the business community and attain the objective of "unit thinking and unit action" to which the NAM, for example, was committed.[8]

Turning toward the more "practical" kind of inter- and intrabusiness communication, careful interpretation is still required. Largely it consists of descriptions of general and particular situations in industrial relations — mostly of situations defined as "problems." Their causes are analyzed, importance discussed; what should be done about them is explained, and expected results of remedial action given. Some of the material is apparently pure reportage — "We had this problem; after deliberation, this is what we did about it; and this is what happened." Some is more obviously didactic — "This worked for us; it can work for you, too, and you should try it."[9]

But one cannot verify that the "facts" as reported are accurate rather than selected to make a particular case, or even fabrications. For, on closer examination, even "practical" arguments are supported by estimates, predictions, received opinions, and value judgments, and the courses of action proposed are frequently justified by reference to ideological distortions of the past and present, and apocalyptic visions of the future.

Proceedings and publications of the American Management Association contain much of this mixed material. The AMA's conferences were regular assemblies of men with special interest in or responsibility for aspects of industrial relations. It was dominated by large and technically advanced companies. Its proceedings were concerned with the current preoccupations of practical men. Its object was to increase the effectiveness of member companies' policies by diffusing information, experience, and advice about best practice. The AMA's purpose was, in a sense, to promote unit thinking and unit action in a way similar to the NAM. In so doing, it did not rely on strictly "practical" reasoning: AMA speakers and writers, like those of the NAM — indeed, not infrequently they were the same men — used ideological appeals in calling on the rest of the business community to engage in a struggle for power and authority within and outside the workplace.[10]

The difficulty with such sources is therefore the familiar one of disentangling fact from opinion, but in a heightened and sometimes intractable form. Used with care, they will carry a fair burden of interpretation. But some questions they just will not answer. How did a particular policy work out *in practice?* What relative importance should one ascribe to various possible reasons for its success, or failure? How did workers or the public react to attempts to influence them?

These are admittedly large defects, but it would be wrong to make too much of them. If we try to "accentuate the positive" without entirely "eliminating the negative," it becomes clear that these materials are good evidence *for some things.* They provide a generally reliable guide to the workings of the business mind in action and to the way businessmen looked at the world, and that is how they have been used.

In addition, of course, I have not been utterly dependent on materials generated by the business community. For labor relations, in particular, the voluminous, but necessarily one-sided records of the United Automobile Workers cast some light into the shadier recesses of the automobile manufacturers' behavior. Press coverage and the investigations and reports of government bodies further served to check the accuracy of what businessmen claimed to be "facts."[11]

Other kinds of materials used include briefs presented in pleadings before courts or administrative tribunals, testimony in Congressional hearings, newspaper advertisements, employee handbooks and newspapers, and "how-to" instructional manuals for managers, as well as most of the extant scholarly literature. Full descriptions and, where appropriate, comments on the sources are included in the notes, from which nothing used that was of any importance has been omitted.

Notes

INTRODUCTION

1 David Rogers and Ivar E. Berg, "Occupation and Ideology: the Case of the Small Businessman," *Human Organization* 20 (1961): 103–8 esp., for a helpful critique of earlier studies.

2 Useful contemporary studies of the large corporation include: Robert A. Gordon, *Business Leadership in the Large Corporation* (Washington, D.C.: Brookings, 1945); and Paul E. Holden et al., *Top-Management Organization and Control* (Stanford: Stanford Univ. Press, 1941). For peak associations, see Robert A. Brady, *Business as a System of Power* (New York: Columbia Univ. Press, 1943), pp. 199–215; Alfred S. Cleveland, "Some Political Aspects of Organized Industry" (Ph.D. diss., Harvard Univ., 1946); and Richard W. Gable, "A Political Analysis of an Employers' Association — the National Association of Manufacturers" (Ph.D. diss., Univ. of Chicago, 1950).

3 "The Nine Hundred," *Fortune* 46:6 (Nov. 1952): 132–35, 232–36; William Lloyd Warner and James C. Abegglen, *Big Business Leaders in America* (New York: Harper, 1955); William E. Henry, "The Business Executive: The Psychodynamics of a Social Role," *American Journal of Sociology* 54 (1949): 286–91; Arthur W. Kornhauser, "Attitudes of Economic Groups," *Public Opinion Quarterly* 2 (1938): 260–68; Richard Centers, "Attitude and Belief in Relation to Occupational Stratification," *Journal of Social Psychology* 27 (1945): 159–85; Otto Glanz, "Class Consciousness and Political Solidarity," *American Sociological Review* 23 (1958): 375–83.

4 Murray Seider, "American Big Business Ideology: A Content Analysis of Executive Speeches," *American Sociological Review* 39 (1974): 802–13; Floyd Hunter, *Community Power Structure: A Study of Decision Makers* (Chapel Hill: Univ. of North Carolina Press, 1953), pp. 9–24, 74–79, for a fine por-

211

trait of a local business elite; the continuing vitality of power structure research, and its contributions to an understanding of the business community's membership and influence, can be seen in, for example, Michael Useem, "The Social Organization of the American Business Elite," and Gwen Moore, "The Structure of a National Elite Network," *American Sociological Review* 44 (1979): 553–72, 673–92.

5 See, for example, Robert H. Wiebe, *Businessmen and Reform: A Study of the Progressive Movement* (Cambridge, Mass.: Harvard Univ. Press, 1962); and Robert A. Dahl, "Businessmen and Politics: A Critical Appraisal of Political Science," *American Political Science Review* 53 (1959): 1–34, from which comes the Key quotation at p. 16, note 36. Rogers and Berg, "Occupation and Ideology," suggested part of the way to meet these objections.

6 Theodore Lowi, "American Business, Public Policy, Case-Studies, and Political Theory," *World Politics* 16 (1964): 678–715, for the identification of such issues; Seider, "American Big Business Ideology," for an analysis of saliency.

7 Richard T. Averitt, *The Dual Economy: The Dynamics of American Industry Structure* (New York: Norton, 1968), pp. 1–2.

8 Cleveland, "Some Political Aspects of Organized Industry," pp. 188–235 esp., for an identification of the "active minority" in the NAM; Michael Useem, "Which Business Leaders Help Govern?" *Insurgent Sociologist* 9, pts. 2–3 (Fall 1979–Winter 1980): 107–20, for a contemporary parallel.

9 Frederick H. Harbison, "Constructive Rivalries in Modern Labor-Management Relations," in *College Forums on Current Economic Issues* (New Wilmington, Pa.: The Economic and Business Foundation, Inc., 1948), pp. 13–23, esp. p. 20.

CHAPTER 1: THE PROBLEM OF INDUSTRIAL RELATIONS

1 "Government Spending Is No Substitute for the Exercize of Capitalistic Imagination," *Fortune* 18:3 (Sept. 1938): 63.

2 Thomas C. Cochran, *Business in American Life: A History* (New York: McGraw-Hill, 1972), pts. 3–4; and Herman E. Krooss, *Executive Opinion: What Businessmen Said and Thought on Economic Isues, 1920–1960* (Garden City: Doubleday, 1970), chs. 3–4 esp., for an excellent overview. On business-government partnership, see recent revisionist studies of Herbert Hoover, esp. Ellis W. Hawley, "Herbert Hoover, the Commerce Secretariat, and the Vision of an 'Associative State,' 1921–1928," *Journal of American History* 61 (1974): 116–40; to which Joan Hoff Wilson, *Herbert Hoover: Forgotten Progressive* (Boston: Little, Brown & Co., 1975), pp. 289–300, provides an excellent bibliography.

3 For the labor movement in the 1920s, see esp. the classic account by Irving Bernstein, *The Lean Years: A History of the American Worker 1920–1933* (Baltimore: Pelican, 1966), ch. 2. Other useful interpretations include Mark Perlman, "Labor in Eclipse," in John Braeman et al., eds., *Change*

and Continuity in Twentieth-Century America: The Twenties (Columbus: Ohio State Univ. Press, 1968), pp. 147–78; and Ronald Radosh, "The Corporate Ideology of American Labor Leaders from F. Gompers to Hillman," *Studies on the Left* 6, pt. 6 (Nov.–Dec. 1966): 66–88, esp. 69–72, 77–79.

4 Bernstein, *Lean Years*, ch. 3, and Robert R. R. Brooks, *When Labor Organizes* (New Haven: Yale Univ. Press, 1937), chs. 3, 5, contain good analyses of the thinking and practice of belligerent employers, and H. M. Gitelman, "Perspectives on American Industrial Violence," *Business History Review* 47 (1973): 1–23, is an important assessment of its consequences.

5 Bernstein, *Lean Years*, ch. 3; Grant N. Farr, *The Origins of Recent Labor Policy: University of Colorado Studies, Series in Economics No. 3* (Boulder: Univ. of Colorado Press, 1959), pp. 12–20; Stephen J. Scheinberg, "The Development of Corporation Labor Policy, 1900–1940" (Ph.D. diss., Univ. of Wisconsin, 1966), pp. 152–66. Scheinberg's study was extremely useful throughout this chapter, and is one of the few systematic and thorough accounts of its subject. But its "corporate liberal" interpretation of business behavior will not stand scrutiny.

6 Daniel Nelson, *Managers and Workers: Origins of the New Factory System in the United States, 1880–1920* (Madison: Univ. of Wisconsin Press, 1975), and Norman J. Wood, "Industrial Relations Policies of American Management 1900–1933," *Business History Review* 34 (1960): 403–20, both emphasize operating problems within the expanding enterprise as the stimulus to managerial action. Nelson further stresses the critical importance of the war in the best and most concrete study of scientific management, personnel work, and welfare capitalism yet published. On the two former topics, see also Harry Braverman, *Labor and Monopoly Capital: The Degradation of Work in the Twentieth Century* (New York: Monthly Review Press, 1974), pts. 1–2; Samuel Haber, *Efficiency and Uplift: Scientific Management in the Progressive Era* (Chicago: Univ. of Chicago Press, 1964); Don D. Leschier and Elizabeth Brandeis, "Working Conditions and Labor Legislation," in John R. Commons et al., *History of Labor in the United States, 1896–1932*, vol. 3 (New York: Macmillan, 1935), chs. 16–17; Henry Eilbirt, "The Development of Personnel Management in the United States," *Business History Review* 33 (1959): 345–64.

7 Stuart D. Brandes, *American Welfare Capitalism, 1880–1940* (Chicago: Univ. of Chicago Press, 1976); David Brody, "The Rise and Decline of Welfare Capitalism," in Braeman et al., eds., *Change and Continuity: The Twenties*, pp. 147–78; Robert W. Dunn, *The Americanization of Labor: The Employers' Offensive against the Trade Unions* (New York: International Publishers, 1927), chs. 8–11; Homer J. Hagedorn, "A Note on the Motivation of Personnel Management: Industrial Welfare 1885–1910," *Explorations in Entrepreneurial History* 10 (1958): 134–39; Leschier and Brandeis, "Working Conditions and Labor Legislation," pp. 316–21; Nelson, *Managers and Workers*, ch. 6; Scheinberg, "Development of Corporation Labor Policy," chs. 2–3. On the NCF, see Marguerite Green, *The National Civic Federation and the American Labor Movement, 1900–1925* (Washington,

D.C.: Catholic Univ. of America Press, 1956), fuller and less tendentious than James Weinstein's essays in his *The Corporate Ideal in the Liberal State: 1900–1918* (Boston: Beacon Press, 1968), chs. 1, 2, 5 esp. See also Bruno Ramirez, *When Workers Fight: The Politics of Industrial Relations in the Progressive Era, 1898–1916* (Westport, Conn: Greenwood, 1978), ch. 8.

8 Bernstein, *Lean Years*, pp. 157–74; Brandes, *American Welfare Capitalism*, ch. 13; Brody, "Rise and Decline of Welfare Capitalism"; Dunn, *Americanization of Labor*, ch. 6; C. Ray Gullett and Edmund R. Gray, "The Impact of Employee Representation Plans upon the Development of Management-Worker Relationships in the United States," *Marquette Business Review* 20 (1976): 95–101 — an interesting study based on case-study research and polling of managers in companies concerned; Lescohier and Brandeis, "Working Conditions and Labor Legislation," ch. 18; Nelson, *Managers and Workers*, pp. 156–62; Scheinberg, "Development of Corporation Labor Policy," chs. 4–7.

9 Sumner H. Slichter, "The Current Labor Policies of American Industries," *Quarterly Journal of Economics* 43 (1929): 393–435.

10 Henry S. Dennison, "Management," in Committee on Recent Economic Changes of the President's Conference on Unemployment, *Recent Economic Changes*, vol. 2 (New York: McGraw-Hill, 1929), ch. 3; Morrell Heald, *The Social Responsibilities of Business: Company and Community, 1900–1960* (Cleveland: Case Western Reserve Univ. Press, 1970), esp. ch. 4; Krooss, *Executive Opinion*, chs. 1–4.

11 Bernstein, *Lean Years*, pt. 2; Brody, "Rise and Decline of Welfare Capitalism"; Albert U. Romasco, *The Poverty of Abundance: Hoover, the Nation, the Depression* (New York: Oxford Univ. Press, 1965).

12 Irving Bernstein, *Turbulent Years: A History of the American Worker 1933–1941* (Boston: Houghton Mifflin, Sentry ed., 1971), pp. 19–22; Ellis W. Hawley, *The New Deal and the Problem of Monopoly: A Study in Economic Ambivalence* (Princeton: Princeton Univ. Press, 1966), chs. 1, 2; Richard S. Tedlow, *Keeping the Corporate Image: Public Relations and Business, 1900–1950* (Greenwich, Conn.: JAI Press, 1979), ch. 3.

13 Irving Bernstein, *The New Deal Collective Bargaining Policy* (Berkeley and Los Angeles: Univ. of California Press, 1950), chs. 1–3; Bernstein, *Lean Years*, ch. 2; Farr, *Origins of Recent Labor Policy*, ch. 4 esp.

14 Bernstein, *Turbulent Years*, chs. 2–6; Scheinberg, "Development of Corporation Labor Policy," pp. 162–65; Sidney Fine, *The Automobile under the Blue Eagle* (Ann Arbor: Univ. of Michigan Press, 1963).

15 U.S. Department of Labor, Bureau of Labor Statistics, "Characteristics of Company Unions 1935," *Bulletin No. 634* (Washington, D.C.: Government Printing Office, 1938).

16 Charles R. Milton, *Ethics and Expediency: A Critical History of Personnel Philosophy* (Columbia, S.C.: Univ. of South Carolina Press, 1970), chs. 4–5; Scheinberg, "Development of Corporation Labor Policy," pp. 165–69 esp.; U.S. Congress, Senate, Committee on Education and Labor pursuant

to Senate Resolution 266 (74th Cong.), *Labor Policies of Employers' Associations*, pt. 3, *The National Association of Manufacturers*, 76th Cong., 1st sess. (Washington, D.C.: Government Printing Office, 1939), pp. 89–98.

17 Scheinberg, "Development of Corporation Labor Policy," pp. 165–69 esp.; Thomas G. Spates, "An Analysis of Industrial Relations Trends," *Personnel Series No. 25* (New York: AMA, 1937), esp. pp. 16, 18.

18 Bernstein, *New Deal Collective Bargaining Policy*, chs. 5 ff.; Bernstein, *Turbulent Years*, chs. 5, 7; David O. Bowman, *Public Control of Labor Relations: A Study of the National Labor Relations Board* (New York: Macmillan, 1942), pp. 28–57; Harry A. Millis and Emily C. Brown, *From the Wagner Act to Taft-Hartley: A Study of National Labor Policy and Labor Relations* (Chicago: Univ. of Chicago Press, 1950), pt. 1; Robert R. R. Brooks, *Unions of Their Own Choosing: An Account of the National Labor Relations Board and Its Work* (New Haven: Yale Univ. Press, 1939), ch. 1.

19 Bowman, *Public Control*, for the NLRB's difficulties; and Harold S. Roberts, *The Rubber Workers: Labor Organization and Collective Bargaining in the Rubber Industry* (New York: Harper, 1944), ch. 8, for illustrations.

20 David Brody, "The Emergence of Mass-Production Unionism," in John Braeman et al., eds., *Change and Continuity in Twentieth-Century America: Modern America No. 1* (Columbus. Ohio State Univ. Press, 1964), pp. 221–62, and "The Expansion of the American Labor Movement: Institutional Sources of Stimulus and Restraint," in Stephen E. Ambrose, ed., *Institutions in Modern America: Innovation in Structure and Process* (Baltimore: Johns Hopkins Univ. Press, 1967), pp. 11–36, for the best analytical accounts of the "rise of labor." AFL unions lack the CIO's evident sex appeal, but their membership gains were actually larger — see Christopher L. Tomlins, "AFL Unions in the 1930s: Their Performance in Historical Perspective," *Journal of American History* 65 (1979): 1021–42.

21 Committee on Education and Labor, *The NAM*, ch. 4; Gable, "A Political Analysis of an Employers' Association," pp. 94–135; Frederick Rudolph, "The American Liberty League, 1934–1940," *American Historical Review* 56 (1950): 19–33.

22 Jerold S. Auerbach, "The La Follette Committee and the CIO," *Wisconsin Magazine of History* 48 (1964): 3–20; Joseph A. Fry, "Rayon, Riot, and Repression: The Covington Sit-Down Strike of 1937," *Virginia Magazine of History and Biography* 84 (1976): 3–18; Louis G. Silverberg, "Citizens' Committees: Their Role in Industrial Conflict," *Public Opinion Quarterly* 5 (1941): 17–37; and Keith Sward, "The Johnstown Strike of 1937," in George W. Hartmann and Theodore Newcomb, eds., *Industrial Conflict: A Psychological Interpretation* (New York: Cordon, 1939), pp. 74–102, on the use of community pressures against strikers. See also "The Industrial War," *Fortune* 16:5 (Nov. 1937): 104–10; Sidney Fine, *Sit-Down: The General Motors Strike of 1936–1937* (Ann Arbor: Univ. of Michigan Press, 1969), pp. 235–36.

23 Auerbach, "La Follette Committee and the CIO"; Jerold S. Auerbach, "The La Follette Committee: Labor and Civil Liberties in the New Deal,"

Journal of American History 51 (1964): 435–59. On the climate of opinion, see Alfred W. Jones, *Life, Liberty, and Property: A Story of Conflict and a Measurement of Conflicting Rights* (1941; New York: Octagon Books, 1964) — based on field work in Akron, but of wider significance.

24 Roberts, *Rubber Workers*, chs. 7, 8; Robert Ozanne, *A Century of Labor-Management Relations at McCormick and International Harvester* (Madison: Univ. of Wisconsin Press, 1967), ch. 9 — uniquely valuable as a history of industrial relations based on free access to extensive corporate records in an important firm; Bernstein, *Lean Years*, pp. 646–63; Brooks, *Unions of Their Own Choosing*, chs. 4, 6.

25 Nelson Nauen Lichtenstein, "Industrial Unionism under the No-Strike Pledge: A Study of the CIO During the Second World War" (Ph.D. diss., Univ. of California-Berkeley, 1974), ch. 2; Roberts, *Rubber Workers*, ch. 10.

26 "The Industrial War," p. 180.

27 Frederick H. Harbison and John R. Coleman, *Goals and Strategy in Collective Bargaining* (New York: Harper, 1951), ch. 2; Richard C. Willcock, "Industrial Management's Policies Toward Unionism," in Milton Derber and Edwin Young, eds., *Labor and the New Deal* (1957; New York: Da Capo, 1972), pp. 277–315, esp. 303–11. Willcock's excellent short study is the best in print on this issue. This chapter leans on it heavily.

28 Clarence J. Hicks, *My Life in Industrial Relations: Fifty Years in the Growth of a Profession* (New York: Harper, 1941), p. 111.

29 Walter Galenson, "The Unionization of the American Iron and Steel Industry," *International Review of Social History* 1 (1956): 8–40 at 24–25, and "The Industrial War," pp. 105–7, 168, on the role of "principles" in motivating managers to persistent antiunionism. Reinhard Bendix, *Work and Authority in Industry: Ideologies of Management in the Course of Industrialization* (New York: John Wiley, 1956), pp. 254–87; Gable, "A Political Analysis of an Employers' Association," ch. 2; James W. Prothro, *The Dollar Decade: Business Ideas in the 1920s* (Baton Rouge: Louisiana State Univ. Press, 1954); and Francis X. Sutton et al., *The American Business Creed* (Cambridge: Harvard Univ. Press, 1956), on business ideology. See also "The Industrial War," p. 162; and for the ideological framework within which businessmen responded to the New Deal, the best general study is Robert E. Lane, *The Regulation of Businessmen: Social Conditions of Government Economic Control* (New Haven: Yale Univ. Press, 1954), nicely complemented by Thomas R. Winpenny, "Henning Webb Prentis and the Challenge of the New Deal," *Journal of the Lancaster County Historical Society* 81 (1977): 1–24, a revealing study of an NAM activist, Liberty Leaguer, and president of an anti-union firm.

30 Walter H. Uphoff, *Kohler On Strike: Thirty Years of Conflict* (Boston: Beacon Press, 1966), chs. 1–4; Ernest Dale, *The Great Organizers* (New York: McGraw-Hill, 1960), ch. 4; John D. Ubinger, "Ernest Tener Weir: Last of the Great Steelmasters, Part II," *West Virginia Magazine of History* 58 (1975): 487–507; Rudolph, "American Liberty League"; and George Wolfs-

kill, *The Revolt of the Conservatives* (Boston: Houghton Mifflin, 1962). For the Du Ponts, see also Edward L. Bernays, *Biography of an Idea: The Memoirs of Public Relations Counsel Edward L. Bernays* (New York: Simon & Schuster, 1965), pp. 542–43.

31 Peter Seitz, "Changes in Management's Philosophy of Industrial Relations," in L. Reed Tripp, ed., *Proceedings of the Ninth Annual Meeting of the Industrial Relations Research Association, 1956* (New York: Industrial Relations Research Association, 1957), pp. 100–108 at p. 108. Seitz's comments reward attention.

32 Harbison and Coleman, *Goals and Strategy in Collective Bargaining*, ch. 2.

33 Frederick H. Harbison and Robert Dubin, *Patterns of Union-Management Relations: United Automobile Workers (CIO)–General Motors–Studebaker* (Chicago: Science Research, 1947), chs. 1, 2, 4; interview, Andrew Court (formerly of Labor Economics Section, GM), Detroit, 14 November 1974; Leroy H. Kurtz, "Policy — the Conscience of Business," in *Developing Public and Industrial Relations Policy: General Management Series No. 140* (New York: AMA, 1947), pp. 23–33; Peter F. Drucker, *The Concept of the Corporation* (New York: John Day, 1946).

34 Interview, Ralph Deedes, Jr. (Labor Relations Section, GM), Detroit, 5 November 1974; "The Chrysler Operation," *Fortune* 38:4 (Oct. 1948): 103–5, 151–54; "Chrysler's Hundred Days," *Fortune* 41:6 (June 1950): 70–72; Garth L. Mangum, "Taming Wildcat Strikes," *Harvard Business Review* 38:2 (Mar.–Apr. 1960): 88–96 at 92 (example 2); Robert M. MacDonald, *Collective Bargaining in the Automobile Industry: A Study of Wage Structure and Competitive Relations* (New Haven: Yale Univ. Press, 1963), pp. 314, 317–29; Sumner H. Slichter et al., *The Impact of Collective Bargaining on Management* (Washington, D.C.: Brookings, 1960), pp. 784–86; Carl D. Snyder, *White Collar Workers and the UAW* (Urbana: Univ. of Illinois Press, 1973), pp. 32, 46–47, 54.

35 Donald E. Wray, "The Community in Labor-Management Relations," in W. Ellison Chalmers et al., *Labor-Management Relations in Illini City* (Champaign: Univ. of Illinois Press, 1953), 1: 70–74.

36 Ozanne, *A Century of Labor-Management Relations*, pp. 178–79.

37 *Organization of Personnel Administration: Studies in Personnel Policy* (hereafter cited as *SPP*) *No. 73* (New York: NICB, 1946) — case studies of Armstrong Cork Co., Caterpillar Tractor Co., General Foods Corp., Johns-Manville Co., and Thompson Products, Inc. — all exemplars of best practice, with articulate and politically active managements.

38 Milton, *Ethics and Expediency*, ch. 5.

39 William H. McPherson, *Labor Relations in the Automobile Industry* (Washington, D.C.: Brookings, 1940), pp. 150–52, esp. p. 151; Robert R. R. Brooks, *As Steel Goes . . . : Unionism in a Basic Industry* (New Haven: Yale Univ. Pres, 1940), pp. 200–203.

40 Cyrus S. Ching, "Problems in Collective Bargaining," *Journal of Business* (Jan. 1938): 33–42 at 40.

41 Ching, "Problems in Collective Bargaining," p. 37. See also his *Review and*

Reflection: A Half-Century of Labor Relations (New York: B. C. Forbes & Sons, 1953), ch. 4 esp.

42 Ching, "Problems in Collective Bargaining," pp. 40–42, and *Review and Reflection*, pp. 46–48; Oral History Interview with Cyrus S. Ching, August–Septembe. 1965, John Truesdale, Interviewer (typescript in Labor-Management Documentation Center, Cornell University, Ithaca, N.Y.), pp. 19–20; Paul W. Litchfield, *The Industrial Republic: Reflections of an Industrial Lieutenant* (Cleveland, Ohio: privately printed, 1946), pp. 95–104 esp. (by the president of Goodyear Tire); and Roberts, *Rubber Workers*, esp. ch. 7.

43 Ching, "Problems in Collective Bargaining," p. 42.

44 Ching, *Oral History*, p. 377; Roberts, *Rubber Workers*, pp. 333–34; Bernstein, *Turbulent Years*, 610–13; H. L. R. Emmet, "Industrial Justice and the Labor Union," *Management Record* 3:2 (Feb. 1941): 17–21; James J. Matles and James Higgins, *Them and Us: Struggles of a Rank-and-File Union* (Englewood Cliffs, N.J.: Prentice-Hall, 1974), esp. chs. 5–6; Ruth Susan Meyerowitz, "The Development of General Electric's Labor Policies, 1922–1950" (M.A. thesis, Columbia Univ. 1969), ch. 1; Harry A. Millis, ed., *How Collective Bargaining Works: A Survey of Experience in Leading American Industries* (New York: Twentieth Century Fund, 1942), ch. 14, esp. pp. 747–60; Herbert R. Northrup, *Boulwarism: The Labor Relations Policies of the General Electric Co.* (Ann Arbor: Univ. of Michigan Press, 1963), ch. 2, esp. p. 14; Ronald Schatz, "The End of Corporate Liberalism: Class Struggle in the Electrical Manufacturing Industry, 1933–1950," *Radical America* 9: 4 & 5 (July–Aug. 1975): 187–205.

45 See also below, ch. 2, n. 14.

46 Bernstein, *Turbulent Years*, pp. 607–10; Milton Derber, "Electrical Products," in Millis, ed., *How Collective Bargaining Works*, ch. 14, pp. 790–801 esp.; Donald Robinson, "Champ Strike Deflector," *Nation's Business* 36: 9 (Sept. 1948): 43–45, 61; and, for an unflattering picture, "Edward F. McGrady: Salesman of 'Industrial Peace,'" in Bruce Minton and John Stuart, *Men Who Lead Labor* (New York: Modern Age Books, 1937), ch. 3, esp. pp. 55–63, 80–84; Scheinberg, "Development of Corporation Labor Policy," pp. 184–85; Ralph Lind, "Union Agreements and Contracts," in *Personnel Series No. 34* (New York: AMA, 1938), pp. 4–20.

47 General Motors Corporation, *Fourth Conference for College and University Educators: Personnel Administration and Industrial Relations, 16–29 June 1948* (processed verbatim transcript), afternoon sess., 29 June 1948, pp. 5–6; Lloyd Ulman, *The Government of the Steel Workers Union* (New York: John Wiley, 1962), chs. 1–2; Morris L. Cooke and Philip Murray, *Organized Labor and Production* (New York: Harper, 1940); Clinton S. Golden and Harold J. Ruttenberg, *The Dynamics of Industrial Democracy* (New York: Harper, 1942). Cooke was a long-established, liberal proponent of scientific management; much of Golden and Ruttenberg's work was first published in the *Harvard Business Review*, like *Fortune* a house journal of managerial progressivism.

48 *Organization of Personnel Administration*, p. 40; Cleveland, "Some Political Aspects of Organized Industry," pp. 233–34; Thomas G. Spates, "Management's Responsibility in Industrial Relations," in *Informed Leaders for Better Understanding: Proceedings of the 23d Silver Bay Industrial Conference* (hereafter cited as *Procs. SBIC*), 24–27 July 1940 (New York: Association Press, 1940), pp. 9–19 at p. 15. The Silver Bay conferences were held under the auspices of the Y.M.C.A., an organization which had been present at the creation of welfare capitalism in the last decades of the nineteenth century, and which had maintained its connections with businessmen interested in the enlightened handling of personnel problems. The Silver Bay conference reports rival those of the AMA as a guide to the thinking of an increasingly representative sample of industrial management about industrial relations problems in the 1940s.

49 Spates, "Analysis of Industrial Relations Trends," pp. 18, 23–24.

50 Spates' analysis can be traced further in his "Spark Plugs of Democracy," *Personnel* 18 (1942): 187–94, and "The Competition for Leadership in a Welfare Economy," in *The Practical Meaning of Management Statesmanship: Personnel Series No. 124* (New York: AMA, 1949), pp. 3–11. For Thompson Products, see *Organization of Personnel Administration*, pp. 76–83, and Raymond S. Livingstone (Vice President, Personnel) "Labor Relations in a Non-Unionized Company," in *Personnel Series No. 99* (New York: AMA, 1946), pp. 3–15. On GE's post-1946 policies, see Meyerowitz, "Development of GE's Labor Policies," pp. 79–94; Northrup, *Boulwarism*, ch. 4 esp.; Schatz, "End of Corporate Liberalism"; and below, concluding sec. of ch. 5. Both Thompson Products' President Crawford and General Foods' President Colby M. Chester rose to the presidency of the NAM, while their respective personnel men, Livingstone and Spates, pushed the conservative line in the AMA and other business forums. Firms whose chief executives were articulate "leaders" of the business community, featuring in the NAM's active minority and other business pressure groups, increasingly provided officers, speakers, and (presumably) membership in erstwhile liberal or progressive organizations like the AMA. Such organizations lost their liberal coloration, while practical conservative managements adopted progressive and sophisticated techniques of man-management. These facts help make AMA and SBIC conference reports, for example, increasingly useful guides to business thought and practice.

51 Scheinberg, "Development of Corporation Labor Policy," was almost as helpful as Willcock, "Industrial Management's Policies Toward Unionism," in providing preliminary ideas and information for this chapter. But Scheinberg leaves one with the impression that union-management accommodation was the sole important progressive response to the rise of labor. Willcock, and Douglass V. Brown and Charles A. Myers, "The Changing Industrial Relations Philosophy of American Management," in L. Reed Tripp, ed., *Proceedings of the Ninth Annual Meeting of the Industrial Relations Research Association, 1956*, pp. 84–99, are much more balanced. As my later analysis, pp. 198–99, suggests, I part company with simplistic,

New Leftist interpretations of the "corporate liberal" motivation underlying industrial relations policy.

52 Bernstein, *Turbulent Years*, ch. 13; Merlyn S. Pitzele, "The New Tactics for Labor Peace," address delivered at the 13th NAM Institute on Industrial Relations, 30 October 1947 (mimeographed), pp. 5–6. Pitzele, Labor Editor of McGraw-Hill's *Business Week*, was one of the most perceptive commentators on the industrial relations scene. (Copy in L-MDC)

53 Harold F. Browne, "Taking Stock of Labor Relations," *Management Record* 1 (Jan. 1939): 3–4 at 3. The NICB's inauguration of a monthly magazine to keep its members informed about industrial relations developments, to supplement its occasional *Studies in Personnel Policy*, is a sign of the times— indicative of the saliency of industrial relations problems in businessmen's minds, and of the acute need they felt for information and guidance, a need business organizations satisfied with an increasing range of publications, better-attended conferences, and membership services.

54 George D. Blackwood, "The United Automobile Workers of America 1935–1951" (Ph.D. diss., Univ. of Chicago, 1951), pp. 134–36; Roberts, *Rubber Workers*, pp. 156–61; Ulman, *Government of the Steel Workers Union*, ch. 1; Lichtenstein, "Industrial Unionism under the No-Strike Pledge," ch. 2.

55 C. Wright Mills, *The New Men of Power: America's Labor Leaders* (1948; reprint ed., New York: Augustus Kelley, 1971); see also, if you can understand it, Peter Friedlander, *The Emergence of a UAW Local, 1936–1939: A Study in Class and Culture* (Pittsburgh: Univ. of Pittsburgh Press, 1975), chs. 7–8.

56 Browne, "Taking Stock," pp. 3–4

57 Ibid., p. 4.

58 Senator H. Styles Bridges, "Foreman Again Carries the Ball," *Supervision* 1:8 (Oct. 1939): 5. The beginning of publication of this magazine by the National Association of Foremen (NAF), a Dayton, Ohio-based organization sponsored by midwestern antiunion firms (especially National Metal Trades Association members), is another sign of the times. Foremen were beginning to show serious signs of discontentment and union-consciousness: see below, ch. 2. Increased support for the NAF, set up to meet the industrial relations crises of the First World War, was one way for managements to try to increase the morale, loyalty, and effectiveness (as managerial agents) of their supervisory subordinates.

59 *NAM Labor Relations Bulletin*, nos. 29 (Jan. 1939) and 30 (Sept. 1939); Gable, "A Political Analysis of an Employers' Association," pp. 287–88.

60 Figures from Krooss, *Executive Opinion*, pp. 193–94; "Industry's Position on Labor Legislation" and Roy W. Moore (Chairman, Employment Relations Committee), "Why the Wagner Act Should Be Amended," *NAM Labor Relations Bulletin* 29 (Jan. 1939): 3, 7. At the same time, Du Pont clan member and GM vice-chairman Donaldson Brown, an original Liberty Leaguer, guided the NAM toward the liberal-sounding "Declaration of Principles" which raised the banner of the "public interest" to the masthead of the NAM's public relations campaign. (Heald, *Social Responsibilities of*

Business, pp. 196–97.) The language was perhaps a little milder, the media were exploited with vigor and sophistication, but the message remained unchanged in essentials—Tedlow, *Keeping the Corporate Image*, ch. 3 esp. In labor as in public relations, the NAM's apparent retreat from reaction was largely tactical; at that date, changes in its public positions were little more than cosmetic.

Chapter 2: Labor Relations in the 1940s

1 "Money and Real Weekly Earnings During Defense, War, and Reconversion Periods," *Monthly Labor Review* 64 (1947): 983–96 at 984; H. M. Douty, "Review of Basic American Labor Conditions," in Colston E. Warne et al., eds., *Yearbook of American Labor*, vol. 1, *War Labor Policies* (New York: Philosophical Library, 1945), ch. 2.
2 John M. Blum, *V Was for Victory: Politics and American Culture During World War II* (New York: Harcourt Brace Jovanovich, 1976), esp. chs. 4, 7; David Brody, "The New Deal and World War II," in John Braeman et al., *The New Deal*, vol. 1, *The National Level* (Columbus, Ohio: Ohio State Univ. Press, 1975), pp. 267–309; and Richard Polenberg, *War and Society: The United States 1941–1945* (Philadelphia: J. B. Lippincott Co., 1972), esp. chs. 1, 3, on the general political climate. For business-government relations, see Paul A. C. Koistinen, "Mobilizing the World War II Economy: Labor and the Industrial-Military Alliance," *Pacific Historical Review* 42 (1973): 443–78; Roland N. Stromberg, "American Business and the Approach of War, 1935–1941," *Journal of Economic History* 13 (1953): 58–78; and Jim F. Heath, "American War Mobilization and the Use of Small Manufacturers, 1939–1943," *Business History Review* 46 (1972): 295–319.
3 In addition to sources cited in note 2 above, see esp. Barton J. Bernstein, "The Automobile Industry and the Coming of the Second World War," *Southwestern Social Science Quarterly* 47 (1966): 22–33, and the enjoyable, impassioned contemporary account by Bruce Catton, *The War Lords of Washington* (New York: Harcourt Brace & World, 1948).
4 Bruno Stein, "Labor's Role in Government Agencies During World War II," *Journal of Economic History* 17 (1957): 397–408; James C. Foster, *The Union Politic: The CIO Political Action Committee* (Columbia, Mo.: Univ. of Missouri Press, 1975), esp. chs. 1–3; John D. Greenstone, *Labor in American Politics* (New York: Vintage Books pbk. ed., 1970), ch. 2; Joseph Gaer, *The First Round: The Story of the Political Action Committee* (New York: Duell, Sloan, & Pearce, 1944).
5 For the labor movement in wartime, see Joshua Freeman, "Delivering the Goods: Industrial Unionism During World War II," *Labor History* 19 (1978): 570–93; Sidney Lens, *Left, Right, and Center: Conflicting Forces in American Labor* (Hinsdale, Ill.: Harry Regnery Co., 1949), ch. 19; Aaron Levenstein, *Labor Today and Tomorrow* (New York: Alfred A. Knopf, 1946); Nelson N. Lichtenstein, "Industrial Unionism under the No-Strike

222 / Notes to Pages 43–49

Pledge: A Study of the CIO During the Second World War" (Ph.D. diss., Univ. of California–Berkeley, 1974); Art Preis, *Labor's Giant Step: Twenty Years of the CIO* (New York: Pathfinder Press pbk. ed., 1972), chs. 10–22; Joel Seidman, *American Labor from Defense to Reconversion* (Chicago: Univ. of Chicago Press, 1953); Warne et al., eds., *War Labor Policies*.

6 "Extent of Collective Bargaining and Union Recognition in 1945," *Monthly Labor Review* 62 (1946): 567–71 esp.; Fred H. Joiner, "Developments in Union Agreements," in Colston E. Warne et al., eds., *Labor in Postwar America* (Brooklyn: Remsen Press, 1949), ch. 2, esp. pp. 28–29.

7 "Money and Real Weekly Earnings"; Douty, "Review of Basic American Labor Conditions," in Warne et al., eds., *War Labor Policies*. In *War Labor Policies*, see also chs. 7, 10, 11.

8 All of the works cited in note 5, above, discuss these issues. But see also Irving Bernstein, *Turbulent Years: A History of the American Worker 1933–1941* (Boston: Houghton Mifflin, Sentry ed., 1971), pp. 752–67; William H. Davis, "The Influence of the NDMB's Experience on the NWLB," in National War Labor Board, *Termination Report* (Washington, D.C.: Government Printing Office, 1947–49), 1:xii–xv, on the NDMB and the "Captive Mines" Dispute; and Noel Sargent (Secretary, NAM), *War Control of Labor* (New York: NAM, n.d.), esp. pp. 3–4, 11, for industry's position.

9 "The Wartime Industry-Labor Conference of December 17–23, 1941," NWLB, *Termination Report*, vol. 2, appendix K-3, pp. 1038–44.

10 On the question of "representativeness," see below, ch. 4; for the NWLB, see Robert G. Dixon, "Tripartism in the National War Labor Board," *Industrial and Labor Relations Review* 2 (1949): 372–90; Dexter M. Keezer, "Observations on the Operations of the National War Labor Board," *American Economic Review* 36 (1946): 233–57; NWLB, *Termination Report*, esp. vol. 1; Allan R. Richards, *War Labor Boards in the Field* (Chapel Hill: Univ. of North Carolina Press, 1953); Warne et al., eds., *War Labor Policies*, esp. chs. 3–7; Edwin E. Witte, "Wartime Handling of Labor Disputes," *Harvard Business Review* 25 (1946): 168–89.

11 For wildcat strikes, see below, ch. 2. For detailed statistical analysis of the upsurge of unrest, see "Strikes and Lockouts in 1944," *Monthly Labor Review* 60 (1945): 957–73, esp. 967; and "Work Stoppages Caused by Labor-Management Disputes in 1945," *Monthly Labor Review* 62 (1946): 718–35, esp. 718–19 and 723.

12 James McGregor Burns, "Maintenance of Membership: A Study in Administrative Statesmanship," *Journal of Politics* 10 (1948): 101–16; Frank P. Graham, "The Union Maintenance Policy of the War Labor Board," in Warne et al., eds., *War Labor Policies*, pp. 145–59; Lichtenstein, "Industrial Unionism under the No-Strike Pledge," ch. 4. Graham was the NWLB public member who wrote the "Little Steel" decision.

13 William B. Given, Jr. (President), "Human Relations in Brake Shoe," in *Messages to the Brake Shoe Organization* (n.p.: American Brake Shoe Co., privately printed, Sept. 1945), pp. 41–45; H. W. Jones, Jr. (President, American Tube Bending Co.), letter of 28 November 1941 and speech of 1 Decem-

ber 1941 reprinted in "A Significant Labor Decision," *Personnel* 20 (1943): 182–85; Dissenting Opinion of Industry Members in Humble Oil & Refining Co. Case, 1 April 1944, in NWLB, *Termination Report*, 1: 368–72. The above are representative of the continuing "Open Shop" strain in employers' expressed opinions about unionism. Given was an articulate chief executive with a flair for self-publicity and an idiosyncratic managerial style which appealed to managerial progressives; Jones's antiunion rhetoric was declared permissible by the federal courts, extending the bounds of "employer free speech" under the Wagner Act; the Humble case was one of the most important in the NWLB's life (see below, ch. 4). These are not isolated or insignificant statements. See also analysis of Montgomery Ward case in editorial, "A War Issue," *Christian Science Monitor*, 27 April 1944 (clipping from Royal Institute for International Affairs collection, Nuffield College, Oxford — hereafter RIIA).

14 This understanding of the world-view of the labor relations experts is based on manifestoes and rationales by doyens of the profession, including Lloyd K. Garrison, "Proposal for a Labor-Management Board and a Charter of Fair Labor Practices," *University of Chicago Law Review* 14 (1947): 347–62, and "Trends and Principles Established in Wartime Bargaining," in *Management's Stake in Collective Bargaining: Personnel Series No. 81* (New York: AMA, 1944), pp. 19–34; Harry A. Millis, "Credo: On Collective Bargaining," in Louis G. Silverberg, ed., *The Wagner Act: After Ten Years* (Washington, D.C.: Bureau of National Affairs, 1945), pp. 123–25; Wayne Morse, "Industrial Peace and the Taft-Hartley Act," in Emmanuel Stein, ed., *Issues in Collective Bargaining and the Taft-Hartley Act: Proceedings of the First Annual New York University Conference on Labor* (Albany and New York: Matthew Bender, 1948), pp. 575–96; Sumner H. Slichter, *The Challenge of Industrial Relations: Trade Unions, Management, and the Public* (Ithaca, N.Y.: Cornell Univ. Press, 1947); George W. Taylor, *Government Regulation of Industrial Relations* (New York: Prentice-Hall, 1948). Decisions of the NWLB, discussed and reprinted in its *Termination Report*, esp. vols. 1 and 2, are also an important source.

15 NWLB, *Termination Report*, 1: 124–29, 148.

16 Raymond S. Livingstone, "Settling Disputes without Interrupting Production," *Management Record* 4 (1942): 385–91, for an especially good statement of this position by Thompson Products' vice-president for personnel, an NAM activist.

17 James W. Towsen (Personnel Director, West Virginia Pulp and Paper Co.), "Negotiation of Labor Contracts," in *Better Industrial Relations for Victory: Procs. 26th SBIC, 28–31 July 1943* (New York: Association Press, 1943), pp. 99–104 at pp. 102–3.

18 Blackwood, "United Automobile Workers of America 1935–1951," pp. 415, 430, 447–48; "Grievance Procedure," *NAM Industrial Relations Bulletin* 30 (Sept. 1939): 15–20; Staughton Lynd, ed., "Personal Histories of the Early CIO," *Radical America* 5 (May–June 1971): 49–76 at 74–75; Harry A. Millis, ed., *How Collective Bargaining Works: A Survey of Experience in*

Leading American Industries (New York: Twentieth Century Fund, 1942), pp. 556–60 (steel), 602–8 (autos).

19 Ed Jennings, "Wildcat! The Wartime Strike Wave in Auto," *Radical America* 9:4 & 5 (July–Aug. 1975): 77–113; Lichtenstein, "Industrial Unionism under the No-Strike Pledge," ch. 7; "UAW Adopts Drastic Strike Ban; Provocation No Excuse for Men," *New York Times*, 27 February 1944, and "How the Auto Workers Are Needled into Striking," *PM*, 27 February 1945 (both clippings RIIA); Opinion of Public Member George W. Taylor in 1943 Chrysler case in NWLB, *Termination Report*, 1:342–46. For similar problems in the steel industry, see "What's Itching Labor?" *Fortune* 26:5 (Nov. 1942): 101–2, 228–36 at 228–29.

20 Nathan P. Feinsinger, "Impact of the National War Labor Board on Collective Bargaining," in NWLB, *Termination Report*, 2:555–63; Paul R. Hays, "The National War Labor Board and Collective Bargaining," *Columbia Law Review* 44 (1944): 409–32 at 411–13.

21 C. F. Mugridge (Management Consultant), "Negotiating a Labor Contract," in *Personnel Series No. 91* (New York: AMA, 1945), pp. 41–48 at p. 42.

22 NWLB, *Termination Report*, 1: 67–68.

23 Jesse Freidin and Francis J. Ulman, "Arbitration and the National War Labor Board," *Harvard Law Review* 58 (1945): 309–60; Robert W. Fleming, *The Grievance Arbitration Process* (Urbana: Univ. of Illinois Press, 1965), pp. 14–18; NWLB, *Termination Report*, 1: 65–67, 112, 121, 131.

24 Sumner H. Slichter et al., *The Impact of Collective Bargaining on Management* (Washington, D.C.: Brookings, 1960), pp. 742–46.

25 Steve Du Brul (Director, Social and Economic Relations), "Authority and Responsibility in Industrial Management" (Talk delivered before the Institute of Public Affairs, University of Virginia, 14 July 1934), in Department of Public Relations, General Motors Corporation, *The Responsibility of Management* (Detroit: The Corporation, n.d. but processed 1945 or 1946), pp. 4–10. Du Brul, a rather shadowy figure, played a large part in the development, implementation, and articulation of GM's industrial relations strategy from the early 1930s until 1950. (Interview, Andrew Court, Detroit, 14 November 1974.) He had something of a reputation as a hatchet-man on behalf of Du Pont's controlling interest.

26 "A Statement of General Motors Policies Governing Its Relations with Factory Employees," 15 August 1934 (n.p. or privately printed; copy in Vertical File, Walter P. Reuther Library, Archives of American Labor History and Urban Affairs, Wayne State University, Detroit—hereafter cited as AALH), p. 5. This statement laid out the standards and objectives which were to guide GM throughout its subsequent relationship with the UAW. It deserves to be better known. Frederick H. Harbison and Robert Dubin, *Patterns of Union-Management Relations: United Automobile Workers (CIO)–General Motors–Studebaker* (Chicago: Science Research, 1947), pp. 49, 81–82; Millis, ed., *How Collective Bargaining Works*, pp. 606–7.

27 Ludwig Teller, *Management Functions under Collective Bargaining: the*

Rights and Responsibilities of Management in a Union Relationship (New York: Baker, Voorhis & Co., 1947), chs. 3–4.

28 Clarence O. Skinner (Washington Representative, Automotive and Aviation Parts Mfrs., Inc.; Alternate Industry Member, NWLB; formerly with GM), "The Fringe Issues," in *Trends in Union Demands: Personnel Series No. 95* (New York: AMA, 1945), pp. 6–14 at p. 10.

29 NWLB, *Termination Report*, 1:105.

30 Teller, *Management Functions under Collective Bargaining*, p. 53, 56.

31 George Hodge (Manager, Labor Relations, International Harvester Co.), "Management Principles in Collective Bargaining," in *Personnel Series No. 95*, pp. 3–6 at pp. 4, 6; "Improving Management's Score at the Bargaining Table: A Panel Session," in *Personnel Series No. 91*, pp. 49–63 at pp. 49–51, 53–56.

32 "Management Functions Recognized by the War Labor Board," *Personnel* 21 (1944): 242–56, esp. secs. 1, 4–20. The report emphasized that the "Board itself has on occasion amended agreements to return to management, functions it has bargained away" (ibid., p. 242). NWLB, *Termination Report*, 1:110.

33 See, for example, Lawrence Stessin, "Is the Arbitrator Management's Friend in Discipline Cases?" *Monthly Labor Review* 82 (1959): 373–75, on the character of developing case law.

34 George W. Taylor, "The Function of Collective Bargaining," in *Personnel Series No. 81*, pp. 3–19 at p. 6.

35 Bryce M. Stewart and Walter J. Couper, *Reconversion in Industrial Relations: Industrial Relations Monograph No. 13* (New York: Industrial Relations Counselors, Inc., 1946), p. 11. This publication by the oldest industrial relations consultancy, founded with Rockefeller money, serving the Special Conference Committee and a growing list of blue riband firms in the 1920s and 1930s, is one of the most important guides to management thinking and strategy in industrial relations in the 1940s; Almon E. Roth (President, National Federation of American Shipping; Chairman, San Francisco Employers' Council; Industry Member, NWLB), "War's Impact on Labor Relations," in *Meeting Personnel Requirements of Reconversion: Personnel Series No. 94* (New York: AMA, 1945), pp. 16–25 at pp. 19–20; S. T. Williamson and Herbert Harris, *Trends in Collective Bargaining: A Summary of Recent Experience* (New York: Twentieth Century Fund, 1945), pp. 181–84; Lee H. Hill and Charles R. Hook, Jr., *Management at the Bargaining Table* (New York: McGraw-Hill, 1945), pp. 66–67 — like the Stewart-Couper monograph, a conservative managerial manifesto.

The steel industry's was the largest and most celebrated joint wage restructuring plan. See Robert Tilove, "The Wage Rationalization Program in United States Steel," *Monthly Labor Review* 64 (1947): 967–82, and Katherine Stone, "The Origins of Job Structures in the Steel Industry," *Review of Radical Political Economics* 6:2 (1974): 113–73 at 155–56.

36 Roth, "War's Impact," pp. 18–19, and Egbert H. Van Delden (Director of

Industrial Relations, Libbey-Owens-Ford Glass Co.), "Problems of Industry-Wide Collective Bargaining," in *Personnel Series No. 95*, pp 14–24 at p. 15.

37 Fred W. Climer (Vice-President, Goodyear Tire and Rubber Co.), "Management Experience in the Rubber Industry," and Garnet L. Paterson (Counsel, United Rubber Workers–CIO), "Problems Encountered in the Rubber Industry," both in *Proceedings of the Conference on Industry-Wide Collective Bargaining, 14 May 1948* (Philadelphia: Univ. of Pennsylvania Press, 1949), esp. pp. 3–4, 56–59; Cyrus Ching, "The Growth of Industry-Wide Bargaining," in *Economic Factors in Labor Relations: Personnel Series No. 109* (New York: AMA, 1947), pp. 20–35.

38 See debate in "Should Collective Bargaining Be Limited to Local Areas?" *Modern Industry* 12:5 (15 Nov. 1946): 116–28. See also below, ch. 4.

39 Neil W. Chamberlain, *The Union Challenge to Management Control* (New York and London: Harper & Bros., 1948). The title for the section deliberately echoes Chamberlain's to reflect my debts, which are substantial. However, neither our analyses nor our concerns exactly coincide.

40 Based on impressionistic study of business press, conference proceedings, etc. See also Lee H. Hill, "Company Organization of Manpower," address delivered before AMA, Chicago, 10 February 1943 (typescript in Allis-Chalmers file, Labor-Management Documentation Center — hereafter cited as L-MDC — Cornell University, Ithaca, N.Y.), esp. pp. 1–6. Hill was one of the most important management strategists in the industrial relations field — see below, ch. 3. But fourteen months after Pearl Harbor, in a speech designed, in part, to remind his audience of longer-term considerations and identify developing problems needing their attention, he stressed that the "salient problem of the moment is to organize manpower for most effective utilization" (p. 2) and that, though managers could and "should plan for the future after the war, first we must win the war, and the present demands nearly all of our energies" (p. 6). At that early date, the degree of strategic awareness displayed even by Hill was low, his plans unformed — purely tactical concerns predominated.

41 Thomas R. Jones, "The Scope of Collective Bargaining," in *Personnel Series No. 81*, pp. 40–51 at p. 42.

42 Managerial analyses include Teller, *Management Functions under Collective Bargaining*, and Hill and Hook, *Management at the Bargaining Table*, as well as Stewart and Couper, *Reconversion in Industrial Relations*. Less valuable, but representative, contributions to the debate are Stephen F. Dunn (Industry Member, Detroit Regional WLB), *Management Rights in Labor Relations* (Grand Rapids, Mich.: Woodbeck Publishing Co., 1946), and Henry Clifton, Jr., "Management Functions," in Stein, ed., *Proceedings of First Annual NYU Conference on Labor*, ch. 4. Chamberlain's was the most important scholarly contribution to the debate, but see also the works of Bakke and Turnbull, cited below.

43 E. Wight Bakke, "Labor and Management Look Ahead," in *Reconciling Labor and Management Philosophies: Personnel Series No. 98* (New York:

AMA, 1946), pp. 9–25 at p. 13, and *Mutual Survival: the Goal of Labor and Management* (New Haven: Yale Univ. Press, 1946), pp. 5–8; John G. Turnbull, "A Study on the Management Prerogatives Issue," *Personnel* 25 (1948): 106–24 at 109, 112.

44 Works in this vein include Martin Glaberman, *Wartime Strike: The Struggle against the No-Strike Pledge in the UAW During World War II* (Detroit: Bewick ed., 1980); Jennings, "Wildcat! The Wartime Strike Wave in Auto"; Lichtenstein, "Industrial Unionism Under the No-Strike Pledge"; and Preis, *Labor's Giant Step*, esp. ch. 21; and are criticized in Freeman, "Delivering the Goods: Industrial Unionism During World War II."

45 For the background to these Hearings, see Automobile Manufacturers Association, *Freedom's Arsenal: The Story of the Automotive Council for War Production* (Detroit: The Association, privately printed, 1950), ch. 6.

46 Jennings, "Wildcat! The Wartime Strike Wave in Auto," p. 98; General Motors Corporation, *Here Is the Issue: Facts Concerning the UAW-CIO Strike against General Motors* (Detroit: The Corporation, privately printed, 10 Jan. 1946), p. 2; U.S. Congress, Senate, Special Committee to Investigate the National Defense Program, *Hearings, Part 28: Manpower Problems in Detroit* (Washington, D.C.: Government Printing Office, 1945), pp. 13,444–45, 13,447.

47 F. D. Newbury, "Wages and Productivity—the Problems Involved," in *Economic Fundamentals of Collective Bargaining: Personnel Series No. 103* (New York: AMA, 1946), pp. 3–18 at pp. 5–6 esp. Newbury was in charge of Westinghouse's own postwar planning—see his "A Forecast of Business Prospects," *Harvard Business Review* 25 (1947): 273–88.

48 L. Clayton Hill (Vice-President, AMA Production Divison), "How Can We Meet This Challenge—'Higher Wages, No Price Increases,'" in *Developments in Production and Management Engineering: Production Series No. 162* (New York: AMA, 1945), pp. 3–11 at p. 7. The theme of the entire Fall Production Conference in 1945, "Get Back on the Cost Beam," was chosen in recognition of the seriousness of this problem—see Hill's "Production Problems and Policies," in *Modern Management Practices and Problems: General Management Series No. 139* (New York: AMA, 1947), pp. 8–14 at p. 10.

49 Norman Matthews, testimony in *Manpower Problems in Detroit*, pp. 13, 332–34; George W. Taylor, "Problems and Policies of the NWLB," in *Personnel Series No. 91*, pp. 3–19 at p. 8; C. Canby Balderston, "What Has Been Happening to Employee Compensation?" *Personnel* 21 (1945): 266–71 at 271; "Where to Trim Those War-Swollen Costs," *Modern Industry* 12:4 (15 Oct. 1945): 82–84.

50 Irving J. Phillipson (Director of Industrial Relations), address given at Joint Botany Worsted Mills-Textile Workers Union of America, CIO, Training Program, 19 September 1946 (mimeographed—copy in Corporations File, L-MDC), p. 7. Botany Mills and the Textile Workers mounted this joint training program for supervisors and shop stewards to try to improve the company's productivity after wartime slippage. Arthur Kolstad, "Em-

ployee Attitudes Before the War and Now," *Personnel* 20 (1943): 138; Hill, "How Can We Meet This Challenge—'Higher Wages, No Price Increases,'" p. 6; Carl C. Harrington, "The Decline in Labor Productivity," *Mill and Factory*, May 1946, reprinted in *Management Review* 35 (1946): 336–38; *Reducing Absenteeism: SPP No. 46* (New York: NICB, 1942), p. 34.

51 H. F. Howard (President, Manufacturing, Fruehauf Trailer Co., Detroit), in "What Is a Fair Day's Work? A Panel Session," in *Management Techniques for Increasing Productivity: Production Series No. 163* (New York: AMA, 1946), pp. 28–51 at p. 36; for the significance of the effort bargain, see Maurice Kilbridge, "The Effort Bargain in Industrial Society," *Journal of Business* 33 (1960): 10–20.

52 "What Has Become of Discipline?" *Factory Management and Maintenance* 103:6 (June 1945): 82–87 at 87; Elmer W. Earl, Jr., *Personnel Practices in Factory and Office*, II: SPP No. 59 (New York: NICB, 1943), p. 22, table 59.

53 See, in particular, reports of incidents at Borg-Warner Corporation's Norge Products Division Plant in Muskegon, Michigan, and at Ford Motor Co.'s Edgewater, N.J., plant, widely regarded as test cases—"Firing of Strikers Is Upheld by WLB," *New York Times*, and "Industrial Discipline Upheld," *Journal of Commerce*, both 17 May 1944; "Detroit Labor Debate: Auto Firms Will Warn Mead Group: Unions Try to Manage Our Business," *Wall Street Journal*, 6 March 1945; NWLB, *Termination Report*, 1:110; "Says Union Forces Men to Ease Off" and "Ford, UAW Argue on Slowdown," *Detroit Free Press*, 22 and 24 January 1944 (all clippings from RIIA collection); Teller, *Management Functions under Collective Bargaining*, pp. 81, 87.

54 Jonas Silver and Everett Kassalow, *Seniority in the Automobile Industry April 1944* (Washington, D.C.: U.S. Department of Labor, Bureau of Labor Statistics, processed report), pp. 3, 31.

55 *Manpower Problems in Detroit*, p. 13, 320.

56 James F. Lincoln, "The Lincoln Electric Company Incentive Plan," in *Industrial Engineering for Better Production: Production Series No. 153* (New York: AMA, 1944), pp. 34–40 at p. 34.

57 Agnes E. Meyer, *Journey Through Chaos* (New York: Harcourt, Brace & Co., 1944), pp. 252–68; Al Nash, "A Unionist Remembers: Militant Unionism and Political Factions," *Dissent* 24 (Spring 1977): 181–89.

58 George S. Moore (Manager, Industrial Relations), "The Story of Joe Workman," address delivered 8 June 1948 (mimeographed, copy in Information File, L-MDC), pp. 2–8; *Manpower Problems in Detroit*, pp. 13, 286–90; Harbison and Dubin, *Patterns of Union-Management Relations*, pp. 160–62; David W. Rust (Vice-President), "A Plan to Share Cost Savings with Employees," in *Personnel Series No. 103*, pp. 19–25 at pp. 19–20.

59 See, for example, William F. Whyte, *Pattern for Industrial Peace* (New York: Harper & Bros., 1951), chs. 2–5, for an interesting study of a militant local in the steel fabricating industry. More generally, see Garth L. Mangum, "Taming Wildcat Strikes," *Harvard Business Review* 38:2 (Mar.–Apr. 1960): 88–96; Slichter et al., *Impact of Collective Bargaining*, pp. 331,

492–95, 666, 818–20; and Richard Herding, *Job Control and Union Structure: A Study on Plant-Level Industrial Conflict in the United States, with a Comparative Perspective on West Germany* (Rotterdam: Univ. of Rotterdam Press, 1972), esp. pp. 30–31, 41–42, 346–49.

60 Supervisors and Foremen of Williamson Heater Co., "How Does Top-Management Look at Cost Control?" in *Building a Cost-Minded Organization: Production Series No. 160* (New York: AMA, 1945), pp. 24–31, quoted material from p. 27.

61 *Manpower Problems in Detroit*, pp. 13, 370–93.

62 "Detroit's Labor" and "Labor Reconversion," *Wall Street Journal*, 16 December 1944 and 14 May 1945 (clippings from RIIA collection).

63 Hill, "Production Problems and Policies," esp. pp. 10, 12; "Where to Trim Those War-Swollen Costs"; "What Will Happen to Wages," *Factory Management and Maintenance* 103: 6 (June 1945): 82–87 at 87.

64 Selig Perlman, "The Basic Philosophy of the American Labor Movement," *Annals of the American Association of Political & Social Science* 274 (Mar. 1951): 57–63 at 59 ff.

65 For Hill's role, see also below, ch. 3.

66 Harold W. Story (Vice-President), "Communist Influence in Labor Unions," address delivered at the 52d Congress of American Industry, 4 December 1947 (NAM press release, mimeographed—copy in Record Series L-2, L-MDC).

67 Statement of Allis-Chalmers Manufacturing Company in Negotiations With Local 248, United Automobile Workers of America-CIO, before a panel of the National War Labor Board, 6 July 1942 (processed), pp. 68, 42–51.

68 Statement of Allis-Chalmers, pp. 73–77; Elinore M. Herrick (Director, Personnel and Labor Relations, Todd Shipyards Corp.), "Application of Seniority Provisions," in *The Collective Bargaining Agreement in Action: Personnel Series No. 82* (New York: AMA, 1944), pp. 17–19; Frederick Harbison, "Seniority in Mass-Production Industries," *Journal of Political Economy* 48 (1940): 851–64; Charles E. Wilson (President, GM) to UAW Top Negotiating Committee, 18 February 1946 (typed transcript in Walter P. Reuther Pre-Presidential Materials, Box 2, Folder 12, AALH).

69 Statement of Allis-Chalmers, pp. 37–39, 48–49, 54–61; *We Work in a Great Tradition at Allis-Chalmers* (employee handbook, privately printed, 1944—copy in Corporations File, L-MDC), pp. 28–29.

70 Chamberlain, *Union Challenge to Management Control*, pp. 268–85.

71 Chamberlain, *Union Challenge*, esp. chs. 4–6 and appendices.

72 Van A. Bittner (Labor Member, NWLB), "As Labor Sees It," in *Toward a National Labor Policy: Personnel Series No. 72* (New York: AMA, 1943), pp. 9–19 at p. 13. See also Labor representatives' position at November 1945 Conference, ch. 4 below.

73 Hill and Hook, *Management at the Bargaining Table*, pp. 60–75; Hill, "Management's Rights and How to Retain Them," in *Proceedings of the 27th SBIC* (New York: Association Press, 1944), pp. 30–47.

74 *Manpower Problems in Detroit*, pp. 13,568–74.
75 "Patterns for Power: An Account of the Reuther Plan and Other CIO Plans for Control of the Nation's Industry," Automotive Council Exhibit No. 15, *Manpower Problems in Detroit*, pp. 13,626–28; Clinton S. Golden and Harold J. Ruttenberg, *The Dynamics of Industrial Democracy* (New York: Harper & Bros., 1942), chs. 8–11 and appendix; Frederick Harbison, "Steel," in Millis, ed., *How Collective Bargaining Works*, pp. 546, 567–69.
76 Julius Emspak, "Labor-Management War Production Councils," *Science and Society* 7 (1943): 83–96; Dorothea de Schweinitz, *Labor and Management in a Common Enterprise* (Cambridge: Harvard Univ. Press, 1949).
77 Richard Leonard (Vice-President, UAW-CIO), address before the Industrial Relations Council of Metropolitan Boston, 8 May 1946 (mimeographed copy in Information File, L-MDC), pp. 1–3; Harbison and Dubin, *Patterns of Union-Management Relations*, pp. 37–41; Katherine Pollack Ellickson, "Labor's Recent Demands," *Annals of the American Association for Political and Social Science* 248 (Nov. 1946): 6–10.
78 In addition to the sources cited in ns. 4 and 5 above, see John Harding, "The 1942 Congressional Elections," *American Political Science Review* 38 (1944): 41–58; John R. Moore, "The Conservative Coalition in the United States Senate, 1942–1945," *Journal of Southern History* 33 (1967): 368–76; and Julie Meyer, "Trade Union Plans for Social Reconstruction in the United States," *Social Research* 11 (1944): 491–505.
79 Stephen K. Bailey, *Congress Makes a Law* (New York: Columbia Univ. Press, 1950), esp. chs. 1–3, 5–7; Barton J. Bernstein, "The Removal of War Production Board Controls on Business, 1944–1946," *Business History Review* 39 (1965): 243–60.
80 Everett M. Kassalow, "New Patterns of Collective Bargaining," in Richard A. Lester and Joseph Shister, eds., *Insights into Labor Issues* (New York: Macmillan, 1949), esp. pp. 119–27; Murray W. Latimer, "Social Security in Collective Bargaining," in Stein, ed., *Proceedings of First Annual NYU Conference on Labor*, pp. 1–32; Arthur F. McClure, *The Truman Administration and the Problems of Postwar Labor* (Cranbury, N.J.: Associated University Presses, 1969), esp. chs. 4, 5. Less comprehensive than McClure, but more analytical, are Barton J. Bernstein's articles, "The Truman Administration and Its Reconversion Wage Policy," *Labor History* 6 (1965): 214–31, and "The Truman Administration and the Steel Strike of 1946," *Journal of American History* 52 (1966): 791–803.
81 The best account of the strike and its issues is in Harbison and Dubin, *Patterns of Union-Management Relations*, esp. pp. 35–37, 71–72, 86–90. Blackwood, "The UAW," pp. 244–54, gives a sympathetic exposition of the connection between strike issues and strategy and Reuther's "New Industrial Philosophy"; Irving Howe and B. J. Widick, *The UAW and Walter Reuther* (New York: Random House, 1949), ch. 6, offer an equally sympathetic, near-contemporary, yet quite reliable insiders' account; Lichtenstein, "Industrial Unionism under the No-Strike Pledge," pp. 694–705, concentrates on the linkage between Reuther's tactics and strategy and internal

UAW politics; while Barton J. Bernstein, "Walter Reuther and the General Motors Strike of 1945–1946," *Michigan History* 49 (1965): 260–77, focuses narrowly on the wage issue and the negotiating tactics of the two parties. See also discussion of GM strike below, ch. 5.

82 Levenstein, *Labor Today and Tomorrow*, pp. 210–11.

83 The metaphors, and the ideas they represented, were in common use at the time — see the alarmist analyses of Goetz A. Briefs, *Can Labor Sit in the Office? Sociological Aspects of Union-Management Cooperation* (New York: NICB, July 1948), esp. pp. 9–18; John Lyon Collyer (President, The B. F. Goodrich Co.), "America's Decade of Decision," remarks at 25th Anniversary of Industrial Relations Counselors, Inc., New York City, 22 May 1951 (copy in Information File, L-MDC).

84 For background, see J. Carl Cabe, "Foremen's Unions: A New Development in Industrial Relations," *University of Illinois Bulletin*, vol. 44 no. 44 (18 March 1947); Ernest Dale, *The Unionization of Foremen: Research Report No. 6* (New York: AMA, 1945); Robert H. Ferguson, "The Unionization of Foremen" (Ph.D. diss., Cornell Univ., 1948). Statistics from U.S. Department of Labor, Bureau of Labor Statistics, "Union Membership and Collective Bargaining for Foremen," *Bulletin No. 745* (Washington, D.C.: Government Printing Office, 1943); survey evidence in Opinion Research Corporation, "Trends in Foremen Thinking — 1948," *The Public Opinion Index for Industry* (Princeton, N.J.: privately circulated, March 1948), p. 27, and "Here's Your Modern Foreman," *Modern Industry* 14:1 (15 July 1945): 54–64 at 62; quotation from Carroll E. French (Director, Industrial Relations Dept., NAM), "Management's Program for Making Collective Bargaining Work," address delivered before the Industrial Relations Council of Metropolitan Boston, 8 May 1946 (mimeographed — copy in Information File, L-MDC), p. 2.

85 For the making of the modern foreman, see Daniel Nelson, *Managers and Workers: Origins of the New Factory System in the United States, 1880–1920* (Madison: Univ. of Wisconsin Press, 1975), esp. ch. 3; on the foreman in the 1920s, see J. David Houser, *What the Employer Thinks: Executives' Attitudes toward Employees* (Cambridge, Mass.: Harvard Univ. Press, 1927), pp. 160–65, and Don D. Lescohier and Elizabeth Brandeis, "Working Conditions and Labor Legislation," in John R. Commons et al., *History of Labor in the United States, 1896–1932*, vol. 3 (New York: Macmillan, 1935), pp. 324–29; on the transformation of the supervisory role, see Cabe, "Foremen's Unions," pp. 7–10; Richard C. Edwards, *Contested Terrain: The Transformation of the Workplace in the Twentieth Century* (New York: Basic Books, 1979), esp. chs. 2, 4, 7; Kenneth H. Kolker, "The Changing Status of the Foreman," *Bulletin of the Business History Society* 22 (1948): 84–105; Thomas B. Patten, Jr., *The Foreman: Forgotten Man of Management* (New York: AMA, 1968), pp. 13, 17–20; "The Changing Position of Foremen in American Industry," *Advanced Management* 10 (1945): 155–56.

86 Golden and Ruttenberg, *Dynamics of Industrial Democracy*, pp. 4–22, 40–42, 128–29.

87 Cabe, "Foremen's Unions," esp. pp. 11–13, 17–19; Kolker, "Changing Status of the Foreman," p. 98; Patten, *The Foreman*, pp. 87–90.
88 Millis, ed., *How Collective Bargaining Works*, pp. 547–49, 672–74, 775, 790, 798–99; Slichter et al., *Impact of Collective Bargaining*, ch. 29 — for these two patterns of managerial response; Robert Dubin, "Decision-Making by Management in Industrial Relations," *American Journal of Sociology* 54 (1949): 292–97, on the "reign of rules."
89 See works of Cabe, Kolker, and Patten, cited in n. 87 above.
90 Ira B. Cross, Jr., "When Foremen Joined the CIO," *Personnel Journal* 18 (1940): 274–83; William H. McPherson, *Labor Relations in the Automobile Industry* (Washington, D.C.: Brookings, 1940), pp. 22–23; Harry W. Anderson (Vice-President for Industrial Relations), "Introduction" in *The Supervisory Personnel Program of the General Motors Corporation: Personnel Series No. 78* (New York: AMA, 1944), pp. 3–5; Harold F. Browne, "Foremen and Unions," *Management Record* 6 (1944): 215–19.
91 Cabe, "Foremen's Unions," pp. 20–28; Charles C. Smith, *The Foreman's Place in Management* (New York: Harper & Bros., 1946), esp. chs. 4, 5, 8, 9. Smith was a NAM staff expert on supervisory problems. His account of them is remarkably frank, his analysis penetrating. See also Browne, "Foremen and Unions," pp. 216, 218; George C. Willis, "Why Do Foremen Unionize?" in *Proceedings of the 27th SBIC* (1944), pp. 114–20; Harry W. Anderson, *Should Management Be Unionized? Personnel Series No. 90* (New York: AMA, 1945), p. 5; C. G. McQuaid, "Detroit Foremen Fight for Recognition," *Industrial Relations* 2:2 (June 1944): 6–7, 33–34; "Foremen's Compensation," *Industrial Relations* 2:9 (Jan. 1945): 11–12, 32–33. (The *Industrial Relations* magazine referred to was a monthly publication of the Dartnell Corporation of Chicago, and directed at a readership among midwestern manufacturing management, especially from medium-sized firms. It is not to be confused with the similarly-named academic periodical put out by the University of California Industrial Relations centers at Berkeley and Los Angeles for the past two decades.)
92 For the history of the FAA, see Cabe, "Foremen's Unions," pp. 32–37; Dale, *Unionization of Foremen*, esp. pp. 8–17; General Motors Corporation, *History of the Movement to Organize Foremen in the Automobile Industry* (Detroit: The Corporation, 1 May 1945, processed); Charles P. Larrowe, "A Meteor on the Industrial Relations Horizon: The Foremen's Association of America," *Labor History* 2 (1961): 259–94.
93 As well as secondary accounts cited above, see testimony of FAA officers in U.S. Congress, House, Military Affairs Committee, *Hearings on HR 2239, HR 1742, HR 1728 and HR 992: Bills Relating to the Full Utilization of Manpower*, 78th Cong., 1st sess., 1943 (Washington, D.C.: Government Printing Office, 1943), pp. 354, 678–79 (hereafter cited as *Full Utilization of Manpower*); and in U.S. Congress, Senate, Committee on Labor and Public Welfare, *Hearings on S. 249*, 81st Cong., 1st sess., 1949 (Washington, D.C.: Government Printing Office, 1949), pt. 4, pp. 2161–63 (hereafter cited as *1949 Senate Labor Hearings*). See also interview between the au-

thor, Dennis East, and Carl Brown, in AALH. Brown was one of the FAA's founders, and successively president of Ford Willow Run Chapter, national Ford organizer and membership director, and finally national FAA president from 1948 until its demise. The oral history contains some information otherwise unobtainable—FAA records have been lost, scattered, or destroyed, and FAA officers and activists have not been systematically searched out and interviewed.

94 *Full Utilization of Manpower*, p. 679.

95 Herbert R. Northrup, "The Foreman's Association of America," *Harvard Business Review* 23 (1945): 187–202.

96 Bureau of Labor Statistics, "Union Membership and Collective Bargaining for Foremen"; Cabe, "Foremen's Unions," pp. 36, 38.

97 See sources cited in notes 84, 91, 92 above, and Herbert R. Northrup, "Unionization of Foremen," *Harvard Business Review* 21 (1943): 496–504. General Motors' leadership of business opinion can be followed in the Corporation's *History of the Movement to Organize Foremen;* in Anderson, *Should Management Be Unionized?*; and in "Should Management Be Unionized? A Statement by General Motors," advertisement in New York *Journal of Commerce* 12 April 1945 (clipping in RIIA collection). Chrysler's position is made explicit in its *Shall the Rank and File Boss the Plants?* (Detroit: The Corporation, 10 April 1946, privately printed)—a version of a brief presented to the NLRB by its counsel.

98 J. A. Voss (Director of Industrial Relations, Republic Steel Co.), in *Full Utilization of Manpower*, p. 139.

99 William T. Gossett (Counsel, Ford Motor Co.), in *1949 Senate Labor Hearings*, pt. 4, p. 2169. Cf. responsibilities of foremen in the event of work stoppages in *Ford Motor Company Supervisor's Manual* (privately circulated, February 1948—copy in Corporations File, L-MDC), pp. 230, 301.

100 Elbert M. Cushing (Director of Industrial Relations, U.S. Rubber Co.), in U.S. Congress, House, *Hearings before a Special Subcommittee of the Committee on Education and Labor on HR 2032*, 81st Cong., 1st sess., 1949 (Washington, D.C.: Government Printing Office, 1949), p. 461 (hereafter cited as *1949 House Labor Hearings*).

101 General Motors, *History of the Movement to Organize Foremen*, p. 18; *1949 Senate Labor Hearings*, pp. 3369–71, 3040–41; *1949 House Labor Hearings*, p. 351; Chrysler Corporation, *Shall the Rank and File Boss the Plants?* p. 40.

102 Gossett, in *1949 Senate Labor Hearings*, pt. 4, p. 2169.

103 Charles E. Wilson (President, General Motors), in *Full Utilization of Manpower*, p. 76.

104 The case, involving the Washington D.C. area of the Great Atlantic and Pacific Tea Co., is discussed in "Store Managers as 'Employes,'" [New York] *Journal of Commerce*, 23 July 1946 (clipping from RIIA collection).

105 C. C. Carlton (Vice-President, Motor Wheel Corp.; President, Automotive Manufacturers' Association), in *Full Utilization of Manpower*, pp. 109–10.

CHAPTER 3: THE "VIEW FROM THE TOP"

1 Title taken, with grateful acknowledgment, from Robert L. Heilbroner's contribution in Earl F. Cheit, ed., *The Business Establishment* (New York: John Wiley, 1964), pp. 1–36. Heilbroner's is an important discussion of the changing nature of the American big businessman's "conservatism."

2 "Reconversion Time Is Cost-Cutting Time," *Management Review* 34 (1945): 122–24; Boyce F. Martin, "What Business Learns from War," *Harvard Business Review* 21 (1943): 358–68; F. D. Newbury, "Wages and Productivity– the Problems Involved," in *Economic Fundamentals of Collective Bargaining: Personnel Series No. 103* (New York: AMA, 1946), pp. 3–18 at pp. 6–7, 13.

3 Newbury, "Wages and Productivity," pp. 13–14; L. Clayton Hill, "Production Problems and Policies," in *Modern Management Practices and Problems: General Management Series No. 139* (New York: AMA, 1947), pp. 8– 14; Jules Backman, "Productivity, Wages and Prices," in *Economic Factors in Labor Relations: Personnel Series No. 109* (New York: AMA, 1947), pp. 3– 13. Cf. "The Time for Low Production Costs Is Now," *Factory Management and Maintenance* 103: 8 (Aug. 1945): 81–82. This was the magazine's fifth annual National Production issue: five of its ten case studies of successful productivity-raising programs emphasized manpower management.

4 A. L. Kress, "Job Classification under Cost Reduction," in *Wages and Production Costs: Production Series No. 159* (New York: AMA, 1945), pp. 32– 36 at p. 33; cf. "What's Happening to Productivity," *Modern Industry* 12:5 (15 Nov. 1946): 49–64 at 51–52.

5 Albert Raymond (Management Consultant), "Labor Productivity and Technical Advances," in *Management Techniques for Increasing Labor Productivity: Production Series No. 163* (New York: AMA, 1946), pp. 17–27 at p. 17.

6 Charles F. Roos, "Economic Considerations for Production Executives," in *Production Series No. 163*, pp. 5–16 at p. 16; cf. "What's Happening to Productivity," *Factory Management and Maintenance* 105:9 (Sept. 1947): 66–69 at 67.

7 Henry Ford II, "The Challenge of Human Engineering," address before the Society of Automotive Engineers, Detroit, 9 January 1946 (n.p., Ford Motor Co. private print, 1946), p. 6; and "One Solution to Our Problems," address at Commonwealth Club, San Francisco, 8 February 1946 (n.p., n.d.), pp. 5–7. Copies from Detroit Public Library, AALH.

8 *Proceedings of the Conference on Productivity, 4 June 1949, Milwaukee* (processed – copy in Information File, L-MDC); Ewan Clague (Commissioner, Bureau of Labor Statistics), "The Facts on Productivity," address before the Society for the Advancement of Management, New York, 6 December 1946 (mimeographed – copy in Information File, L-MDC); "Labor Output Check Now Available," *Modern Industry* 12:1 (15 July 1946): 174– 76; and "To Hunt Yardstick for Productivity," *Modern Industry* 12:4 (15 Oct. 1946): 118.

9 Guy B. Arthur, Jr., "The Status of Personnel Administration in Manage-

ment," in *Management's Internal "Public" Relations: Personnel Series No. 102* (New York: AMA, 1946), pp. 29–41 at pp. 33–34; Frances Spodick, "Making Foremen Discipline-Conscious," *Personnel* 20 (1944): 339–42 at 339; Joseph L. Trecker, "The Economic Justification for Investment in Plant Assets," in *Production Policies for Increased Output: Production Series No. 169* (New York: AMA, 1947), pp. 10–19.

10 W. S. Woytinsky, "What Was Wrong in Forecasts of Postwar Depression?" *Journal of Political Economy* 55 (1947): 142–51; the clearest and most sophisticated analysis of the likely political effects of the economy's failure to operate at an optimum level after the war came from businessmen associated with the Committee for Economic Development, for which see ch. 7 below.

11 See esp. Alonzo L. Hamby, *Beyond the New Deal: Harry S. Truman and American Liberalism* (New York: Columbia Univ. Press, 1973), chs. 1, 2; and Norman D. Markowitz, *The Rise and Fall of the People's Century: Henry A. Wallace and American Liberalism, 1941–1948* (New York: Free Press, 1973), chs. 1–5. For the barest outlines of the debate on the American economy's supposed tendency toward "secular stagnation," see Ernst W. Swanson and Emerson P. Schmidt, *Economic Stagnation or Progress* (New York: McGraw-Hill, 1946), and George Terborgh, *The Bogey of Economic Maturity* (Chicago: Machinery and Allied Products Institute, 1945), representing conservative business and market economics; Seymour E. Harris, ed., *Postwar Economic Problems* (New York: McGraw-Hill, 1943), and Benjamin Higgins, "The Doctrine of Economic Maturity," *American Economic Review* 36 (1946): 133–41, for the views of liberal Keynesians.

12 On the war economy, see Dr. Edwin G. Nourse (Chairman, Council of Economic Advisers), "The Employment Act and the Economic Future," address before the 51st Congress of American Industry, 6 December 1946 (NAM press release, mimeographed—copy in record series L-2, L-MDC), pp. 6–7; Erwin H. Schell, "Current Changes in Management Operating Policy," in *Guides to Management Operating Policy: Production Series No. 171* (New York, AMA, 1947), pp. 3–9 at p. 4. For business uncertainties and anticollectivism, see copy of letter, George A. Sloan to Paul Hoffman, 4 June 1943, Marion B. Folsom Papers, University of Rochester, Rochester, N.Y.; and Richard S. Tedlow, *Keeping the Corporate Image: Public Relations and Business, 1900–1950* (Greenwich, Conn.: JAI Press, 1979), pp. 118–21.

13 On wartime conservatism, see John Robert Moore, "The Conservative Coalition in the United States Senate, 1942–1945," *Journal of Southern History* 33 (1967): 368–76; and Donald R. McCoy, "Republican Opposition During Wartime," *Mid-America* 49 (1967): 174–89. For conservative businessmen's program, the best sources are conference addresses to the NAM's annual Congresses of American Industry, e.g. "Make Way for Prosperity," program statement by Board of Directors, NAM, 3 December 1946 (mimeographed—copy in Record Series L-2, L-MDC).

14 Walter B. Weisenburger, *Challenge to Industry: An Address Delivered be-*

fore the 51st Congress of American Industry (New York: NAM, privately printed, January 1947 — copy in record series L-2, L-MDC).

15 Henry Ford II, "Production for Peace and Freedom," address before members of the Automotive and Aviation Parts Manufacturers, Inc., Cleveland, 29 September 1947 (copy from AALH), p. 7. Emphases in original.

16 J. D. Zellerbach, "American Industry's Stake in the World Situation," *California Personnel Management Association* (hereafter cited as *CPMA*) *Management Report No. 1* (San Francisco: CPMA, 1948), pp. 57–62; Richard Glen Gettell, "International Economic Policy," and C. D. Jackson, "Domestic Economic Policy," in *New Goals in Economic and Labor Policies: General Management Series No. 144* (New York: AMA, 1949), pp. 21–26 and 27–31; Fred C. Crawford, "On Guard for Freedom," address before 52d Congress of American Industry, New York City, 5 December 1947, pp. 1–8 (NAM press release, mimeographed, copy in record series L-2, L-MDC).

17 On managerial ideologies, see Herman E. Kroos, *Executive Opinion: What Businessmen Said and Thought on Economic Issues, 1920–1960* (Garden City: Doubleday, 1970), chs. 2, 11; Francis X. Sutton et al., *The American Business Creed* (Cambridge: Harvard Univ. Press, 1956); and Heilbroner, "The View From the Top."

18 The question, "To Whom and for What Ends Is Corporate Management Responsible?" has provoked a vigorous debate, well reviewed in Edward S. Mason, "The Apologetics of Managerialism," *Journal of Business* 31 (1958): 1–11, and Henry G. Manne, "The 'Higher Criticism' of the Modern Corporation," *Columbia Law Review* 62 (1962): 399–432.

19 "Trends in Union Contract Clauses," in *The New Pattern of Labor Relations: Personnel Series No. 79* (New York: AMA, 1944), pp. 27–34 at p. 27.

20 For the emergence of this absolutist theory of owners' and employers' prerogatives, see Rowland Berthoff, "The 'Freedom to Control' in American Business History," in David H. Pinkney and Theodore Ropp, eds., *A Festschrift for Frederick B. Artz* (Durham, N.C.: Duke Univ. Press, 1964), pp. 158–80; Lee H. Hill, "Using Management Rights in Day-to-Day Labor Relations," in *The Collective Bargaining Agreement in Action: Personnel Series No. 82* (New York: AMA, 1944), pp. 11–17 at pp. 11–12.

21 Hill, "Using Management Rights," p. 12.

22 Congressman Short in *Full Utilization of Manpower*, p. 154.

23 Clarence B. Randall, *Full Utilization of Manpower*, p. 88. (Randall was vice-president of Inland Steel Co., and an important figure in the NAM.)

24 Ludwig Teller, *Management Functions under Collective Bargaining: The Rights and Responsibilities of Management in a Union Relationship* (New York: Baker, Voorhis & Co., 1947), p. 114; R. C. Smyth and M. J. Murphy, *Bargaining with Organized Labor* (New York: Funk & Wagnalls, 1948), p. 132 (Smyth and Murphy had been responsible for industrial relations at the Bendix Aviation Corporation's Radio Division plant in Baltimore — see also their important "Discipline: A Case Study in the Development and Application of a Discipline Procedure," *Factory Management and Maintenance* 103:7 [July 1945]: 97–104); C. C. Carlton (Vice-President, Motor Wheel

Corp.; President, Automotive Manufacturers Association), in *Full Utiliza-tion of Manpower*, p. 109; Sam Lewisohn (President, Miami Copper Co.; founder member, AMA), *Human Leadership in Industry: The Challenge of Tomorrow* (New York: Harper & Bros., 1945), pp. 6, 69–81.

25 Thomas R. Jones, "The Scope of Collective Bargaining," in *Management's Stake in Collective Bargaining: Personnel Series No. 81* (New York: AMA, 1944), pp. 40–51 at p. 45; Lee H. Hill and Charles R. Hook, Jr., *Manage-ment at the Bargaining Table* (New York: McGraw-Hill, 1945), pp. 7–8, 57–58.

26 Hill, "Using Management Rights in Day-to-Day Labor Relations," p. 12.

27 Hill and Hook, *Management at the Bargaining Table*, p. 58; see also Andre Maximov, "Safeguarding Management's Functions," *Personnel* 22 (1946): 391–401, and discussion of prerogatives issue at November 1945 President's Labor-Management Conference, below, ch. 4.

28 Hill and Hook, *Management at the Bargaining Table*, p. 58; Elinore M. Herrick, "Application of Seniority Provisions," in *The Collective Bargain-ing Agreement in Action: Personnel Series No. 82* (New York: AMA, 1944), pp. 17–19 at p. 19.

29 W. Homer Hartz (for the U.S. Chamber of Commerce), in U.S. Congress, Senate, Committee on Labor and Public Welfare, *Hearings on S. 55 and S.J. Res. 22*, 80th Cong., 1st sess., 1947 (Washington, D.C.: Government Printing Office, 1947), p. 881.

30 On "unitary" and "pluralistic" managerial ideologies, the best analytical discussion, drawn from the British experience but more generally applica-ble, is by Alan Fox; see esp. his "Managerial Ideology and Labor Relations," *British Journal of Industrial Relations* 4 (1966): 366–78, for a clear state-ment. "Pluralistic" rhetoric from American managers of the 1940s is rare and comparatively insignificant. Almost all of the sources cited in this work are supersaturated with unitary assumptions, but for particularly good ex-amples see comments of Harry Coen (Vice President, Industrial Relations), in General Motors Corporation, *Third Conference for College and Univer-sity Educators: Personnel Administration and Industrial Relations, 16–30 June 1947* (processed report — copy in L-MDC), pp. 112–19, and sources cited in notes 13 and 16 to chapter 2, above.

31 For the "good worker" see esp. statements from executives of Thompson Products Corp., who took a clear and (more or less) consistent line — Stanley R. Black, "Earning Employee Backing," in *College Forums on Current Economic Issues* (New Wilmington, Pa.: The Economic and Business Foun-dation, 1948), pp. 25–43; Raymond S. Livingstone, "Labor Relations in a Non-Unionized Company," in *Personnel Series No. 99* (New York: AMA, 1946), pp. 3–15. See also ch. 7, below.

32 For the soft metaphors, see in particular firms' induction and orientation handbooks for new employees, of which there are excellent collections in the L-MDC Corporations File — fine examples include *Your Life With Calco* (Bound Brook, N.J.: Calco Chemicals Division, American Cyanamid Corp., 1944), esp. pp. 3, 12; *You and Your Job at Bird & Son, Inc.* (E. Wal-

pole, Mass.: Bird & Son, Inc., 1945), esp. pp. 2–4, 30; and *Your Job at Hill-side* (Hillside, N.J.: Bristol-Myers Co., 1943). For militaristic metaphors, see esp. communications addressed by management to supervision, or discussions of the foreman problem, incl. William F. Wise (President, American Propellor Corporation), "Foremen, Top Sergeants of the Production Army," *Supervision* 4:10 (Oct. 1942): 12, 31; Louis Ruthenberg (Chairman, Servel, Inc. — staunch antiunion firm, pillar of the NAM, and supporter of rightist causes; later, one of the founder members of the John Birch Society), "Foremen Field Generals in Battle for America," *Supervision* 11:11 (Nov. 1949): 11; and American Steel Foundries, "Foremen Today . . . Leaders of Industry Tomorrow," *Manage* 1:1 (Sept. 1948): 51. Understandably, managers of antiunion, authoritarian firms, speaking to what they expected to be a sympathetic audience, were most inclined to use crude and overt militaristic metaphors. But in fact the language of American management is in any case full of expressions whose first application was in the discussion of modern war-making — one thinks particularly of the "line and staff" organization, and of the preoccupation with "morale." Possibly this is simply because of the historical priority of armies as large-scale, complex, hierarchical, and deliberately planned efficient social organizations. Another possible explanation for the appeal of military — and "team" — metaphors to the 1940s generation of senior executives must surely be their upbringing in the first great age of organized sport (especially collegiate football), and the impact of American military adventures and involvements upon them. Personal service as World War I officers may deserve greater weight than the general cult of arms — in the 1940s, some senior executives continued to be referred to by their military rank, e.g. Colonel Herman Steinkraus of Bridgeport Brass. But Teddy Roosevelt and, later, Knute Rockne certainly made their contributions to the language, imagery, and folklore of American management.

33 Naturally enough, comments on the problems of industrial discipline and the restoration of productivity in the 1940s are most pervaded by this pessimistic view — see, for example, Arthur, "Status of Personnel Administration in Management," p. 33, and discussion in ch. 7, below. It is also exposed in businessmen's testimony before Congressional committees about the foreman problem. Quotation from Guy W. Vaughan (President, Curtiss-Wright Aircraft Corp.), in *Full Utilization of Manpower*, p. 198.

34 James W. Prothro, *Dollar Decade: Business Ideas in the 1920s* (Baton Rouge: Louisiana State Univ. Press, 1956), pt. 1; M. M. Olander (Personnel Director, Owens-Illinois Glass Co., Toledo), "The Problem of Supervision in the Defense Program," in *For National Unity — Better Industrial Relations: Procs. 24th SBIC, 23–26 July 1941* (New York: Association Press, 1941), pp. 20–27 at p. 23; managers' self-image in, e.g., "Act Management!" (editorial), *Supervision* 7:2 (Feb. 1945): 3; Harry Woodhead (President, Consolidated Vultee Aircraft Corporation), "Management Must Manage," and "Am I My Brother's Keeper?" (editorial), *Supervision* 8:10 (Oct. 1946): 4, 3; Charles W. Perrelle (President, Gar Wood Industries), "Leader Selection,"

Supervision 8:12 (Dec. 1946): 4–5 at 4. *Supervision* and, from 1948, *Manage*, were organs of the National Association of Foremen, now National Management Association, a body set up during the First World War mobilization in Dayton, Ohio, under the inspiration of the National Cash Register Co., a pioneer in personnel management. The NAF was devoted to increasing the effectiveness of foremen, and to improving their loyalty and identification with managerial values and goals. For this reason, its publications, and the speeches of the antiunion, authoritarian corporate leaders who promoted it in the 1940s, are especially rewarding sources of articulate conservative managerial thinking. On the NAF, see Charles C. Smith, *The Foreman's Place in Management* (New York: Harper & Bros., 1946), ch. 7; and Frank H. Irelan (President, NAF; General Manager, Delco Products Division of GM), "The Purposes and Objectives of the National Association of Foremen," in *Proceedings of the First Annual Conference of Educational Directors in Industry 17–18 March 1944 at Columbus, Ohio, Conducted under the Auspices of the National Association of Foremen* (n.p., n.d.), pp. 8–10.

35 Charles P. Taft, "What Is Ahead for Management and Labor?" in E. Clark Worman, ed., *Better Relations through Better Understanding: Procs. 29th SBIC* (New York: Association Press, 1947), pp. 67–88 at p. 86. Taft was reporting sentiments expressed at a recent conference in Pittsburgh. Cf. ch. 7, below.

36 Douglas McGregor, *The Human Side of Enterprise* (New York: McGraw-Hill, 1960), esp. ch. 3.

Chapter 4: Recovery Of The Initiative, I

1 See discussion in ch. 2 and notes for ch. 2, above. These matters are also discussed in my "Responsible Unionism and the Road to Taft-Hartley: Public Policy and the Domestication of American Labour," paper delivered to the annual conference of the British Association for American Studies, April 1978 (copies available from author). See also, for a detailed study of the NLRB's work, Christopher L. Tomlins, "The State and the Unions: Federal Labor Relations Policy and Organized Labor Movement in America, 1935–1955" (Ph.D. thesis, Johns Hopkins University, 1980), esp. Chs. 4–6.

2 National War Labor Board, *Termination Report: Industrial Disputes and Wage Stabilization in Wartime*, 3 vols. (Washington, D.C.: Government Printing Office, 1947–49), 2:2, 4; "President Moves for Labor Peace," *New York Times*, 11 December 1941, p. 34 (hereafter *NYT*); "No Strike Policy Adopted by AFL," *NYT*, 16 December 1941, p. 25; "A War Labor Board (editorial), *NYT*, 31 December 1941, p. 16; "The Wartime Industry-Labor Conference of December 17–23 1941," NWLB, *Termination Report*, vol. 2, appendix K-3, pp. 1038–44.

3 NWLB, *Termination Report*, 2:2, 6; Allan R. Richards, *War Labor Boards in the Field* (Chapel Hill: Univ. of North Carolina Press, 1953), p. 90;

NWLB, *Termination Report*, vol. 2, appendix G-2; Aaron Levenstein, *Labor Today and Tomorrow* (New York: Alfred A. Knopf, 1946), pp. 65–70; Edwin E. Witte, "Wartime Handling of Labor Disputes," *Harvard Business Review* 25 (1946): 169–89 at 187; "Two Back Union Security," *NYT*, 19 January 1942, clipping from RIIA collection; Cyrus S. Ching, *Review and Reflection: A Half-Century of Labor Relations* (New York: B. C. Forbes & Sons, 1953), p. 58; Lapham quoted in Nelson N. Lichtenstein, "Industrial Unionism under the No-Strike Pledge: A Study of the CIO During the Second World War" (Ph.D. diss., Univ. of California-Berkeley, 1974), p. 195.

4 Thomas R. Jones, "The Scope of Collective Bargaining," in *Management's Stake in Collective Bargaining: Personnel Series No. 81* (New York: AMA, 1944), pp. 40–51 at pp. 47, 48; James Tanham (Vice-President, The Texas Co., and industry member, NWLB), "Management's Case Before the War Labor Board," in *Practical Techniques of Collective Bargaining: Personnel Series No. 86* (New York: AMA, 1944), pp. 30–38; Clarence O. Skinner, "The Fringe Issues," in *Trends in Union Demands: Personnel Series No. 95* (New York: AMA, 1945), pp. 7–14 at pp. 7–8, 13.

5 Richards, *War Labor Boards in the Field*, pp. 75–80 esp.

6 "The War Against Labor," *PM*, 14 August 1944; "Industry on WLB Asks a Court Test on Union Security," *NYT*, 30 April 1944; NWLB, *Termination Report*, 1: 89–91, 368–72; Henrietta M. Larson and Kenneth W. Porter, *History of Humble Oil and Refining Company: A Study in Industrial Growth* (New York: Harper, 1959), pp. 600–606; for the Ward dispute, see "Do We Want a Wave of Postwar Strikes?" (editorial), *Chicago Sun*, 24 April 1944; "Sewell Avery against the Government at War," *Chicago Sun*, 26 April 1944; "Avery Says Policies He Fights Mean 'Dictator Government,'" *New York Herald-Tribune*, 28 April 1944 — all clippings from RIIA collection. The Ward case was a cause célebre, and as such accounts of it are found in the standard sources cited in note 5, chapter 2. It also occasioned a Congressional investigation.

7 Richard W. Gable, "A Political Analysis of an Employers' Association — the National Association of Manufacturers," (Ph.D. diss., Univ. of Chicago, 1950), p. 423; Drew Pearson, "The Washington Merry-Go-Round," *Washington Post*, 27 April 1944; "Employers' Standing with WLB Improves," *New York World Telegram*, 22 January 1945; Jones, "Scope of Collective Bargaining," p. 47 — clippings from RIIA collection. Interestingly, it was about this time (winter-spring 1943–44) that the old-established, "progressive" New York firm of Industrial Relations Counselors, Inc., began the research which led to the publication of Bryce M. Stewart, Walter J. Couper, et al., *National Collective Bargaining Policy: Industrial Relations Monograph No. 9* (New York: Industrial Relations Counselors, Inc., 1945) — see "Report of the Committee on Labor Policy," (Oct. 1945), Box 786, General Records of the Department of Commerce, National Archives, Washington, D.C., p. 1 (I thank Prof. Kim McQuaid for this reference); and discussion of report below.

8 Colston E. Warne et al., eds., *Yearbook of American Labor, I: War Labor*

Policies (New York: Philosophical Library, 1945), pp. 534–35; Allan R. Richards, "Tripartism and Regional War Labor Boards," *Journal of Politics* 14 (1952): 72–103, esp. 93–96. Cf. Robert G. Dixon, "Tripartism in the National War Labor Board," *Industrial and Labor Relations Review* 2 (1949): 372–90, who believed that industry members remained, on balance, less well-prepared and closely connected to their constituents than did labor — particularly CIO — representatives.

9 Raymond S. Smethurst (NAM General Counsel), "What's Ahead in Government Policy and Regulations," and Melvin H. Baker (President, National Gypsum Co.; Chairman, NAM Committee on Industrial Relations Policy), "Labor Peace and Production," in *Labor Relations Today and Tomorrow* (New York: NAM, n.d. — but addresses were delivered to December 1944 Congress of American Industry), esp. pp. 8–12, 26–30; Henning W. Prentis, Jr. (President, Armstrong Cork Co., and formerly president of NAM), "Government's Place in Postwar Labor-Management Relations," address delivered at 257th Meeting of the NICB, New York, 20 January 1944 (Lancaster, Pa.: privately printed, n.d.; copy from Armstrong Cork Co. archives), esp. pp. 8–10. "Employer free speech" and other aspects of developing NLRB policy and judicial interpretation are discussed in Harry W. Millis and Emily C. Brown, *From the Wagner Act to Taft-Hartley: A Study of National Labor Policy and Labor Relations* (Chicago: Univ. of Chicago Press, 1950).

10 "The Chrysler Operation," *Fortune* 38:4 (Oct. 1948): 103–5, 151–54; Johnston's developed views are to be found in his *America Unlimited* (Garden City, N.Y.: Doubleday Doran, 1944).

11 Lichtenstein, "Industrial Unionism under the No-Strike Pledge," p. 684; Levenstein, *Labor Today and Tomorrow*, pp. 273–78; "Text of New Charter for Labor and Management," [New York] *Journal of Commerce*, 29 March 1945; "Business, Labor Frame Peace Code," *NYT*, same date, p. 16 — clippings from RIIA collection.

12 "Industry Group Seeks Law to Curb Strikers," *Journal of Commerce*, 29 March 1945 (clipping from RIIA collection); "More Specific Code Needed, NAM Says," *NYT*, same date, p. 16; "NAM Backs the Aims of New Labor Code," *NYT*, 7 April 1945, p. 19; "Industry to Fight Union of Foremen," *NYT*, 10 April 1945, p. 15; "NAM Offers Aid on Labor Charter," *NYT*, 24 April 1945, p. 26; "Eric Johnston's Code Gets Cool Reception," *Industrial Relations* 2:12 (Apr. 1945): 11.

13 John Scoville, *The Theory of Collective Bargaining* (n.p., n.d.; copy from Information File, L-MDC), p. 3.

14 U.S. Senate, Special Committee to Investigate the National Defense Program, *Hearings, Part 28: Manpower Problems in Detroit* (Washington, D.C.: Government Printing Office, 1945), pp. 13,781–82; Romney speeches — "Why Does the Auto Union Cause So Much Trouble in the Automotive Industry?" (privately printed, 1945; copy in AALH), esp. p. 12; "A Dangerous First Step — Reconversion Brings American Industry to the Crossroads," delivered before the NICB, 20 September 1945 (n.p.: Automotive Manufac-

turers' Association, 1945; copy in Detroit Public Library — hereafter cited as DPL); "Labor-Management Cooperation: Some Major Obstacles," delivered before the Detroit Rotary Club, 20 November 1946 (privately printed; copy in AALH), esp. pp. 10–13.

Automotive industry antiunionism typically combined extremist rhetoric and practice with a brand of "classical liberal" economics in which combinations of workers had no place. GM staff member Steve Du Brul (see ch. 2, note 25) exemplified it by reading Henry C. Simons' famous "Some Reflections on Syndicalism" (*Journal of Political Economy* 52 [1944]: 1–25) into the record during the 1945–46 GM-UAW negotiations and at the same time dropping a serious public relations "clanger" by joining with members of the Fruehauf family (truck builders) and others to organize the stridently right-wing Society of Sentinels at the height of the reconversion strike wave. (Interview with Andrew Court, 13 November 1974; R. J. Thomas [President, UAW-CIO] press release of 7 January 1946; Walter P. Reuther to Charles E. Wilson, 8 January 1946; and UAW-CIO Top Negotiating Committee to President Truman, 22 January 1946 — all in folders 7–8, UAW-GM collection, Series VI and VII, AALH.)

15 Arthur F. McClure, *The Truman Administration and the Problems of Postwar Labor* (Cranbury, N.J.: Associated University Presses, 1969), esp. chs. 3–5; Clark Kerr, "Employer Policies in Industrial Relations, 1945–1947," in Colston E. Warne et al., eds., *Labor in Postwar America* (Brooklyn: Remsen Press, 1949), esp. p. 47. Kerr's piece first explained the *significance* of what went on in the immediate postwar period of American industrial relations, and contributed largely to the genesis of this work.

16 List of delegates from U.S. Department of Labor, Division of Labor Standards, *The President's National Labor-Management Conference, November 5–30, 1945: Summary and Committee Reports: Bulletin No. 77* (Washington, D.C.: Government Printing Office, 1946), pp. 84–85; NWLB, *Termination Report*, 2:6; identification of active minority in NAM from Alfred S. Cleveland, "Some Political Aspects of Organized Industry" (Ph.D. diss., Harvard Univ., 1946), pp. 207–17 — thirteen of the thirty-six firms represented at the Conference were drawn from the 125 firms which had dominated NAM policymaking and provided most of its funds from 1934 to 1946. Allowing for nonmanufacturing firms and trade association representation, these thirteen were a majority of industry representatives, and played the decisive part in the working committees on the most controversial issues.

17 Stewart and Couper, *National Collective Bargaining Policy*, passim; "Report of the Committee on Labor Policy," pp. 2–8; committee membership from "BAC — Membership of Committees, May, 1946," Box 17, Alfred Schindler Papers, Harry S. Truman Library, Independence, Missouri (I thank Prof. Kim McQuaid for this reference); U.S. Department of Labor, Division of Labor Standards, *The President's National Labor-Management Conference*, pp. 84–85; identification of active minority in NAM from Cleveland, "Some Political Aspects of Organized Industry," pp. 207–17. My analysis here follows closely, and leans on, Kim McQuaid's discussion in an

unpublished manuscript of his in my possession. For his generosity in sharing his findings he is to be doubly thanked.

18 George W. Taylor, *Government Regulation of Industrial Relations* (New
York: Prentice-Hall, 1948), p. 232. NWLB Chairman Taylor also chaired
the conference, and left an excellent discussion of it in his book.

19 General Motors Corporation, *Fourth Conference for College and University Educators: Personnel Administration and Industrial Relations, 16 – 29
June 1948* (processed transcript – copy in L-MDC), morning sess., 29 June
1948, p. 12; U.S. Department of Labor, *President's National Labor-
Management Conference*, pp. 44–47.

20 U.S. Department of Labor, *President's National Labor-Management Conference*, pp. 47–49; Irving Bernstein, "Recent Legislative Developments
Affecting Mediation and Arbitration," and Edgar L. Warren, "The Conciliation Service: V-J Day to Taft-Hartley," *Industrial and Labor Relations
Review* 1 (1948): 406–20 and 351–62.

21 U.S. Department of Labor, *President's National Labor-Management Conference*, pp. 54–55.

22 Ibid., pp. 55–56.

23 Fred H. Joiner, "Developments in Union Agreements," and Kerr, "Employer Policies in Industrial Relations," both in Warne et al., eds., *Labor in
Postwar America*, chs. 2, 3, esp. pp. 34–35. See also below, ch. 5.

24 U.S. Department of Labor, *President's National Labor-Management Conference*, pp. 68–70.

25 Taylor, *Government Regulation of Industrial Relations*, p. 237; U.S. Department of Labor, *President's National Labor-Management Conference*,
p. 87. Labor representation on the committee was not of the same caliber,
and included the right-winger James Carey (Electrical Workers) and the
Steel Workers' accommodationist staff expert Clinton Golden, later to become a notable evangelist for union-management cooperation. Such men
could be expected to be understanding toward management claims.

26 U.S. Department of Labor, *President's National Labor-Management Conference*, p. 58.

27 Ibid., pp. 58–60; cf. R. C. Smyth and M. J. Murphy, *Bargaining with Organized Labor* (New York: Funk and Wagnalls, 1948), p. 133; Ludwig
Teller, *Management Functions under Collective Bargaining: The Rights
and Responsibilities of Management in a Union Relationship* (New York:
Baker, Voorhis, and Co., 1947), pp. 381–84.

28 U.S. Department of Labor, *President's National Labor-Management Conference*, pp. 59–62.

29 Ibid., pp. 25–28.

30 Lee H. Hill, "Why the Washington Conference Failed," *Factory Management and Maintenance* 104:1 (Jan. 1946): 100–103.

31 NAM, *The Public and Industrial Peace* (New York: NAM, 1946); McClure,
Truman Administration and Problems of Postwar Labor, esp. chs. 6–9;
Millis and Brown, *From the Wagner Act to Taft-Hartley*, chs. 8–9.

32 Gable, in "Political Analysis of an Employers' Association," ch. 6 and ap-

pendices 8–15, analyzes the making of the NAM's labor program. He had access to committee minutes and departmental position papers, which he reproduces verbatim. His analysis and documentation have both been used heavily in the account which follows, but for somewhat different purposes from his own. Our analyses tally, and his sources are of better quality than those which were otherwise available to me, though their message is the same. See contemporary accounts and analyses — from the press ("NAM Policy Seeks Peace in Industry, Federal Economy," *NYT*, 6 December 1946, p. 1; "Head of NAM Pledges to Carry Out New Liberalized Labor Program," *NYT*, 7 December 1946, p. 5; "NAM Group Seeks Labor Act's Repeal," *NYT*, 23 December 1946, p. 1); the trade press ("Renovation in NAM," *Fortune* 38:1 [July 1948]: 72 ff. at 168; "Here's Industry's Target" [editorial], *Modern Industry* 15:1 [15 Jan. 1947]: 156); and from the NAM itself (Clarence Randall, "A New Federal Labor Policy," address before the 51st CAI, 5 December 1946 [NAM News Bureau press release, mimeographed]).

NAM's dead files have been deposited at the Eleutherian Mills-Hagley Foundation Library in Greenville, Delaware. But the archivists have been unable to locate minutes of the crucial Board of Directors' meeting which confirmed the policy of seeking amendment, not repeal, of the Wagner Act.

33 Minutes of meeting of 16 October 1946 in Gable, "Political Analysis of an Employers' Association," appendix 12, p. 515. Theodore Iserman, Chrysler attorney and advisor to the Republican majority on the Senate Labor Committee in 1947, gave an additional reason: repeal would allow industrial states with prolabor administrations and legislatures to continue to apply Wagner Act principles to intrastate employment relations. Federal preemption would close that loophole. Taft-Hartley, as enacted, only allowed state laws to be controlling if they were *harsher* than federal policy in prohibiting union security agreements utterly, facilitating and encouraging the spate of "right-to-work" laws in the newly industrializing states of the South and West. Iserman's analysis, and the subsequent behavior of Congress, are revealing. See Iserman, *Industrial Peace and the Wagner Act: How the Act Works and What to Do About It* (New York: McGraw-Hill, 1947), p. 68, and discussion of Taft-Hartley provisions at pp. 122, 127 below; Gable, "Political Analysis of an Employers' Association," appendix 14 (working draft for meeting of 18 November 1946), p. 522.

34 See Carroll E. French, "A Constructive Approach to Collective Bargaining Negotiations," introduction to *Preparing to Negotiate* (NAM Industrial Relations Department Management Memo No. 2, March 1947, processed — copy in Information File, L-MDC); Gable, "Political Analysis of an Employers' Association," p. 249.

35 Gable, "Political Analysis of an Employers' Association," p. 295.

36 Ibid., p. 522 (working paper for 18 November 1946 meeting), p. 515 (minutes of 16 October 1946 meeting), and pp. 296–305. See also analysis of personnel management in ch. 6, below.

37 Gable, "Political Analysis of an Employers' Association," pp. 272–73. This was the full recommendation of the Program Committee, which the Board

of Directors shortened, and its similarity to Taft-Hartley's legislative philosophy is striking — see U.S. Congress, House, Committee on Education and Labor, *Report No. 245: Labor-Management Relations Act, 1947*, 80th Cong., 1st sess., 1947 (Washington, D.C.: Government Printing Office, 1947), esp. pp. 4, 7–8, 10–11 — hereafter cited as *Hartley Committee Report*; Fred A. Hartley, Jr., *Our New National Labor Policy — The Taft-Hartley Act and the Next Steps* (New York: Funk and Wagnalls, 1948), esp. ch. 9; Iserman, *Industrial Peace and the Wagner Act*, pp. 78–83; *Labor-Management Relations Act of 1947, Public Law 101*, 80th Cong., Title I, Sec. 1 — hereafter cited as *Taft-Hartley*.

38 "A Labor Management Policy to Benefit America," in *Make Way for Prosperity* (as approved by the Board of Directors), 3 December 1946 (mimeographed — copy in record series L-2, L-MDC), p. 2; *Taft-Hartley*, Title I, sec. 8 (b)(3) and Sec. 9(c)(1)(B).

39 Gable, "Political Analysis of an Employers' Association," p. 273 — "peaceful procedures" were the Board of Directors' words, "voluntary arbitration" the Program Committee's. Cf. *Taft-Hartley*, esp. secs. 8(d) and 10(1).

40 "A Labor Management Policy to Benefit America," p. 2. In 1947 the House majority (*Hartley Committee Report*, proposed sec. 9[f][1], pp. 35–36) and four Republican hard liners in the Senate committee attempted to limit or prohibit multi-employer bargaining — U.S. Congress, Senate, Committee on Labor and Public Welfare, *Report No. 105, Pt. 1: Federal Labor Relations Act of 1947*, 80th Cong., 1st sess. (Washington, D.C.: Government Printing Office, 1947), p. 51 — hereafter cited as *Taft Committee Report*. But they failed — in the Senate committee and on the floor of the Senate, as well as in House-Senate conference. The business community was, in any case, divided on this issue. See Jesse Freidin, *The Taft-Hartley Act and Multi-Employer Collective Bargaining* (Philadelphia: Univ. of Pennsylvania Press, 1948).

41 "A Labor Management Policy to Benefit America," p. 2; cf. *Hartley Committee Report*, proposed sec. 2(II)(B)(vi); only a vestige of this survived in the final Act — *Taft-Hartley*, Title II, sec. 209(b).

42 "A Labor Management Policy to Benefit America," pp. 2–3; Emily Clark Brown, "Free Collective Bargaining or Government Intervention?" *Harvard Business Review* 25 (1946): 190–206; *Taft-Hartley*, esp. sec. 8(b)(4), (6) and sec. 10(k)(I).

43 "A Labor Management Policy to Benefit America," p. 3; Gable, "Political Analysis of an Employers' Association," pp. 504, 524, 529. The House majority proposals outlawed the closed shop, but permitted union security or membership-maintenance agreements, subject to a majority vote of the workers involved in a secret ballot, the union's meeting certain standards of internal democracy, and the employer's assent. Senator Ball (Rep., Minn.) was in favor of the unconditional "right to work." The final Act accepted the House version, with less detailed internal regulation of unions and no employer right to reject a union security provision against the vote of a majority of his workers. *Hartley Committee Report*, esp. pp. 31–34 and 39,

and proposed sec. 8(b)(c) and sec. 9(g), pp. 53–54 and 57. However, as noted above (n. 32, this chapter), state provisions could be more restrictive — Hartley, *Our New National Labor Policy*, esp. p. 72.

44 "A Labor Management Policy to Benefit America," p. 3; *Hartley Committee Report*, pp. 13–17, 33; *Taft-Hartley*, sec. 2(II), sec. 8(c) and sec. 14(a).

45 Holcombe Parkes (Vice-President, Public Relations Division, NAM), "Building on Faith," address delivered before 52d CAI, New York City, 3 December 1947 (NAM press release, mimeographed, copy in record series L-2, L-MDC), pp. 4–7; Richard W. Gable, "NAM: Influential Lobby or Kiss of Death?" *Journal of Politics* 15 (1953): 254–73, esp. 267–69, 272; Gerard D. Reilly, "The Legislative History of the Taft-Hartley Act," *George Washington Law Review* 29 (1960): 285–300, esp. 289–90; Millis and Brown, *From the Wagner Act to Taft-Hartley*, ch. 10, esp. pp. 367, 369–71, 377. John W. Scoville's extremist pamphlet, *Labor Monopolies — OR Freedom* (New York: Committee for Constitutional Government, 1946) had a wide free distribution to members of Congress and other influential figures. It was a call for repeal of the Wagner and Norris-La Guardia Acts. For Ingles' connections, see U.S. Congress, House, *Hearings before a Special Subcommittee of the Committee on Education and Labor on HR 2032*, 81st Cong., 1st sess., 1949 (Washington, D.C.: Government Printing Office, 1949), p. 185. Ingles' special concern was lobbying against government sanction for supervisory unionism; his special target was the FAA.

The longest and most detailed study of the making of the Taft-Hartley law, rather after the manner of Stephen K. Bailey's *Congress Makes a Law: The Story of the Employment Act of 1946* (New York: Columbia Univ. Press, 1950), is Seymour Z. Mann's "Congressional Behavior and National Labor Policy — Structural Determinants of the Taft-Hartley Act" (Ph.D. diss., Univ. of Chicago, 1951). Mann was Millis and Brown's research assistant on *From the Wagner Act to Taft-Hartley*, and the *best* of his work is reproduced there, more or less verbatim. The most interesting aspect of it, however, results from his in-depth interviews with and study of Senators Taft, Ball, Ives (N.Y.) and Morse (Oreg.). Though the dissertation is excessively long and awfully written, it rewards close attention.

46 Hartley, *Our New National Labor Policy*, esp. pp. 22–30, 55–56, 63; *Hartley Committee Report*, esp. pp. 16–17, 21–23, 28–33, 38–39; *Taft-Hartley*, Title II, secs. 206–210. Cf. Gable, "A Political Analysis of an Employers' Association," pp. 508–10, 516, 523–24, 528–30. Iserman, *Industrial Peace and the Wagner Act*, pp. 76–77, was the source of the "confidential personnel" provision. Chrysler had exceptional difficulties with the unionization of its white-collar workers — Carl D. Snyder, *White-Collar Workers and the UAW* (Urbana: Univ. of Illinois Press, 1973), pp. 32, 46–7. That the close fit between the House majority proposals and extremist suggestions made by the Committee for Constitutional Government and the defeated minority within the NAM was not accidental is suggested in Mann, "Congressional Behavior and National Labor Policy," pp. 459–60.

47 Stephen K. Bailey and Howard D. Samuel, *Congress at Work* (London:

Douglas Saunders, 1953), ch. 15, and James T. Patterson, *Mr. Republican: A Biography of Robert A. Taft* (Boston: Houghton Mifflin, 1972), ch. 23, add to the sources cited in n. 44 above. R. Alton Lee, *Truman and Taft-Hartley: A Question of Mandate* (Lexington: Univ. of Kentucky Press, 1966), provides an interesting discussion of the different constituencies of Congressmen and Senators, but otherwise adds little to our understanding of the legislative process. Mann, "Congressional Behavior and Labor Policy," esp. chs. 8, 10, 12, is the most thorough discussion of these issues.

48 For press bias, see Philip Ash, "The Periodical Press and the Taft-Hartley Act," *Public Opinion Quarterly* 12 (1948): 266–71; for a critique which should make us wonder how accurate poll data on public support for labor law reform was, see Arthur W. Kornhauser, "Are Public Opinion Polls Fair to Organized Labor?" *Public Opinion Quarterly* 10 (1946): 484–500; Parkes, "Building on Faith," pp. 4–5; Murray W. Edelman, "Government's Balance of Power in Labor-Management Relations," *Labor Law Journal* 2 (1951): 31–35.

49 Remarks of Raymond S. Smethurst at Labor Relations Session of the 52d CAI, New York City, 4 December 1947 (NAM press release, mimeographed, record series L-2, L-MDC); Carroll E. French, "Industrial Relations and a Free Enterprise Economy," address before the Oklahoma A & M Industrial Relations Conference, 5 October 1949 (mimeographed — copy in record series L-2, L-MDC); Wheeler McMillen, "The Miracle of 1948," address before the 53d CAI, New York City, 3 December 1948 (NAM Press Release, mimeographed — copy in record series L-2, L-MDC); James C. Foster, *The Union Politic: The CIO Political Action Committee* (Columbia, Mo.: Univ. of Missouri Press, 1975), ch. 6; Ben Aaron, "Amending the Taft-Hartley Act: A Decade of Frustration," *Industrial and Labor Relations Review* 11 (1958): 327–38.

The NAM maintained a proprietary interest in Taft-Hartley through the Eisenhower years, relying on the presidential appointing power rather than on further legislation in a Democratic Congress to encourage the NLRB's increasingly conservative interpretation of the law — Frank W. McCulloch and Tim Bornstein, *The National Labor Relations Board* (New York: Praeger, 1974), pp. 61–62. When the opportunity came for further labor law revision, in the aftermath of the McClellan Committee's investigations of labor racketeering, NAM, the U.S. Chamber of Commerce, and other conservative interest groups were able to capitalize on their links with the administration — Alan K. McAdams, *Power and Politics in Labor Legislation* (New York: Columbia Univ. Press, 1964), esp. pp. 68–75, 211. The resulting Landrum-Griffin Act, in whose drafting and passage many of Taft-Hartley's architects had a hand, represented in a number of respects the elaboration and completion of the original program of subjecting labor unions and their activities to restrictive federal intervention. This is particularly true of the secondary boycott provisions and the "Bill of Rights" for union members.

50 Philip H. Burch, Jr., "The NAM as an Interest Group," *Politics and Society*

4 (1973): 97–130. This is not to say, however, that the big business community became less organized, or less involved in the politics of labor relations. Rather, it developed a plurality of organizations (e.g. the Business Council, Business Roundtable) instead of the old preeminence of the NAM; but they can still pull together to support further tightening of labor law, or to oppose any liberalization—D. Quinn Mills, "Flawed Victory in Labor Law Reform," *Harvard Business Review* 57:3 (May–June 1979): 92–102.

51 William J. Baade, Jr., *Management Strategy in Collective Bargaining Negotiations: How to Negotiate and Write a Better Contract* (New London, Conn.: National Foremen's Institute, 1950), pp. 65–66, and General Motors Corporation, *Sixth Conference for College and University Educators: Personnel Administration and Industrial Relations, 17–29 August 1950* (processed transcript), first session, p. 8, on the problems for a "right to work" management caused by Taft-Hartley; on welfare funds, see ch. 6, below.

52 Smethurst, "Remarks" of 4 December 1947, p. 2; French, "Industrial Relations and a Free Enterprise Economy," p. 2; "Reaction to Taft-Hartley Act," *Management Record* 9 (1947): 217–21 at 217; John L. McCaffrey (President, International Harvester Corporation), "Management Policy under the Taft-Hartley Act," in *Industrial Relations under the Taft-Hartley Law: Personnel Series No. 112* (New York: AMA, 1947), pp. 14–25 at p. 15; "Should Management Waive Its Right to Sue Unions?" *Modern Industry* 14:4 (15 Oct. 1947): 112–20 at 113–18; Egbert H. Van Delden, "Management Experience under the Labor Management Relations Act," in *Problems and Experience under the Labor-Management Relations Act: Personnel Series No. 115* (New York: AMA, 1948), pp. 14–25 at p. 15; "ABC's of the New Labor Law," *Modern Industry* 14:2 (15 Aug. 1947): 54–64 at 54; Carroll E. French, "Management Views the National Labor Policy," address delivered at Univ. of N. Carolina, Chapel Hill, 12 May 1949 (mimeographed —copy in record series L-2, L-MDC). See also "How Practical Personnel Men Think the Labor Law Will Work," *Factory Management and Maintenance* 105:8 (Aug. 1947): 81–96 and 105:9 (Sept. 1947): 84–96.

53 The business assessment was probably more realistic than that of its Congressional sponsors—Mann, "Congressional Behavior and National Labor Policy," esp. pp. 388–90, 410, 453–54; Robert Abelow, "Management Experience under the Taft-Hartley Act," Joseph Shister, "The Impact of the Taft-Hartley Act on Union Strength and Collective Bargaining," and Clyde W. Summers, "A Summary Evaluation of the Taft-Hartley Act," all in *Industrial and Labor Relations Review* 11 (1958): 360–70, 339–51, 405–12; George W. Brooks, *The Sources of Vitality in the American Labor Movement: New York State School of Industrial and Labor Relations Bulletin No. 41* (Ithaca, N.Y.: NYSSILR, July 1960).

54 Frank Rising, (General Manager, Automotive and Aviation Parts Manufacturers, Inc.), "New Issues in Collective Bargaining," address at 52d CAI,

New York City, 4 December 1947 (NAM press release, mimeographed — copy in Record Series L-2, L-MDC).
55 Walter H. Wheeler, Jr., "Profit Sharing — the Spark That Jumps the Gap," address before the 19th Pacific Coast Management Conference of the California Personnel Management Association, 20 April 1948 (distributed by Connecticut General Life Insurance Co., Hartford, Conn.), p. 2.

CHAPTER 5: RECOVERY OF THE INITIATIVE, II

1 See discussion in chapters 2 and 3 above; and James C. Olson, "Is Your Company Prepared for Rough Weather?" *Harvard Business Review* 25 (1947): 595–608. See also trend of commentaries in business magazines, e.g. "Clearing the Decks for Competition," *Modern Industry* 11:2 (Feb. 1946): 40–43; "Are You Headed for a Sales Collapse?" *Modern Industry* 13:1 (July 1946): 50–51; "Trimming the Fat from Indirect Labor Costs," *Modern Industry* 13:2 (Feb. 1947): 34–39; and "Lower Costs: Will Break-Even Point Break You?" *Modern Industry* 14:3 (Sept. 1947): 54–64.

2 Everett Kassalow, "New Patterns in Collective Bargaining," in Richard A. Lester and Joseph Shister, eds., *Insights into Labor Issues* (New York: Macmillan, 1949), ch. 5; Clark Kerr, "Employer Policies in Industrial Relations, 1945–1947," in Colston E. Warne et al., eds., *Labor in Postwar America* (Brooklyn: Remsen Press, 1949), ch. 3; and discussion above, ch. 2.

3 James C. Foster, *The Union Politic: The CIO Political Action Committee* (Columbia, Mo.: Univ. of Missouri Press, 1975), ch. 4.

4 David Levinson, "Left-Wing Labor and the Taft-Hartley Law," *Labor Law Journal* 1 (1950): 1079 ff.; David J. Saposs, *Communism in American Unions* (New York: McGraw-Hill, 1959), pts. 4–5. Recent scholarship has been somewhat more sympathetic toward the "Communist-controlled" unions than its Cold War-era predecessors — see esp. Bert Cochran, *Labor and Communism: The Conflict That Shaped American Unions* (Princeton, N.J.: Princeton University Press, 1977), chs. 10–12; and Roger Keeran, *The Communist Party and the Auto Workers Unions* (Bloomington: Indiana Univ. Press, 1980), ch. 11.

5 Daniel Hamberg, "The Recession of 1948–1949 in the United States," *Economic Journal* 62 (1952): 1–14.

6 George W. Taylor, "The Functions of Collective Bargaining," in *Management's Stake in Collective Bargaining: Personnel Series No. 81* (New York: AMA, 1944), pp. 3–19 at pp. 6–8.

7 General Motors Corporation, *Third Conference for College and University Educators: Personnel Administration and Industrial Relations, 16–30 June 1947* (privately circulated, processed transcript), first session, 16 June 1947, p. 22; Nelson N. Lichtenstein, "Industrial Unionism under the No-Strike Pledge: A Study of the CIO During the Second World War" (Ph.D. diss., Univ. of California-Berkeley, 1974), pp. 327–32.

8 "Guns *and* Butter: The Paradox of Collective Dealing," *Personnel* 18 (1942): 322–38 at 334. The anonymous article is a most important early statement of realistic collective bargaining strategy and tactics.

9 Press releases on UAW-GM contract ordered by NWLB, dated March 1945, in Walter P. Reuther-Pre-Presidential Materials (hereafter cited as WPR PPM), Box 9, AALH.

10 Clarence O. Skinner, "The Fringe Issues," in *Trends in Union Demands: Personnel Series No. 95* (New York: AMA, 1945), pp. 6–14 at pp. 7–8; Thomas R. Jones, "The Scope of Collective Bargaining," in *Personnel Series No. 81*, pp. 40–51 at p. 48; James Tanham, "Management's Case before the War Labor Board," in *Practical Techniques of Collective Bargaining: Personnel Series No. 86* (New York: AMA, 1944), pp. 30–38 at pp. 32–38; Dale Purves (Associate Industry Member), "Essential Factors Necessary in Presenting a Case before the WLB," in *More Production through Sound Industrial Relations: Proceedings of the 25th SBIC* (New York: Association Press, 1942), pp. 33–41.

11 William M. Leiserson, "What's Evolving in Wartime Labor Relations," in *Personnel Series No. 86*, pp. 18–30 at pp. 18–19, reported that some large national firms were the last strong bastions of antiunionism in the business community. Practical acceptance of the new world of labor relations was more general. And the overt expression of "open shop" attitudes, even by executives of the least-reconciled corporations, was practically eliminated. This may have been a response by businessmen to the clear public support for "responsible" labor unionism and the fundamentals of national labor relations policy. In this circumstance, it was good public relations to present an image of the business community as law-abiding and seeking "cooperation" with labor, not confrontation. See *Aftermath of the Strikes: The Public Opinion Index for Industry* (Princeton, N.J.: Opinion Research Corporation, April 1946, processed), "Green Page" and pp. 2–3; Elmo Roper, "Public Opinion," in *Toward a National Labor Policy: Personnel Series No. 72* (New York: AMA, 1943), pp. 20–23 at p. 21, and "The Public Looks at Business," *Harvard Business Review* 27 (1949): 167–75 at 171.

12 For an understanding of managerial labor relations reform, see, in addition to the sources cited in notes 2, 6, 7, 8, and 10, the following: *Books and pamphlets* — William J. Baade, Jr., *Management Strategy in Collective Bargaining Negotiations: How to Negotiate and Write a Better Contract* (New London, Conn.: National Foremen's Institute, 1950); Russell L. Greenman, *Getting Along with Unions* (New York: Harper & Bros., 1947); Lee H. Hill, *Pattern for Good Labor Relations* (New York: McGraw-Hill, 1947); Industrial Relations Department of the NAM, *Preparing to Negotiate* (New York: NAM, March 1947); R. C. Smyth and M. J. Murphy, *Bargaining with Organized Labor* (New York: Funk & Wagnalls, 1948); Staff of the Executives' Labor Letter, *How to Handle Collective Bargaining Negotiations: Bargaining Techniques and Strategy* (Deep River, Conn.: National Foremen's Institute, 1944, processed); Bryce M. Stewart and William J. Couper, *Reconversion in Industrial Relations: Industrial Relations Monograph No.*

13 (New York: Industrial Relations Counselors, Inc., 1946). *Articles and addresses*—Guy B. Arthur, Jr., "Techniques of Successful Labor Arbitration," *Personnel* 21 (1945): 297–304; *Collective Bargaining Developments and Representative Union Agreements: SPP No. 60* (New York: NICB, 1944), p. 3 esp.; Jules Justin, "Presenting Management's Case to the Arbitrator," *Factory Management and Maintenance* 106:3 (Mar. 1948): 119–21; C. F. Mugridge, "Negotiating a Labor Contract" and "Improving Management's Score at the Bargaining Table: Report of a Panel Session," both in *Personnel Series No. 91* (New York: AMA, 1945), pp. 41–48, 49–63; "Negotiating the Labor Agreement: an Open Forum," in *Negotiating and Interpreting the Labor Agreement: Personnel Series No. 110* (New York: AMA, 1947), pp. 17–30; Leonard J. Smith, "Common-Sense Collective Bargaining," *Personnel* 21 (1944): 162–65.

The above list is illustrative rather than exhaustive.

13 See ch. 1, above.

14 For representative statements of their views, see Eric Johnston, *America Unlimited* (Garden City, N.Y.: Doubleday Doran, 1944), esp. ch. 14; Robert W. Johnson, *Or Forfeit Freedom* (Garden City, N.Y.: Doubleday, 1947), esp. chs. 13–15; Louis J. A. Villalon, ed., *Management Men and Their Methods: Fifteen Case Studies in Executive Techniques* (New York: Funk and Wagnalls, 1949), ch. 1. From the labor side, see Edward T. Cheyfitz, *Constructive Collective Bargaining* (New York: McGraw-Hill, 1947)— Golden and Ruttenberg had had their say before the war, in *The Dynamics of Industrial Democracy* (New York: Harper & Bros., 1942), a work of elemental importance.

15 Russell W. Davenport, "Enterprise for Everyman," *Fortune* 41:1 (Jan. 1950): 55 ff.; Transcript of Joint Botany Worsted Mills—Textile Workers Union of America, CIO, Training Program (mimeographed, copy in Corporations File, L-MDC), esp. Inaugural Session, 18 September 1946. The latter provides an interesting illustration of the kinds of political and economic pressures which reinforced managements' and unions' ideological preferences for cooperation: the management was interested in industrial peace and union cooperation in restoring cost-control and competitiveness in the postwar period; the union wanted to protect its members' jobs in a high-cost northern textile producer against southern competition, and to demonstrate to managements of southern mills, which it was vainly trying to organize, just how "responsible" and helpful it could be.

16 On corporate liberalism, see the extended discussion in ch. 7, below; see also David W. Eakins, "The Development of Corporate Liberal Policy Research in the United States 1885–1965" (Ph.D. diss., Univ. of Wisconsin, 1966), p. 385; "Business, Labor Frame Peace Code," *NYT*, 29 March 1945, p. 16; Research and Policy Committee of the CED, *Collective Bargaining: How to Make It More Effective* (New York: CED, February 1947), p. 4; "Truman Names Twelve to Taft Act Panel," *NYT*, 19 December 1947, p. 22.

17 Victor R. Reuther, *The Brothers Reuther and the Story of the UAW* (Boston: Houghton Mifflin, 1976), esp. ch. 24; Ronald Radosh, *American La-*

bor and United States Foreign Policy (New York: Random House, 1969), esp. ch. 10, ch. 14, pp. 435–38; D. Graham Hutton, *We Too Can Prosper: The Promise of Productivity* (New York: Macmillan, 1953); Herbert O. Eby (Labor Relations Director, Pittsburgh Plate Glass), "Gearing Our Labor Relations to the New Order," *CPMA Management Report No. 1* (1948): 42–56; J. D. Zellerbach, "American Industry's Stake in the World Situation," *CPMA Management Report No. 1* (1948): 57–62. Zellerbach was also U.S. Employers' Delegate to the International Labor Organization.

18 Glenn Gardiner (Vice-President, Forstmann Woollen Co.), "How Labor-Management Cooperation Can Be Achieved," in *Planning and Administering Effective Incentives: Production Series No. 172* (New York: AMA, 1947), pp. 18–23 at p. 19.

19 Frederick H. Harbison and John R. Coleman, *Goals and Strategy in Collective Bargaining* (New York: Harper, 1951), pp. 55–60; Cheyfitz, *Constructive Collective Bargaining*, p. 51. See also Alexander R. Heron (Director of Industrial Relations, Crown-Zellerbach Corp.), *Sharing Information With Employees* (Palo Alto, Calif.: Stanford Univ. Press, 1942), esp. ch. 21; J. W. Ballantine and J. M. True, *Transmitting Information through Management and Union Channels* (Princeton, N.J.: Princeton Univ. Press, 1949), including a study of Johnson & Johnson's practice.

20 Alexander R. Heron, *Beyond Collective Bargaining: Toward Understanding in Industry, 3* (Palo Alto, Calif: Stanford Univ. Press, 1948); Alan Fox, *Beyond Contract: Work, Power and Trust Relations* (London: Faber and Faber, 1974), esp. chs. 6–7, for a helpful discussion of the limits on managerial "pluralism" in Western industrial societies.

21 Richard A. Lester's *As Unions Mature: An Analysis of the Evolution of American Unionism* (Princeton, N.J.: Princeton Univ. Press, 1958), pp. 39–43 esp. — written, ironically, just before the second wave of management's industrial relations "counteroffensive" which was set off by the Eisenhower recession — reflects this optimistic view; Clinton S. Golden and Virginia D. Parker, eds., in *Causes of Industrial Peace under Collective Bargaining* (New York: Harper, 1955), gather together case studies conducted in the late 1940s, and draw conclusions in pt. 1, esp. ch. 6; Harbison and Coleman, in *Goals and Strategies*, draw on the widest range of studies.

22 Solomon Barkin (Director of Research, Textile Workers Union of America), "Labor's Code for a Private Enterprise Economy," *Labor Law Journal* 2 (1952): 840–45 esp. 844–45, shows how acceptable progressive nostrums were even to liberalism's social democratic fringe; Harbison and Coleman, *Goals and Strategy*, p. 137.

23 Herbert R. Northrup and Harvey A. Young, "The Causes of Industrial Peace Revisited," *Industrial and Labor Relations Review* 22 (1968): 31–47.

24 Stewart and Couper, *Reconversion in Industrial Relations*, pp. 27, 37.

25 See secondary accounts of the strike cited in ch. 2, note 81. In addition, this account rests on an interview with Andrew Court, formerly of the company's Labor Economics staff (Detroit, 13 November 1974) and on extensive research in company and union archives and publications. The most impor-

tant documents explaining strike issues are: *For the union* — Walter P.
Reuther, address on Mutual Broadcasting System, 26 October 1945 (transcript in UAW-GM collection, AALH, Series VI and VII, Box 1); UAW-GM
Department, Supplementary Brief in Reply to Corporation Brief of 7 November 1945: "General Motors' Plan for Longer Hours, Lower Wages,
High Prices, Mass Unemployment, Inflation, and Economic Imperialism,"
9 November 1945 (same location); "Purchasing Power for Prosperity: The
Case for Maintaining Take-Home Pay without Increasing Prices," Sum-
mary and Special Briefs Presented to the President's Fact-Finding Board in
the UAW-CIO-General Motors Corporation Wage Dispute, 21 December
1945 (same location); Victor G. Reuther, "Responsibility of the General
Motors Corporation to GM Employees and the Nation," transcript of
broadcast address at meeting of the Union for Democratic Action, New
York, 15 January 1946 (same location). *For the company* — General Motors'
Reply to UAW-CIO Brief Submitted in Support of Wage Demand for 52
Hours' Pay for 40 Hours' Work, transmitted over signature of Harry W. Anderson, vice-president for industrial relations, 7 November 1945 (copy in
DPL); Alfred P. Sloan, Jr., and Charles E. Wilson, *Here Is the Issue* (De-
troit: General Motors Corporation, 30 December 1945 — copy in DPL); and
sources cited in ns. 26, 27 below. *For both sides together* — Statements of
George Romney (Automobile Manufacturers' Association) and Walter
Reuther in *Town Meeting*, bulletin of America's Town Meeting of the Air
(sponsored by the *Readers' Digest*), 11 October 1945.

26 Unpublished manuscript by Harry D. Garrett (formerly GM Labor Relations Staff), pp. 112–50, for a succinct, factual, and chronological account
of the strike and negotiations (GM Labor Relations Library); Andrew
Court Interview.

27 Walter G. Merritt (Attorney), *General Motors' Statement before Fact-
Finding Board, 28 December 1945* (Detroit: The Corporation, 1946), p. 4.
GM's sensitivity on this issue is explained when one understands the central-
ity of financial planning as the cardinal management control device at GM
— see H. Thomas Johnson, "Management Accounting in an Early Multidi-
visional Organization: General Motors in the 1920s," *Business History
Review* 52 (1978): 490–517; and Thomas Cochran, "The Sloan Report:
American Culture and Business Management," *American Quarterly* 29
(1977): 476–86. For the propaganda battle, see Statement of R. J. Thomas,
president of the UAW-CIO, and of Walter Reuther, 20 November 1945
(mimeographed — copy in UAW-GM Collection, Series VI, Box 1, Folder 4,
AALH), p. 4; *The General Motors Strike: The Public Opinion Index for Industry* (Princeton, N.J.: Opinion Research Corporation, December 1945,
processed); and *Aftermath of the Strikes*, p. 6.

28 Elwin J. Corbin (Chairman, National Negotiating Committee), letter no.
50 re: Procedure for Local Union Strike Demands, 19 September 1945, in
"Letters to Locals" File, WPR PPM Box 2, AALH: General Motors Corporation, *Fourth Conference for College and University Educators: Personnel
Administration and Industrial Relations, 16–29 June 1948* (privately circu-

lated, processed verbatim transcript), afternoon session, 16 June 1948, p. 28. The national contract was only subject to "reopening," i.e. renegotiation, in the wages clauses. So other issues had to be pressed locally.

29 Charles E. Wilson (President, GM) to NWLB, 2 October 1942, reprinted in *Information Concerning the UAW-CIO Strike at General Motors for Members of General Motors Management* (privately circulated, processed, 18 December 1945, copy from GM Labor Relations Library), pp. 63–65; "GM Proposals to Strike Out of Contract Provisions Inserted by NDMB/NWLB" (press release of 13 February 1946, copy in WPR Collection, Box 8, Folder 10, AALH). GM even printed such clauses in a different color in copies of the April 1945 agreement it distributed—see example in WPR PPM Box 2, Folder 11.

30 Harry W. Anderson, Letter to International Union, UAW-CIO, 17 December 1945, reprinted in *Information Concerning the UAW-CIO Strike*, pp. 60–62.

31 Ibid.; "Union Wins Fight against Corporation Demands" (press release, mimeographed, copy in WPR PPM Box 2, Folder 9, AALH), p. 3—for GM's supplementary proposals of 12 February 1946. For the union's assessment of these demands, see "General Motors Offers Us Five Cents for the Union," *GM National Strike Bulletin* 3:13 (13 Feb. 1946), in WPR PPM Box 2, Folder 12, AALH.

32 General Motors Corporation, *The General Motors Strike—The Facts and Their Implications: A Special Message To General Motors Stockholders* (Detroit: The Corporation, 18 April 1946), issued over signature of Alfred P. Sloan, Jr.

33 Richard Herding, *Job Control and Union Structure: A Study on Plant-Level Industrial Conflict in the United States* (Rotterdam: Rotterdam Univ. Press, 1972), p. 130; General Motors Corporation, *Here Is the Issue: Facts Concerning the UAW-CIO Strike against General Motors* (Detroit: The Corporation, 10 January 1946); Andrew Court Interview. GM's Public Relations Department—one of the highest-ranking and most solidly established in all industry—put in a remarkably powerful performance during the great strike; and GM management displayed a real sense of "responsibility," as they judged it, for the business community's interests in general.

34 Allan Nevins and Frank E. Hill, *Ford: Decline and Rebirth: 1933–1962* (New York: Charles Scribner's Sons, 1963), chs. 10, 12–13; with Ernest F. Breech, "The Ford Spirit," address at Ford Motor Co.'s 50th Anniversary Management Conference, Dearborn, Michigan, 19 May 1953 (privately printed), pp. 2–6; Henry Ford II, "One Solution to Our Problems," address at Commonwealth Club, San Francisco, 8 February 1946 (privately printed), pp. 4–7—from AALH.

35 Manton M. Cummins (Director of Labor Relations), "Industrial Relations in the Automobile Industry," address before the students of the Institute of Industrial Relations, College of the Holy Cross, Worcester, Mass., 7 April 1948 (mimeographed, copy in DPL), esp. pp. 5, 10–11. For an account of Ford's postwar negotiations containing much reprinted material, and with

an interpretation which this account generally follows, see Benjamin Selekman et al., *Problems in Labor Relations* (New York: McGraw-Hill, 1950),
pp. 288–98, and Stephen Fuller (with Ruth C. Hetherston), *A Key to Problems in Labor Relations* (New York: McGraw-Hill, 1950, processed).

36 For typical GM political credos and attitudes to organized labor, see
Charles E. Wilson, "The Great Delusion: Where Marx Went Wrong," address before the American Society of Mechanical Engineers, Stevens Hotel,
Chicago, 16 June 1947 (pamphlet, n.d., copy in L-MDC) — an irresistible title; *Minutes of General Motors Corporation Conference for College and
University Educators: Personnel Administration and Industrial Relations*
(privately circulated, mimeographed), morning session, 27 June 1946, p. 6–
14, for statements of vice-presidents Anderson and Coen, and Steve Du
Brul. See also ch. 4, n. 14, and ch. 7, below, for the radical rightist causes
with which GM executives associated themselves. GM was still effectively
controlled by a large Du Pont minority stockholding at this time. This may
have accounted for its top management's "entrepreneurial" style, as surely
did the very large individual shareholdings executives accumulated through
the generous bonus plan. (Andrew Court Interview.) For Ford, see Henry
Ford II, "A Political Challenge to Business and Industry," address before
the Economic Club of New York, 28 April 1949 (privately printed, copy in
L-MDC), and, on McNamara, Jan G. Deutsch, *Selling the People's Cadil-
lac: The Edsel and Corporate Responsibility* (New Haven, Conn.: Yale
Univ. Press, 1976), pp. 56–60, 65–71.

37 On the white-collar problem, see Carl D. Snyder, *White Collar Workers
and the UAW* (Urbana, Ill.: Univ. of Illinois Press, 1973), pp. 32, 38–41, 43;
The Editor, "Management Revisions of Union Agreements," *Personnel* 34
(1945): 425–27; and Mel B. Lindquist to National Ford Council, 14 November 1945 (in Ford Department–UAW, Box 1, Folder 4, AALH), for the
thirty-one demands and their rationale.

38 Apparently the Labor Relations Staff had been trying to move in this direction for some years — Malcolm Denise, "Labor Relations and Implementation of Policy — 1942, 1944, and 1945," as quoted in George Heliker, "Heliker Report," Frank Hill Papers, Henry Ford Museum, Dearborn, Mich.,
pp. 300–307. Staff member Denise claimed significant success: independent
confirmation is lacking, there is considerable contradictory evidence from
management and union sources about the actual effectiveness of these policies, and, in any event, the opinion of the new managerial regime in 1945–
46 was that the situation was still, more or less, a mess.

39 Henry Ford II, "The Challenge of Human Engineering," address before the
Society of Automotive Engineers, Detroit, 9 January 1946 (privately printed,
copy in AALH). Booton Herndon, *Ford: An Unconventional Biography of
the Two Henry Fords and Their Times* (London: Cassell, 1970), includes a
fascinating account of the drafting of this speech — it was a definite public
relations ploy on the part of Ford's counsel, Earl Newsom, and reflected the
opinions of the entire senior executive group, not just of Young Henry — pp.
192–94.

40 Richard Leonard (Director, Ford Department UAW-CIO), address before the Industrial Relations Council of Metropolitan Boston, 8 May 1946 (mimeographed, copy in L-MDC), pp. 1–6 esp.; copy of final contract (in Ford Department–UAW, Box 1, Folder 10, AALH), esp. Articles IV (Management Responsibility) and V (Union Responsibility); for intra-union opposition to its terms, see Leonard to Bugas, 8 April 1946, in Folder 14, and Telegram from Bert Hoffman (Secretary, International Skilled Trades Councils), in Folder 15. The UAW convention rejected the "excluded categories" clause—Snyder, *White Collar Workers*, p. 40, and Tony Nicol to Leonard, 19 February 1946, in Folder 19.

41 Robert M. MacDonald, *Collective Bargaining in the Automobile Industry: A Study in Wage Structure and Competitive Relations* (New Haven, Conn.: Yale Univ. Press, 1963), pp. 325–26; Selekman et al., *Problems in Labor Relations*, pp. 331–39; Mel B. Lindquist (Superintendent of Labor Relations), "Responsibility in Collective Bargaining," address before the Pittsburgh Section of the Society of Automotive Engineers, 25 April 1946 (mimeographed, copy in DPL), p. 2.

42 Ibid., pp. 3–4.

43 Ibid., p. 7.

44 Selekman et al., *Problems in Labor Relations*, esp. pp. 301–4.

45 Ibid., pp. 305–6; clipping of 28 May 1947 from *Detroit Free Press*, in VF-Foremen and Supervisors, AALH; Archie A. Pearson (Manager, Training Department), "The Ford Foreman Program," talk given at AMA Production Conference, Chicago, 19 November 1948 (processed, copy in L-MDC); interview with Carl Brown, 13 November 1974.

46 John L. McCaffrey, "Management Policy under the Taft-Hartley Law," in *Industrial Relations under the Taft-Hartley Law: Personnel Series No. 112* (New York: AMA, 1947), pp. 3–8 at pp. 4–5; Harry A. Millis and Emily C. Brown, *From the Wagner Act to Taft-Hartley: A Study of National Labor Policy and Labor Relations* (Chicago: Univ. of Chicago Press, 1950), pp. 637–38; Selekman et al., *Problems in Labor Relations*, pp. 310–59; "Turning Point," *Fortune* 39:4 (Apr. 1949): 189–91.

47 Herding, *Job Control and Union Structure*, pp. 121, 140–41, and "Tighter Discipline for More Output," *Modern Industry* 15:2 (Feb. 1948): 46–48, on other companies' performance; Lindquist, "Responsibility in Collective Bargaining," p. 6; Maurice D. Kilbridge, "The Effort Bargain in Industrial Society," *Journal of Business* 33 (1960): 10–20 at 13; John S. Bugas, "Labor Relations and Productivity," address before the AMA, New York City, 2 October 1947 (processed, copy in AALH), and "Industrial Relations—Unfinished Business," address at the Institute of Industrial Relations, College of the Holy Cross, Worcester, Mass., 27 April 1949 (processed, copy in L-MDC); the results of the Roper Survey—remarkably frank in its disclosure of a bad situation—are in *Report of Management Meeting: March 1947* (Industrial Relations Department, Ford Motor Co., processed, copy in L-MDC); the program of remedial action is sketched in R. E. Roberts

(Director of Employee Relations), "Human Relations in Industry," an address (1948, mimeographed, copy in DPL).

48 Cummins, "Industrial Relations in the Automobile Industry," p. 13; cf. Mel B. Lindquist, "Preparation for Collective Bargaining," address before the National Forum on Trucking Industrial Relations (Ford News Bureau, 31 January 1950, processed, copy in L-MDC); and note *Personnel*'s equivocal reaction to the inauguration of Harvard's trade union fellowship program — it might make stewards and officials more "responsible"; on the other hand, it would also make them even smarter than management representatives: "Labor Leaders Go to School," *Personnel* 19 (1942): 517–18.

49 *Aftermath of the Strikes*, p. 6; interview with Ralph Deedes (GM Labor Relations Staff), Detroit, November 1974. Coen had been particularly hostile, attributing "socialistic desires" to Reuther, opining that the latter's philosophy of industrial democracy via collective bargaining "came from foreign countries," and dismissing Reuther's sophisticated arguments as "all this crap" and "Horse Shit." On the last point, one has some sympathy with him. "Excerpts of Transcript of UAW-GM Negotiations," WPR PPM Box 2, pp. 11, 24, 16, 34 (AALH).

50 The best accounts of these negotiations are to be found in presentations made before GM's annual semi private conferences for academic industrial relations specialists, where it tried both to pick their brains and to convince them of the justice of its cause. See General Motors Corporation, *Fourth Conference*, verbatim transcript of morning session, 16 June 1948, pp. 6–18; afternoon session, same date, pp. 1–3, 44–45; afternoon session, 29 June 1948, p. 9; General Motors Corporation, *Sixth Conference for College and University Educators: Personnel Administration and Industrial Relations, 17–29 August 1950* (privately circulated, processed transcript), sessions of 17 August, esp. pp. 3–9. The best assessments of the 1948 and 1950 contracts are Frederick H. Harbison, "The General Motors–United Automobile Workers Agreement of 1950," *Journal of Political Economy* 58 (1958): 397–411 (best read together with his and Robert Dubin's excellent *Patterns of Union-Management Relations: United Automobile Workers (CIO)–General Motors–Studebaker* [Chicago: Science Research Associates, 1947]), and "The Treaty of Detroit," *Fortune* 42:1 (July 1950): 53–55. Kathyanne Groehn El-Messidi, "Sure Principles Midst Uncertainties: The Story of the 1948 GM–UAW Contract" (Ph.D. diss., Univ. of Oklahoma, 1976), is disappointingly short on analysis or original material — particularly so in the light of the fact that, as daughter of a former GM executive, she had excellent access to GM archives and interviewed numerous once-senior men. Unfortunately, she felt bound to keep most of her interesting findings confidential — which is tantalizing.

51 Harry W. Anderson (Vice-President), "The Job Ahead in Industrial Relations," address delivered before the Northern Ohio Personnel and Executive Conference, Cleveland, October 1948, in *1949 Industrial Management Symposium* (New York: Consolidated Reporting Co., processed), pp. 1–6;

General Motors Corporation, *Sixth Conference*, transcript of 17 August session, p. 4 — remarks of Harry Anderson. Reuther had always run a "tight ship" in the GM Department, but after defeating his factional opponents in 1946–47, and extirpating remaining opposition "cells" in locals thereafter, he was much freer to act super-responsibly. Irving Howe and B. J. Widick, *The UAW and Walter Reuther* (New York: Random House, 1949), chs. 7–9, 11; Frank Marquart, *An Auto Worker's Journal: The UAW from Crusade to One-Party Union* (University Park, Pa.: Pennsylvania State Univ. Press, 1975), chs. 8–10; Jack Steiber, *Governing the UAW* (New York: John Wiley & Sons, 1962), ch. 5.

52 General Motors Corporation, *Sixth Conference*, transcript of 17 August session, pp. 7–8; Selekman et al., *Problems in Labor Relations*, pp. 365, 371.

53 Fred Joiner, "Developments in Union Agreements," in Colston E. Warne et al., eds., *Labor in Postwar America* (Brooklyn, N.Y.: Remsen Press, 1949), esp. pp. 34–35; Ralph W. Lind, "Salient Characteristics of Post-War Union Agreements," in *New Concepts in Collective Bargaining: Personnel Series No. 97* (New York: AMA, 1946), pp. 17–34 at pp. 20–22, 24–30; "New Trends in Labor Clauses," *Modern Industry* 11:5 (May 1946): 49–64. "Beefing up" of clauses on productivity standards, seniority, and the workings of the grievance procedure, always to management's advantage, characterized postwar bargaining rounds. Gwilym A. Price (President, Westinghouse Electric), "Right to Manage Reestablished by Strike," *Factory Management and Maintenance* 104:9 (Sept. 1946): 280–82.

54 Ruth Susan Meyerowitz, "The Development of General Electric's Labor Policies, 1922–1950" (M.A. thesis, Columbia Univ., 1969), pp. 54–56, 70–76. Cf. Daniel T. Pierce (Assistant to the President, Sinclair Oil Co.), "How the Union Disillusioned Us," *Factory Management and Maintenance* 104:1 (Jan. 1946): 94–97, for another ex-"progressive" company's tale of militancy and woe. The evidence suggests a fatal flaw in corporate liberal policies for union-management accommodation: the unions' inability to deliver their members' reliable acceptance of managerial demands. For similar accounts of the breakdown of cooperative union-management relations in the early twentieth century, see David Montgomery, *Workers Control in America: Studies in the History of Work, Technology, and Labor Struggles* (Cambridge: Cambridge Univ. Press, 1979), esp. ch. 3; and Bruno Ramirez, *When Workers Fight: The Politics of Industrial Relations in the Progressive Era, 1898– 1916* (Westport, Conn.: Greenwood, 1978), chs. 5–7 esp.

55 Robert Ozanne, *A Century of Labor-Management Relations at McCormick and International Harvester* (Madison: Univ. of Wisconsin Press, 1967), pp. 210–13.

56 Supplemental Agreement of 15 February 1946, in WPR PPM Box 2, Folder 12, AALH (GM's President Wilson was illustrating to Reuther the kind of agreement he wanted).

57 Robert Tilove, "The Wage Rationalization Program in United States Steel," *Monthly Labor Review* 64 (1947): 967–82 at 981–82; John A. Stephens

(Vice-President, Industrial Relations), "Significance of the Contract between the Steel-Producing Subsidiaries of U.S. Steel and the United Steelworkers," in *Developing Public and Industrial Relations Policy: General Management Series No. 140* (New York: AMA, 1947) pp. 3–14 at p. 7. Local disputes over working practices and manning levels, however, remained common — Herding, *Job Control and Union Structure*, ch. 2, esp. pp. 134–39. Elimination of these disputes was a major issue in the 1959–60 strike.

58 Walter Geist (President), "Allis-Chalmers' Experience with a Left-Wing Union," *Factory Management and Maintenance* 105:3 (Mar. 1947): 80–82; "International Harvester's Attack on Radical Labor Leadership," *Factory Management and Maintenance* 105:12 (Dec. 1947): 66–73; "How One Union Swept Out the Communists," *Factory Management and Maintenance* 106:11 (Nov. 1948): 66–69; A. B. Martin (Assistant Manager, GE Oakland and San Jose Works), "A Bid for Employee Cooperation," *CPMA Management Report No. 14* (1948): 1–10; James J. Matles and J. Higgins, *Them and Us: Struggles of a Rank-and-File Union* (Englewood Cliffs, N.J.: Prentice-Hall, 1974), esp. ch. 13.

59 Old-style antiunionism in the North in the 1950s chiefly affected the UAW — with celebrated incidents at the Perfect Circle Corp.'s New Castle, Indiana plant, and the Kohler Company's in Wisconsin — see Walter H. Uphoff, *Kohler on Strike: Thirty Years of Conflict* (Boston: Beacon Press, 1966), chs. 5–11. Northrup and Young, "Causes of Industrial Peace Revisited"; William B. Harris, "The Breakdown of Studebaker-Packard," *Fortune* 54:4 (Oct. 1956): 139–41, 222–32.

60 "Chrysler's Hundred Days," *Fortune* 41:6 (June 1950): 70–72.

61 For the later 1940s, see Samuel L. H. Burk (Director of Industrial Relations, Pittsburgh Plate Glass), "Labor Relations and Hindrances to Full Production," *CPMA Management Report No. 19* (1948): esp. 7–12. For the 1950s, see Leonard R. Sayles and George Strauss, *The Local Union: Its Place in the Industrial Plant* (New York: Harper, 1953); and James W. Kuhn, *Bargaining in Grievance Settlement: The Power of Industrial Work Groups* (New York: Columbia Univ. Press, 1961). For the counteroffensive of the late 1950s, see Garth L. Mangum, "Taming Wildcat Strikes," *Harvard Business Review* 38:2 (Mar.–Apr. 1960): 88–96; Kilbridge, "The Effort Bargain," pp. 13–17; Herbert R. Northrup, "Management's 'New Look' in Labor Relations," *Industrial Relations* 1:1 (Oct. 1961): 9–24; and George Strauss, "The Shifting Power Balance in the Plant," *Industrial Relations* 1:3 (May 1962): 65–96. On the 1959–60 steel strike and its repercussions, see John Herling, *Right to Challenge: People and Power in the Steelworkers' Union* (New York: Harper & Row, 1972).

62 E. Robert Livernash, "How Effectively Are Management and Unions Living Together?" in Dan H. Fenn, Jr., ed., *Management's Mission in a New Society* (New York: McGraw-Hill, 1959), pp. 238–52, esp. 247–49, presenting the chief conclusions of Sumner H. Slichter et al.'s massive study of *The Impact of Collective Bargaining on Management* (Washington, D.C.:

Brookings Institution, 1960). Mangum's work was also part of this project. MacDonald's *Collective Bargaining in the Automobile Industry* illustrates the effectiveness of "realism" quite exhaustively.

The realistic strategy acquired the status of indisputable conventional wisdom — see Industrial Relations Division, NAM, *Check Points for Sound Collective Bargaining* (New York: NAM, November 1958); Le Roy Marceau, ed., *Dealing With a Union* (New York: AMA, 1969). It now informs what is euphemistically known as "conflict management," whose practitioners dress up an antilabor hard line in impenetrable jargon.

63 See Lester, *As Unions Mature;* Stanley Aronowitz, *False Promises: The Making of American Working-Class Consciousness* (New York: McGraw-Hill, 1973), esp. ch. 4. For the best assessment of the significant — if limited — achievements of the postwar American labor movement, see the new essays on "The Uses of Power" in David Brody, *Workers in Industrial America: Essays on the Twentieth Century Struggle* (New York: Oxford Univ. Press, 1980).

64 See Richard Edwards, *Contested Terrain: The Transformation of the Workplace in the Twentieth Century* (New York: Basic Books, 1979), esp. ch. 11; Sumner Rosen, "The United States: A Time for Reassessment," in Solomon Barkin, ed., *Worker Militancy and Its Consequences 1965–1975: New Directions in Western Industrial Relations* (New York and Washington, D.C.: Praeger, 1975), ch. 10.

65 Lemuel Boulware, *The Truth about Boulwarism: Trying to Do Right Voluntarily* (Washington, D.C.: Bureau of National Affairs), esp. chs. 1, 4, 13, is interesting, and communicates the ideological fervor of GE's union-bashing program, but is not especially reflective or analytical. For detail and criticism, see Matles and Higgins, *Them and Us*, esp. ch. 16; Meyerowitz, "Development of General Electric's Labor Policies," pp. 79–94 esp.; Herbert R. Northrup, *Boulwarism: The Labor Relations Policies of the General Electric Co. — Their Implications for Public Policy and Management Action* (Ann Arbor: Univ. of Michigan Press, 1964).

CHAPTER 6: BEYOND COLLECTIVE BARGAINING

1 See sources cited in ch. 1, notes 5–7.

2 H. F. Johnson (President, S. C. Johnson & Son, Inc. — Johnson Wax), "Will Industry Adopt Voluntary Profit Sharing without Tax Incentive Legislation," an address, 15 March 1947 (mimeographed copy in Information File, L-MDC).

3 Peter F. Drucker, *The Practice of Management* (London: Heinemann, 1955), p. 242. See also Paul H. Douglas, "Plant Administration of Labor," *Journal of Political Economy* 27 (1919): 544–60, for a description and analysis of the "state of the art" at the end of the First World War.

4 See sources cited in ch. 1, note 6.

5 Ross Young, *Personnel Manual for Executives* (New York: McGraw-Hill,

1947), p. 2; Elmer W. Earl, Jr., *Personnel Factors in Factory and Office, II: SPP No. 59* (New York: NICB, 1943), p. 5. The NICB's studies of best and actual practice were an important aid to the standardization and improvement of managerial performance in this field.

6 William Donald, "Effective Executive Personnel Administration," *Personnel* 10 (1933): 46–64; Geneva Seybold, *Company Organization Charts: SPP No. 64* (New York: NICB, 1944), *Written Statements of Personnel Policy, SPP No. 79* (New York: NICB, 1947), and *Company Rules — Aids to Teamwork: SPP No. 95* (New York: NICB, 1948); D. B. Harris (Director of Industrial Relations, Humble Oil and Refining Co.), "Industrial Relations Organization and Personnel Administration," *Personnel* 19 (1943): 674–85. Cf. Robert Dubin, "Decision Making by Management in Industrial Relations," *American Journal of Sociology* 54 (1949): 292–97.

7 Charles R. Hook, *Principles behind Employer-Employee Harmony* (New York: NAM, n.d. — text of address delivered 8 December 1939); A. L. Kress, "A Sound Compensation Structure — the Foundation of Morale," in *Morale Factors in Production: SPP No. 54* (New York: NICB, 1943), pp. 3–4; S. Avery Raube, *Factors Affecting Employee Morale: SPP No. 85* (New York: NICB, 1947).

8 Loren Baritz, *The Servants of Power: A History of the Use of Social Science in American Industry* (1960; New York: Science Editions, 1965), esp. chs. 1–4, for the classic critical account of the origins and application of industrial psychology.

9 Edmund C. Lynch, "Walter Dill Scott: Pioneer Industrial Psychologist," *Business History Review* 42 (1968): 149–70; Walter D. Scott et al., *Personnel Management: Principles, Practices, and Point of View* (New York: McGraw-Hill, 1941), esp. chs. 1–2; Whiting Williams, *Mainsprings of Men* (New York: Charles Scribner's Sons, 1925). Williams was an important practicing personnel man and popularizer of industrial psychology, whose career spanned the time from the First World War to the Cold War. Through the 1940s, empirical research had made little impact on industrial psychology's prescriptive view of worker motivation.

10 Whiting Williams, *What's on the Worker's Mind: By One Who Put on Overalls to Find Out* (New York: Charles Scribner's Sons, 1921), written after field work conducted at the height of the post-First World War strike wave, is an important source for this prescriptive view of the role of personnel work. Williams also provides telling descriptions of the harsh and careless man-management customary in American industry at the time, and preaches the need for a "new leadership" — for which see also David R. Craig and W. W. Charters, *Personal Leadership in Industry* (New York: McGraw-Hill, 1925); Glenn Frank, *The Politics of Industry: A Footnote to the Industrial Unrest* (New York: The Century Co., 1919); and J. David Houser, *What the Employer Thinks: Executives' Attitudes toward Employees* (Cambridge: Harvard Univ. Press, 1927), esp. pt. 2.

11 Charles R. Milton, *Ethics and Expediency: A Critical History of Personnel Philosophy* (Columbia, S.C.: Univ. of South Carolina Press, 1970), ch. 4;

Don D. Lescohier and Elizabeth Brandeis, "Working Conditions and Labor Legislation," in John R. Commons et al., *History of Labor in the United States, 1896–1932* (New York: Macmillan, 1935), 3:324–9; Houser, *What the Employer Thinks*, pp. 160–65.

12 On the rise of personnel departments in the 1930s, see esp. Thomas G. Spates, "Management's Responsibility in Industrial Relations," in *Informed Leaders for Better Understanding: Proceedings of the 23rd SBIC, 24–27 July 1940* (New York: Association Press, 1940), pp. 9–19; Joseph E. Moody (Manager, Industrial Relations, York Corporation), "Industrial Relations Problems of Smaller Industries," in *Better Industrial Relations for Victory: Proceedings of the 26th SBIC, 28–31 July 1943* (New York: Association Press, 1943), pp. 87–93; case studies in *Organization of Personnel Administration: SPP No. 73* (New York: NICB, 1945); accounts of two progressive firms — Henrietta M. Larson and Kenneth W. Porter, *History of Humble Oil and Refining Company: A Study in Industrial Growth* (New York: Harper & Bros., 1959), ch. 15; and Robert Ozanne, *A Century of Labor-Management Relations at McCormick and International Harvester* (Madison: Univ. of Wisconsin Press, 1967), pp. 178–80.

For record-keeping and the "reign of rules," see Raymond S. Livingstone, "Policies for Promotion, Demotion, and Discharge," in *For National Unity — Better Industrial Relations: Proceedings of the 24th SBIC, 23–26 July 1941* (New York: Association Press, 1941), pp. 82–89; Leonard C. Bajork, "The Foreman as a Labor Relations Man," *Supervision* 4:6 (June 1942):4–5; Frank M. Knox, "A Guide to Personnel Record Keeping," *Personnel* 19 (1942): 540–61; "Employment Records," *NAM Labor Relations Bulletin* 33 (Sept. 1940): 37.

13 Guy B. Arthur, Jr. (Vice-President, AMA Personnel Division), "Changing Aspects of the Personnel Function in Management," in *Modern Management Practices and Problems: General Management Series No. 139* (New York: AMA, 1947), pp. 3–8 at pp. 3–5; Egbert H. Van Delden, "Government Policies and Personnel Management," *Management Review* 34 (1945): 178–81 at 178–79; Garret L. Bergen (Personnel Manager, Retail Division, Marshall Field & Co.), "War's Lessons in Personnel Administration," in *Meeting Personnel Requirements of Reconversion: Personnel Series No. 94* (New York, AMA, 1945), pp. 26–47, esp. pp. 27–28, 32–38, 40.

14 Glenn Gardiner (Vice-President, Forstmann Woollen Co.), "The Operating Executive and the Personnel Department," in *Personnel Functions and the Line Organization: Personnel Series No. 121* (New York: AMA, 1948), pp. 3–12; examples of comprehensive personnel services in aircraft plant in Agnes E. Meyer, *Journey Through Chaos* (New York: Harcourt, Brace & Co., 1944), pp. 268–85; "In-Plant Feeding Is Here to Stay," *Industrial Relations* 2:6 (Oct. 1944): 20–22; Howard Dratch, "The Politics of Child Care in the 1940s," *Science and Society* 38 (1974):167–204; "Solving the Shopping Problem," *Personnel* 21 (1944): 66–67; Louise M. Snyder (Bell Aircraft Corp.), "Counseling — Bridge between Management and Workers," *Factory Management and Maintenance* 103:1 (Jan. 1945): 129–33; Kathleen

North, "Counseling for Men by Men," *Factory Management and Maintenance* 103:2 (Feb. 1945): 119–20. Jeanne L. and Harold L. Wilensky, "Personnel Counseling: the Hawthorne Case," *American Journal of Sociology* 57 (1951): 265–80, is an excellent, critical, insider's study of the application of this device.

15 John C. Aspley and Eugene Whitmore, eds., *The Handbook of Industrial Relations* (Chicago: Dartnell, 1943), esp. chs. 8, 9, 27, 31, 35–36, and 39, gives a full and detailed account of these characteristic wartime activities.

16 Herbert G. Heneman, Jr., "Labor Cost and the Personnel Director," *Personnel* 21 (1945): 292–96; Howard M. Dirks, "Appraising the Personnel Department," in *Practical Operating Problems in Personnel Administration: Personnel Series No. 129* (New York: AMA, 1949), pp. 3–9; Arthur, "Changing Aspects of the Personnel Function in Management," pp. 3–5 esp.

17 Dr. Reign H. Bittner (Director, Personnel Research, Owens-Illinois Glass Co.), "Selection, Training, and Promotion of Employees," in *Lectures on Personnel Management* (Urbana: Univ. of Illinois Institute of Labor and Industrial Relations, 1949; processed), pp. 58–71; General Motors Corporation, *Sixth Conference for College and University Educators: Personnel Administration and Industrial Relations, 17–29 August 1950* (processed transcript), 18 August 1950 session, pp. 52–54.

18 Clarence J. Valir, "Job Evaluation and Wage Determination," in *Lectures on Personnel Management* (1949), pp. 29–56, esp. pp. 29–30; Samuel L. H. Burk, "Job Evaluation," in *The Industrial Relations Problems We Face Today: Proceedings of the 27th SBIC* (New York: Association Press, 1944), pp. 141–45; Baritz, *Servants of Power*, pp. 160–63; "New Emphasis on Personnel Ratings," *Personnel* 19 (1943): 702; Guy Wadsworth, Jr., "Seniority and Merit Rating in Labor Relations," in *Advances in Methods of Personnel Evaluation: Personnel Series No. 107* (New York: AMA, 1947), pp. 22–32.

19 Staff of the Foremen's Letter, *A Report on Foremanship Attitudes* (Deep River, Conn.: National Foremen's Institute, Inc., n.d. — mid-1940s, from internal evidence); "Here's Your Modern Foreman," *Modern Industry* 14:1 (July 1947): 54–64 at 60; "What Foremen's Unions Want," *Factory Management and Maintenance* 105:4 (Apr. 1947): 62. The literature analyzing the problem and proposing or describing remedial action is vast, but most of the core program is to be found summarized in "Answers to the Foreman Problem," *Modern Industry* 15:6 (June 1948): 40–44, and in Ernest Dale, *The Development of Foremen in Management: Research Report No. 7* (New York: AMA, 1946).

20 Robert K. Burns, "Unionization of the White Collar Worker," in *Negotiating and Interpreting the Labor Agreement: Personnel Series No. 110* (New York: AMA, 1947), pp. 3–16; Lawrence A. Appley, "Management's Responsibility to Its Forgotten People," in *Personnel Series No. 91* (New York: AMA, 1945), pp. 34–40; Merlyn S. Pitzele, "The Outlook for White-Collar Unionism," *Management Review* 33 (1944): 184–89; Carl Dean Snyder, *White Collar Workers and the UAW* (Urbana: Univ. of Illinois Press, 1973), pp. 32, 46–47.

21 *Working with GM: A Handbook for Salaried Men and Women* (Detroit: The Corporation, October 1946), esp. pp. 13–15, 22; General Motors Corporation, *Sixth Conference*, transcript of session of 18 August 1950, pp. 56–58; Snyder, *White Collar Workers and the UAW*, pp. 29–30, 51, 95–96, 103–4. Such policies soon became accepted best practice — see Industrial Relations Division, NAM, *Satisfying the Salaried Employee* (New York: NAM, 1962). Other examples of their successful application are to be found in Mark D. McColloch, "White Collar Electrical Machinery, Banking, and Public Welfare Workers, 1940–1970" (Ph.D. diss., Univ. of Pittsburgh, 1975), esp. chs. 2–3, 5–6.

22 Research Institute of America, Inc., *Facing a Union Drive* (New York: The Institute, 1946), esp. pp. 6, 21–22; "How Southern Plants Are Meeting Operation Dixie," *Modern Industry* 12:2 (Aug. 1946): 51–64; case study of Thompson Products in *Organization of Personnel Administration: SPP No. 73 (1945)*, pp. 75–84, illustrating progressive personnel administration as sophisticated antiunionism. For the continuing importance of this, see Richard Edwards, *Contested Terrain: The Transformation of the Workplace in the Twentieth Century* (New York: Basic Books, 1979); Fred K. Foulkes, *Personnel Policies in Large Nonunion Companies* (Englewood Cliffs, N.J.: Prentice-Hall, 1980); Daniel Q. Mills, *Labor-Management Relations* (New York: McGraw-Hill, 1978), pp. 50–66; and Industrial Relations Division, NAM, *Dealing with Employees as Individuals* (New York: NAM, 1960), demonstrating that the "Open Shop" idea has not died — simply been renamed.

23 Stephen Habbe, "How Not to Have Grievances," *Management Record* 9 (1949): 247–49; "Stopping Grievances Before They Grow," *Modern Industry* 13:2 (Feb. 1947): 49–62; Herbert R. Northrup, "The Case for Boulwarism," *Harvard Business Review* 41:5 (1963): 86–97; R. E. Roberts (Director of Employee Relations, Ford Motor Co.), "Human Relations in Industry," an address, 1948 (mimeographed, copy in DPL); *Industrial Relations Round Table Discussion: Report of Management Meeting No. 12* (Ford Motor Co. Industrial Relations Dept., Oct. 1948, processed); General Motors Corporation, *Fourth Conference for College and University Educators: Personnel Administration and Industrial Relations, 16–29 June 1948* (privately circulated, processed verbatim transcript), afternoon session, 18 June 1948; Robert W. Johnson, *Or Forfeit Freedom* (Garden City, N.Y.: Doubleday, 1947); James De Camp Wise (President), "Positive Management Action in Human Relations," in *The Practical Meaning of Management Statesmanship: Personnel Series No. 124* (New York: AMA, 1949), pp. 20–31.

24 Robert Dubin, "Industrial Workers' Worlds: A Study of the 'Central Life Interests' of Industrial Workers," *Social Problems* 3 (1956): 131–42, questioned these basic propositions; Walter J. Conley, ed., *Some Proposals to Management: A Suggested Approach to Sound Industrial and Public Relations* (Rochester, N.Y.: Industrial Management Council, February 1950). In nonunion Rochester, this "progressive" manifesto, produced by the Industrial Relations Group of the Council's Personnel Steering Committee, still

managed to make no direct reference to unionism — as a problem, or even as a significant factor in industrial relations policy. Given favorable circumstances, managerial unilateralism survived undiluted.

25 As well as the references given in ch. 1, note 7, see Edward Berkowitz and Kim McQuaid, "Businessman and Bureaucrat: The Evolution of the American Social Welfare System, 1900–1940," *Journal of Economic History* 38 (1978): 120–42, esp. 120–30; Murray W. Latimer, "Social Security in Collective Bargaining," in Emanuel Stein, ed., *Issues in Collective Bargaining and the Taft-Hartley Act: Proceedings of the 1st Annual New York University Conference on Labor* (Albany and New York, N.Y.: Matthew Bender, 1948), pp. 1–32 at pp. 2–4; Francis M. Wistert, *Fringe Benefits* (New York: Reinhold Publishing, 1959), pp. 3, 36.

26 *What Employers Are Doing for Employees: A Survey of Voluntary Activities for Improvement of Working Conditions in American Business Concerns: NICB Studies, No. 221* (New York: NICB, March 1936).

27 Latimer, "Social Security in Collective Bargaining"; John M. Brumm, "Unions and Health Insurance" and Abraham Weiss, "Union Welfare Plans," in J. B. S. Hardman and Maurice F. Neufeld, eds., *The House of Labor: Internal Operations of American Unions* (New York: Prentice-Hall, 1951), chs. 23, 22.

28 Raymond Munts, *Bargaining for Health: Labor Unions, Health Insurance, and Medical Care* (Madison: Univ. of Wisconsin Press, 1967), esp. pp. 9–12, notes at pp. 259–60; Industrial Relations Division, NAM, *Management Faces the Pension Problem* (New York: NAM, October 1949), p. 4.

29 Hardman and Neufeld, eds., *House of Labor*, chs. 25–27, 41; "Three-Ring Circus for Union Members" (on Ford Local 600), *Modern Industry* 13:3 (Mar. 1947): 136; C. W. M. Hart, "Industrial Relations Research and Social Theory," *Canadian Journal of Economic and Political Science* 15 (1949): 53–73; cf. "Billy Rose of Labor Relations," *Modern Industry* 14:6 (Dec. 1947): 67–74, on Bausch and Lomb Co.

30 See notes 21–24 above; see also Stanley Aronowitz, *False Promises: The Shaping of American Working-Class Consciousness* (New York: McGraw-Hill, 1973), pp. 25, 36–40. This is particularly true with respect to what Richard Edwards terms the "subordinate primary" section of the labor market, i.e. traditional blue-collar and routine white-collar employment, often unionized — see his *Contested Terrain*, esp. pp. 170–73, 189–91.

31 Herman W. Steinkraus (President, Bridgeport Brass Co.; Chairman, NAM Committee on Labor Negotiations), "Pattern for Labor Relations," in *Labor Relations Today and Tomorrow* (New York: NAM, n.d. — but address delivered December 1944), pp. 13–18 at p. 18; on workers' desires, see also Elmo Roper, "Public Opinion," in *Toward a National Labor Policy: Personnel Series No. 72* (New York: AMA, 1943), pp. 20–23, esp. pp. 21–22; cf. Merle Curti, "The Changing Concept of 'Human Nature' in the Literature of American Advertising," *Business History Review* 41 (1967): 235–57. Personnel administration's view of motivation was much more old-fashioned and rationalistic than the advertisers'.

32 "Billy Rose of Labor Relations," p. 68; Appley, "Management's Responsibility to Its Forgotten People," p. 38; and, for the best versions of this aspect of the personnel rationale, statements of General Foods and Thompson Products—for General Foods, see Thomas Spates' articles and addresses cited in ch. 1, note 50; for Thompson Products, see Raymond S. Livingstone, "Settling Disputes without Interrupting Production," *Management Record* 4 (1942): 385–91; and Stanley Black (Assistant to Vice-President Livingstone), "Earning Employee Backing," in *College Forums on Current Economic Issues* (New Wilmington, Pa.: Economic and Business Foundation, 1948), pp. 25–43. Other firms also espoused this philosophy, most notably General Electric in its "Boulwarist" period—cf. James J. Nance (President, Hotpoint, Inc.), "Top Management Views the Job Ahead in Industrial Relations," in *Personnel Series No. 124* (1949), pp. 32–39.

33 For the history of this technique, see Baritz, *Servants of Power*, pp. 124–27, 149–55; Houser, *What the Employer Thinks*, ch. 8; Arthur Kornhauser, "Psychological Studies of Employee Attitudes," *Personnel* 21 (1944): 170–89. For descriptions of cases, and discussions of its value, see Harold B. Bergen (Management Consultant), "Determining Employee Attitudes," in *Proceedings of the 23d SBIC* (1940), pp. 127–33, and "Measuring Attitudes and Morale in Wartime," *Management Record* 4 (1942): 101–4; F. F. Bradshaw and Herbert E. Krugman (Management Consultants), "Making the Most of Morale Surveys," *Personnel* 25 (1948): 18–22; J. T. Burke (Westinghouse), "Sensing Employee Attitudes," in *Addresses on Industrial Relations 1939* (Ann Arbor: Univ. of Michigan Press, 1939), pp. 25–30; Tom N. Boggs and Louis L. Maness (Le Tourneau Mfg. Co.), "How to Conduct Employee Opinion Surveys," *Factory Management and Maintenance* 104:3 (Mar. 1946): 90–94; "How to Find Out What Your Workers Think about You," *Factory Management and Maintenance* 106:8 (Aug. 1948): 81–91; Charles E. Swezey (Armstrong Cork Co.), "Surveys to Build Understanding," in *Personnel Series No. 129* (1949), pp. 16–21; James C. Worthy (Sears, Roebuck & Co.), "Discovering and Evaluating Employee Attitudes," in *Influencing and Measuring Employee Attitudes: Personnel Series No. 113* (New York: AMA, 1947), pp. 13–22. Notable survey users included General Electric, General Motors, Ford, Thompson Products, and Standard Oil of New Jersey.

34 Sources cited in n. 33 above are only a sampling of those available on this subject; but among the dozens of commentators, only one, to my knowledge, rates the 'cathartic' effect of the procedure anywhere near as high as the beneficial impact of consequent improvement in company policies and behavior—Robert C. McMurry, in *Handling Personality Adjustment in Industry* (New York: Harper & Bros., 1944), pp. 40–54. This only reflects the prevailing managerial opinion that employees were at least partly rational, and that experience was the great educator. This contrasts sharply with the psychologizing strain in the well-known Mayoite school of "human relations" studies—cf. Wilensky and Wilensky, "Personnel Counseling," 273–77; Harold L. Sheppard, "The Social and Historical Philosophy of Elton

Mayo," *Antioch Review* 10 (1950): 396–406 at 399 — of whose practical, as opposed to rhetorical, influence upon management in general before the 1950s there is scant evidence. Even "human relations training" for foremen in the 1940s was little more than attempts to inculcate the principles of the "new foremanship" first expounded during the First World War. The manipulative management of men antedated Mayo and the Hawthorne studies; the practical impact of the latter in the 1940s scarcely went beyond some parts of the Bell System and associated companies.

35 For the origins of this softer supervisory style, see works on the "new foremanship" — Charles R. Allen, *The Foreman and His Job* (Philadelphia: J. B. Lippincott, 1922), pts. 7–8; Eugene Grace (President, Bethlehem Steel), "A Successful Executive's View on Foremanship in Industry," in Policyholders' Service Bureau, Group Insurance Division (hereafter cited as PSB, GID), *Foreman Training Plans* (New York: Metropolitan Life Insurance Co., — hereafter cited as MLIC — n.d. but not earlier than 1928), pp. 49–50; Cyrus McCormick, Jr. (International Harvester), *Foreman Training — Essential to Plant Self-Government* (Washington, D.C.: Chamber of Commerce of the USA, June 1926). Versions of the same theme occur repeatedly in the 1940s — in instruction manuals (George H. Fern, *Training for Supervision in Industry* [New York: McGraw-Hill, 1945], esp. ch. 6; Glenn Gardiner, *How to Create Job Satisfaction: A Manpower Maintenance Manual for Foremen* [New York: Elliott Service Co., 1943]; Palmer J. Kalsem and N. M. Johnston, Jr. [of the Glenn L. Martin Co., Baltimore], *Practical Supervision* [New York: McGraw-Hill, 1945]), and in numerous articles and pamphlets — Armstrong Cork Co., *The Supervisory Six* (Lancaster, Pa.: The Corporation, 1945); Lemuel R. Boulware, "How Big Is Our Job?" address delivered before the AMA Personnel Conference, Chicago, 17 February 1948 (privately printed — copy in L-MDC), pp. 6–9; H. H. Carey (General Foods), "Consultative Supervision and Management," *Personnel* 18 (1942): 286–95; Eastman Kodak Co., *Principles of Supervision* (n.p.: The Corporation, Dec. 1947); M. A. Heidt (Vice-President, Industrial Relations, Bendix Aviation Corp. — a GM affiliate), "Stimulating Cooperation among Management, Foreman, and Worker," in *Strengthening Management's Channels of Communication: Personnel Series No. 116* (New York: AMA, 1948), pp. 16–21, esp. p. 17; Ralph Lee, "Man to Man on the Job," in *Management Training for Foremen: Personnel Series No. 78* (New York: AMA, 1944), pp. 24–26; Raymond F. Livingstone (Thompson Products), "Settling Disputes without Interrupting Production," p. 390; examples of "best practice" in *Organization of Personnel Administration: SPP No. 73*, pp. 13 (Armstrong Cork), 40 (General Foods); *Better Supervision: Training within Industry Bulletin No. 4* (Washington, D.C.: Office of Production Management-Labor Division, Nov. 1940). The last reference is extremely interesting — the "new foremanship" developed in response to labor supply difficulties and the need for all-out, uninterrupted production in the First World War; it found renewed favor as a result of similar circumstances during the Second World War, and, *via* the federally sponsored, management-

staffed Training Within Industry organization's job relations training program, was taught to over two million newly promoted foremen. Quoted material from Robert A. Sutermeister, "Training Foremen in Human Relations," *Personnel* 20 (1943): 6–14 at 10.

The effectiveness of management's investment in "human relations training" in changing supervision's actual leadership styles may be doubted. The pedagogic techniques employed were usually authoritarian—formal lectures —or crudely manipulative—the "discussion group," guided towards predetermined conclusions. These could produce verbal acceptance of the principles of "leading, not bossing," etc., but had little apparent effect on foremen's actual behavior in the workplace. Experience of a punitive leadership style at the hands of their own superiors told them what the real policies of the organization were; and, in the workplace, they continued to rely on the usual combination of threats and favors. Leland P. Bradford, "The Future of Supervisory Training," *Personnel* 22 (1945): 6–12, esp. 6–7; Edwin A. Fleishman, *A Study of the Leadership Role of the Foreman in an Industrial Situation (with Special Implications for Leadership Training): A Summary of Research Conducted with the Cooperation of the International Harvester Co.* (Columbus, Ohio: Personnel Research Board, Ohio State University, 1951, mimeographed); Schuyler Dean Hoslet, "Training in Human Relations: A Review and Evaluation," *Personnel* 23 (1946): 85–97. More sophisticated instructional techniques apparently enjoyed greater success— Allan H. Tyler (American Type Founders, Inc.), "A Case Study of Role Playing," *Personnel* 25 (1948): 136–42.

For a detailed study of these matters, see Karen Louise Jorgensen-Esmaili, "Schooling and the Early Human Relations Movement: With Special Reference to the Foreman's Conference, 1919–1939" (Ph.D. thesis, Univ. of California-Berkeley, 1979), esp. Chs. 2, 3.

CHAPTER 7: HEARTS AND MINDS: THE SEARCH FOR PUBLIC FAVOR

1 Ralph E. Flanders, *The Function of Management in American Life: Lectures Delivered at the Seventh Annual Stanford Business Conference, 19–23 July 1948* (Palo Alto, Calif.: Stanford Univ. Press, 1949), p. 8.
2 See, in particular, Marguerite C. Green, *The National Civic Federation and the American Labor Movement, 1900–1925* (Washington, D.C.: Catholic Univ. of America Press, 1956); Morrell Heald, *The Social Responsibilities of Business: Company and Community, 1900–1960* (Cleveland: Case Western Reserve Univ. Press, 1970); and James Weinstein, *The Corporate Ideal in the Liberal State: 1900–1918* (Boston: Beacon Press, 1968) chs. 1, 2, 5 esp.
3 The history of this liberal group is only now being written. See, in particular, the work of Kim McQuaid, esp. "The Frustration of Corporate Revival During the Early New Deal." *The Historian* (Aug. 1979): 682–704, and "The Business Advisory Council of the Department of Commerce, 1933–

1961: A Study in Corporate-Government Relations," in Paul Uselding, ed., *Research in Economic History* (Greenwich, Conn.: JAI Press, 1976), 1:171–97; and Robert M. Collins, "Positive Business Responses to the New Deal: The Roots of the Committee for Economic Development, 1933–1942," *Business History Review* 52 (1978): 342–68.

4 Flanders, *Function of Management in American Life*, pp. 22–25.

5 See letters of Donaldson Brown (GM) and J. Howard Pew (Sun Oil), printed in Richard S. Tedlow, *Keeping the Corporate Image: Public Relations and Business, 1900–1950* (Greenwich, Conn.: JAI Press, 1979), pp. 118–20.

6 Karl Schriftgeisser, *Business Comes of Age* (New York: Harper & Bros., 1960), p. 6 — an excellent official history of the CED.

7 Robert A. Brady, "The C.E.D. — What Is It and Why?" *Antioch Review* 4 (1944): 21–46; David Eakins, "The Development of Corporate Liberal Policy Research in the United States 1865–1965" (Ph.D. diss., Univ. of Wisconsin, Madison, 1966), ch. 7; Tedlow, *Keeping the Corporate Image*, pp. 121–25. A good and convenient source of primary material on the origins and activities of the CED is to be found in the papers of Marion B. Folsom, at the University of Rochester, N.Y., library. Folsom, Treasurer of Eastman Kodak Company, was a long-time BAC activist and a founder member of the CED, as well as its first secretary.

8 Walter B. Weisenburger, "Challenge to Industry," address delivered before the 51st Congress of American Industry (New York: NAM, privately printed, 1947), p. 5. The liberalization of NAM rhetoric was noted at the time — see "Renovation in NAM: Industry's Intransigent Spokesman Now Says 'Yes' as Well as 'No,'" *Fortune* 38:1 (July 1948): 72 ff.

9 Walter H. Wheeler, Jr. (President, Pitney-Bowes), "Industry's New Responsibility," *Management Review* 38 (1949): 646–51 at 650.

10 Tedlow, *Keeping the Corporate Image*, p. 123.

11 Ralph E. Flanders, "Address of Award," in *The Henry Lawrence Gantt Memorial Medal: Personnel Series No. 101* (New York: AMA, 1946), pp. 7–15 at p. 15. Flanders was chairman of the CED's Research and Policy Committee; the award went to Paul Hoffman, CED chairman and perhaps the most influential corporate liberal of the period.

12 For representative examples of CED thinking on this score, see Paul G. Hoffman, "The Survival of Free Enterprise," *Harvard Business Review* 25 (1946): 21–27; and his *Management's Responsibility to Capitalism: An Address* (New York: CED, 1947).

13 Elmo Roper, "Public Opinion," in *Toward a National Labor Policy: Personnel Series No. 72* (New York: AMA, 1943), pp. 20–23; and Elmo Roper, "The Public Looks at Business," *Harvard Business Review* 27 (1949): 167–75. Cf. Dr. George Gallup, "Main Street Rates the Issues," address delivered before the 52d Congress of American Industry, 3 December 1947 (NAM press release, mimeographed — copy in record series L-2, L-MDC); for Robinson, see analysis presented at pp. 189–91. Some elements in the NAM had evidently learnt the lesson Roper was trying to teach — see Ira

Mosher (NAM Chairman), "Making Regular Jobs Regular," address before the 50th Congress of American Industry, 5 December 1946 (NAM press release, mimeographed — copy in record series L-2, L-MDC). Mosher himself grew so committed to the idea of the importance of employment security that he became a consultant advising firms on what they could do to increase it. The NAM did not go so far, but its earnest encouragement of the adoption of "progressive" personnel administration in the later 1940s did reflect a growing sophistication in its political approach.

14 Wheeler, "Industry's New Responsibility," p. 647.

15 For this analysis, see also Calvin B. Hoover, *The Economy, Liberty, and the State* (New York: Twentieth Century Fund, 1959), ch. 7, as well as articles and addresses of Ralph Flanders and Paul Hoffman, cited in ns. 1 and 11–12 above.

16 See, for example, Henning W. Prentis (President, Armstrong Cork Co.; ex-Chairman, NAM), *Competitive Enterprise Versus Planned Economy* (New York: NAM, Aug. 1945) — a passionate and powerful affirmation of faith in the American business system, representative in its argument but notable for its eloquent presentation of theses countless other businessmen at the time turned into banal clichés.

17 A. B. Martin (Plant Manager, General Electric Co.), "A Bid for Employee Cooperation," *CPMA Management Report No. 14* (San Francisco: CPMA, 1948), pp. 4–5.

18 Curtis, "Current Human Problems in Quality and Productivity," in E. Clark Worman, ed., *Responsibilities and Opportunities in Human Relations: Proceedings of the 31st SBIC* (New York: Association Press, 1949), pp. 17–20 at p. 18; cf. Guy B. Arthur, "The Status of Personnel Administration in Management," in *Management's Internal "Public" Relations: Personnel Series No. 102* (New York: AMA, 1946), pp. 29–41 at p. 33; Rodney Chase (Director, Public and Industrial Relations, Chase Copper and Brass Co.), "The Public Relations of Management's Labor Relations," in *Developing Public and Industrial Relations Policy: General Management Series No. 140* (New York: AMA, 1947), pp. 15–22 at pp. 15–16.

19 "Trends in Employee Thinking on Simple Economics," *The Public Opinion Index for Industry* 8:2 (Feb. 1950): 34–35; cf. NAM, *Fallacies about Our Private Enterprise System* (1940; New York: NAM, March 1944). The "fallacious beliefs" for which the ORC was testing were the most frequently repeated, and understandably worrying, in managerial analyses of the climate of public opinion — understandably, because they related to real issues of public policy in areas where the business system's record of performance was vulnerable.

20 "Trends in Employee Thinking on Simple Economics," p. 45; cf. Eli Chinoy, "The Tradition of Opportunity and the Aspirations of Automobile Workers," *American Journal of Sociology* 57 (1952): 453–59; "The Fortune Survey," *Fortune* 35:1 (Jan. 1947): 5–16, esp. 5, 6, 12; "The Fortune Survey," *Fortune* 35:5 (May 1947): 5–12.

21 "What the Factory Worker Really Thinks about Productivity, Nationaliza-

tion of Industry, and Labor in Politics," *Factory Management and Mainte-nance* 104:1 (Jan. 1946): 82–88, at 82–85.

22 "What the Factory Worker Really Thinks — About His Job; Unemployment; and Industry's Profits," *Factory Management and Maintenance* 105:12 (Dec. 1947): 86–92 at 87; "What the Factory Worker Really Thinks about Productivity . . . ," pp. 89–90; "Trends in Employee Thinking on Simple Economics," p. 29. Claude Robinson's ORC was the polling agency favored by McGraw-Hill, publishers of *Factory*, as well as by the blue-riband, public relations–conscious firms which supported the *Index*.

23 "What the Factory Worker Really Thinks about Union Behavior and Industry Earnings," *Factory Management and Maintenance* 104:11 (Nov. 1946): 81–88 at 88; "Trends in Employee Thinking on Simple Economics," p. 44.

24 "What Employees Say about Management's Leadership," *The Public Opinion Index for Industry* 12:7 (July 1954): 3.

25 Austin S. Iglehart (President, General Foods), "A Challenge to American Management," *Management Review* 37 (1948): 274–76 at 274.

26 The classic account of both these movements, lampooning the second, is William H. Whyte, Jr., *Is Anybody Listening? How and Why Business Fumbles When It Talks with Human Beings* (New York: Simon & Schuster, 1952). When the title article was first published in *Fortune* (42:3 [September 1950]: 77–83, 167–78), it produced the greatest volume of reader response in the twenty-year history of that mouthpiece of business liberalism, much of it agreeing with Whyte's slashing attack on the crudities of business propaganda. It also produced an interesting retort from Earl Bunting, managing director of the NAM, the organization more committed than any other to the Campaign and accordingly one of Whyte's prime targets — see Earl Bunting, *Industry Looks at Its Relations with Employees* (New York: NAM, 1950). Whyte's argument, and his sarcastic tone, are foreshadowed in an address by Fritz J. Roethlisberger, director of the Hawthorne studies and one of the fathers of the "human relations" school of industrial psychology — "A 'New Look' for Management," in *Worker Morale and Productivity: General Management Series No. 141* (New York: AMA, 1948), pp. 11–22. Roethlisberger was evidently appalled at the degree to which management in general remained unimpressed by, or ignorant of, industrial psychology with its emphasis on interpersonal communications, though managers had adopted the slogans of "human relations" more or less wholesale.

See also Employee Relations Department, Standard Oil of New Jersey, *A Special Report: What Should Esso Be Doing in the Field of Economic Education for Employees?* (privately circulated, processed, 1 April 1950 — copy in Corporation File, L-MDC). This contains an evaluation of the "Great Free Enterprise Campaign" full of critical detail, leading to a policy recommendation that Esso should steer clear of it and concentrate on "Communications in Industry."

27 Wallace F. Bennett (President, NAM), "Preface" to *Employee Communications for Better Understanding* (New York: NAM, June 1949). The pamphlet

was designed to encourage member firms to become more active in selling free enterprise to their *own* workers, complementing NAM's national advertising and "information" programs.

28 Charles R. Hook, *Principles behind Employer-Employee Harmony* (New York: NAM, n.d. but address delivered 8 December 1939), p. 13; but see Robert Dubin, "Industrial Workers' Worlds: A Study of the 'Central Life Interests' of Industrial Workers," *Social Problems* 3 (1956): 131–42.

29 John Lyon Collyer (President, B. F. Goodrich Co.), "America's Decade of Decision," remarks at 25th Anniversary of Industrial Relations Counselors, Inc., New York City, 22 May 1951 (privately printed — copy in Information File, L-MDC).

30 Bunting, *Industry Looks at Its Relations with Employees*, p. 13.

31 *Interpreting the Company through the Employee Publication: The Public Opinion Index for Industry* (Princeton, N.J.: ORC, November 1947, processed), pp. 41, 33.

32 Geneva Seybold, "Put the Reason with the Rule," *Management Record* 10 (1948): 541–43; Robert A. Sutermeister, "How to Interest the Employee in His Job," *Personnel* 21 (1944): 131–38; "The Problem of Boredom," *Management Record* 10 (1948): 567–75. The best original sources to examine for such a message, and its associated imagery, are employee orientation manuals and company newspapers, of which good collections exist in the libraries and archives of the Industrial Relations Section, Princeton University, and the New York State School of Industrial and Labor Relations, Cornell University. Their titles alone are often quite revealing — "Getting Along as a Member of the NCR Family," "GM Folks," "The ARMCO-Operator," "We" (Allis-Chalmers), "The Wingfoot Clan" (Goodyear Tire and Rubber).

33 Marver H. Bernstein, "Political Ideas of Selected American Business Journals," *Public Opinion Quarterly* 17 (1953): 258–67, and Francis X. Sutton et al., *The American Business Creed* (Cambridge, Mass.: Harvard Univ. Press, 1956), describe and dissect this ideology in great detail; Sherman Rogers, *Why Kill the Goose?* (Irvington-on-Hudson, N.Y.: Foundation for Economic Education, 1947), and *Business in a Democracy* (New York: NAM, 1942), are representative examples of propaganda materials used in the attempt to disseminate it.

34 For descriptions of such media and their message, and instruction in their preparation and use, see the following: books — John C. Aspley and Eugene Whitmore, eds., *The Handbook of Industrial Relations* (Chicago: Dartnell, 1943), chs. 27–31, 40–42; Glenn and Denny Griswold, eds., *Your Public Relations — the Standard Public Relations Handbook* (New York: Funk & Wagnalls, 1948), esp. chs. 9, 10, 22, 28–30; Alexander R. Heron, *Sharing Information with Employees* (Palo Alto, Calif.: Stanford Univ. Press, 1942) — a pioneering work by the head of Crown Zellerbach's industrial relations department; Robert Newcomb and Marg Sammons, *Speak Up, Management! How to Communicate with Employees and the Public* (New York: Funk & Wagnalls, 1951) — by the leading specialists in employee communi-

cations media; Robert W. Peters, *Communications within Industry: Principles and Methods of Management-Employee Interchange* (New York: Harper & Bros., 1949) — by the head of employee relations research of Standard Oil of New Jersey (cf. last reference in note 26 above), containing valuable survey evidence of best and standard pratice; Fred Rudge, *Economic Information for Employees: Helping Employees Understand the Operation of Their Own Company as a Prerequisite to Their Understanding of the American Business System* (New London, Conn.: National Foremen's Institute, 1952); articles and pamphlets — too numerous to mention, but see esp. *How to Tell Your Company's Story* (New York: Research Institute of America, 1947), for excellent illustrations of tabular, graphical, and other ways of explaining away the size of corporate profits. For sample survey evidence on the use of various media, see "How Management in a Hundred Plants Gets Information to Workers," *Factory Management and Maintenance* 104: 7 (July 1946): 114–17; "Industry's Communications Systems 1950," *The Public Opinion Index for Industry* 8:10 (Oct. 1950); *Personnel Practices in Factory and Office (Revised): SPP No. 88* (New York: NICB, 1947), tables 66–70, 178–81, pp. 27–28, 57. The NICB survey most usefully relates media use to plant size, demonstrating, as one would expect, increased use of formal media and structured contacts or meetings in larger plants, where problems of employee morale were greater, informal methods more difficult to use and less adequate, and staff resources for supporting communications programs more numerous.

35 Tedlow, *Keeping the Corporate Image*, ch. 3; Strother H. Walker and Paul Sklar, "Business Finds Its Voice," *Harper's Monthly Magazine* 176 (Jan., Feb., Mar., 1938): 113–23, 317–29, 428–40; Theodore S. Repplier, "Advertising Dons Long Pants," *Public Opinion Quarterly* 9 (1945): 269–78; and J. A. R. Pimlott, "Public Service Advertising: The Advertising Council," *Public Opinion Quarterly* 12 (1948): 209–19.

36 Thomas D'A. Brophy (President, American Heritage Foundation), "We Found an Abiding Faith," *Manage* 1: 10 (June 1949): 12, 32–33; "Film Kicks Off Admen's PR Plan for Industry," *Modern Industry* 15:3 (Mar. 1948): 97–98; Leonard I. Pearlin and Morris Rosenberg, "Propaganda Techniques in Institutional Advertising," *Public Opinion Quarterly* 16 (1952): 5–26; "'Plan for Action' Helps Industry with Its Public Relations," *Factory Management and Maintenance* 106:10 (Oct. 1948): 108–10; "Plant Gives Company Facts in Local Ads," *Factory Management and Maintenance* 105:6 (June 1947): 100–101; "Selling Begins at Plant Home Town," *Modern Industry* 16:6 (Dec. 1948): 50–53. Allegheny-Ludlum Steel Co.'s community program attracted great attention — like General Electric's similar commitment to the Free Enterprise Campaign, it was sparked off by a realization of the depth of local hostility towards itself and business power revealed in the bitter 1946 strikes; see Hiland G. Batchellor (President), "Let's Make Workers Feel They Belong," *Factory Management and Maintenance* 106:2 (Feb. 1948): 90–93; Lamar Kelly (Manager, Public Relations Department),

"A Grass Roots Public Relations Program," in Metropolitan Life Insurance Co., *Community Relations — Selected Cases* (New York: The Corporation, 1950, processed), pp. 45–48.

37 I thank Prof. Richard S. Tedlow of Harvard Business School for his helpful comments on an earlier draft of this section. Some of the points he made have been incorporated into this paragraph. For survey evidence, see Burton R. Fisher and Stephen B. Wiley, *Big Business as the People See It: A Study of a Socio-Economic Institution* (Ann Arbor: Univ. of Michigan Press, 1951), pp. ix–x, xii; "What Employees Say about Management's Leadership," *The Public Opinion Index for Industry* 12:7 (July 1954): 10, 16, 20–21. This is the kind of inchoate class-consciousness John C. Leggett calls "skepticism" — see his "Uprootedness and Working-Class Consciousness," *American Journal of Sociology* 68 (1963): 682–92.

38 On the question of business encouragement of the post-Second World War Red Scare, see Peter H. Irons, "American Business and the Origins of McCarthyism: The Cold War Crusade of the United States Chamber of Commerce," in Robert Griffiths and Athan Theoharis, eds. *The Specter: Original Essays on the Cold War and the Origins of McCarthyism* (New York: New Viewpoints, 1974), pp. 74–89.

39 Lemuel R. Boulware, "How Big Is Our Job?" address delivered before the AMA Personnel Conference, Chicago, 17 February 1948 (privately printed pamphlet — copy in L-MDC), p. 13.

40 Leonard W. Trestor (Director, CCUS, and Chairman, Committee on Advertising), "Free Enterprise — How Long Can It Survive?" address delivered before the Rotary Club of Marion, Ohio, 11 January 1949 (mimeographed copy in L-MDC), p. 1. Trestor's is an optimistic, reflective speech.

41 L. J. Fletcher (Director, Training and Community Relations, Caterpillar Tractor Co.), "Telling Your Story to the Plant and Community," *CPMA Management Report No. 15* (San Francisco: CPMA, 1948), p. 12.

42 Gallup, "Main Street Rates the Issues," p. 2; cf. Martin Dodge (Management Consultant), "Does Management Get Its Message Across to Employees?" in *Management's Internal "Public" Relations: Personnel Series No. 102* (New York: AMA, 1946), pp. 3–14. This theme was also commonplace.

43 This vision of society was much more common in business' public rhetoric of the 1920s — James W. Prothro, *The Dollar Decade: Business Ideas in the 1920s* (Baton Rouge: Louisiana State Univ. Press, 1954), esp. pt. 1 — but persisted into the 1930s and 1940s; see Robert A. Brady, *Business as a System of Power* (Morningside Heights, N.Y.: Columbia Univ. Press, 1943), esp. pp. 288–93. Cf. Stanley R. Black, "Earning Employee Backing," in *College Forums on Current Economic Issues* (New Wilmington, Pa.: Economic and Business Foundation, 1948), pp. 25–43 at p. 29.

44 Morris Sayre (President, Corn Products Refining Co. — how appropriate! — and NAM), "We Owe It to America," address delivered before the 53d Congress of American Industry, New York City, 3 December 1948 (NAM Press Release, mimeographed — copy in L-MDC), p. 8; Otis A. Pease, *Responsibilities of American Advertising* (New Haven, Conn.: Yale Univ. Press,

1958); Repplier, "Advertising Dons Long Pants"; "The Nine Hundred," *Fortune* 46:6 (Nov. 1952): 132–35, 232–36 at 135, 232; Mabel Newcomer, *The Big Business Executive: The Factors That Made Him, 1900–1950* (New York: Columbia Univ. Press, 1955), pp. 107–8; Trestor, "Free Enterprise — How Long Can It Survive?" pp. 2–3; Brophy, "We Found an Abiding Faith," pp. 12, 32–33.

45 Merle Curti, "The Changing Concept of 'Human Nature' in the Literature of American Advertising," *Business History Review* 41 (1967): 335–57; Chase, "Public Relations of Management's Labor Relations," p. 19; Austin M. Fisher and Fred G. Rudge, "Employee Manuals—a Key to Improved Employee Relations," *Personnel* 22 (1946): 288–91 at 289; Dodge, "Does Management Get Its Message across to Employees?" p. 8; L. C. Morrow, "Management Outlook in Labor Relations," *CPMA Management Report No. 10* (San Francisco: CPMA, 1948), pp. 9–10.

46 This would also seem to be the conclusion of detailed studies of business support for the hard right in the 1950s and early '60s — see Philip H. Burch, Jr., "The NAM as an Interest Group," *Politics and Society* 4 (1973): 97–130; Fred J. Cook, "The Ultras," *The Nation*, 23 June 1962, pp. 565–606; and Alan F. Westin, "Anti-Communism and the Corporations," *Commentary* (Dec. 1963): 479–87.

47 U.S. Congress, House, Select Committee on Lobbying Activities, *Hearings*, 81st Cong., 2d sess. (Washington, D.C.: Government Printing Office, 1950), pt. 5, pp. 32, 121, 243, and pt. 4, pp. 69–71 (hereafter cited as *Lobbying Hearings*).

48 George Wolfskill, *The Revolt of the Conservatives: A History of the American Liberty League, 1934–1940* (Boston: Houghton Mifflin, 1962), pp. 58–60; *Lobbying Hearings*, pt. 8, pp. 54, 62–64; Alfred S. Cleveland, "Some Political Aspects of Organized Industry" (Ph.D. diss., Harvard Univ. 1946), pp. 207–17; Richard W. Gable, "A Political Analysis of an Employers' Association—the NAM" (Ph.D. diss., Univ. of Chicago, 1950), pp. 229–31.

49 Ford, through its own Foundation, almost single-handedly supported a more sophisticated, CED-backed public information program, the Joint Council on Economic Education, for which see *Summary Report of the JCEE 1948–1951* (New York: The Council, 1951), pp. 9–11. Ford's contribution to the JCEE was $105,000—twenty-one times as much as Ford alone gave its rival; the latter's total receipts from corporate givers, 1946–50, were only eight and a half times the size of that one donation. *Lobbying Hearings*, pt. 8, pp. 52, 14–20. This illustrates a problem with using a contribution list as a hard-and-fast guide to a company's endorsement of a pressure group's program: some firms supported conflicting pressure groups, and only where one has information on the pattern of a firm's political contributions can one assess the significance of any particular one; and the size of some contributions the FEE received—given by fellow businessmen in response to personal approaches—was not such as to prove that a firm's commitment to, or even knowledge of, its aims was very deep. So the FEE

master list is not a perfect guide: however, in the case of many of the firms on it, corroborative evidence of the conservative character of their managements is given by the tone of political statements their chief executives were wont to issue, the other organizations they supported, and the labor or public relations policies they followed.

50 *Lobbying Hearings*, pt. 8, pp. 12–20.
51 Clinton S. Golden and Virginia Parker, eds., *Causes of Industrial Peace under Collective Bargaining* (New York: Harper & Bros., 1955), pp. 82–99. The management is criticized for its conservatism in Herbert R. Northrup and Harvey A. Young, "The Causes of Industrial Peace Revisited," *Industrial and Labor Relations Review* 22 (1968): 31–47 at 35, suggesting that Libbey-Owens-Ford's good labor relations were the result of peculiar market conditions and management appeasement rather than of any active and conscious "progressive" policy. So this exception is probably neither serious nor very significant.

CHAPTER 8: EPILOGUE: "GETTING EVERYBODY BACK ON THE SAME TEAM"

1 Raymond S. Livingstone, "The Changing Concept of the Personnel Function," in *Industrial Applications of Medicine and Psychiatry: Personnel Series No. 130* (New York: AMA, 1949), pp. 18–31.
2 Ibid., p. 19.
3 Ibid., p. 19.
4 Ibid., p. 20.
5 Ibid., p. 20.
6 Ibid., p. 21.

A NOTE ON SOURCES

1 Thomas C. Cochran, "A Plan for the Study of Business Thinking," *Political Science Quarterly* 62 (1947): 82–90.
2 Gary D. Saretzky, "North American Business Archives: Results of a Survey," *American Archivist* 40 (1977): 413–19.
3 Madison: University of Wisconsin Press, 1967.
4 Interview, Warner Pflug, Detroit, 3 November 1974; interview, Ralph Deedes, Detroit, 5 November 1974. Some of GM's sensitivity may have resulted from the publication of William Serrin's *The Company and the Union: The "Civilized Relationship" of the General Motors Corporation and the United Automobile Workers* (New York: Knopf, 1973).
5 "The Nine Hundred," *Fortune* 46:6 (Nov. 1952): 132–35, 232–36 at 133. The later and much larger sample by William Lloyd Warner and James C. Abegglen showed a similar result—a median age of fifty-four for some

8,500 executives of vice-presidential rank and above. *Big Business Leaders in America* (New York: Harper, 1955), p. 210.

6 Arthur H. Cole, *Business Enterprise in Its Social Setting* (Cambridge: Harvard Univ. Press, 1959), ch. 4, esp. pp. 78, 82–91.

7 General Motors, Ford, and General Electric were especially important contributors of information from the ranks of large firms. Of business associations, trade-based bodies like the Automobile Manufacturers Association and the National Metal Trades Association were of some importance, but those crossing industry lines were much more so — the Chamber of Commerce of the United States, Committee for Economic Development, National Industrial Conference Board, and above all the National Association of Manufacturers and the American Management Association.

From the huge output of the business press, I selected for particular attention periodicals emphasizing industrial relations matters: *Factory Management and Maintenance*, bellwether in the conservative flock of McGraw-Hill's trade papers, and its smaller more progressive rival, *Modern Industry; Industrial Relations; Supervision* and *Manage*, from the National Association of Foremen; NICB publications from the *Studies in Personnel Policy* series and the *Management Record;* AMA periodicals *Personnel* and *Management Review*, and transcripts of its conference series — the *Personnel, Production*, and *General Management Series*. Some general-interest business periodicals of different political persuasions — *Fortune*, the *Harvard Business Review, Nation's Business* (official CCUS publication), and *U.S. News and World Report* — were examined in depth; others, particularly *Business Week*, the *Wall Street Journal*, and the New York *Journal of Commerce*, were given much less attention as their chief concern was news reporting rather than providing the longer, more detailed, evaluative articles common in the other organs.

Consultancy and business-service agencies providing material included the Policyholders' Service Bureau of the Group Insurance Division, Metropolitan Life Insurance Co. — an unexpected, but rich, source; Industrial Relations Counselors, Inc.; Opinion Research Corporation; the Research Institute of America; and the National Foremen's Institute.

In addition, books written by and for businessmen, either about immediate problems or about managerial techniques, were of some use. Publishing houses whose output was most valuable included Funk & Wagnalls, Prentice-Hall, McGraw-Hill, and Harper & Row.

Most of the material referring to particular firms and business organizations, and much of that from consultancy and service agencies, was found in the extensive vertical-file collections at the Walter P. Reuther Memorial Library and the Public Library in Detroit, and at the Princeton University Industrial Relations Section and the Labor-Management Documentation Center at the New York State School of Industrial and Labor Relations, Cornell University. Much of this matter is ephemeral, and it seems to have been little used. For an explanation of why it began to be collected so intensively in the 1940s, and a description of it, see Tim Mason, "Class Conflict and Scientific Management in American Industry: Guides to the Literature," *History Workshop* 3 (Spring 1977): 81–82.

8 Fine examples of NAM Congress of American Industry rhetoric include Ira Mosher, "Making Regular Jobs Regular," address delivered 5 December 1946; Fred C. Crawford, "On Guard for Freedom," address delivered 5 December 1947; and J. Howard Pew, "The NAM's Public Relations Program," address delivered 3 December 1947 — all mimeographed press releases in Record Series L-2 at the Labor-Management Documentation Center at Cornell. Other NAM publications in the same holdings are, however, much more practical and down-to-earth: when the NAM aimed to inform its members rather than inspire them, its tone was much less extreme. *Unit Thinking and Unit Action* was the title of a significant NAM pamphlet (New York: 1935).

9 Magazines designed for practicing managers are particularly full of this material — *Modern Industry, Mill and Factory,* and *Factory Management and Maintenance* are about the most rewarding. See, for example, M. J. Murphy and R. C. Smyth (Bendix Radio Division, Bendix Aviation Corporation), "Discipline: A Case Study in the Development and Application of a Discipline Procedure," *Factory Management and Maintenance* 103:7 (July 1945): 97–104; and A. V. Larson, "Worker Opinion Survey Did a Good Job for Us," *Factory Management and Maintenance* 104:9 (Sept. 1946): 156–57.

10 List of Officers, *Management Review* 31:5 (May 1941): back cover; and pamphlet, *Training for and by Management in the Principles and Methods of Management* (New York: AMA, [late 1940s]). For AMA conference rhetoric paralleling that of the NAM, see Thomas Roy Jones, "The Scope of Collective Bargaining," in *Management's Stake in Collective Bargaining: Personnel Series No. 81* (New York: AMA, 1944), pp. 40–51; and Harry W. Anderson, *Should Management Be Unionized? Personnel Series No. 90* (New York: AMA, 1945). The close fit between AMA and NAM rhetoric in the 1940s is natural, as both organizations became increasingly representative of industrial management. Rather than representing "progressive" managerial and traditional entrepreneurial groups respectively, as they had tended to do in the 1920s, by the 1940s they were both expressions of the new "practical conservative" synthesis within American management — a growing consensus on strategy and tactics, under big business leadership.

11 The main UAW sources used were the Pre-Presidential Materials in the Walter P. Reuther Collection, and the Ford and General Motors Department files. The most valuable public documents were the 1943 *Hearings* of the House Military Affairs Committee (cited as *Full Utilization of Manpower*), especially good on the foreman problem and outspoken expressions of the "unitary ideology"; the 1945 *Hearings* of the Senate Committee Investigating the National Defense Program (cited as *Manpower Problems in Detroit*), full of material on the loss of labor discipline; the 1947 and 1949 *Hearings* of the House and Senate Labor Committees concerned with the passage and proposed repeal of the Taft-Hartley Act, which also demon-

strated the depths of businessmen's concern about the foreman problem and the degree of their interest in those provisions of Taft-Hartley relating to it; the 1950 *Hearings* of the House Select Committee on Lobbying Activities, on business pressure groups; publications of the Department of Labor, particularly the *Monthly Labor Review* and *Bulletins* of the Bureau of Labor Statistics; and reports of the National War Labor Board and 1945 President's National Labor-Management Conference. An approach I did not use, but which might be very rewarding for someone wanting to know about grassroots labor-management relations and the implementation of federal policy in the field, would be to search the case-files of the NLRB, the National and Regional War Labor Boards, the U.S. Conciliation Service (after 1947 Federal Mediation and Conciliation Service), the War Manpower Commission, State Mediation Boards, and the field representatives of the military procurement agencies in industrial states. The growing number of studies of the wildcat strike problem in the automobile industry, for example, have scarcely scratched the surface of what might well be a valuable body of material. Press coverage — which was much more useful to me in providing an initial understanding of what was going on than its representation in the notes would suggest — was supplied from the clipping files of the Royal Institute for International Affairs at Nuffield College, Oxford. These files were compiled in political-intelligence gathering activities during the Second World War designed to inform the U.K. about domestic American affairs. They are very extensive, classified into sensible subject categories, and sample a larger range of metropolitan, regional, and special-interest dailies and weeklies than most research libraries hold. I made greatest use of the Labour Unions, Labour Rights, Labour Politics, and WLB-NLRB series.

Index

281

JACKET DESIGNED BY GARY G. GORE
COMPOSED BY METRICOMP, GRUNDY CENTER, IOWA
MANUFACTURED BY INTER-COLLEGIATE PRESS, INC.,
SHAWNEE MISSION, KANSAS
TEXT IS SET IN CALEDONIA, DISPLAY LINES IN CENTURY SCHOOLBOOK

Library of Congress Cataloging in Publication Data
Harris, Howell John, 1951–
The right to manage.
Includes bibliographical references and index.
1. Industrial relations — United States — History.
2. Industry — Social aspects — United States —
History. I. Title.
HD8072.H2874   331'.0973   81-69820
ISBN 0-299-08640-2   AACR2